LINUX® ON THE MAINFRAME

John Eilert
Maria Eisenhaendler
Dorothea Matthaeus
Ingolf Salm

PRENTICE
HALL
PTR

PRENTICE HALL
Professional Technical Reference
Upper Saddle River, NJ 07458
www.phptr.com

Library of Congress Cataloging-in-Publication Data

Linux on the mainframe / John Eilert … [et al.].
    p. cm.
    ISBN 0-13-101415-3 (pbk.)
    1. Linux. 2. Operating systems (Computers) I. Eilert, John.
    QA76.76.O63L54553 2003
    005.4'469--dc21   2003048813

Editorial/production supervision: *Patti Guerrieri*
Composition: *Maria Eisenhaendler*
Cover design director: *Jerry Votta*
Cover design: *Nina Scuderi*
Manufacturing manager: *Alexis R. Heydt-Long*
Acquisitions editor: *Jeffrey Pepper*
Editorial assistant: *Linda Ramagnano*
Marketing manager: *Kate Hargett*

© 2003 Pearson Education, Inc.
Publishing as Prentice Hall Professional Technical Reference
Upper Saddle River, New Jersey 07458

Prentice Hall books are widely used by corporations and government agencies for training, marketing, and resale.

Prentice Hall PTR offers excellent discounts on this book when ordered in quantity for bulk purchases or special sales. For more information, please contact: U.S. Corporate and Government Sales, 1-800-382-3419, corpsales@pearsontechgroup.com. For sales outside of the U.S., please contact: International Sales, 1-317-581-3793, international@pearsontechgroup.com.

All company and product names mentioned herein are the trademarks or registered trademarks of their respective owners.

Printed in the United States of America

First Printing

ISBN   0-13-101415-3

Pearson Education LTD.
Pearson Education Australia PTY, Limited
Pearson Education Singapore, Pte. Ltd.
Pearson Education North Asia Ltd.
Pearson Education Canada, Ltd.
Pearson Educación de Mexico, S.A. de C.V.
Pearson Education — Japan
Pearson Education Malaysia, Pte. Ltd.

About Prentice Hall Professional Technical Reference

With origins reaching back to the industry's first computer science publishing program in the 1960s, and formally launched as its own imprint in 1986, Prentice Hall Professional Technical Reference (PH PTR) has developed into the leading provider of technical books in the world today. Our editors now publish over 200 books annually, authored by leaders in the fields of computing, engineering, and business.

Our roots are firmly planted in the soil that gave rise to the technical revolution. Our bookshelf contains many of the industry's computing and engineering classics: Kernighan and Ritchie's *C Programming Language*, Nemeth's *UNIX System Adminstration Handbook*, Horstmann's *Core Java*, and Johnson's *High-Speed Digital Design*.

PH PTR acknowledges its auspicious beginnings while it looks to the future for inspiration. We continue to evolve and break new ground in publishing by providing today's professionals with tomorrow's solutions.

PRENTICE
HALL
PTR

Trademarks

The following terms are trademarks of the IBM Corporation in the United States or other countries or both:

1-2-3	IMS	SP
CICS	Lotus	System/360
DB2	MQSeries	System/370
DB2 Connect	MVS	Tivoli
DB2 Universal Database	Multiprise	Tivoli Enterprise Console
DirMaint	OS/390	TotalStorage
ECKD	PR/SM	VM/ESA
ESCON	Parallel Sysplex	VSE/ESA
Enterprise Storage Server	Processor Resource/Systems Manager	WebSphere
Enterprise Systems Architecture/370	RACF	e-business on demand
FICON	RAMAC	eServer
FlashCopy	RMF	z/Architecture
Footprint	Redbooks	z/OS
GDPS	S/370	z/VM
Geographically Dispersed Parallel Sysplex	S/390	zSeries
IBM	S/390 Parallel Enterprise Server	

Java and all Java-based trademarks and logos are trademarks or registered trademarks of Sun Microsystems, Inc. in the United States, other countries, or both.

Microsoft, Windows, Windows NT, and the Windows logo are trademarks of Microsoft Corporation in the United States, other countries, or both.

Intel is a trademark of Intel Corporation in the United States, other countries, or both.

UNIX is a registered trademark of The Open Group in the United States and other countries.

Linux is a registered trademark of Linus Torvalds in the United States, other countries, or both.

Other company, product, and service names may be trademarks or service marks of others.

Contents

Foreword: Linux in the Emerging On Demand World

The future of e-business: e-business on demand

When the Internet burst out of the research community in the mid-1990s, it inaugurated one of the most fruitful, creative periods in the history of the information technology industry. Businesses began exploiting this new means of communicating with the larger world. And they experienced levels of integration that enabled their employees to begin acting more quickly and collaborating more effectively. What emerged was a new model called "e-business."

If anything, the market forces that inspired the e-business phenomenon have intensified. Especially in these difficult economic times, companies are looking for new levels of efficiency. Beyond that, the marketplace is compelling them to become more competitive: to find better ways to attract and retain customers, develop better products in more innovative ways and get them to market faster, and to form and extend more productive value chains. In short, they need to take e-business integration to an entirely new, much more profound level.

Even as those market forces press upon business, the technology to achieve this next level of integration has been advancing at an incredible pace. The Internet itself has continued to evolve in reach, capability, and reliability, assimilating ever more powerful, sophisticated, and less expensive technologies, and exploiting higher bandwidth.

All the while, it has been incorporating open standards, like XML-based Web services and the Open Grid Services Architecture. These, in turn, are transforming the Internet into a distributed computing platform capable of unprecedented integration and sharing of compute resources and applications.

This confluence of market forces and technological capabilities has prepared the way for the next step in e-business: e-business on demand. IBM Chairman Sam Palmisano captured its essence last October when he defined an on demand business as "an enterprise whose business processes—integrated end-to-end across the company and with key partners, suppliers and customers—can respond with speed to any customer demand, market opportunity, or external threat."

Such an enterprise displays four characteristics. First, it is *responsive*. Information is available in such an immediate fashion that the enterprise can meet any challenge contemporaneously, as it is emerging, when a customer demand or a market opportunity is fresh and before a threat has had time to become established.

That enterprise is *focused* on its core competencies and the things that make it stand out from its competitors. It can be focused because, in an on demand operating environment, the business does not have to pay a lot of attention to its IT infrastructure.

Likewise, an on demand business is *resilient*. Its operating environment has achieved a degree of automation that permits it to be self-managing—to regulate itself in an autonomic fashion, just as the human autonomic nervous system controls our basic functions without our having to think about them. The infrastructure is available day-in and day-out.

The final property of an on demand enterprise is that it is *variable*. It is variable in the sense that the business can strike the most favorable balance between large, upfront investments in IT assets and the variable costs associated with tapping into the IT resources of a service provider.

The importance of open standards to an on demand business

Making all this possible are open standards that permit the constituent parts of a vast heterogeneous infrastructure to connect and communicate.

With the proliferation of open standards-based technologies like Web services and with open Grid protocols and open middleware, a business can attain unprecedented levels of integration. With integration and standards comes a degree of automation that permits the operating environment to virtualize everything in the infrastructure, so users don't have to deal with its complexity. They can simply use the resource without having to care about how it works or even where it is.

That gives customers unheard-of flexibility in the ways they acquire and manage information technology. Virtualized resources can exist in the enterprise or at a service provider. Sharing the same standards as the service provider, the enterprise can call on the provider to satisfy peak computing demand or even all its needs. With that kind of flexibility, an enterprise can strike the most efficient balance between fixed capital investments and variable costs.

An on demand business is a more efficient business as well, because open standards that permit the formation of computing grids allow an enterprise to share computing resources, thus optimizing the installed base of information technology. And, in a world in which estimated 24-hour server utilization approximates two to five percent for Intel processor-based servers, 10 percent for UNIX® servers, and 60 percent for mainframes, even marginal increases in efficiency count.

Finally, open standards facilitate communication among systems. And systems that can share information about their respective states make for an infrastructure that is more autonomic. So it is resilient and working day after day, around the clock.

On demand boils down to a company that is poised to compete minute-by-minute, day-by-day, all year long in a marketplace constantly growing more dynamic, fluid, and unpredictable.

On demand, Open Source and Linux

If the movement toward e-business on demand teaches us anything, it is that innovation and openness are indivisible. The recent history of the IT industry also shows that the most effective way to evolve those standards is in a democratic, collaborative community capable of agreeing on standards, implementing them, and evolving them *de facto* in the light of actual marketplace experience. (The only alternative—doctrinaire, *de jure* imposition of a single monolithic standard—is incompatible with the heterogeneity of the modern infrastructure and with the customer's natural interest in choice.)

In fact, the Open Source community contributed the technologies that were used to build much of the Internet itself—technologies such as TCP/IP, sendmail, and Apache. But perhaps the most successful technology to emerge from the Open Source community recently has been Linux.

For one thing, Linux is more than just software. It is a movement, a culture peopled by thousands of developers all over the world who constantly refine and improve the code and contribute it back to the community. Because of this open approach, Linux has become a symbol of collaboration and innovation—a celebration of the entrepreneurial spirit of the world's software developers.

The result of this uniquely collaborative approach is a truly elegant piece of software that works on any type of computer hardware—everything from set top boxes to mainframes, and everything in between. In fact, one could say with confidence that it will even run on computer hardware that has not yet been invented. Customers thus get unprecedented flexibility and freedom of choice.

Linux and the on demand business

Linux is about the lowest-cost operating-system alternative on the market, which accounts for its growing appeal in the world of business and government. Just as important, Linux is ideally suited for the emerging on demand world because it can contribute so much to making a business responsive, variable, focused, and resilient.

For example, to begin moving toward an on demand operating environment, one must first simplify the data center. That requires, among other things, consolidating many distributed servers into one. And Linux, more than any other technology, allows the workloads of hundreds, even thousands, of distributed servers to be consolidated on a single mainframe.

Server consolidation—a prime benefit of Linux on the mainframe—can result in fewer servers to maintain, fewer IT staff required, and less floor space and power consumption to pay for. The savings can then be invested in further transforming business processes, integrating them, and virtualizing the system environment. The result is an environment that is more responsive and a cost structure that is more variable.

Being open, Linux lets a customer deploy applications across many different hardware architectures running the operating system, resulting in a more integrated operating environment, less time spent connecting applications and processes, and more focus on the business. This Linux-based integration results in significant cost savings—savings which, again, can be reinvested in transforming the business.

Honeywell Corporation, the large industrial sector conglomerate, implemented a Linux/mainframe solution that simplifies its business immensely with a single point of entry to 20 distinct strategic systems and makes operations more resilient with automatic rerouting to backup systems should the primary fail. And not having to worry about 20 different sign-ons lets Honeywell engineers focus more on their business.

The Open Source operating system also lends itself readily to utility-like computing and consequently a more variable cost structure. Any business can tap into a Linux-based, zSeries mainframe, for example, and acquire the processing power it needs in the same way that it obtains electricity—on demand and paid for on a usage basis.

Mobil Travel Guide, instead of investing in its own equipment, will use Linux-based mainframe virtual servers and Enterprise Storage servers at IBM's e-business hosting centers and pay for only the computing power they consume. Mobil, in turn, will offer customers on demand travel services, including 24-hour enroute travel support. As a result, Mobil moves toward a more variable cost structure, becomes more responsive and, since it does not have to worry about IT, can focus more on its own business. In short, it takes a major step toward becoming an on demand business.

Despite the bursting of the dot-com bubble, companies around the world still recognize the value inherent in all the open technologies and standards that have emerged in the Internet era. They see their potential for making a business more *responsive*, *focused*, and *resilient*, and moving it toward a more *variable* cost structure. More than any other operating system, Linux, with its roots in the Open Source community that built so much of the Internet, can be an integrating platform that capitalizes on all those creative forces unleashed by the Net to turn a business into an on demand business.

Somers, NY, April 2003

Irving Wladawsky-Berger
Vice President Technology and Strategy, IBM Server Group

Preface

Both the Linux and the mainframe communities are understandably interested in the unique concepts and benefits of Linux on the mainframe. In this book, we define mainframe as being IBM's enterprise servers, that is, S/390 and zSeries servers.

This guide is for anyone seeking technical or market insight regarding Linux on the mainframe. It is for the business person who looks for opportunities to consolidate servers, reduce the complexity of an infrastructure, or reduce IT costs. It is also written for the IT architect who wants to plan for, design, and implement the solutions. It is for all those who are interested in this solution.

This book gives an overall perspective of the concepts that make this solution unique. It is a practical guide which helps you to reach an informed decision as to whether Linux on the mainframe is for your business. It shows examples of business solutions for Linux on the mainframe, and examples of how systems can be designed and built.

While this book is not a tutorial or how-to book, it references a wealth of material that provides details about specific technical topics.

Part 1, "Linux on the Mainframe – an Introduction," describes technologies that possess inherent, strong values on their own merits so that they should be considered as options for your IT projects. This part includes an introduction to Linux, an introduction to the mainframe, and an introduction to Linux on the mainframe.

Part 2, "Planning for Linux," discusses the early decision points that allow a Linux on the mainframe solution to effect the bottom-line project value. Apart from these decision points, this part illustrates, with the help of two sample companies, the spectrum of possibilities open to you. It also presents a total cost-of-ownership discussion on how Linux on the mainframe can facilitate substantial savings in the enterprise.

Part 3, "Is Linux on the Mainframe for Me?" is about the technical foundations that bring unique value to running applications in a Linux-on-the-mainframe environment. Virtualization, communications, and security are among the topics discussed. For example, this part describes how it is possible to have hundreds of Linux servers on one mainframe machine.

Part 4, "Making the Most of Linux on the Mainframe," is about the challenge that Linux on the mainframe means to systems management. How can you preserve the benefits of tight systems management schemes that help to make mainframe environments so reliable and, at the same time, allow Linux to act as an engine for the rapid change that the market-

---

place demands today? This part explores the opportunities that Linux on the mainframe offers for managing availability, data, performance, and security.

Part 5, "Running Applications," outlines the spectrum of uses for Linux images, ranging from independent servers to components in an integrated multi-platform environment with traditional mainframe operating systems. There is also a section with considerations for those who want to port applications from other platforms.

Part 6, "Reference," provides technical details about specific Linux and mainframe functions and capabilities. It also points to some of the key software that is available to your Linux-on-the-mainframe solution, including applications, middleware, and systems management and performance tools.

We have attempted to make the various topics as independent as possible, but, as with any system-level solution, all parts are interrelated. There is a fair amount of cross-referencing to allow you to find sections where a related topic is covered in more detail.

The book is the result of collaboration among three current IBM employees and one retired IBM employee. Our sources are companies that use Linux on the mainframe, customer visits, and other IBM colleagues. The book, its purpose, and structure are an outgrowth of what we have learned.

Terminology used in this book

In the UNIX world of a single-application-per-hardware machine, the term *system* is often used synonymously with *server*. It usually refers to a hardware machine and the software that runs on it. In the mainframe environment with multiple operating systems, each running several applications on virtualized hardware, *server* no longer corresponds to a single hardware machine.

In this book, we use *system* either in a non-mainframe context or as a general term that includes the mainframe hardware and all its software, encompassing all operating systems and applications. To narrow the scope to a particular instance of an operating system, we use *image*. When referring to the scope of an application, we say *server*. Sometimes we take a user's view of an application as a single *server* even if its implementation involves multiple *images.*

The following table lists some other words that are used differently in the UNIX and mainframe worlds. Depending on the context, we use both terminologies.

UNIX/Linux term	Mainframe term
systems administrator	system programmer
network management	systems management
boot	IPL
4–processor machine	4–way
main memory	main storage
disk	DASD
scheduler	dispatcher

For a complete list of abbreviations and special terms used in this book, see "Glossary."

Disclaimer

The authors have made a reasonable effort to ensure that the information in this book is accurate. The authors do not offer any warranties or representations nor accept any liabilities related to the information contained in the book.

The information contained in this book is distributed on an "as is" basis without any warranty of any kind, either expressed or implied and including, but not limited to, the implied warranties of function of the technologies and concepts or merchantability or fitness for a particular purpose. The use of this information or the implementation of any of these techniques is the reader's responsibility and depends on the reader's ability to evaluate, to implement, and to integrate the techniques into the reader's operational environment. Readers attempting to adapt these techniques do so at their own risk.

The names chosen for the example companies, ISPCompany and StoreCompany are purely fictional and are in no way intended to resemble or represent real existing companies. If such an incidence should occur, it is purely coincidental.

Opinions expressed in this book, as well as any errors or omissions, are strictly those of the authors. The contents of this book in no way reflect the official opinions or positions of the International Business Machines Corporation.

Acknowledgements

This book has been a team effort.

We thank Ulrike Wicke and Tim Kane for their ongoing support. Their belief in the value of this effort made this book possible.

Special thanks go to Dr. Karl-Heinz Strassemeyer, Distinguished Engineer, the mentor of this book, for his vision and encouragement.

Also, we thank Herbert Kircher, Heather Kahan, Thomas Klein, Karl Klink, Thomas Rozmus, Hubertus Barthold, and Alexander Stark for their professional advice and support.

We especially acknowledge the following experts for their contributions:

Christoph Arenz	Introducing Linux and Introducing Linux on the mainframe
Reinhard Buendgen	Achieving higher availability
Paul Gallagher	Achieving higher availability and communications reference
Andreas Herrmann	Debugging and dump analysis
Michael Holzheu	Debugging and dump analysis
Reed Mullen	The value of virtualization
Eberhard Pasch	Performance and capacity planning
Holger Smolinski	Data management
Peter G Spera	Security considerations
Horst Weber	Systems management and running applications

Many thanks also go to the following people for many hours of discussion and review:

Ingo Adlung	Alan Altmark	Erich Amrehn
Utz Bacher	D. J. Barrow	Debbie Beatrice
Oliver Benke	Klaus Bergmann	Boas Betzler
Bill Bitner	John L. Czukkermann	Bernhard Dierberger
Juergen Doelle	Timothy Hahn	Horst Hummel
Eginhard Jaeger	Jan-Rainer Lahmann	Tom Laudati
Scott Loveland	Hans Dieter Mertiens	Carlos Ordonez
Chris Panetta	Franziska Peterthalner	Milagros Portocarrero
Stephen Record	Nancy Scala	Raimund Schröder
Martin Schwidefsky	Horst Sinram	Joe Temple
Hanns-Joachim Uhl	Bob Visanji	Ulrich Weigand
Romney White	Eva L. Yan	

Joel Hermann, briefing manager, deserves our gratitude for his professional advice and collegial support.

We would like to thank the ITSO teams for permitting us to use images from Redbook publications, in particular from *Linux on IBM eServer zSeries and S/390: ISP/ASP Solutions*, SG24-6299. Thanks to the many other people who have helped us with this book.

Thanks to the team at Prentice Hall PTR for their support. Special thanks to Jeffrey Pepper, our editor, for his diligent work. We are grateful to all who helped preparing the book for publication, especially Kate Hargett, Patti Guerrieri, and Mary Loudin. Also, we would like to mention Jamie Milazzo from the Pearson Technology Group for providing innovative publishing concepts for this book.

Part 1.
Linux on the Mainframe
– an Introduction

The processor (hardware) and the operating system form the supporting structure of an application server. Choosing the right hardware and operating system can relieve you of many management chores and provide you with the flexibility to focus on other important aspects of the system. One important business aspect is the applications you want to run on the system. You can gain a business advantage from choosing to host certain applications (or parts of applications) on Linux on the mainframe. Among other things, Linux brings new technology and applications to the mainframe.

The first chapter of this part introduces Linux. We look at the role of Open Source in Linux development and the status of Linux today.

This is followed by an introduction to the mainframe. We look at what the long history of the mainframe means to its quality and usefulness today.

The third chapter of this part describes how Linux and the mainframe fit together. We take a look at the IBM porting effort, describe how Linux behaves on the mainframe, and list some of the benefits of running Linux on the mainframe.

Chapter 1.
Introducing Linux

This chapter introduces Linux. Linux is the UNIX-like kernel of an operating system initially developed by Linus Torvalds at the University of Helsinki in the early 1990s. Hundreds of programmers that were connected through the Internet helped develop Linux into a full-function operating system. In this chapter we explore these questions:

- What does Linux offer as an enterprise-class operating system?
- What is the role of Open Source in Linux development?
- How can Linux run on the mainframe architecture?

1.1 Benefits of the Linux operating system

Today, Linux is a worthy alternative to other well-known operating systems. As an operating system, Linux offers benefits such as:

- Full functionality.

  Like other operating systems, Linux has components for systems management, security, and performance. Throughout its history, Linux has been enhanced with additional functions as they have been needed, at rapid speed.

- Architecture independence.

  Linux started out as a personal computer (PC) operating system, but enthusiasts soon ported it to other platforms. Linus Torvalds himself ported it to the Alpha platform and, while doing so, introduced an abstraction layer between the hardware and the operating system. This allows the system to be compiled on different hardware architectures but still use the same source code. Thus, only small adjustments had to be made in the kernel to let Linux run on the mainframe. The way Linux is written allows for wide variety in hardware architecture. For example, when running on the mainframe, Linux uses the mainframe I/O structure with no problems.

- Support for standards and new technologies.

  Thanks to the many active Linux developers, Linux is fast to adopt new technologies. Linux was one of the early operating systems to support 64-bit addressing. 64-bit addressing combined with sufficient random access memory (RAM) allows the central processing unit (CPU) to pull more data into memory and operate on it directly, thus increasing performance.

- Linux is an Open Source project.

  Linux is an example of Open Source development with many active developers working together to provide functionality, enhance performance, and ensure support of devices.

To fully appreciate the last point, we need to discuss Open Source in more detail.

1.2 The role of the Open Source community

The idea of Open Source plays a major role in Linux development. In this section, we will look at what Open Source is, what it means for software to be Open Source, and what it means for Linux to be Open Source.

The definition of Open Source can be found on the organization's Web site, http://www.opensource.org.[1] Open Source code is licensed under a variety of licenses, all of which provide access to the source code and the right to modify it.

1.2.1 Peer review means quality

How can something put together by a disparate group of programmers have high quality? Put yourself in their shoes. Any code you submit to the Open Source project is scrutinized by a lot of people. You cannot hide behind object code either, so delivering "spaghetti code" that works is not good enough. You do not want to be the laughing stock of the cybernetic neighborhood, do you? Therefore, you will work to create high quality code.

1.2.2 Licenses

Commercial software usually comes with a license that regulates its use. Open Software is no exception. The Open Source community recognized that when others use someone else's intellectual property, there must be rules that regulate users' rights and obligations. The Open Source Initiative provides a procedure for certifying software licenses as Open Source licenses.

One of the core ideas of Open Source software from a user's point of view is that a license grants you certain rights:

- You have the right to receive the source code for the software along with any binary version of the software.

---

[1] A discussion of the Open Source philosophy is given in *The Cathedral and the Bazaar* by Eric Raymond.

- You have the right to modify the software according to your own needs or to expand the software with further functionality.

- You have the right to redistribute the software, including your modifications or without them.

Because you receive the source code with the object code, you are not dependent on a software vendor for support of the code. You will not find yourself locked in a situation where you are forced to upgrade your software just because your current version goes out of service.

Two of the most prominent licenses are the GNU General Public License (GPL) and the BSD (from the University of California, Berkeley) license. While both licenses meet the Open Source definition (given at `http://www.opensource.org`), they differ substantially in their terms.

The Linux operating system consists of several portions of software called *packages* that are licensed under different Open Source licenses.

1.2.3 Linux as an Open Source project

When Linus Torvalds started work on "Linus' UNIX" operating system in 1991, he was aware of the work the Open Source community was doing. He derived his work from the academic MINIX operating system written by Andrew S. Tanenbaum. Although Torvalds' project started out as a private enterprise, it quickly became independent of the MINIX project and became a global, widespread project, especially when Torvalds released his work as Open Source software under the GPL. The Internet made this possible; it played an important role in the Linux and Open Source movements.

Open Source projects attract many of today's best programmers because of their simple and sensible premise: Let us work as a team, because together we are faster and smarter than each one alone.

A brief history of Linux

Linux was developed with the help of many volunteer programmers and "wizards" across the Internet, allowing anyone with enough know-how to develop and change the system. Table 1-1 shows the rapid development of Linux in the early years.

Table   *1-1. Linux history: the early years*

Year	Event
1991	• August: Linus Torvalds sends a request over the Internet asking if other program-mers are interested in helping him with the project. In the first six months, he received over 600 responses. • September: Torvalds puts version 0.01 out on an FTP server for others to look at. • October: Torvalds announces the first generally available version of Linux, version 0.02.
1992	• March: Torvalds increases the version number to 0.95, to reflect his expectation that the system would soon be ready for an "official" release.
1993	• December: The Linux kernel is still at version 0.99.pl14, slowly approaching 1.0. (Generally, software is not assigned the version number 1.0 until it is deemed com-plete or bug-free.)
1994	• March: Linux 1.0 is announced at the Department of Computer Science at the Uni-versity of Helsinki. • The first commercial Linux distribution, Red Hat Linux, is introduced.

What's in a name?

What is Linux? Ask three different people and you may get the following three answers:

• The operating system *kernel*, offering the basic services of process scheduling, virtual memory, file management, and I/O—what Linus Torvalds started.

• A complete system consisting of the kernel plus the many applications that it runs: com-pilers, editors, graphical interfaces, games, and so on—what Linus Torvalds and thou-sands of others are developing in the Open Source community.

• What you get when you buy, for example, "SuSE Linux 8.0" in your local software store—what a distributor has chosen to combine into an easily installable product.

None of the above answers is right or wrong. Those who look at Linux as just the kernel of an operating system have a point, as other parts that make up the full operating system come from Open Source projects, such as GNU.

There are also people who think of Linux as what we refer to as a *Linux distribution*. Some-times the association is so strong that they use the name of the distribution instead of Linux when talking about the operating system (Red Hat, SuSE, and Turbolinux, to name a few). This is easy to understand, given that a Linux distribution is what you are probably dealing with when you run Linux.

However, for the purposes of this book, we will use "Linux" to mean the complete operating system. When we talk about the kernel, we will call it the *kernel* or the *Linux kernel*. When we talk about a combination of programs you can buy from SuSE or others, we will call it a *distribution*.

IBM and Linux

IBM does not provide a Linux distribution. However, IBM is an active participant in the Open Source community. IBM delivers Open Source code that is either actively integrated into the official source code repositories of the various projects or packages or helps to integrate it.

1.3 The role of distributions

A distribution is a collection of various development projects (most of them are under constant development) that work together. Distributors select the packages with the versions that provide the right levels of new functionality, while at the same time assuring a level of stability, reliability, and maintainability. This must be achieved for the software packages of the individual projects and also for them working together. For some packages—for example, for the so-called *core packages* of the GNU development and build-environment—this is especially important.

A distribution includes applications with the operating-system packages. Among the most popular applications are Web-serving applications (such as Apache) and file and print serving applications (such as Samba). A lot of solutions can be built directly from the Open Source applications that come with the distribution. The distribution also contains installation scripts, configuration files, system administration tools, and documentation. Distributions often provide maintenance and support for the products they include, education, and sometimes certification.

Some distributions exist for very specific solutions. For Linux running on personal computer (PC) based systems, for example, there are distributions that focus on firewall solutions, while others focus on mail-serving, Web serving, or other solutions.

It is possible to create your own Linux by going to the Open Source projects and selecting what you want. However, building your own operating system is not a trivial task. When building your own Linux system, you pay with the work you put in, whereas a commercial distribution has a monetary cost. The cost covers, for example, the packaging, documentation, and testing which the distributor has done. Distributions often offer service and support.

1.3.1 Choosing a distribution

What criteria should you use when selecting a distribution? The answer depends on your situation. However, there are generally two ways to arrive at it: You can do an internal study or get consultant services.

Criteria to consider when choosing a Linux distribution are:

- Does the distribution contain and support most of the functionality and applications that you need? One way to find this out is to install the distribution and test it in your environment.

- What kind of middleware do you want to run? Who provides support for it? The middleware owner or your service provider?

Distributions that are available for Linux on the mainframe at the time of this writing include Red Hat, SuSE, and Turbolinux.

1.3.2 The role of a distributor

Distributors usually play an active part in Open Source development projects. The major distributors employ Open Source developers. For example, a distributor may employ compiler developers and developers working on the kernel.

Distributors actively drive some Linux development (for example, the compiler), depending on their business needs or the platforms they want to support. Distributors also support special projects where they see value for their customers (for example, a journaling file system). They run stress tests and actively search for security holes. They compile documentation and simplify installation. They provide support for their distribution and offer services and education.

Actively participating in Open Source projects means that distributors are giving something back to the community. In this way, everyone benefits from their work.

1.3.3 What about maintenance and support?

How do you plan to maintain an Open Source operating system like Linux? Are your employees going to do it? Are you getting a contract? To whom you turn for maintenance can depend on whether the system is for test or production purposes.

Maintenance from the Open Source community

Using Open Source software gives you options in the way the software is maintained. Normally, the provider of the software offers some level of maintenance. If not, you always have the choice (apart from looking for other software) of either maintaining it yourself or subcontracting the work to another company. The source is available for you to work with.

While chances are good that a request for a repair job to the Open Source community will get you a quick answer, there is no guarantee that anybody in the Open Source world will treat you as a 24-hour priority customer. If your business requires quick responses to maintenance requests, you may want a maintenance contract. Distributors normally offer maintenance and support for their distributions.

Maintenance from a subcontractor

If you are getting a contract, consider that you may have to recompile the Linux kernel in order to include needed functionality. This must be allowed under the terms of your maintenance contract. We will discuss maintenance and support in Chapter 16, "System Administrator Tasks."

1.4 Linux structure

The Linux operating system consists of a kernel and tools. Figure 1-1 shows the structure of the operating system with the kernel shaded. The diagram is not to scale. The kernel is significantly smaller than the tools and application portions.

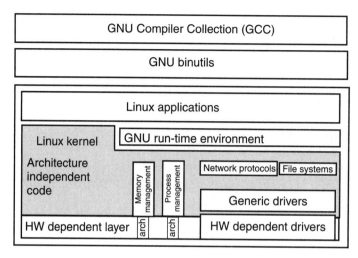

Figure   1-1. The Linux structure

Linux kernel

A kernel is the program that controls the allocation of the machine's resources to the other programs that are running. Though a kernel is an essential part of an operating system, it is useless on its own. It can serve a useful purpose only as part of a complete operating system. Linux is a UNIX-like system and, as such, it contains most UNIX features such as multitasking, virtual memory, memory management, and TCP/IP networking.

GNU Compiler Collection (GCC)

GCC is a versatile and sophisticated compiler that can compile programs written in several different languages to run on many different hardware platforms. Languages supported include C, C++, Objective-C, Ada, Fortran, and Java. GCC is usually supplied with a Linux distribution, but is also available for download on the Internet.

GNU Binary Utilities

These are a set of utilities supplied as part of a Linux distribution. For example, the utility *ar* can be used to extract files from the archive file. Also included in the package are the linker ld and the assembler as. If you have acquired Linux as part of a distribution, binutils would have been included with the distribution. If you need to upgrade to the latest release of binutils, go to
`http://www.gnu.org/directory/index.html`.

Note: If you ever need to upgrade your kernel, GCC, glibc, or binutils, you must ensure that the new version is compatible with the rest of your operating system and that you follow the guidelines for compiling the new version. You may also need to recompile some of your programs, making sure you specify the correct libraries.

Linux applications

A distribution normally bundles various applications (such as word processors, spread sheets, Internet browsers, Web servers, fax programs, and graphics programs). Additionally, sophisticated applications are available from many suppliers.

Device drivers

A device driver is a file or program that enables communication between a computer and a specific peripheral device such as a printer. For Linux to be able to use a device, the associated device driver must be available to the Linux kernel. This can be accomplished either by compiling the device driver with the kernel or by making the driver available as a module. Details of the available mainframe device drivers and comprehensive information about their use are documented in *Device Drivers and Installation Commands.*[2]

Runtime environment

To run an application that has already been compiled, you need various support programs and files. A runtime environment provides these items. A runtime environment can simply be a directory that contains the necessary files, such as glibc or libgcj (created by compiler GCJ for Java) or the libg2c library (created by G77 Fortran compiler, part of GCC). Whereas a Java applet can rely on a Web browser to run a Java application, a user needs a Java virtual machine and various support programs and files. This collection of software constitutes a Java runtime environment. Various suppliers provide Java runtime environments for download. See, for example, IBM Developer Kit and Runtime Environment for Linux:

http://www.ibm.com/developerworks/java/jdk/118/linux/jre-info.html,

or Java 2 Platform, Standard Edition (J2SETM):

http://java.sun.com/j2se/1.3/runtime.html.

---

2 www.software.ibm.com/developerworks/opensource/linux390/.

1.5 Summary

Today, Linux is an enterprise-level operating system. It is robust and exploits numerous standards and new technologies.

Linux is an example of an Open Source project. Distributions include Open Source tools in their packages. The actual expense for using this operating system in your business can be significantly less than for other operating systems.

Open Source signifies freedom for developers to work on projects in which they take an interest. This is an attractive premise, and many talented developers work on Open Source projects. The scrutiny of many Open Source community members makes code quality high.

Distributions solve a perceived problem with Open Source: who is responsible for ongoing software support? Distributors (and others such as IBM Global Services) take care of support and maintenance in a legally binding way.

Chapter 2.
Introducing the Mainframe

To understand what the mainframe offers to Linux, you need some basic knowledge of the mainframe's architecture and design. It is difficult to find a concise and easy-to-read mainframe overview. In this chapter, we provide a brief introduction for those who are new to the mainframe.

In this chapter, we discuss the following questions:

- How did the mainframe develop?
- What distinguishes the mainframe from other platforms?
- What does the mainframe of today offer?

2.1 The mainframe's birth

Before 1940, a "computer" was a human being who did calculations using paper and pencil. *Digital* or *electronic computers* were developed to relieve the human computer of boring, iterative calculation work. An electronic computer performed calculations much faster than a human could and did not get tired. An important aspect of the electronic computer was that it could store a program. This distinguished the computer from an adding machine.

The first electronic computers were housed in several cabinets consisting of steel frames with metal covers. The most important cabinet—the *main frame*—housed the circuitry that performed calculations. The other cabinets housed power units and peripheral devices such as tape drives.

The very first IBM mainframe was installed half a century ago in IBM world headquarters (see Figure 2-1). It consisted of a room-sized set of cabinets housing the units for the 701 Defense Calculator. The 701 was the first large-scale, high-speed, stored-program electronic computer to be produced in volume by IBM.

Figure 2-1. The room-sized 701, IBM's first mainframe. IBM announced installation of the first machine in 1953. The 701 main frame is at the back of the room on the right. The other cabinets include three power units, a dual magnetic tape drive to the left, and card units to the right. (Photograph courtesy of IBM Archives.)

The 701 was capable of performing thousands of instructions per second: 2000 instructions when multiplying and dividing, and up to 16,000 when adding and subtracting. The average instruction execution rate was 14,000 instructions per second. Compared to the manual computing common at the time, this was an overwhelming achievement. One day of digital computer time was equivalent to 500 years of pencil and paper calculations.

The 701 may have been the first large-scale electronic mainframe, but it was built for special engineering and scientific purposes, not for commercial transaction processing. It did not have a general-purpose operating system (OS), and it could run only custom-made programs. However, its success encouraged IBM to make a computer for the commercial market. To find all-purpose mainframes as we know them today, we must go forward to the 1960s.

2.2 General-purpose computer architecture

Around 1960, there were many computer systems in the marketplace, each developed for a specific purpose. Some were optimized, for example, to do accounting, others to solve engineering problems or to help scientists with complex calculations. At the time, about 80% of the total customer cost of the IT environment was spent on hardware. Therefore, fully exploiting the capabilities of a piece of hardware was crucial for an efficient IT operation.

To efficiently use IT resources, it was sometimes desirable to move a program between computers. This was not easy. Figure 2-2 illustrates the relationship between the hardware, or electronic layer, and the program, application, or user layer at that time. To move between different computers, it was necessary to rewrite programs, because the interface to the programs was different for each machine.

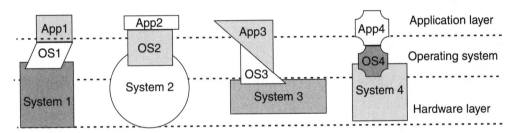

Figure 2-2. Four computer systems, each with a different interface to applications and operating system

In response this problem, Gene Amdahl, Fred Brooks, and Gerry Blaauw envisioned and implemented the IBM System/360 (S/360)[3] architecture. The five-member S/360 family of computers was announced in 1964.

The basis for S/360 was the idea that computing could be abstracted so that a very broad range of problems could be solved within the confines of a single computer architecture. In fact, we can say that all computing can be reduced to the following operations:

1. Get some data.

2. Perform some computation (or manipulation) on that data.

3. Save the data that resulted from the computation.

---

3 The "360" in the name stands for the 360 degrees of a full circle (not for the 1960s when it was invented).

The IBM team distinguished between *architecture*, which is the theoretical behavior of the system, and *design*, which is an implementation of the architecture. They designed machines that implemented the general architecture in a way that allowed subsets of the problem space to be solved better (faster or more cost-effectively) on one model compared to another model. For example, some models of the S/360 family, such as the model 95, were considered to be supercomputers. The model 65 was the workhorse, top-of-the-line business computer, and the model 25 was for small businesses. All three used the same architecture across a wide range of applications.

2.3 Distinguishing features of the mainframe

Let us go deeper into the structure of three main resources defined by the S/360 architecture.[4] It is this structure and implementation that distinguishes the mainframe from other vendors' computer implementations and that can give some significant value to your business opportunity.

The mainframe is based on the von Neumann computer model (see Figure 2-3), with these main parts:

- The CPU is the processing unit, responsible for executing instructions.

- The memory[5] holds data to be manipulated.

- The I/O system takes care of communication with external devices.

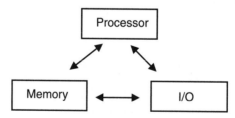

Figure   2-3. The von Neumann computer model

---

[4] In this book, we will use *mainframe architecture* to mean any of these architectures: S/360, S/370, S/390, or z/Architecture. If we refer specifically to the 64-bit architecture of the zSeries 900, we will use the term z/Architecture.

[5] Memory is called *storage* in the mainframe world.

2.3.1 Central processing unit

In this section, we will take a look at how the architecture and design of the central processing unit (CPU) contributes to the reliability and scalability of the mainframe. The design aims to optimize the workloads that are run on the machine.

Architecture of CPU

The architecture of the CPU defines *data integrity* and *work separation*. Data integrity means that an instruction either completes accurately or the reason for the error can be found. One instruction is executed at a time. If it does not complete, the architecture defines how this will be handled. In other words, the mainframe is self-checking.

Work separation alludes to the fact that the CPU can run in either of two modes: supervisor (or privileged) mode and problem mode. The two states ensure that only properly authorized programs, like the operating system itself, can perform critical actions. At the same time, user programs can run without fear of their interfering with another program's or operating system's data. To protect data, *storage protect keys* were initially used. Later, technologies such as virtual memory and address spaces were developed.

The mainframe architecture defines the order in which instructions are to be processed as "next sequential instruction" (NSI). However, in the mainframe design there are two exceptions to the sequential rule: branching and interrupts. When branching, the program branches to an address specified in a branching instruction instead of executing the next instruction as specified. Interrupts signal external events that have an impact on the sequence in which instructions are executed.

A little known fact is that, statistically, every fifth instruction is a branch. So while the mainframe architecture defines it as an NSI machine, the CPU is designed around the fact that processing is constantly going down different paths. In the CPU design, a lot of effort has gone into ensuring that both branching and interrupts are handled as efficiently as possible. These efforts are ultimately the reason for the speed of processing.

Multitasking

Early systems processed work as it came in as a job unit. Each job was processed as a whole, and only one job was processed at a time. Jobs often had to wait (for example, for information from a printer or a tape drive), and the CPU was idle much of the time, as illustrated in Figure 2-4. The speed of the external devices was much slower than that of the CPU.

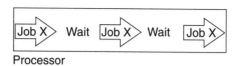

Figure   2-4. An active job causes the CPU to be idle while the program is waiting for I/O

In contrast to a personal computer, a mainframe is designed to support many users at the same time. On a PC, you might not really care how busy the CPU is, because you are the only user on it. On the mainframe, thousands of different pieces of work compete for processing resources. Finding a way to keep the CPU working while a job waited would increase the amount of work the CPU could process. The solution was *multitasking*. Multitasking means that when a job waits for I/O, another job can be processed, as illustrated in Figure 2-5.

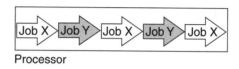

Figure   2-5. Multitasking: While one job waits, another can be processed

In order to implement multitasking, a technique was needed to switch control from one job to another. This switching is achieved by *interrupts*. An interrupt is an event that alters the sequence in which the CPU executes instructions, as illustrated in Figure 2-6.

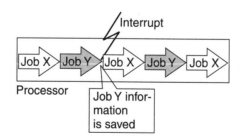

Figure   2-6. Interrupts alter the execution sequence of instructions

An interrupt can be planned (specifically requested by the program) or unplanned (caused by an event that is not related to the executing task). See Chapter 21, "Mainframe Reference" for more details on the interrupt technique. Interrupts and multitasking are possible because the relevant information about the interrupted program is captured and saved. This is called *state handling* and allows the CPU to continue executing a program where it left off.

The interrupt technique enables a program to wait for work without consuming significant resources, as the program does not need to constantly check if there is work to be processed. Programs will be called by an interrupt when data for processing are available.

Multiprocessing

Even the most efficient CPU can execute only one instruction at a time. As the workload increases, thousands of jobs can wait for a single CPU. In this situation, it might make sense to add CPUs. Two or more CPUs processing simultaneously make up a *multiprocessor*. Multiprocessing on the mainframe was introduced with the S/370 architecture in 1970.

Increasing the number of CPUs increases the demand on the operating system. Linux is an operating system that handles multiprocessors fairly well, as we shall see in Chapter 3, "Introducing Linux on the Mainframe."

Today's mainframe (for example, the zSeries 900) is a *Symmetric Multiprocessor* (SMP)[6] with up to 16 CPUs as illustrated in Figure 2-7.

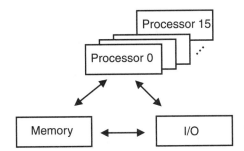

Figure 2-7. An SMP with 16 CPUs

A mainframe CPU can sustain a utilization of over 90% over long periods of time.

---

6 "Symmetric" means that from the point of view of any one CPU, the rest of the machine looks the same. At the same time, from the point of view of the memory, all CPUs behave identically. In other words, all CPUs can do the same tasks and have access to the same memory and the same I/O devices.

2.3.2 Memory

Memory's task is to serve data to the outside world. Memory either receives data and stores data safely, or gives data out. Memory serves many masters, including the CPUs and the I/O subsystem. This being the case, memory is optimized to do its job quickly and provide for data integrity while doing it. The memory subsystem does multitasking and knows how to keep track of all the requests for data. For example, when a program tries to use data that it shouldn't, an interrupt occurs, and a program is brought in to handle the problem.

Architecture of memory

Initially, the architecture defined a flat, real memory space. Memory was addressable by bytes, half words, full words, and double words (see Figure 2-8). Eventually, quadwords (4 words) and page were added for addressing, depending on the instruction or I/O operation being run.

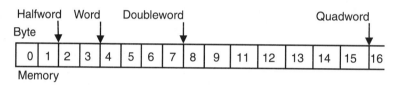

Figure   2-8. Memory can be visualized as a horizontal string starting at zero and extending to the limit of memory

As CPU speed increased, it was only a matter of time before a CPU could execute more programs in a given period of time than it could hold in its own storage. Again, the CPU was idle for periods of time. The solution was to bring pieces of a program into memory (or real storage) instead of the entire program. The program pieces, called *pages,* were fixed in size (4 KB today). Each page was assigned a unique address defined by the first byte of the page. That address was called the *virtual address.* The CPU kept track of which pages were in real storage and which it would have to get by way of a table that listed the page addresses for the program that was executing. Thus, memory was no longer limited to the size of real storage, but to the number of virtual addresses (see Figure 2-9).

The benefit which programmers see from virtual addressing is that the program is freed from the constraints of real memory. Programmers can still address memory as if it were a flat array. The operating system resolves the addressing at runtime by paging.[7]

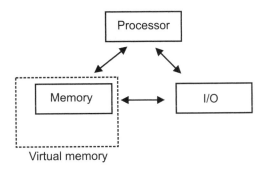

Figure 2-9. Virtual memory lets programs address a virtual address range. Only a subset may be residing in real memory at any time.

Address spaces—full range of memory, yet isolation guaranteed

What is an *address space* on the mainframe? An address space is a range of contiguous virtual storage addresses that the operating system creates. A small portion of an address space is reserved for system data and programs, but most of an address space is available for user data and programs.

The first version of IBM's OS operating system to use virtual memory, the Single Virtual Storage (SVS) system, removed the constraint on real storage and provided a single 16-megabyte virtual address space to be divided among all tasks.

When more than one program is running on a computer, the issue of isolation becomes important. Programs must not be allowed to write into memory reserved by others. There are several techniques for doing this, including allocating a separate piece of real memory to every program. Real memory is divided into "n" pieces, plus an overhead for the operating system.

Only six months after the release of SVS in 1972, the Multiple Virtual Storage (MVS) operating system introduced the concept of one full range of virtual addresses per program running. That is, each address space would represent 16 MB of virtual memory, as illustrated in Figure 2-10.

---

7 Paging is I/O, so you might expect it to take a relatively long time. But paging is a much more efficient I/O than if the program itself would have to handle it.

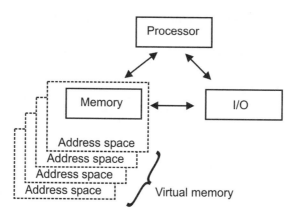

Figure 2-10. S/370 architecture defined the address space to have the full range of addressing from 0 to 16 MB. MVS put each job or user in a separate address space.

Design of memory

From the beginning, the CPU was an expensive resource, and customers wanted to take full advantage of it. Hence, the goal of machine designers was to keep the CPU busy. The CPU had to be fed continually with data from memory, which in turn was fed from the I/O subsystem. The designers came up with the *cache* concept which allowed the CPU to access and process data faster. The mainframe today uses multiple levels of cache and separates data cache from instruction cache.

The architecture requires that each CPU has the same view of memory. In the design of the memory structure, it must be guaranteed that CPUs and I/O have the same view of memory. This is called *cache coherence* and requires some fairly complex design if done at the hardware level. Some architectures handle cache coherence at the programming level, which means that the cache must be "visible" to the programs. However, this can introduce problems with scaling and may lead to data integrity problems if the software misbehaves. The mainframe architecture thus does not define cache and cache is designed to hide the complexity of cache coherence. Thus, no operating system on the mainframe has to worry about cache, as it might on other architectures.

Table 2-1 shows an overview of memory development on the mainframe. Real storage addressing has progressed from 24-bit to 64-bit addressing. Virtual memory space has followed the increases in real addressing.

Table   2-1. Examples showing memory hierarchy development

Architecture	Memory addressing	Memory design (examples)
S/360	24-bit real addressing allows addressing of 16-MB memory.	Machine model 30 had a 64-KB memory. The 360/85 in 1969 was the first production machine with cache memory.
S/370	24-bit real addressing allows addressing of 16-MB memory.	Machine models 158 and 168 introduced multiprocessing and virtual memory.
S/390	31-bit real addressing allows addressing of 2-GB memory.	On the S/390 Parallel Enterprise Servers Generation 5 and 6, memory can be varied from 1 GB to 32 GB.
z/Architecture	64-bit addressing allows addressing of 16-EB* memory.	On the IBM eServer zSeries 900, memory varies from 5 GB on the 101 model to 64 GB on the 2C9 and 216 models.

*EB stands for "exa bytes" and equals 2^{60} bytes or approximately 1 153 000 000 000 000 000 bytes.

2.3.3 Input/Output system

In contrast to other architectures that use I/O bus systems, the mainframe uses *I/O channels*. An I/O channel is a processor that manages the data movement between memory and external devices under the control of *channel programs*. In other words, I/O on the mainframe is managed independently of the CPUs. Architecturally, only the independent and overlapped execution aspects are specified and not whether a separate CPU is required for each real channel. For example, on the IBM zSeries machines, a single System Assist Processor (SAP) might control up to a hundred channels and the associated hardware interfaces.

Design of I/O

We have mentioned that it is possible for a mainframe CPU to be consistently busy more than 90% of the time. This requires that the CPU be given a steady stream of work to do. One of the potential bottlenecks in some system designs is the I/O design.

The central CPUs can process data at nanosecond speed. The rest of the computer system should be able to feed the CPUs information, and receive it from them, at the speed that they need it. Hence, there must be a balance between the CPUs, the memory, and the I/O. Let's take a look at data processing from the I/O perspective.

The simple, early approach to I/O was the following: Send out requests for data to a device, wait for data to be returned (the job is said to enter a *wait state*), and then continue processing. This is illustrated in Figure 2-11.

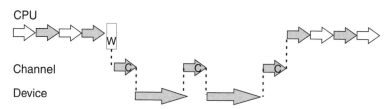

Figure   2-11. Simple I/O system design

Figure 2-11 shows quite a gap in processing while the I/O device is busy. In order to keep the CPU busy, mainframe designers decided to use this gap for other processing. The CPU would continue with other waiting work until an I/O interrupt signaled that the I/O operation was complete (Figure 2-12).

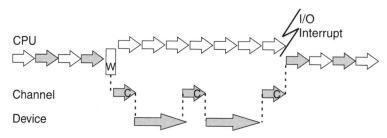

Figure   2-12. Mainframe I/O processing.   The CPU can process other tasks while some tasks are waiting for I/O.

On early systems with 500 KB of real storage, three to five users (or programs) running simultaneously was the rule. As the CPU became faster, the idle time became significant again, as all programs were processed up to a point where they waited for I/O. It thus became possible for the CPU to load and initiate even more work. With the help of virtual memory (see 2.3.2, "Memory" in this chapter), it was possible to significantly increase CPU utilization.

Over the years, further improvements were made to I/O handling. Notice the two large gaps on the middle line (channel) in Figure 2-12. This means that the channel could execute another channel program that talks to a different device. By contrast, on the bottom line (device) the middle gap is small; the device should not do anything else until this data action is processed. While Figure 2-12 shows the principle of how a program is interrupted to wait for I/O, it doesn't show the proportions of time. I/O from DASD typically takes five orders of magnitude longer than a CPU cycle. For example, if we were to slow down the CPU so that a cycle lasted one second, the I/O operation would take days.

Over time, the mainframe's I/O system was optimized to keep feeding the CPUs data, allowing them to do other work while waiting for data.

Mainframe I/O processing

In the S/360 computing systems, a channel decodes the channel program, which in turn is composed of CCWs. Channels are not the same as the physical cabling; rather, they are a logical construct. The *path*, on the other hand, is the actual physical path that data can take to a device, as illustrated in Figure 2-13.

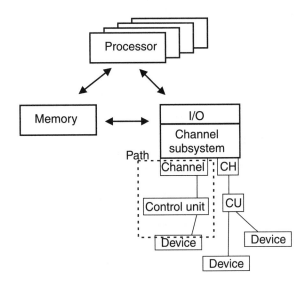

Figure 2-13. Mainframe I/O subsystem. Channels are connected to control units to which devices connect.

Each external device can be connected to one or more channels to allow for high bandwidth and reliability for data access on the external devices.

Channels make it possible to overlap requests to a disk to connect as soon as it is not active elsewhere and check the existing data on the disk to determine if and when what type of data transfer may occur—all done without any interaction with the CPU. Only upon completion of the channel program (or exception termination) is the CPU made aware of what has occurred. The CPU is not involved in the data movement.

As shown in Table 2-2 , the mainframe I/O subsystem has evolved from an initial maximum of 8 channels. Each channel is capable of transferring data as needed between memory and external devices independently and coincidently with other channel and CPU access to memory. This capability allows for the high data transfer rates required to sustain multiprocessing activities on up to 16 CPUs.

Table 2-2. Examples showing I/O development

Architecture	Channels	Machine models
S/360	8 Parallel	Model 67
S/390	Either of: • 96 Parallel • 256 ESCON • 36 FICON	S/390 Parallel Enterprise Servers Generation 5 and 6
z/Architecture	• 88 Parallel • 256 ESCON • 96 FICON • 96 FICON Express • 24 OSA-Express • 4 HiperSockets	IBM eServer zSeries 900

2.4 From real to virtual

"Virtual" is a word used by other manufacturers today. Virtual on one machine is not the same as on other machines. On the mainframe it is not only the memory that can be virtualized. On the mainframe, virtualization has been part of the design for over 30 years. It is the key factor that allows you to do consolidation on the mainframe. For more details on virtualization, see Chapter 7, "The Value of Virtualization."

2.4.1 The roots of z/VM

In the 1960s, hardware was expensive, and it was imperative to use a computer as economically as possible, that is, to run it as much of the time as possible. The machine was needed to run existing business applications, and also to test new programs. Ideally, each tester needed a full machine with all the hardware and software available. Thus, there was a need for an operating system environment that allowed multiple users to use a single machine. Within IBM, two approaches were taken to meet the need: the Time-Sharing System (TSS) and what was to become the Virtual Machine (VM) operating system.

Time sharing allows multiple users to share the use of the operating system. Virtual machines allow multiple operating systems to share the same machine hardware.

2.4.2 Virtual machines

The VM operating system started its days as an unofficial project. Wanting to build a time-sharing system for S/360 but realizing that the "official" TSS project would not be able to provide the sophisticated testing platform that they needed, developers at the Cambridge Scientific Center started work on the Cambridge Monitor System (CMS)[8] at the end of 1964.

It was to be a new kind of operating system, a system that would provide not only virtual memory, but entire virtual machines. In the virtual machine model, the hardware resources of a computer system are managed by one computer program, the Control Program (CP). Users' activities are managed by an operating system (CMS is one such OS). Developers saw that the cleanest way to protect users from one another was to use the S/360 *Principles of Operations* manual to describe the user's interface to the CP. Each user would have a virtual S/360 machine image in software created by the CP. The virtual machine image appears to be actual computer hardware to the programs running in that virtual machine, including operating systems and application programs. The idea of a virtual S/360 was new, but what was really important about their concept was that nobody until then had seen how elegantly a virtual machine system could be built, with very minor hardware changes and not much software.

The CMS developers worked under a very early S/360 operating system until they got enough of CMS together so that they could start it stand-alone from a card reader. In 1972, IBM announced VM/370 as an operating system together with S/370 models 370/158 and 370/168. Today, this operating system has evolved into what is now called z/VM.

Virtualization, stemming from the time-sharing concept and the need to virtualize the hardware, made IBM go back and look at the mainframe architecture and extend it to ensure the isolation needed for the virtual machines and to allow the virtualization Control Program to optimize performance.

z/VM is an important reason why Linux on the mainframe is so attractive. The "guest operating system" capability of VM, along with the guest isolation provided by the virtual machine concept, makes it possible to run hundreds of Linux servers under z/VM.

Figure 2-14 shows a typical system with z/VM and Linux running as guest operating systems, side by side with other operating systems. z/VM itself can also run under z/VM (as a test environment, for example).

---

[8] This is now known as the "Conversational Monitor System."

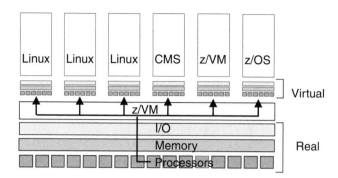

Figure 2-14. Linux as guest operating systems under z/VM

2.4.3 Logical partitioning (LPAR)

Some of the concepts of virtualization were so fundamental that it made sense to take them down below the architecture level. This became the logical partitioning (LPAR) and Processor Resource/Systems Manager (PR/SM) concepts.

Regardless of the number of central processors, a mainframe today can be divided logically into parts, giving the appearance of multiple different, totally separated and isolated computers to the users and to the system operator. A single zSeries 900 server today can be divided into as many as 15 logical partitions (LPARs).

For each LPAR, you can define the architecture and resources (central processors, central storage, and channels). A separate operating system can be installed and used in each LPAR. The operating systems in the LPARs can be different; you can run any mainframe operating system. An example is shown in Figure 2-15.

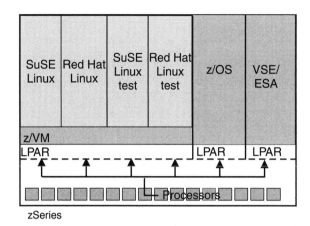

Figure 2-15. Linux images on one of two LPARS in a system

2.4.4 LPAR versus VM

With VM, resources can be dedicated to a guest operating system or virtualized. A virtualized resource appears to a program as a real resource that it can use fully. In fact, the resource is shared. With LPAR, resources can be dedicated (for the partition to use fully) or shared with other partitions. Table 2-3 shows the virtualization capabilities of VM and LPAR.

Table 2-3. Comparing LPAR and VM virtualization capabilities

	VM	LPAR
CPU	Virtual or dedicated	Dedicated or shared
Memory	Virtual or dedicated	Dedicated
Channels or devices	Virtual or dedicated	Dedicated or shared
Number of images supported	Hundreds	15

2.5 Summary

The mainframe and hardware have undergone a long evolution. The evolution has resulted in the well-known attributes of reliability, availability, and scalability. From its 24-bit, single CPU, real storage origins it has developed into architectured, 64-bit, SMP machines with virtualization not only of storage, but also of CPU and I/O resources. A single server is capable of supporting hundreds of operating system images.

The mainframe today is a multipurpose machine, optimized for data processing in a business environment and it continues to evolve in response to new business needs.

Chapter 3.
Introducing Linux on the Mainframe

From a project undertaken by a handful of developers, Linux on the mainframe has become an official component of IBM's mainframe strategy. This union of traditional proprietary computing and Open Source elements helps to bring e-business applications from distributed servers to a single platform where they can be more easily managed.

Looking at the Linux evolution and the evolution of the mainframe architecture, it becomes obvious that both have a specific background and their specific reasons for certain design decisions. In this chapter, we focus on bringing these two thoughts together. We will explore questions such as the following:

- Why does Linux fit the mainframe?

- How does Linux fit the mainframe?

3.1 Why Linux fits the mainframe

Linux can run on the mainframe because the mainframe is a general-purpose machine architected to support many programming models. Linux, in turn, is designed to be architecture-neutral except for a very thin architecture-dependent layer. Thus, the implementation of Linux on the mainframe came down to recompiling it for the mainframe architecture, and reimplementing Linux's architecture layer.

3.1.1 The mainframe is independent of the operating system

The IBM mainframe architecture was designed without a specific operating system in mind.[9] This is still true today. IBM's zSeries architects do not simply enrich the platform with new operating system features or new hardware functions; they primarily have the evolution of the platform in mind. Currently, the operating systems available for the zSeries mainframe are: z/OS, VSE/ESA, z/VM, TPF and, most recently, Linux.

---

[9] See *Principles of Operation* for an in-depth look at zSeries architecture.

3.1.2 Linux is independent of the hardware architecture

Linux grew to become a more architecture-independent operating system. Since the first port from Intel to the Alpha architecture in 1995, one design principle has been to clearly distinguish between architecture-dependent and architecture-independent code in the Linux kernel. The same holds for the GNU essential packages (like the C compiler and runtime library) which supported a variety of architectures even before Linux was released in 1991.

3.1.3 Fitting Linux into the mainframe portfolio

The Linux and Open Source development approach was taken for the port of Linux to the mainframe. But from the beginning, it was clear that production work had to run on Linux on the mainframe and that Linux had to run side by side with traditional mainframe operating systems in the data center. In this setting, qualities such as reliability, availability, serviceability, scalability, manageability, and security were important and had to be considered for Linux on the mainframe.

The unique hardware platform values of the mainframe are used by Linux. Fast time-to-market is also a factor when Linux is chosen in favor of a z/OS solution. Often a solution embraces both Linux and a traditional operating system, such as z/OS or VSE/ESA, in an integrated environment (that is, on the same machine). For example, since VSE/ESA does not provide a Java environment, Linux can host the Java components in an integrated VSE/ESA and Linux solution.

3.2 What was done to fit Linux onto the mainframe

Let us take a look at how the IBM team ported Linux to the mainframe and how the mainframe Linux distributions have developed.

IBM calls Linux on the mainframe "Linux for S/390" or "Linux for zSeries." Don't let the "for" confuse you. The Linux that IBM ported on the mainframe *is the same* Linux that is out there on the Internet. What the developers at IBM did was contribute a new architecture for inclusion in the Linux source tree—the zSeries (and S/390) architecture. Linux for zSeries supports the 64-bit z/Architecture in both real mode and virtual mode on zSeries CPUs. Linux for S/390 supports the 31-bit S/390 architecture and will also run on zSeries in 31-bit mode. The Linux code maintainers did not need to modify the common code, nor did they have to change the Linux system structure. (See Figure 3-1.) The new architecture code was accepted into the Linux code tree and is now a standard part of the Linux kernel.[10]

For the friends of the mainframe, let it be said that no changes were needed in the zSeries or S/390 architecture. No adaptation layer was required. The bottom line is that Linux runs on the mainframe architecture, period. The goal of the developers at IBM is to combine the strengths of Linux and the mainframe, not to reinvent a mainframe-specific Linux.

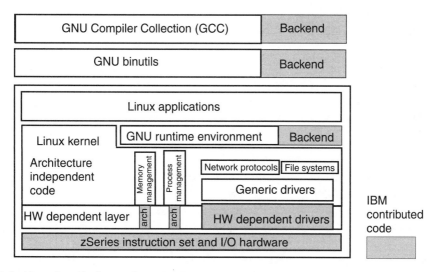

Figure   3-1. Linux for zSeries system structure

So how much code *was* added by IBM? The patches to the kernel that are needed to build Linux for the mainframe, at the time of writing, boil down to between 0.5% in the areas of glibc, gdb, gcc, and strace, up to 0.8% for the binutils, and about 2% in the Linux kernel. These were changes due to the system environment, the CPU architecture, and device support.

3.2.1 Porting Linux to the mainframe

Despite the fact that Linux is mostly developed on PCs and the majority of users run Linux on a PC, the design of Linux has been architecture-independent since its early days. Given the availability of a well-defined and well-documented hardware architecture, a working platform-specific compiler, and an operating system that has proven to be easily portable, what else do you need to bring it to the mainframe? Just a team of skilled programmers

---

[10] You can even see this code on your PC Linux. It is in the code tree that ships with all Linux distributions.

who were very enthusiastic about Open Source, Linux, and how this could fit on the mainframe!

Within a few weeks, the programmers could show that there were no technical obstacles that prevented the port of Linux to the mainframe architecture. From the start, it was clear that this had to be more than just a proof of technology. Therefore, the Linux kernel design was carefully studied and analyzed. Two objectives had to be met:

- The port had to become an official part of the Linux source. The platform-independent part of the Linux kernel must run unchanged on the zSeries architecture. The new code had to integrate seamlessly with the old, without impacting other architectures or violating the design and coding styles of Linux.

- The port had to run on the basic architecture definition of zSeries as documented in the *Principles of Operation*, the reference description. No emulation layer, or other "glue" code, could be used, nor could any extensions to the existing zSeries architecture be required.

   While an emulation layer approach typically helps avoid porting problems and thus leads to fast results, it comes with some major disadvantages. You typically have a performance degradation, and you have another layer of code that has to be maintained and synchronized with both the layer beneath (the architecture) and the layer above (the operating system). The Linux for zSeries programmers wanted to avoid using an emulation layer and meet the challenge of a technically clean solution. The "right thing to do" was to implement Linux on the pure architecture definition.

The work progressed rapidly, thanks to the clear separation between architecture-specific and architecture-independent parts in Linux. (The code for the former is placed in subdirectories for each architecture.) Because it is all Open Source code, it could be used as template and be adapted smoothly for the S/390 architecture. The majority of the architecture-dependent part for S/390 was written by developers at the IBM laboratory in Boeblingen, Germany, in 1998 and 1999.

Some special considerations went into the design of unique mainframe characteristics and how they relate to the Linux design. One example is the I/O channel subsystem of S/390 and the interrupt concept of Linux. Other presumed issues simply vanished. One example was the assumption that S/390 computes EBCDIC data only. Few people realize this, but the S/390 architecture is actually code-page neutral. Thus Linux works as a pure ASCII operating system on the mainframe.

3.2.2 Spreading the word—the Linux install fest

The first set of patches from IBM that enabled Linux to run on a mainframe were released to the Open Source world in December 1999. In 2000, the first commercial Linux for S/390 distribution (from SuSE) based on these patches became available.

To bring the mainframe and the Linux worlds together, and to increase the number of installations, IBM sponsored an installation party with the potential administrators of Linux on the mainframe. It was called an "install fest" because it was run from Germany. (You may have heard of the October Fest in Munich.)

There was no way that customers could bring in their heavyweight mainframes and disk subsystems over long distances to the location of the install fest as they would for a Linux user group PC install fest. The install fest had to be run remotely and without impact on the parts of the system that were running production work.

Materials were sent to participants in advance—planning guides, installation documentation, Linux distributions for the mainframe and also for desktop systems—to help participants become familiar with Linux. The actual installation took place during conference calls with four to seven participants who were ready to install Linux on their mainframes. For some of them, this was their first contact with Linux. The phone calls were staged by time zone, as several continents were involved—North and South America, Europe, and Asia.

The idea worked well. There was a great overall satisfaction with the ease of the process, the quality of help, and the speed of the installation. A lot of people expected an installation of a mainframe operating system to be a tedious task, given their prior experience with traditional mainframe operating systems. Installing Linux during a three-hour phone conference was a new experience.

Many customers overcame the initial hurdle of dealing with a new operating system on their mainframes. Furthermore, some mainframe experts showed their Linux system to Linux experts who had never dealt with the mainframe platform before, but were familiar with Linux on the PC and UNIX worlds. To a great degree, experts from both sides could talk about the same thing despite their different backgrounds. These technical contacts created synergy by getting the various technical people together and having them learn from each other.

Table 3-1 shows the rapid development of Linux on the mainframe.

Table   3-1. A brief history of Linux on the mainframe

Year	Event
1998	• December: Marist College in Poughkeepsie, New York, starts the Linux-390 mailing list: http://www.marist.edu/htbin/wlvindex?linux-390.
	• Several IBM employees participate in an unofficial capacity.
1999	• December: IBM announces its source modifications to the Linux kernel and tool chain. Linux for S/390 will run under VM, in LPAR, and in basic mode.
	• December: Patches for Linux for S/390 are released to the Open Source community through the IBM DeveloperWorks server.
2000	• January: Marist College releases pre-built files for a simplified install of Linux for S/390.
	• January: IBM initiates a Linux unit under senior executive Irving Wladawsky-Berger.
	• February: LinuxWorld in New York City and Paris. First technical demonstration of Linux on S/390.
	• May: SuSE and TurboLinux distributions announced.
	• August: SuSE Install Fest.
	• October: IBM commits support for 64-bit Linux (for zSeries).
	• November: TurboLinux Install Fest.
	• November: SuSE 31-bit distribution available.
	• December: IBM and other middleware for Linux on zSeries start roll-out.
	• December: 64-bit Linux patches submitted to Open Source.
2001	• January: TurboLinux 31-bit available.
	• March: Tape and disk device driver enhancements released.
	• December: Red Hat 31-bit available.
2002	• April: SuSE 64-bit available.
	• May: Exploitation of zSeries hardware (Cryptography and HiperSockets).
	• May: SCSI devices supported.
	• June: Red Hat 64-bit available.
	• November: SuSE SLES 8 (both 31-bit and 64-bit) powered by UnitedLinux launched.
2003	• New offerings including middleware enhancements.

3.3 How Linux fits the mainframe

Once Linux was ported to the mainframe, it turned out that its behavior on this platform was quite good. In fact, with Linux on the mainframe, you can:

- Scale with the workload

- Utilize CPU power

3.3.1 Scale with the workload

It has been claimed by some experts in the industry that Linux running on systems with multi-CPU capability does not scale well. What would be the point in running Linux on a large mainframe with multiple CPUs? Performance measurements, however, clearly show that many Linux applications on a mainframe scale well.

Figure 3-2 illustrates a scalability experiment with a business intelligence workload performed on an IBM zSeries processor. When adding copies of the workload (up to eight), the time that one CPU takes to complete the work increases linearly. The diagram also indicates that when the workload level is kept constant at eight, the time taken to complete the work is halved when an additional CPU is added, then roughly halved again when CPUs are doubled. Finally, we reach a level of eight CPUs running eight workloads.

The ideal scaling behavior of a multiprocessor would be when eight units of work on eight CPUs finish at the same time as one unit of work on one CPU. In Figure 3-2, if you compare the left-most and right-most measurements, they are not far off from that ideal. This experiment clearly indicates that on IBM's mainframe, Linux workloads scale well.

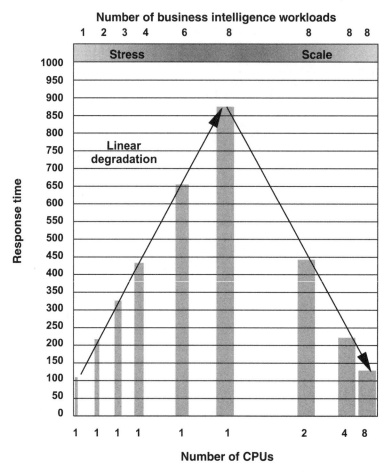

Figure 3-2. Scalability for Linux business intelligence workload. With increased load, response time increases linearly. With added CPUs, it decreases linearly on average.

3.3.2 Utilize CPU power

On the mainframe, you can have hundreds of Linux images. The workload management capabilities of the mainframe let you utilize the mainframe to a higher degree than an average server performing a single task. As an example, consider the four stylized workloads depicted as functions of CPU utilization in Figure 3-3. Each workload exhibits a very different behavior from the others over time, but all of them use about 50% of one CPU. One workload uses 100% of the CPU at times and then goes back down to zero again. The others are less radical, but have their own characteristics.

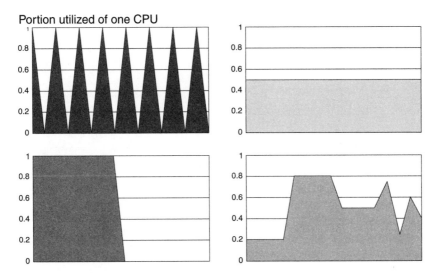

Figure 3-3. Workloads using 50% of one CPU

Each of these workloads has a justification for the machine it is on. The two on the left need their machines due to peaks workloads. The two on the right may be running on systems that do not allow a higher utilization for sustained periods of time due to constraints in the application or another part of the system. As an experiment, we will now consolidate the four workloads on a 4-CPU machine.

When we build a composite of all four workloads, we get the graph shown in Figure 3-4. The average utilization is still 50%. Using a 4-CPU machine that can sustain a higher utilization than 50%, we can reclaim some of the "white-space" and put even more work on it.

Number of CPUs

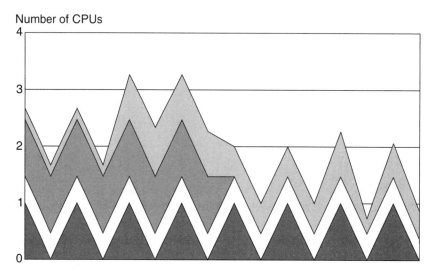

Figure   3-4. Utilization after consolidation—50% utilization of four CPUs

Another alternative is to use only three CPUs. If these workloads were running on VM on a 3-way mainframe, VM would manage them in the following way. You would need to decide what workload was your least favored (for example, the topmost workload) and its peaks would get elongated to the right. Or, you could decide to slow all the workloads down the same amount. Notice that just after the highest peaks there is excess capacity. Despite the slowdown, work would be caught up very quickly.

When can you stay with the 3-way machine and when would you need a 4-way machine? If Figure 3-4 shows a 24-hour day starting at midnight, the first shift has the highest peaks. There is not much room to grow on the first shift. If you needed to add work on the first shift, that would be a reason to go to a larger machine. Similarly, if none of the first shift workloads could afford elongation (for example, if it was real-time work), you would need a 4-way machine.

Most of the time, there is capacity to spare. For the first quarter of the chart, utilization is at 2.2 to 2.3 CPUs. In the second quarter of the chart, average utilization is probably around 2.7 to 2.8. On a mainframe running z/VM or z/OS, that level of utilization is not a problem. In fact, there is room for even more work.

These sample workloads are obviously made up to show different behaviors rather than to provide a good consolidation example. Larger numbers of unpredictably behaving workloads turn out to be statistically favorable for a consolidation solution. Later (see Chapter 6, "Total Cost of Ownership: the Challenge") we will look at what kinds of workloads make a favorable consolidation case.

3.4 Six reasons to run Linux on the mainframe

Many more benefits of running Linux on the mainframe have crystallized than were expected at the time of the first proof of concept. In our talks with companies that use Linux on the mainframe, we have come across more benefits than we can list here. However, let us look at some of the most important ones. All of these will be discussed in greater detail later in the book.

Linux on the mainframe meets several needs of mainframe-based enterprises today:

- Responsiveness.

  Many of the Open Source tools and applications that exist for Linux have become available on the mainframe. You can also test and use new functions earlier (in most cases) on Linux. You can try them out and promote or abandon them, depending upon the result of your tests.

  If a workload is broken up properly and distributed so that the right pieces of work are on Linux, time-to-market can be reduced. Securely isolated Linux images can be set up with ease, together with virtual communications that can be dynamically changed. This flexibility also adds to the time-to-market benefit.

- Close integration.

  Today's applications are typically multitiered, with the back-ends firmly rooted in z/OS and other platforms vying for the other tiers. Linux makes it possible to move the middle-tier close to the z/OS mainframe back-end, which may improve performance and reduce complexity.

  In contrast to z/OS, VSE/ESA does not provide its own Java environment. For VSE/ESA shops, Linux provides the opportunity of running Java applications in close integration with existing VSE/ESA resources.

  Linux as an operating system can span a huge range of machines, from the mainframe to departmental machines to desktop PCs. Similar skills can cover deployment on different platforms. Support people speak a common language and communicate well.

- Virtualization.

  With the virtualization technology found in IBM's z/VM product, you can run tens to hundreds of Linux images on a single mainframe, thus saving on hardware cost.

- New applications.

  A broader selection of applications is available with Linux.

- Safe experimentation.

Running evaluations or proofs of concept are easily done on a mainframe. It is quite easy to fire up a test Linux system without impacting the production workload running on the same machine (provided the spare resources are available).

- Skills are readily available.

  Since Linux is a UNIX-like operating system, a rich set of skills is available in the marketplace and from colleges and universities.

3.5 Summary

IBM is working to make sure that the mainframe can be used advantageously for Linux. Linux fits the mainframe well because of its hardware independence. Linux as an operating system behaves well on the mainframe. It scales and is able to fully utilize CPUs. Reasons to introduce Linux into your enterprise follow:

- Linux inherits availability, reliability, and scalability characteristics from the mainframe hardware.

- Linux is a source of new applications and new technology for e-business. Having new applications on the mainframe means you can use existing infrastructure for testing new ideas. In addition, having them on the mainframe can mean better integration into existing change and problem management procedures and service level agreements.

Part 2.
Planning for Linux

This part starts with an overview of how you can use Linux on the mainframe, thereby introducing sample companies that will be used throughout the book.

Sample projects are presented in the second chapter of this part. We look at how to get started with Linux on the mainframe.

The last chapter in this part discusses total-cost-of-ownership (TCO) analysis and how Linux on the mainframe can have a favorable impact.

Chapter 4.
Overview of What You Can Do with Linux on the Mainframe

Before you deploy Linux on the mainframe, you want to know what kind of business scenario can be advantageous. This book features two example companies: ISPCompany and StoreCompany. These companies demonstrate some typical Linux on the mainframe uses. One typical use is integrating middle-tier servers with z/OS or VSE/ESA. Another is consolidating stand-alone servers not needing integration with other systems. Scenarios that represent an in-between of these are, of course, also possible.

We have chosen two companies because with Linux on the mainframe we can observe two different styles of IT growth that we call *horizontal* and *vertical*. ISPCompany and StoreCompany represent typical businesses that are using Linux on the mainframe differently:

- ISPCompany is an outsourcing business which is growing horizontally and offers server consolidation on a zSeries 900. Refer to Appendix A, "ISPCompany," for more details on this company.

- StoreCompany is a retail company which is growing vertically, as the applications they use need more capacity. Refer to Appendix B, "StoreCompany," for more details on this company.

In this chapter we discuss:

- What growth scenarios can Linux on the mainframe support?
- What are typical Linux on the mainframe business applications?

4.1 Horizontal and vertical growth

What do we mean by horizontal and vertical growth? Horizontal growth is based on the concept of adding more of the same building blocks—in our case, adding server images alongside the existing server images. If you lined these servers up in a row, they would extend out to the horizon, as shown in Figure 4-1.

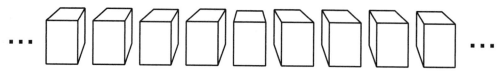

Figure 4-1. Horizontal growth

Such companies usually have a very segmented business where it is simple to segregate and grow by a cloning-like process. ISPCompany (for its outsourcing side of the business) experiences most of its growth from adding more images. For security reasons, each ISPCompany client needs a separate set of images. For ISPCompany's Internet service provider business, it is simple to grow by just adding more images for mail serving or Web serving as more clients sign up.

Vertical growth is based on the concept of an application needing more and more capacity. (See Figure 4-2.) In this case, it is easier to grow the image size than it is to split the work among a set of images. You could visualize this as an image growing upward:

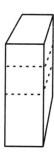

Figure 4-2. Vertical growth

Both the horizontal and vertical growth scenarios can map well to zSeries:

* Horizontal: It is relatively easy to create another Linux image using cloning techniques supported by z/VM. Some IT shops measure the time needed to set up a new server in a matter of minutes!

* Vertical: A zSeries mainframe can currently grow to a 16-way SMP. Its memory and cache structure allow a single application to exploit that entire multiprocessor capacity. Such a machine is efficient at both utilizing multiprocessor capacity and running multiple processes. Linux is developing into an environment that can handle workloads using several CPUs efficiently. There are various Capacity Upgrade on Demand options available.

4.2 ISPCompany and its new business application

ISPCompany offers two types of services:

- Mail serving and Web serving: infrastructure server consolidation of clients' low-utilized servers. (See Figure 4-3.) ISPCompany can put up to several hundred of these servers on one mainframe and can save substantially on overall cost. There is no need for stand-alone machines and their respective cables.

- Outsourcing: complete or partial hosting of other companies' computer systems on the mainframe. ISPCompany offers a spectrum of services that ranges from supplying the bare iron through providing applications, helpdesk, and backup/restore services.

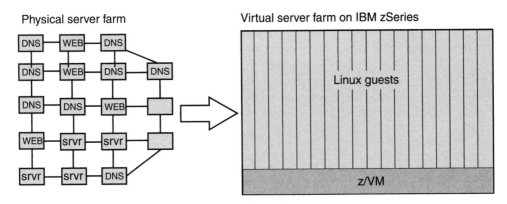

Figure   4-3. ISPCompany infrastructure server consolidation

See Appendix A, "ISPCompany" for a more complete story of ISPCompany's development.

In our example, ISPCompany has been approached by a client to outsource its small server farm. This opportunity for ISPCompany is handled by creating a new set of unique Linux images needed by this client. This is an example of horizontal growth.

4.3 StoreCompany and its business application

StoreCompany is used in this book to demonstrate issues of security, performance, and system management. StoreCompany is the larger of the two example companies. StoreCompany is an established retail company that is looking at using excess capacity to test a new business opportunity.

StoreCompany illustrates two different possibilities for using Linux on the mainframe:

- Back-end integration (Figure 4-4)
- Vertical growth

StoreCompany, a leading department store chain with 85 stores, has been in business for decades, mostly in large cities in the eastern United States. Their IT organization has been very progressive over the years, moving from back office and support functions to actively managing sales and inventory. They have also become involved in business-to-business type transactions with their key suppliers.

Our examples demonstrate the growth of the mainframe side of StoreCompany's IT division as Linux enters the picture in a new business endeavour. After integrating and growing Linux applications on the mainframe, the logical setup of StoreCompany will be as in Figure 4-4 (simplified).

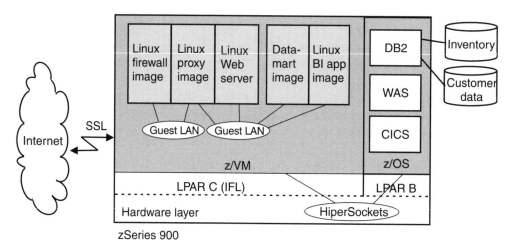

Figure 4-4. StoreCompany's back-end integration

See Appendix B, "StoreCompany" for a more complete story of StoreCompany's development.

StoreCompany is looking to test a new business opportunity. The suggestion is to use spare IFL capacity on the mainframe that hosts a Web-based ordering service and add a catalog of gifts (called "One-of-a-Kind" or OaK). The catalog is based on the inventory database and customer database already in place on the mainframe. Most of the changes related to the implementation of this will turn out to be in the software. If the experiment turns out well, more IFL capacity will be added to a new business intelligence application.

This application will then grow vertically, and the new business opportunity will take off. The hardware for the new business opportunity is mostly in place. See B.6, "Project 3: OaK project" for more details.

4.4 Summary

In this chapter, we have presented two companies with typical Linux projects. ISPCompany supports the infrastructure of various customers with Linux images on the mainframe. This enables ISPCompany to offer lower rates to customers. ISPCompany grows horizontally, adding new Linux images on its mainframe.

StoreCompany, on the other hand, is integrating Linux into the fabric of its enterprise as a system for rapid deployment. Linux on the mainframe gives StoreCompany the opportunity to be very responsive to demands for new applications at a very low risk. StoreCompany will create new Linux images as new prototype projects require. Projects that succeed and grow can justify any additional IFL capacity. Projects that fail simply have their images deleted, and others can then use the resources.

Chapter 5.
Sample Projects

After talking to customers who have finished at least one successful Linux-on-the-mainframe project, we realized that they all followed some basic project management rules. In this chapter, we will share our findings with you.

Some of the material may seem obvious to the experienced project manager, but it is surprising that a large number of projects fail to meet their original objectives because the simple rules-of-thumb presented here were not followed. Thus even the experienced may find this chapter useful as a quick review before moving on to the remaining parts of the book.

The trick is to choose the right project and use the opportunity of fast deployment that Linux gives you. In this chapter, we discuss the following questions:

- What should a Linux-on-the-mainframe team look like?
- What is a suitable project?

5.1 Building a team

In numerous project management classes, building a team for a project is seen as critical. It may be the first thing you consider, even before selecting a specific project.

On the Linux-on-the-mainframe team, you will need people with the right mix of technology skills. This might mean that your team members come from different departments across the company. First, the team will need general IT skills in the form of good system management and control processes. This skill is independent of their technical background and can be provided by people with either a mainframe or a Linux and UNIX background.

Second, the team will obviously need someone who knows how to prepare for a Linux image on the mainframe. Skills that such a person might have include setting up a mainframe, operating it, partitioning it, defining I/O, and setting up z/VM or LPAR.

Last, but not least, the team will profit from someone who has Linux, or at least UNIX, administrator skills.

Apart from these skills related to the technology used, you will also need some skill in the area of the project chosen.

5.2 Choosing the right Linux project

People tell us two things about Linux on the mainframe projects:

- It is easy to get started.

- Using a staged approach works best.

5.2.1 Start small

Our advice is to start small. The bigger the scope of the initial project, the more the entire company is involved, and the harder it will be to succeed. What would constitute a typical small project? In our experience, successful companies started with things like consolidating an infrastructure server on the mainframe or simple (static) Web serving. Choosing a low-attention project allows the team some success without the pressure of company politics. Once some success with Linux is established, that can be used to calm the fears of any doubters. It is important with new technology in a large company to have an early success. Even if the Linux project is simple, it gives you the proof that the technology works and the benefit of undisputable savings (for example, you did not have to buy another server). Once you have the proof that the technology works, you are ready to take the next step. StoreCompany started off with moving the firewall and proxy servers to Linux (see B.4, "Project 1: Firewall and proxy server"). That was a project of limited scope that proved successful.

The second reason for starting small is authority. The Linux-on-the-mainframe team needs the authority to move forward and to use the necessary resources. Big projects need significant resources, which again is often difficult to procure for as yet unproven technology in a company.

5.2.2 Initial server consolidation

For some, this level may be as far as they want to go. Here you might realize some hardware savings because you have consolidated servers on to the mainframe. This is also called simple server consolidation, taking the work from several servers and consolidating that work on one server. See Figure 5-1.

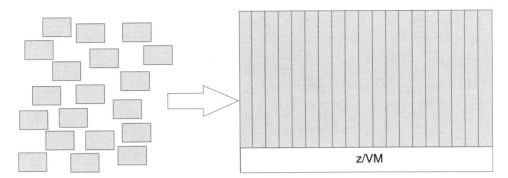

Figure 5-1. Simple server consolidation

With Linux on the mainframe, we continue to use the term *server consolidation*. It also means moving as much work as possible to one server. With Linux, what is often moved to the mainframe are whole images, one by one, including all the resources they need. Often this is done with the help of z/VM, in which case VM controls these guest systems.

Using Linux, this "work migration" is typically simple. There are no worries about how to pack all the things together, and usually the application we are talking about already exists on Linux. Thus, you do not need to migrate code from another operating system or talk your vendor into doing it. The only change that is made is where the image is hosted. Instead of on real, separate hardware, it is now on virtual hardware (LPAR and/or z/VM).

In this case, there frequently are savings on the hardware side, assuming that enough servers are consolidated. How many servers are "enough"? For example, one department store colocated 50 servers by going to Linux on the mainframe. The break-even point depends on your environment.

While what you include in a business case can vary from hardware and software costs to efficiency and ease of management, with Linux on the mainframe you can often make your case. What you have gained is a simplified setup, easy scalability, and improved availability.

Example

If there is already a mainframe present in the enterprise, then to achieve such a consolidation, the price of an Integrated Facility for Linux (IFL) should be considered. If a number of low-utilized servers, N, can be consolidated, that might make up the price for one IFL (see Figure 5-2).

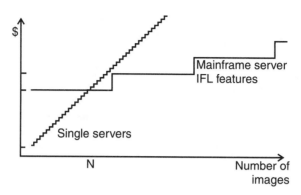

Figure 5-2. Server consolidation cost example

Although this example is oversimplified, it illustrates why most of the larger consolidation cases you may hear about are on z/VM. With LPAR, you can have at the most 15 logical partitions in a z900 or z800, and with one server per partition, that is 15 servers. Under certain circumstances, even fewer images can pay off as a consolidation case.

What if you do not have a mainframe to start with? If you have to buy a whole new machine (say, a model z800 0LF that has one CPU), the cost will obviously be higher than adding one IFL to an existing mainframe. In this case, you need more Linux servers to consolidate for break-even. But the incremental growth path is attractive because if you need more capacity, then an additional CPU does not incur a great cost. By the way, the more Linux images you have, the more hardware sharing (such as sharing LAN adapters) will help save on cables and routers.

5.2.3 Full Linux integration in an enterprise

This second level of server consolidation is more complex because it involves integrating a Linux middle-tier with the legacy back-end systems. Because you have to use middleware and connectors and the like, this is a more complicated project. There are tuning issues as you allocate resources to the back-end and to the middle-tier. There are relative priorities that must be set to get the work done, and so on. Here IBM's WebSphere family of products can be effectively used for developing Linux applications and deploying them on the mainframe. For more information, see
`http://www.ibm.com/software/info1/websphere/index.jsp`.

5.3 Summary

In this chapter, we shared with you some of the lessons we learned when talking with companies that have introduced Linux on the mainframe. Getting started with Linux on the mainframe is easy. We discussed building a team and the importance of choosing a suitable small project to start with. We mentioned cost and break-even considerations.

Customers tell us that Linux on the mainframe helps them streamline operations and simplify management. The mainframe might be more cost-efficient and easier to run than a physical server farm. For details of customer stories, see
http://www.ibm.com/servers/eserver/zseries/os/linux/stories.html.

Chapter 6.
Total Cost of Ownership: the Challenge

Numerous papers have discussed server consolidation in the last few years. The articles illustrate a renewed interest in the mainframe and make a clear financial case for server consolidation and for moving applications to the mainframe. The bottom line is that the initial cost of a mainframe is often counter-balanced and outweighed by long-term profitability. This especially applies to Linux on the mainframe.

If you are considering a project that involves Linux, you will already have a good idea of the business value to your company. To assess the return on investment for the project, you will need to balance the value against the total cost of ownership (TCO). This chapter discusses these questions:

- What are factors to consider in a TCO equation?

- How can the mainframe lower your TCO?

- How can Linux lower your TCO?

- What are examples of how companies save by deploying Linux on the mainframe?

6.1 Total cost-of-ownership factors

As indicated in 4.3, "StoreCompany and its business application," StoreCompany is looking at setting up a new Web catalog with third-party items that StoreCompany would not have to stock. Now it is up to you as "decision maker" to decide whether to give this new idea a try. Naturally, you ask, "What is the cost of this opportunity?" Linux on the mainframe brings some interesting factors to the TCO calculation.

Total cost of ownership attempts to give a picture of total cost of an IT system over a period of time, typically three to five years. A TCO analysis is especially of interest when you are considering any significant change, such as evaluating a new business opportunity, upgrading your servers, or moving locations. This can be contrasted with *total cost of acquisition*, which takes into account only the cost of buying new machinery and associated software but does not include any other costs.

A TCO study is made up of a multitude of factors. Some are quantifiable, such as the typical factors listed in Table 6-1. Other factors are of a more hidden nature and are listed in Table 6-2. Some factors have a particular importance when you are considering the combination of Linux and the mainframe.

In short, calculating TCO is a complicated business, and every organization ultimately must come up with its own method.

Table   6-1. Typical TCO factors (cost of acquisition)

Quantifiable cost factors

Hardware:	Software:	Occupancy:
• CPU, storage • Disks • Network, cables • Maintenance and support	• Operating system • Middleware • Systems management programs • Application software • Maintenance and support	• Space • Power • Lighting, heating, cooling
People, or full-time equivalents (FTEs): • Operators • System administrators • Data administrators	Services: • Contract costs for new projects. • Consultants to guide the project design and deployment	Opportunity factors: • Cost of money (the interest on the loan you took, or the stock you issued) • The deferred costs of not pursuing other opportunities (this gets into the risk of prioritizing business choices)

A typical TCO equation thus sums the cost of hardware, software, occupancy, people, and services. In addition to this, you may want to consider costs of a more hidden nature such as those listed in Table 6-2.

Table   6-2. Hidden TCO factors

Hidden cost factors

Availability factors:	Hardware:	Opportunity factor:
• Duration and frequency of software outage • Cost of backup and restore • Cost of service, debugging, and repair	• Reliability of hardware platform • Flexibility • Freedom of choice (hardware and software vendor)	• Time-to-market • Favorable mentions in the press or influential reference customer

Let us go quickly through the typical TCO factors before we look at what Linux and the mainframe bring to the equation. Note that we will not give you exact numbers for any of the parameters, because every one of these varies throughout the world. For example, labor costs are not uniform across the globe.

6.1.1 Hardware

Hardware usually includes:

- Servers, including not just the machines you need for production, but all of the associated machines, like the backup, development, failover, network infrastructure (firewalls), and test machines.

- Disks and tape (storage), including the data backup for this.

- Network attachment (interface cards and routers and the cables, including fiber).

A physical server costs the same whether its utilization is 100% or 10%. Chances are that not only the test and supporting servers are low-utilized. Typically, the utilization of the production servers is in the 10 – 20% range. It may be worth looking into consolidating that whole set of servers on z/VM. Assuming you do not have work that requires new, dedicated capacity, the virtualization technology offered by z/VM can save you real hardware, such as CPUs, disks, and cabling.

6.1.2 Software

Software cost includes acquisition, plus service and support of the programs used on the system:

- Operating system
- Middleware
- Systems management programs
- Applications

Additionally, software costs generally include the backup software and essential network services such as directory services, messaging, routing security, and network management.

While it is possible to build a Linux system from sources on the Internet for free, this may not be suitable for production systems. With Linux, the operating system cost may be low, especially if the price is based on the number of processors you have (rather than the number of images). The cost of a distribution today may include maintenance.

In fact, for all of the software, you have the option of building it yourself (the cost will be in the development), buying it (and getting the service that goes with a contract), or using Open Source (some cost will be in the support, either in a support contract or as personnel cost).

6.1.3 Maintenance and support

The purpose of a support contract is for an enterprise to have access to a problem reporting mechanism (usually a phone number), including an assurance that problems reported will be fixed. Some software providers offer a single number to call for all of the products in the solution. In other words, they accept responsibility for the solution. Others cover only the products they sell.

The cost of support will be a trade-off between what you want to do yourself versus what the service contract should cover. Part of your TCO analysis might be to decide on the trade-off. It is the time of your staff versus an expense. The range of possibilities in the Linux space is wide. If, for example, you are happy with using mailing lists to find solutions to problems in Open Source programs, the cost of service can be low. You can decide on an umbrella contract that covers everything, such as IBM Global Services offers. Most Linux distributors offer support as well.

6.1.4 Services

Services involve a contract or contracts with a consultant or others who are hired to do something, such as develop a tool. An example of services for Linux on the mainframe could be getting z/VM operational, if you don't have the skills available. Or, if you don't have Linux skill, you could contract that out until your people get their education. Or you could get one of the distributors to come in and set up Linux for you.

You have a lot of control over services. The question is, for the particular solution you are considering, how many services are you going to buy to get the solution up and running?

6.1.5 Occupancy

Servers must be housed somewhere. The cost of the raised floor in square feet, space for access and the control center, and power are usually included in an occupancy parameter for TCO.

Part of what used to make the mainframe a "dinosaur" was the cooling, the raised floor, and the cabling. Today, a mainframe uses less of almost everything than a typical server farm. A mainframe no longer needs a raised floor and has a moderate footprint, as shown in Table 6-3.

Table   6-3. Mainframe (zSeries 900) space requirements

	Minimum configuration, 1 frame	Maximum configuration, 2 frames
Weight	917 kg (2021 lbs)	1866 kg (4113 lbs)
Footprint	1.32 sq. meters (14.2 sq. feet)	2.81 sq. meters (30.3 sq. feet)
Height	200.4 cm (79.8 inches)	200.4 cm (79.8 inches)

Given the availability of high-speed fiber for interconnecting sites, the cost of occupancy may be a less critical factor in the future. You now have more choice as to where you want to locate the equipment. However, consolidating football fields of servers on a mainframe can mean substantial savings in square feet and power (power to run the machine, to cool the machine, power for your staff working there, etc.).

If you think about a typical low-end server (such as a PC) consuming, for example, a kilo-watt, and the biggest z900 mainframe consuming around 15 KW and being capable of functionally replacing numerous low-utilized servers, the cost savings in power can be dramatic.

Example: While a typical configuration of a server farm can cost hundreds of dollars a day in electricity to run, a single z900 running the same workload can be an order of magnitude cheaper. The savings are even more dramatic when the floor space requirements of a server farm are considered. The average server farm can require up to some 10,000 square feet of floor space compared with the much smaller footprint of the mainframe including its peripheral devices, as shown in Table 6-3.

6.1.6 People

Personnel cost is normally measured in units of full-time equivalents (FTEs).

Personnel typically included might be operators, system administrators, and data administrators. The personnel cost can be calculated by multiplying the number of FTEs with a current average salary.

How many machines or servers or how much data one person can handle often depends on the type of task the servers are doing. FTE averages that are sometimes used are shown in Table 6-4.

In general, the more similar the servers in a server environment are, the more servers one FTE can manage.

Table   6-4. Different types of server tasks require different numbers of people per server

Server task	Number of servers per FTE
Large application server, running a CPU-intensive job such as business intelligence or ERP.	1.5 to 3 servers, with the average IT shop having around 2 servers per person.
Small application server, running more specialized applications such as accounting packages or HR programs.	2 to 4 servers, with the average IT shop supporting 3 servers per person.
File and print characterized by very low utilization rates.	10 to 40 servers, with the average person managing 20 servers.
Firewall servers typically characterized by very low utilization rates.	10 to 40 servers, with the average person managing 20 servers.
E-mail servers.	5 to 50 servers supported by each FTE. On average, 10 servers running a typical e-mail application can be supported by each FTE.
Web/Internet applications.	10 to 40 servers running a Web application can be supported by each IT staffer, with the average IT shop managing 15 servers per FTE.
Systems management involves applications that simplify network and applications management such as Tivoli Business Systems Manager.	1 FTE to support 5 to 15 servers. The typical IT staff member could manage 7 systems management servers.

6.2 The mainframe and the TCO equation

What are the mainframe attributes that make it valuable from a TCO perspective?

6.2.1 Availability factors

To assess the impact of an unavailable system and hence what it is worth to you to have the system available, you should consider these factors:

- Staff productivity—If the system is down, parts of your staff cannot perform their jobs. The cost depends on the duration of the outage and how many employees were impacted. How long does it take before the system is up again, and what does a person-hour cost you?

- Damage to the company brand—If the outage is spectacular enough, it will make the news.

- Effect on the share value and hence the value of the company.

Sources of outages generally include software errors and hardware errors. The goal of mainframe hardware development is to have no downtime. Most changes to I/O and most memory upgrades can now be done on the fly, as can some CPU updates.

Statistically, outage-causing errors are most often found in the applications. Just as you decide what hardware to use, you decide what applications to use, whether to buy them, build them yourself, or use Open Source. Choosing software carefully can help in maintaining good availability.

6.2.2 Mainframe availability characteristics

Availability involves reducing the duration and frequency of outages.

The mean time between failures (MTBF) for the mainframe of up to 30 years can be attributed to the mainframe's unique combination of availability features (refer to Chapter 2, "Introducing the Mainframe" for details):

- Redundancy is the most important contributing factor for availability, and it is also the reason why the mainframe is expensive from a cost-of-acquisition point of view. Redundancy gives the mainframe the ability to dynamically replace, frequently with no impact on running programs, failing hardware units like CPUs or memory.

- Error correction code (ECC) is provided in all levels of memory and checking is provided on all buses. When errors are found in either data or logic, they are corrected on the fly, where possible.

Relevant chapter in book: Chapter 11, "Achieving Higher Availability" and Chapter 13, "Availability Management."

6.2.3 Partitioning and virtualization

The value of Linux on the mainframe is in large part due to the possibility of hosting multiple servers on a single hardware machine. On the mainframe, there are two methods for hosting multiple operating systems: logical partitioning (LPAR) and virtualization using z/VM. The mainframe offers the most mature and dynamic partitioning and virtualization technology in the industry.

zSeries LPAR implementation is unique in comparison to the other partitioning implementations available from other hardware vendors. LPAR can exploit the PR/SM microcode, which provides a flexibility superior to that of a static hardware solution. Logical partitions each have their own allocation of memory, and either dedicated or shared processors, as well as dedicated and shared channels for I/O operations.

z/VM presents a unique virtualization approach. It provides each end user with an individual working environment known as a *virtual machine*. The virtual machine simulates the existence of a dedicated real machine, including processor functions, storage, and I/O resources. For example, you can run multiple z/OS and Linux on zSeries images on the same z/VM system that is supporting z/VM applications and end users. As a result, application development, testing, and production environments can share a single physical computer.

Relevant chapter in book: Chapter 7, "The Value of Virtualization."

6.2.4 High utilization rates

The average server farm tends to have low CPU utilization. If you have low utilized Linux (or UNIX) servers, you could run them all on one mainframe, which would then run at a higher utilization. Using Linux guests on z/VM gives you the capability to utilize even more such logical servers. With z/VM, you can also manage the priority of the guests and provide more resources to important guests in a peak situation.

The CPU has historically been considered the "expensive" part of a (mainframe) computer, and the part to utilize fully. The rest of the system should feed the CPU work so that it can run at nearly 100%. It takes clever design to build a fast CPU and the supporting I/O and memory structure to allow "normal" work to be able to drive it to 100% capacity. When we talk about *balance*, we mean that memory and I/O support the CPU.

Thus, in utilizing a mainframe, it is not so much a question of how high the load can be (it can even be 100%). The question is, is there enough workload to keep it busy?

Relevant chapter in book: Chapter 7, "The Value of Virtualization" and Chapter 15, "Performance and Capacity Planning."

6.3 Linux and the TCO equation

Let us look at what Linux considerations can change the TCO equation to your benefit.

6.3.1 Opportunity factors

The importance of nearly 100% availability may argue for many projects being done in z/OS. However, when fast time-to-market is essential, Linux on the mainframe may come into play because for some applications Linux can have adequate availability characteristics while giving you the following:

- Technology (and applications) not available on z/OS that you can exploit for time-to-market. (See Part 5, "Running Applications" for a discussion of the applications and middleware available.)

- Opportunity for rapid change

6.3.2 Time-to-market

Time-to-market has become one of the most important attributes a company can have. If the IT infrastructure is impeding development (or whatever is important to your business, such as marketing), it can be costly in lost business. If this is the case, you might want to consider Linux. The benefits of Linux can be summarized as follows:

- New applications can be available more quickly.

- Applications are simpler to port, as many applications are developed on Linux or UNIX.

- Many applications are available from the Open Source community.

Another kind of time-to-market is the possibility to provide new images quickly to the customer by using z/VM and cloning techniques.

Relevant part of book: Part 5, "Running Applications."

6.4 ISPCompany: TCO considerations

6.4.1 Software

ISPCompany buys most of its software through site licenses (when these are available) and shares savings with its clients. The benefit to their customers is that they get a larger choice for less cost to them.

ISPCompany offers a choice of two distributions to their customers: SuSE and Red Hat. The more consolidated servers there are, the cheaper they become. The more standardized the servers can be, the easier they are to maintain and create.

6.4.2 Occupancy

ISPCompany pays as part of its overhead for the IT infrastructure and utility costs. Its clients do not need the space and utility costs (and the headaches of redundancy, and so forth). They indirectly just pay a share of the costs.

Until the typical company grows big enough to have multiple sites, the IT site and personnel are usually kept where it normally does business, which tends to be a high-rent district. ISPCompany is big, and it is a business for businesses. Hence it does not have to locate in a high-rent district. It also has the ability to attract and keep more talent because it has more job opportunities in IT.

ISPCompany and its clients can save considerably when consolidating servers on the mainframe.

Refer to Appendix A, "ISPCompany" for more details on occupancy.

6.5 StoreCompany: TCO considerations

6.5.1 Software

StoreCompany's software costs will only increase when it adds IFLs or new priced software. In our OaK example, software costs are only an initial cost (probably mitigated by a test license) increase for their DB2 UDB. Software cost always depends on the license conditions. The other software costs are flat until the extra IFL capacity is brought online. And that cost is split amongst all the Linux images!

In our StoreCompany example, a clone can be made of an existing Linux image and some new code needs to be written. The new code manages the presentation of items in the OaK category, assuring that the order is sent to the right artist to be filled, making special offers to customers fitting a certain profile, and serving dynamic Web pages.

6.5.2 Hardware

When trying out a new project, one first tries to use spare capacity. On the mainframe, all spare capacity is aggregated into one machine. The amount of spare capacity to try out new ideas can mean avoiding new hardware acquisitions.

If one adds more capacity for a specific application and it turns out that the application does not need it, it is simple to reconfigure that capacity to the other images. If the new business opportunity does not work out well for StoreCompany, it is easy to reconfigure the system and use any excess capacity for other Linux applications. In contrast, other design implementations may mean that StoreCompany's business intelligence application would be implemented on a stand-alone machine. If the number of visitors to the new catalog turns out to be low, machine resources would be "wasted."

6.6 Summary

It is clear that the cost versus benefit equation for investment in server infrastructures extends well beyond initial acquisition. TCO deals with fundamental variables of IT effectiveness and business performance. Linux on the mainframe offers a highly reliable hardware platform. A large number of low-utilized Linux images can be consolidated with little effort. You can manage them flexibly using the resource-sharing techniques of the mainframe.

Linux on the mainframe is one alternative for implementing your project. You could also choose to implement an application using, for example, z/OS. The decision comes down to the alternatives available and the cost of each. Not only may a project have value in and of itself, but additional value may be realized when using Linux on the mainframe:

- Using Linux as a development platform may give you a considerably shorter development time than other solutions and may offer revenue from a project sooner.

- z/VM and Linux make it possible, for example, to create new Linux images in a matter of minutes instead of days.

What factors you include in a TCO for a Linux-on-the-mainframe project will depend on your model of IT value.

Part 3.
Is Linux on the Mainframe for Me?

This part covers some potential advantages to consider when planning your Linux-on-the-mainframe project in more detail.

First, we explore one of the technologies that makes Linux on the mainframe an interesting proposition: virtualization.

This is followed by a look at one of the most important issues for any enterprise using computers to do their business: security.

Next is a discussion of how to set up Linux on the mainframe, including guest definitions, availability considerations, and file system considerations.

Achieving higher availability discusses how availability can be optimized.

Finally, we examine how Linux and the mainframe communicate with the rest of the world, because this is different from what you may be used to with other Linux platforms.

Chapter 7.
The Value of Virtualization

Virtualization provides valuable support for running large numbers of Linux images on the mainframe. IBM mainframe virtualization technology is found in the z/VM product and in logical partitioning (LPAR). These technologies provide the infrastructure that enable, on one hand, numerous Linux images that use only small amounts of CPU, and, on the other hand, a few Linux images that consume large amounts of CPU to be hosted on a single mainframe. Such deployments might save your company money.

z/VM is the zSeries Virtual Machine operating system. This chapter explains why z/VM is ideally suited for large-scale Linux deployments and server consolidation. z/VM's ability to run hundreds of Linux images on a single machine opens a multitude of business possibilities. Because the powerful mainframe virtualization technology is little understood outside the mainframe world, this chapter should be especially useful for readers not familiar with the mainframe.

In this chapter, we discuss these questions:

- What is z/VM, and how did its virtualization technology develop?
- How does Linux run on z/VM?
- What are the possibilities and benefits of running Linux under z/VM or on an LPAR?

7.1 What is z/VM?

To better understand what is going on today, it is sometimes helpful to revisit the past. In this section, we examine what drove the creation of z/VM and why it plays such a key role in Linux on the mainframe.

Virtual machine (VM) technology development started with the IBM System/360 in the mid-1960s. One reason for developing it was the need for testing facilities. Many software programmers could thus test new programs on the virtual hardware simultaneously.

Another factor driving VM development was the need for multiuser systems. Computers were large and costly. Thus, a need arose for an operating system environment that allowed multiple users to use one machine simultaneously in real-time.

To support testing and multiple users, researchers developed the unique concept of *virtual machines*. In the virtual machine model, the hardware resources of a computer system are managed by a *hypervisor*. VM's hypervisor is called *Control Program (CP)*. Users' activities are managed by an operating system. When users log on to VM, CP creates a unique guest virtual machine for each user. Depending on the guest definition, CP then allows the user to start up an operating system within that guest.

The first commercial VM product offering from IBM, in 1972, was the VM/370 product. Apart from CP, it included a special-purpose operating system called *CMS*, the *Conversational Monitoring System*. CMS has been a component of VM products ever since the delivery of VM/370. The purpose of the CMS operating system is to provide multiple users with a powerful yet simple interactive interface that performs extremely well. Performing well means sub-second response time for hundreds of CMS instances on a single machine. The design for simplicity extends to all aspects of CMS, including the command set and file system. The CMS that offers the VM community a rich set of programming tools and utilities can help manage and automate a virtual Linux server farm running on the current VM product, z/VM.

Guests on z/VM are zSeries operating systems in their own right. The CMS operating system today is different from the other guests in that it no longer runs native on the hardware. The use of CMS has changed from being VM's only interactive end user operating system to also being a home for utility-like functions. For example, TCP/IP or performance management functions can be run in a guest of their own and can be used by other guests.

Similarly, in a Linux-on-the-mainframe environment with many Linux guests, CMS is where scripts get run to automatically restart failing images, or manage switch-over to a hot standby. A system administrator uses CMS to create new images (or CMS is the programmatic interface where the request for the creation of a new Linux image is routed).

Over time, IBM has made investments in hardware, architecture, and microcode, as well as in the VM product itself, to enhance the virtualization technology available with each successive line of mainframe computers.

7.2 How Linux can run on z/VM

At its core, the z/VM operating system is a hypervisor. The hypervisor can present virtual copies of the underlying hardware resources that it controls to operating systems running on a virtual machine. Users can run multiple images of other operating systems as "guests" of the hypervisor, sharing the same single set of real CPUs and I/O facilities, as shown in Figure 7-1.

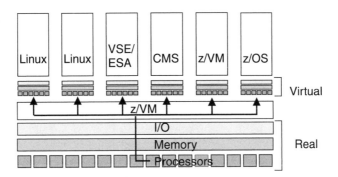

Figure 7-1. Virtualization technology with z/VM. Resources can be virtualized and presented to the user as if each user had his or her own machine.

Any operating system that can run on an S/390 or z/Architecture mainframe can also run under the control of z/VM, that is, in a z/VM-created virtual machine. z/VM faithfully represents the complete mainframe architecture to the guest operating system.

Like any other operating system that runs on the mainframe architecture, *Linux runs on z/VM without any further changes.*

7.3 What does z/VM provide?

z/VM is a mainframe operating system. Linux on the mainframe can particularly benefit from what z/VM provides:

- The hypervisor.

  z/VM's CP component is the hypervisor that manages resources for its guests. The hypervisor includes all the emulation code and an extremely efficient scheduler. The fact that hundreds of users can work concurrently and expect sub-second response times shows the efficiency of the scheduler.

- The CMS operating system.

  CMS has a simple user interface and is used by system administrators to manage both z/VM itself and its guests. It is also used as a utility operating system for various server functions such as TCP/IP.

- A large set of systems management tools.

  In the z/VM directory, system administrators can quickly and easily change the definitions of a guest or create a new guest. z/VM has both a user interface and a command line interface that can be driven by scripts to control the entire environment. z/VM's system administration facility includes functions that help the user create and

manage multiple Linux images. Functions include assigning disks, starting and stop-
ping Linux images, and more. System and hardware resources can be allocated among
multiple Linux guests, which can also be managed by z/VM.

A scripting language (REXX) allows for programmatic response to events; for example,
you can use the programmable operator (PROP) to filter messages from the z/VM operator console. You can specify a REXX program (called a *PROP exit*) to be invoked
whenever a guest logoff message appears. The message includes the name of the
guest that terminated. The exit could then take whatever action was appropriate, such
as restarting the guest. There are also extensive logging capabilities for performance
tracking or debugging.

z/VM has a large, active user community (much like the Open Source community) that
provides tools and scripts for managing a z/VM environment.

- Security and integrity.

z/VM is built on the mainframe architecture that highly values those attributes. We
examine z/VM security and integrity in Chapter 8.

To understand the difference of z/VM compared to other virtualization techniques, we need
to take a look at some technical issues.

Importantly, z/VM allows its guests to take advantage of the underlying mainframe architecture. In the interest of achieving good performance, z/VM guests run as much as possible
as if the hardware were real. Only when z/VM must run privileged instructions for the guest
does it take control from the guest.

In 1985, IBM announced and delivered a microcode assist for its 3081, 3083, and 3084
processor models called *Start Interpretative Execution (SIE)*. The SIE assist reduced the
number of instructions VM had to execute on behalf of a guest operating system. With SIE,
the processor (in interpretative execution mode) could handle more guest I/O instructions
and associated interrupts. Less VM intervention was required, thus significantly improving
guest performance.

The distinguishing factor of z/VM is that all resources can be virtualized. CPU, memory,
disks, and network communications can be virtual (see Chapter 10). Additionally, certain
hardware that is supported on some mainframe models can sometimes be virtualized on
other models. For example, it is possible to use virtual HiperSockets on machine models
that do not support real HiperSockets (such as G5, G6, and Multiprise 3000 servers).

In summary, the guest operating system believes that it owns and controls the hardware.
CP allows the guest control until an instruction occurs that CP must interpret. From the
outside observer's perspective, there is a "duet" of the CP and the guest.

7.4 What is logical partitioning?

Once VM was generally available in 1972, some companies used it to partition machines in order to run different workloads in different partitions. It turned out that for some companies, a simpler partitioning scheme would be just as useful. As a result, some fundamental virtualization concepts were included into the architecture. These concepts became the hardware hypervisor *Processor Resource/Systems Manager (PR/SM)* and the *logical partitions (LPARs)* into which PR/SM could divide a machine. A zSeries 900 or 800 mainframe can run in one of two modes: basic mode or LPAR mode. In basic mode, the entire machine is under the control of a single operating system. In LPAR mode, you can logically divide the machine into partitions so that multiple operating systems can run concurrently.

LPAR partitioning helps companies to exploit the resources of the machine better than if there were no partitioning. LPAR allows companies to have a single machine support both production and test requirements. Initially, companies would bring up the test partition only at off-peak times.

The PR/SM hypervisor of the zSeries 900 can manage up to 15 LPAR "guests." The CPU and channel paths are the two resources that can be logically shared. Central storage must be physically partitioned and assigned to each active partition.

Although the virtualization technology that is best known in the context of Linux on the mainframe is z/VM, there are some occasions where you might consider using an LPAR:

- You might want to take advantage of the cost savings available with Integrated Facility for Linux (IFL). The IFL feature CPUs can be assigned only within an LPAR that is dedicated to Linux, or Linux running on z/VM (see 21.4, "Integrated Facility for Linux (IFL)").

- You might want to have just a few Linux images. Then you might not require the ability of z/VM to handle hundreds of images.

- You might require the certified security offered by LPAR. Typically, you might want to run a few Linux images each in their own LPAR (Figure 7-2). An independent authority has certified LPAR to confirm that LPARs are isolated from one another (see 23.1.1, "LPAR certification"). Depending on your corporate audit policy, a firewall might be an instance where you want an individual Linux in its own LPAR.

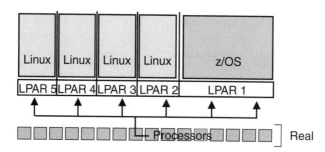

Figure   7-2. Two LPARs, one running z/OS, the other running Linux

Companies can utilize their mainframe with more flexibility using LPARs than using native mode. However, LPAR provides far less flexibility and function than what is available with z/VM.

7.5 Why run Linux on z/VM?

The interest in Linux on the mainframe can be attributed to three things:

- As a source of new technology for mainframe users

- As an opportunity to reduce complexity when deploying an integrated server environment

- As a possibility to host large server farms

z/VM is ideally suited to hosting an integrated Linux server environment, letting companies run applications across multiple images on a single hardware platform. Information technologists can exploit the benefits of having numerous images, each running only one application, and yet limit the costs associated with having unique hardware for each image, as shown in Figure 7-3.

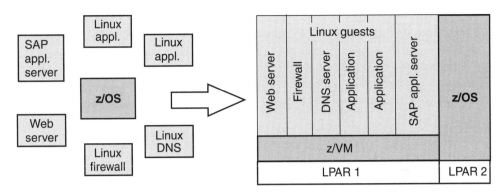

Figure   7-3. Application images can be brought closer to the back-end z/OS (integrated environment)

Many years of product development have made z/VM ideally suited today for Linux deployments. Through the years of product development, z/VM has been designed to support:

- Production systems. Typically, these are single-image operating systems or applications consuming large amounts of CPU, for example, VSE/ESA, or SAP R3 application servers.

- Interactive users. z/VM can support hundreds of CMS users.

- Test environments. These environments can be used for migration, or to test different operating system levels before deploying one.

7.5.1 Why z/VM is ideally suited for hosting large application Linux images

Even today, companies running large z/OS or VSE/ESA systems as guests of z/VM typically have only a few images (maybe just two: one for production and one for testing). The demand on z/VM is to maximize the amount of work that the z/OS or VSE/ESA guests can perform. In the past, this required VM developers to be very efficient in their support of new technologies such as large real memory, advanced disk storage systems, and processor facilities. The goal for supporting guest systems is to give each guest what it needs and get out of the way.

A characteristic of the z/VM operating system that benefits a Linux server environment is the high degree of resource sharing that is achieved with VM's CP. z/VM facilitates sharing processor capacity, main memory, disk devices, channel adapters, network adapters, and practically anything you can attach, connect, or plug into your mainframe among the virtual machines. Note that z/VM allows defining of guests dynamically; no static partitions need to be created ahead of time.

At the same time, if a guest needs sole access to a processor, device, or network resource, that resource can be dedicated to the guest. A hallmark of z/VM is its flexibility in supporting a wide variety of computing requirements. System administrators can mix and match shared resources with dedicated resources on the same z/VM system, and even in the same guest, changing the landscape of the virtual machine configurations, if needed, in a matter of minutes, not hours or days.

7.5.2 Why z/VM is ideally suited to Linux server consolidation

CMS workloads in the past were typically multi-image, interactive workloads. Many companies were deploying hundreds of CMS guests on their VM systems and were asking IBM for enhancements to support that workload. Today, Linux workloads tend to be spread across multiple images and be highly interactive, such as Web-serving workloads. Because of the similarities between Linux workloads and traditional VM workloads, the provisions made to accommodate these workloads also work well for Linux.

The refinements made to VM's scheduler and dispatcher over the course of decades are equally suited for a Linux server environment. This kind of environment requires the facilities to host a large number of images with an unpredictable set of workloads that must meet stringent response-time objectives.

The appeal of z/VM's resource sharing becomes obvious when one considers the amount of wasted resources that typically exist in a discrete server farm environment. It is not unusual for individual servers to have, on average, a utilization rate as low as 3%. Servers with such low utilization are, for example, domain name servers (DNS) where data does not have to be looked up often. A company can have many DNSs. ISPCompany, for example, could have a DNS for each client of its outsourcing business, which adds up to hundreds over time. In general, utilization rates depend on many factors, including:

- The function provided by the application
- Its I/O requirements
- The networking bandwidth
- The number of users or clients who access the application
- The level of technology available in the server itself

Many network infrastructure servers, such as DNSs and firewalls, experience short bursts of activity followed by periods of inactivity. When a server is inactive, its resources are unavailable to other servers that could benefit from additional processor capacity, real memory, network or I/O bandwidth, or disk space. Purchasing server resources to handle application peaks compounds this problem. Processor speed and technology, memory requirements, and all other tangible capital costs associated with a server application are generally measured by how much capacity an application needs when user demand is high. To provide any less resource means potentially falling short of the computing capacity which the application needs at critical times. Unfortunately, this only compounds the waste of system resources when the server is idle or underutilized. (See 3.3.2, "Utilize CPU power.")

In a z/VM world, a server running in a virtual machine can grow or shrink its consumption of available system resources based on application demand. For example, processor cycles that would otherwise be wasted during times of low utilization are available for other images running on the same z/VM system. When resource requirements in a guest exceed expectations, z/VM lets a guest get more cycles or be backed by more real storage, provided no one else with higher priority needs it. Using CP commands, a system administrator can allocate more processor capacity, disk storage, or network bandwidth to the virtual machine when it needs it, not days later. This is possible provided that the virtual resources are available. (It usually takes days to provision a real server to replace the one that no longer meets the customer's need for computing power.)

Figure 7-4 shows many servers with low utilization being consolidated on a mainframe under z/VM.

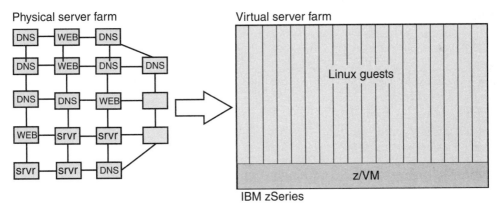

Figure   7-4. Many servers with low utilization can be consolidated on z/VM

There are other costs associated with separate, seldom used servers. When a server goes idle, it still requires energy, floor space, and other environmental costs such as cooling to maintain its connection to the network and be ready for its next transaction. A guest on z/VM does not represent incremental environmental costs, whether active or idle. The environmental cost of a z/VM system is fixed for a given configuration of hardware and wastes resources only if the server farm in aggregate becomes idle or has low utilization. Studies have shown that environmental cost savings can be realized when running a multi-image server environment on z/VM versus a discrete system solution.

7.6 Summary

On a zSeries machine, using LPAR and z/VM for Linux deployments presents a multitude of possibilities not available anywhere else. There can be substantial hardware and floor space savings from using virtualization technology on a zSeries machine. Virtualization technology gives you a flexible server farm environment that can be easily managed and changed in minutes with a few keystrokes.

The purpose of z/VM's efficient virtualization technology is to:

- Allow operating systems to run almost as if they were running on the hardware.
- Maximize the logical sharing of the physical resources such as CPU and central storage.

Much of the appeal of running Linux on the mainframe comes from the ability to run tens to hundreds of Linux images on a single machine.

Chapter 8.
Security Considerations

The details of mainframe security and Linux security are described in numerous technical papers, on Web sites, and in other books. This chapter covers those security aspects of Linux on the mainframe that are likely to influence a decision to run certain types of work, or store certain types of data on the Linux system.

On any platform, total security is an unattainable ideal, but security as a goal must be continually revisited and refined. Each platform comes with a degree of built-in security, and going beyond that means cost and effort. You need to balance the risk you are prepared to take against what you are willing to spend. Thus, when planning a Linux-on-the-mainframe project, you must ask yourself if the project will have sufficient security for a reasonable cost.

New projects and workloads can benefit from tools available in the Linux-on-the-mainframe environment. If you are moving from a traditional server farm, sometimes the tools that you have been using for your current environment are also available for Linux on the mainframe. For a list of security tools, see 25.3, "Security management tools."

Security management is really about risk management. Your goal when analyzing your system security is to reduce the perceived risk. To what level you want to reduce the risk is a question of how much you can spend to get a certain return on your investment. To build a security policy that is both functional and meets operational business needs, you need to balance a combination of physical security, software security, and trust in personnel. Here, it makes sense to spend effort on the areas that will give you the most benefit.

The technology involved in a Linux-on-the-mainframe solution offers some security benefits. In this chapter, we address these questions:

- What role does a security policy play?

- What security does the mainframe contribute to a Linux-on-the-mainframe solution?

- What security do z/VM and Linux contribute to a Linux-on-the-mainframe solution?

- What tools are available?

8.1 The role of security policy

Any computer environment has certain security characteristics, which can be accidental or intentional. For example, to make a computer totally secure, you might turn it off and place it in a locked closet. Arguably, such a computer is physically secure and under little threat of network attacks. It is not likely to be compromised or to affect other machines. However, it also accomplishes little of value to the company. If the computer is turned on, things get more interesting. And if it is attached to the Internet and running an e-business, then things get really interesting.

The mainframe is usually seen as having good security. However, as with any computer, the things required for good security on the mainframe do not come together magically. There is a need for a security policy, instead of letting accidental circumstances dictate security. A security policy is normally used to document desired system behavior. The policy should also guide the implementation of servers so that they have the desirable security characteristics that address various business risks.

A security policy is a comprehensive set of requirements that addresses how users are identified and authenticated, the roles and responsibilities of administrators, the capabilities of administrators and users, password policy, network policy, sharing policy, secure communication, administration of systems, maintenance requirements. Also included are resources and how they are defined and protected, hardening procedures and settings for each of the operating systems, auditing, logging, intrusion detection systems, and firewalls.

In the case of the orphan computer in the closet, the implicit context states that it is to do no work and have no users. Once the computer is turned on, a security policy is needed. The system administrator must determine if a human can manage this policy (typical in the home computer case), or if it must be documented as a procedure to be followed (done by many medium risk businesses), or if tools (like a policy manager) are required to enforce the policy.

Regardless of what kind of environment you are in, you probably already have a security policy in place. When considering a Linux-on-the-mainframe project, you will want to review your policy. Depending on the business value you are looking for from your project, you can follow different strategies. Two examples of objectives for Linux on the mainframe are:

- Business value from consolidation: When Linux images are consolidated on the mainframe, you will probably also have z/VM to manage those images. Then z/VM must be considered in your policy as well. If, in the extreme case, your only goal is to consolidate as economically as possible, the isolation of images given by the hardware and z/VM may be all the additional security you need.

- Business value from the speed-to-market of a business application: When applications running on Linux images interact with applications running on z/OS, the Linux applications should be close to the z/OS back-end, and connected to the z/OS images. In this case, you might need to review the policies that apply for your current environment and how they should be enforced on Linux on the mainframe. The implementation might be different for Linux from what it is for z/OS. For instance, by carefully segmenting the work, you might be able to isolate any new risks.

When evaluating the security policy for a Linux-on-the-mainframe project, you will want to know what risks are involved. We will look at risk assessment in the next section.

8.2 Risk assessment

Security is one of the first considerations for any server environment, whether it is a new system or an existing system that is used for new business opportunities.

All security is about managing risk. We have chosen a risk analysis approach as a framework for security. Using ISPCompany and StoreCompany as concrete examples, we first introduce some general aspects of security. Then we look at more details pertaining to the areas we introduce here, in particular, how they relate to Linux on the mainframe (see Figure 8-1).

Linux is going to be tightly connected to many aspects of your e-business. Connecting the computer system to the Internet (that is, being connected to an external network) dramatically increases the risk of damage from intrusion.

Security is a trade-off between ease of use of the computing resources, business requirements for protection, and expense. There is no magic application or methodology that ensures the security of a system. Like all real-world technical designs, it is a practice of setting and meeting requirements and the consideration of limitations imposed by those requirements. Defending your Linux mainframe server is based on understanding these security requirements, best practices, and experience.

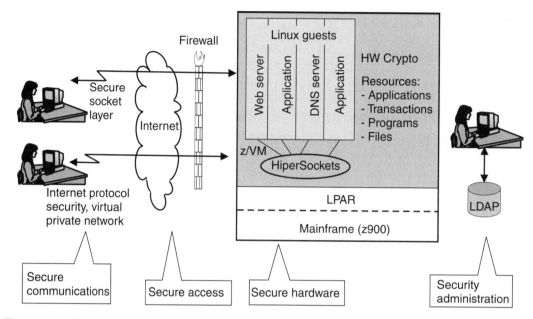

Figure 8-1. Security space: what security covers

Naturally, the primary focus of a company is on its business and not on its systems. The goal of such systems is to support business and overall objectives. All business decisions, in IT or otherwise, are an exercise in the evaluation of the risk of inaction versus the cost of action to reduce risks (real or perceived).

8.2.1 What is risk assessment?

Risk can be defined as "being exposed to injury, pain, or loss." In every situation, your company is exposed to injury or loss. In the business context, there can never be zero exposure. The question is how to minimize that exposure and what level of exposure you can live with. Risk assessment, then, is the art of assessing what level of risk your company can accept.

Areas of risk assessment that pertain to Linux on the mainframe include:

- Hardware: Ensuring physical security of the machine itself and its console

- Network: Establishing secure communications, using encryption, protecting networks from being tapped, and from denial-of-service attacks

- Technology: Using virtualization technology

- Information: Protecting intellectual property (such as specialty applications) and pro- tecting your data, which might be your most valuable asset

- Human: Minimizing the threat of damage by malicious individuals

One way to approach security and make sure that all areas of importance are covered is by performing an extensive risk analysis. This chapter concentrates on problem areas that need to be considered in a Linux-on-the-mainframe solution.

Figure 8-2 shows a typical Web-serving setup, where the machines are separate and dis- crete. Some of the typical attacks on this kind of setup are illustrated.

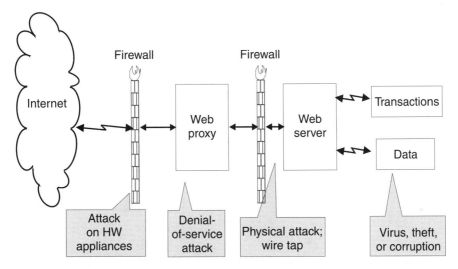

Figure 8-2. Risk areas of typical Web-serving setup

Going back to the examples of business value from Linux on the mainframe, what are examples of risks in those scenarios?

If you are doing simple server consolidation, the images are no longer on individual hard- ware machines. What is the risk from shared hardware? ISPCompany might be wondering how to guarantee that the servers that used to be in separate cages cannot touch each other's data now that they are on one machine. We discuss this in 8.2.3, "Partitioning" and 8.2.4, "Virtual security."

If you are integrating Linux into the existing mainframe environment to work closely with current business applications, one of the Linux images could become compromised. What could an intruder do in a Linux image? We discuss this in 8.4, "Opening the doors."

A Linux-on-the-mainframe environment usually benefits from virtual networks. What are the risks of virtual networking? We discuss this in 8.4.3, "Secure and encrypted communication."

Let us now take a closer look at the risk areas, and see what our example companies have done to reduce risk.

8.2.2 Hardware security

The first security stage is physical access to the floor where the computers are housed. Assuming that ISPCompany, as the typical data center, has tens of servers in one room, the normal way to protect these is to tightly control access to that room. Only the trusted people who work with the servers are allowed there. Often, all the consoles are logged on to save time. As a result, if someone does break in, he or she could tamper with the servers.

Consolidating many servers on the mainframe simplifies the physical security challenge. There are fewer reasons for anybody needing actual access to the physical machine. The system administrator can do most work with the individual servers running under z/VM from the control room.

The mainframe system console

For a direct attack on a system, the (hardware or operating) system console may be the goal of intruders. The mainframe, in contrast to other systems, has a separate hardware system console. (The zSeries operating systems each have their own system consoles.) The physical mainframe system console is shipped with the machine in the form of two IBM laptop computers, one serving as a hot standby backup. They are called *Support Elements (SEs)*. The SE communicates with the internal sub-systems in the machine. For example, it handles initial program loads (IPLs), I/O configuration, LPAR configuration, and microcode updates.

A Support Element is normally not used directly. Instead, commands are sent through the *Hardware Management Console (HMC)* to the SE, as illustrated in Figure 8-3.

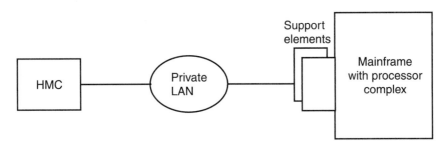

Figure 8-3. The HMC, the SEs, and a mainframe. Commands for operating, monitoring, and maintaining the mainframe are sent through the HMC to the SE, which then issues commands to the central processor complex.

The HMC serves as a single point of control to operate the machines defined to it remotely. The HMC must be connected to the SEs through a LAN. To be physically secure, the LAN that connects the HMC to the SE should be contained within the raised floor and control room. Through the LAN, you can also operate the systems through a Web interface to the HMC. The HMC is often placed in the control room in case staff need to take some hardware-related actions. (Refer to *IBM eServer zSeries 900 System Overview*, SA22-1071, for rules on setting up the HMC.)

Apart from physical isolation in an access-controlled room, the SE and HMC are protected by role-based user IDs and passwords. The HMC has a role-based model for access that provides a second layer of security in addition to logon authentication. *Role-based* means that there are user IDs for certain roles. Even if you have a user ID and a password, you cannot do everything, but only what the role allows.

You can enable remote support for the HMC. This is not automatically enabled.

ISPCompany example

ISPCompany solves the physical access problem by using the conventional method for the outsourcing business. It puts customers' machines in cages, so that any customer has access only to his or her cage. Customer personnel wanting to work in their cage must sign in at the front desk, have badge access to the part of the floor where their cage is, and use a key to open their own cage.

With ISPCompany's mainframes, the mainframes' consoles are connected through a private LAN to the control room, where an HMC acts as a single point of control for those mainframes.

With applications or servers consolidated on the mainframe under Linux, the access problem is now one of logical access rather than physical access. There is little need to touch the actual mainframe. The exception is one or two highly trusted experts who, for example, need to plug in the fiber optic cables to connect new adapters on the server to the fiber network hub. These experts are typically ISPCompany employees. Other situations that call for access to the mainframe are hardware modifications, such as installation of cryptographic cards.

Moving a physical server farm with servers or applications to run on Linux images under z/VM, decreases the risk of physical attack. Instead, security under z/VM, which we examine in detail in 8.2.4, "Virtual security," becomes interesting. You also then need to manage the Linux images "remotely." This can be done with the help of, for example, a virtual private network (VPN) and secure shell (SSH) both of which we discuss later in this chapter.

8.2.3 Partitioning

Logical partitioning (LPAR) provides a flexible alternative for dividing a machine's CPU resources and also guarantees the isolation of the software images running in the individual partitions using the same concepts explained above. The isolation of the partitions is proven by an independent authority. For the most up-to-date information on the technology that provides logical partitioning, see
`http://www.ibm.com/servers/eserver/zseries/security/certification.html`.

8.2.4 Virtual security

A common question asked by technologists interested in running multiple Linux images on z/VM for the first time is, "How good is z/VM's system integrity and security?" The short answer is "very good." The much longer answer offers some additional insight into the technology found in the z/VM product.

Because the z/VM Control Program (CP) and the virtual machine configurations are under the control of the z/VM system administrator, the actual level of system integrity that a company achieves depends on how the z/VM environment is set up and maintained. z/VM is specifically designed to maintain the isolation of one virtual machine from other virtual machines at all times.

The IBM ESA/390 architecture and z/Architecture are at the core of the system's ability to maintain integrity. One crucial aspect of this is the ability to keep each virtual machine isolated from every other virtual machine. This isolation even extends to the CP, because it is logically separate from all virtual machines in the system.

How z/VM keeps it all separate

A special component of the mainframe virtualization technology permits a virtual machine instruction stream to be run on the processor using a single instruction, start interpretive execution (SIE).

When the CP dispatches a virtual machine (that is, executes SIE), details about the virtual machine are provided to the hardware. The SIE instruction runs the virtual machine until the virtual machine receives an interrupt, or wants to perform an operation that either the hardware cannot virtualize or for which the CP must regain control. At that point, SIE performs an exit on behalf of the virtual machine and returns control to the CP, which simulates the instruction or performs the I/O (for example). Once this is done, control is returned to the virtual machine. In this way, the full capabilities and speed of the CPU are available to the virtual machine, and only those instructions that require assistance from or validation by the CP are intercepted.

This mechanism also enables the CP to limit the scope of many kinds of hardware or software failures. When the error can be isolated to a particular virtual machine, only that virtual machine fails. It can be re-initialized (rebooted) without affecting work running in other virtual machines. The CP is designed so that failures that occur in virtual machines do not affect the CP or other virtual machines.

Isolation through address translation

While most platforms today offer virtual memory, zSeries allows an operating system to create separate virtual address spaces. Address spaces enable memory isolation and management. For example, z/VM running natively on a zSeries machine creates a separate address space for each guest. Each address space has an associated set of region, segment, and page tables that contain precise information on the real memory locations being used for the guest. These tables are used by the address-translation hardware to convert virtual memory addresses to real memory addresses. Because these tables are maintained by the operating system and are not accessible by the guests themselves, it is not possible for a guest to read from or write to memory that is used by the operating system itself or another guest.

zSeries takes this capability a step further by supporting two levels of address translation. An operating system running in a virtual machine under z/VM constructs its address-translation tables as usual to isolate and contain the memory for its users. The entire memory of this virtual machine, although viewed by the guest operating system as real memory, is in fact virtual storage as well, defined by another set of translation tables managed by the z/VM CP. Even if an application running on a guest operating system were able to compromise the integrity of the guest, the damage would be limited to that one virtual machine, because of the separate layer of protection provided by zSeries hardware and z/VM.

A virtual machine cannot access an address space owned by another virtual machine unless the address space owner explicitly allows the virtual machine to do so. This capability is controlled through the z/VM directory entry for each guest.

8.3 Before opening the doors: hardening

A process sometimes used in the UNIX and Linux community is *hardening*. A "hardened" system is presumed to be impervious to any currently known attacks, exposures, or vulnerabilities. Every system, Linux or otherwise, should be hardened before being placed on any active LAN. Hardening is not a one-time task. Depending on the level of acceptable risk, triggers must be identified to ensure that the system configuration is revisited as needed. The security policy should contain criteria that trigger a reassessment of the configuration. For example, if a new Internet worm is identified and is known to attack the e-mail server, the security policy must be checked, and systems must be updated and rehardened.

Develop a patch policy

System hardening includes making sure that the latest software patches are applied to the system, especially if they are security-related or apply to any of the security or system management products that are critical to the solution. Once all the patches are installed, the mechanisms into and out of the solution must be evaluated with regards to the solution. This makes it necessary to have a *patch policy* within the security policy.

Get rid of the extra fat

Only those mechanisms required by the solution should remain active. For example, if the work that needs to be done is Web serving and the system will be managed remotely through SSH, it would be prudent to turn off the telnet and mail daemons (among others), because they are not part of the solution and could provide intruders unnecessary routes of attack.

Most standard Linux distributions include features and services to enable a wide scope of functionality and value—usually far more then you need and want on a typical Linux server deployment. Many of the latest Linux distribution releases provide warnings if you attempt to install a service that poses a security risk, such as telnet. We highly recommend that you pay attention to these warnings. Validate that the services running are critical for the function of the Linux server you are configuring.

Related information is in the SANS/FBI list (http://www.sans.org/top20/), including one of the top general vulnerabilities, "Default Install of Operating System and Applications."

Remove unused accounts

Removing insecure user accounts is also part of the hardening process. Some system images are provided with well-known accounts and passwords. Some application install processes leave behind accounts that are well-known and vulnerable. Unnecessary user accounts should be removed, and default or weak passwords should be reset to strong passwords. User authority to access system or application code should be limited as well.

For z/VM, consider including these issues in your security policy:

- After installing a new z/VM system, remember to change the default logon and minidisk passwords for all users in the system directory.

- Do not give virtual machines more authority than they require.

8.3.1 Managing hardening

The hardening of a system must be linked with the management of that system. Every time the kernel is patched or upgraded, or a new application is installed or modified, the state of the system with regard to hardening must be reviewed. This integral step can be performed by any number of scripts available in the Open Source community or from service organizations skilled in this area. For example, scripts are available from Bastille at http://www.bastille-linux.org/. These scripts are yet another example of how Open Source code helps Linux be more secure.

In some scenarios, once an image is hardened it can be used as the starting point for cloning new images as needed. This cloning capability is easily implemented and its value is realized when z/VM manages the images.

The early broad-brush approach to enabling many popular network services, such as telnet or FTP, has left many systems vulnerable. The traditional zSeries customer would rather enable function as needed, and the Linux trend is shifting in this direction.

8.3.2 Tools for managing security on z/VM: DirMaint and RACF

Software products exist that can be used to further enhance the integrity and security of a z/VM system. Two of those products from IBM are optional features of z/VM Version 4 called *IBM Directory Maintenance for z/VM (DirMaint)* and *IBM Resource Access Control Facility for z/VM (RACF)*.

DirMaint provides a safe, efficient, and user-friendly way to maintain the z/VM system directory. Through its command line or full-screen interface, you can quickly and easily add, modify, or delete users from the system directory. See 23.3.1, "DirMaint" for more details. In any z/VM installation where large numbers of virtual servers are being deployed, DirMaint is useful.

RACF is an external security manager. It provides comprehensive security capabilities that extend the standard security implemented by the base z/VM product. RACF controls user access to the VM system, checks authorization for use of both system and virtual machine resources, and audits the use of those resources. Like DirMaint, RACF is packaged as a priced feature of z/VM Version 4 and is pre-installed on the system installation media. See 23.3.2, "RACF" for more details.

8.4 Opening the doors

Now that we have covered some physical and virtual security aspects, let's go to the next step in protecting a machine: allowing users entry.

When StoreCompany created its Linux-on-the-mainframe environment with Linux images and z/OS working together on one machine, one risk (arguably very small) it considered was that of a Linux image being taken over. What could then happen? The Linux image has a connection to z/OS, and someone could theoretically get access to z/OS resources. However, like most z/OS systems, StoreCompany's z/OS resources are under the control of the RACF security manager. It would not be possible to take over z/OS.

If someone very knowledgeable got as far as taking over a Linux image with a connection to z/OS, that person could send commands to z/OS. But the effect of such commands is limited to what the Linux image is authorized to do. For example, if the image belongs to user George, it might be authorized to look at all files associated with George's orders. However, if George's image asks z/OS for the payroll, z/OS recognizes that the image has no authorization to look at this file and will deny access. Hence, with the standard authentication and authorization of the mainframe in place, even if an image were taken over, it would have a very limited scope of access to other systems.

This section covers considerations of allowing users access to the system: authorization, access control, and secure network communications.

8.4.1 Identification and authentication

Identification and authentication provide a first level of protection when permitting entry to the machine. Users identify themselves and give some piece of information that authenticates who they are. For example, users identify themselves by giving a user ID and then give the password associated with that ID.

Identification and authentication in general can be done by many different means, such as certificates, user IDs, and passwords.

When the machine knows who you are, it can decide what you are allowed to do—this is *authorization*. For example, a user ID and password combination gives users access to files, with which they are thus authorized to work. In this case, the files are password pro-tected. The file system provides the security service of allowing access to the file only when presented with the correct password. This method was typical of, for example, batch-oriented S/360 systems. This method has some drawbacks in a large multiuser system, however:

- All files (or programs, or other resources) have their own authentication code. If you want to change it, you must recompile all the programs or all the resources that refer-ence the method.

- If multiple users need access to one file, they must all know the password. It is then hard to tell who did what with that file.

- If users need access to multiple files, multiple passwords are needed.

Instead of permitting access on a per file basis, modern operating systems (like z/OS and Linux) authenticate the user to use an *identity*. Identities are typically stored in a user reg-istry. Both Linux and other mainframe operating systems make use of registries.

For z/OS and z/VM, the user registry of choice is the *Resource Access Control Facility (RACF)*. (Note, however, that RACF for z/OS is different from RACF for z/VM.) RACF is the chief function of the mainframe's *Security Server* and incorporates user identification and authentication, as well as access control, which is discussed in 8.4.2, "Access control." In a Linux-on-the-mainframe context with Linux images running under z/VM, you can use RACF to secure z/VM user IDs and passwords.

Instead of each program having its own authentication code, many Linux distributions now come with Pluggable Authentication Modules (PAMs). If a program is PAM enabled, you can easily switch between several authentication methods. If the Linux images with connectors to z/OS use PAMs, it might be possible to share user ID definitions and passwords with the Linux images.

Example of centralized authentication services

On Linux, the Lightweight Directory Access Protocol (LDAP) can be used with a user registry. An example of how to use PAMs and LDAP to share existing z/OS RACF data is shown here.

An LDAP server can be any general-purpose distributed directory server and can contain many different types of information, from distributed application descriptions and configuration information to user and group definitions.

Imagine an environment like that of StoreCompany with many Linux images running on a mainframe where z/OS is also running. User Peter has an account on z/OS as well as on several of the Linux images. How can you manage many users like Peter from a central point? Using a user registry is one answer. Assume user information is stored centrally in an z/OS LDAP server. PAMs can then be configured to pass authentication requests to the LDAP client, and from the LDAP client to the server. Thus you can share existing RACF information with the Linux systems and keep, for example, passwords protected by RACF, using a special feature of the z/OS LDAP server.

If z/OS runs on the same hardware as the Linux images, HiperSockets communications can be used. HiperSockets is an internal communication method with no physical network parts. Thus no information can be "sniffed." This scenario is illustrated in Figure 8-4.

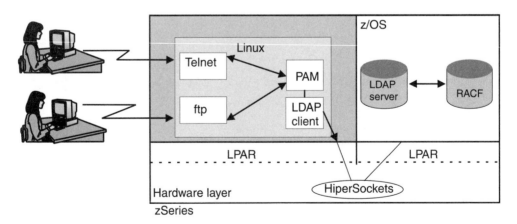

Figure 8-4. RACF information can be shared with Linux systems through using PAM and LDAP

8.4.2 Access control

The use of access control has migrated from a mainframe-only environment to become an integral part of many platforms' security solutions and their security policy management systems. As Linux continued to mature and the number of applications grew, the availability of and need for resource access control became a critical component in the deployment of Linux-based environments.

Access control mechanisms on Linux systems

"Who can do what, where?" is the task that access control performs. There are two types of access control mechanisms:

- Discretionary Access Control (DAC)
- Mandatory Access Control (MAC)

DAC can be used to manage access control in its simplest form in a low-risk environment. The supplied Linux DAC is known as "user," "group," and "other" permission bits on the file system. These bits determine what user or group is allowed to read, write, or execute a particular resource (file, directory, or device). For example, when you access a printer, you are actually writing to a file in the file system. This can be controlled through the "user," "group," and "other" bits. In the simple server consolidation case, this may well be enough.

MACs are used when securing highly confidential data. The user has no control over the classification or labeling of the resources. The security policy requires a security manager, human or automated, to assign sensitivity labels to every subject (users and programs) and all objects (files, directories, and devices). MACs, along with the proper labeling, make up the core of a multilevel security (MLS) policy. The automated implementation of rigorous MACs is found in sophisticated policy management systems where risk must be minimized.

Using DAC, users can choose to share or give away access to a resource under their control. With MAC, this decision is out of their control. At a minimum, groups should be identified and group permissions used to isolate security functions such as user administration, audit, system and application maintenance, system backup, kernel and key operating system executables.

Access control lists (ACLs): Access control lists (ACLs) are another form of the more robust access control case, MAC. They allow the user more flexibility to manage individual resources, but require more knowledge of the system. ACLs give a security administrator the ability to control each user's access at an individual resource level. They list users and what they can do. Taking the "user," "group," and "other" mechanism to the next level by

including ACLs provides an environment with less risk, but yields more system administration overhead.

Certain Linux journaling file systems, such as ext3, are ACL-enabled. These are included
in, for example, the SuSE SLES 8 distribution.

Tools for access control

For an access control solution to successfully enforce the access control list (and hence the
access policy of the system), it must be closely integrated with the kernel's decision points
to avoid various system attacks or spoofing attempts. In the vendor arena, access control
solutions are provided, for example, by IBM Tivoli Access Manager and CA's eTrust suite.
See 25.6, "Tools Web sites" for a list of tools and their Web sites.

In the Open Source area, BestBits, LoMAC, SE Linux, and others all provide various levels
of access control functionality and can run on a zSeries Linux server.

8.4.3 Secure and encrypted communication

Linux provides some potentially useful schemes for more secure communication which are
important for today's e-business environment. In this section, we will cover the most important aspects of secure communication:

- Secure physical communication using Secure Socket Layer (SSL), Virtual Private
  Network (VPN), and mainframe cryptographic functions

- Secure virtual communications over HiperSockets and other virtual communication connections

SSL and key setup

The Secure Sockets Layer (SSL), which is the core technology used to secure Internet
transactions, uses cryptography both for authentication of clients and servers and for data
confidentiality.

One shortcoming of the user ID and password (basic authentication) model is that the password has to be passed from the end point, where the user is, to the physical location where
the application and security registry reside, which may be far away. It is important to ensure
security of the password in transit. On the mainframe, the SSL protocol can be used to
encrypt the password while in transit.

The Open Source version, OpenSSL, is included in many distributions and can be used
with Web servers, such as Apache. OpenSSL is a robust, commercial-grade, full-featured,

and Open Source toolkit that implements the Secure Sockets Layer and Transport Layer Security protocols, as well as a full-strength general-purpose cryptography library. On the mainframe, you can use the hardware cryptographic functions for authentication through OpenSSL.

SSL is a protocol for transmitting documents securely through the Internet. SSL works by using a public key to encrypt data that are used to agree on symmetric encryption keys. These keys, in turn, are used to encrypt data that are transferred over the SSL connection. SSL has several characteristics that can be used by an e-commerce application to communicate with large numbers of users via common Internet browser software:

- SSL can be used to identify and authenticate (with a high degree of trust) server applications to users of the application. For example, this function would be important for a Web marketing application that requests a customer's credit card number. The customer wants to be assured that the application is the one intended and not a "Trojan horse" imposter that is stealing credit card numbers. SSL provides this highly useful security function.

- SSL can be used to establish a private cryptographic communication channel through the Internet between the communicating parties (for example, the customer on the Internet and the Web application server). This channel enables credit card numbers to pass from the customer to the marketing application without being observed. Note that VPNs, which we will discuss later, also provide Internet communication privacy. The difference is that VPNs are generally used for point-to-point communication links that can be shared by multiple applications and that continue for a longer duration than those typically seen with common browsers.

- SSL can be used to identify and authenticate (with a high degree of trust) users of applications to Web application servers. This function is most useful when the application provides function that requires the user to be known to the application. An example is when the application has administrative support function that needs to be individually authorized for execution by only specified individuals (such as payroll functions).

SSL has emerged as the preferred method for securing Web-based transactions on the Internet. It is widely supported in browsers and most Web servers. The first two functions are in common use worldwide, while the third (user identification and authentication using X.509 version 3 digital certificates) is being applied in an increasing number of cases.

For a description of how SSL works, see
http://developer.netscape.com/tech/security/ssl/howitworks.html.

Virtual private networks

Virtual private networks (VPNs) allow remote users safe access to critical system resources and provide safe remote communication, for example, for systems management. VPNs provide a valuable means of doing remote system management securely over the Internet.

VPNs enable encrypted connections from one system to another over the Internet. The part that constitutes the actual connection over the Internet is encrypted, often using OpenSSH (see Figure 8-5) or the IP Security Protocol (IPSec).

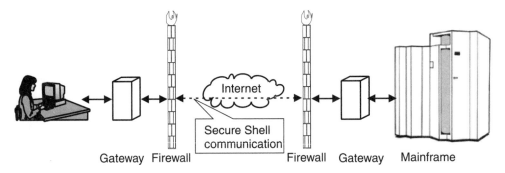

Gateway Firewall   Firewall Gateway   Mainframe

Figure 8-5. Virtual private networks send data over the Internet securely encrypted with SSH or IPSec

There are several uses of VPNs: hardware-based VPNs (usually for encrypting routers), firewall-based VPNs (which include address translation, authentication, alarms, and logging), and stand-alone software VPNs (ideal to use when the connection endpoints are not controlled by the same organization).

Virtual networks should be planned with the same care and attention to security as would be taken for a real, physical network. Networks, virtual or real, must be designed and implemented so that no unauthorized access to data or resources is possible. For system administration tasks, a separate network with secure access is recommended. The ability to define multiple virtual routers gives the ability to completely isolate traffic moving in and out of the S/390 or zSeries server. Highly secure communication between LPARs can be easily handled by using zSeries HiperSockets connections.

Available virtual communication paths under z/VM are summarized in Table 8-1. For more details about them, see Chapter 10, "Communicating in a Virtual Environment."

Table 8-1. Available virtual communication paths with z/VM

Communication	Functionality
Guest LANs	Guest LANs provide multipoint any-to-any virtual shared media connections between guests. As many Guest LANs as are needed can be defined and used simultaneously. To prevent unauthorized connection to a Guest LAN, the creator of the LAN can define it to be restricted, permitting only specific virtual machines to connect to it.
vCTC	vCTC emulates a real CTC adapter (IBM 3088). Each virtual machine defines a vCTCA and then uses the CP COUPLE command to connect the two endpoints. I/O operations to the device are intercepted by the CP, which moves the data between two different virtual machines. Again, data are moved at near memory speeds.

Whenever you use virtual communications technology, there may be no need to encrypt the traffic because the information never leaves the machine. An overview of secure communications can be found in the whitepaper *z/VM Security and Integrity*, GM13-0145. It is available at

`http://www.ibm.com/servers/eserver/zseries/library/techpapers/gm130145.html`.

Cryptography

The use of cryptography has become a common requirement in today's computing environment. Cryptography can be used for confidentiality, authentication, and data integrity. Cryptography is crucial for security on the Internet, banking and finance, and e-business.

Confidentiality is gained when a cryptographic algorithm is used to make the data available to only a trusted group of users. The data are transformed from clear text into cipher text by using an encryption algorithm and a key. The data are unintelligible in cipher text form and can be decrypted only using the correct algorithm and the correct decryption key.

One use of cryptography on Linux on the mainframe is digital signatures. Earlier, authentication was thought of as being done by users entering his or her user ID and password. This is still valid today, but the trend goes towards using digital signatures. This relatively new technology is available and deployable on Linux on the mainframe. Although there are several methods for digital signatures, the most common method in use today is RSA public key cryptography.

Another use of cryptography is the validation of data integrity. Integrity can be validated through the use of a one-way cryptographic function. A hash function is sometimes used by the owner of critical data to come up with a "digest" of the data. Any other user or program can then validate that the data have not been modified by using the same hash function and obtaining the same digest.

zSeries and S/390 servers offer specialized processors for cryptographic operations. In an ISP or ASP environment such as ISPCompany, cryptographic procedures are frequently used for highly secure TCP/IP connections between the server and a user somewhere on the Internet. Applications for firewalls, Web serving, and mail serving also have the requirement to protect data.

Linux and mainframe cryptography: Linux on the mainframe can use the mainframe cryptographic services, thanks to a single device driver for both the newer IBM PCI Cryptographic Accelerator (PCICA) and the older PCI Cryptographic Coprocessor (PCICC). The new PCICA feature is designed to address the high-performance SSL needs of e-business applications. It provides accelerated performance of the complex RSA cryptographic operations used in the SSL protocol.

The older PCICC allows implementation of different cryptographic algorithms and can be used for specialized financial applications, or for secure long-term storage of keys and secrets. Both PCICA and PCICC have earned Federal Information Processing Standard (FIPS) 140-1 Level 4 certification, the highest certification for commercial security awarded by the United States government.

To use a cryptographic coprocessor, the operating system must be able to recognize application requests for cryptography, pass the requests to the cryptographic hardware, and return the result to the application. The driver available for Linux on zSeries and S/390 exploits the PCICA and PCICC cryptographic hardware for the algorithms used by SSL (see Figure 8-6). This exploitation results in significant performance improvements for SSL transactions.

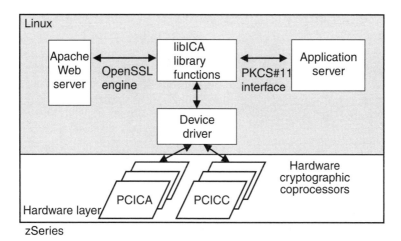

Figure   8-6. The cryptographic device driver for Linux on the mainframe enables openLDAP or openSSL requests

The code for cryptographic support and associated functionality is included in, for example, the SuSE SLES 8 distribution.

Virtual cryptography support—Linux and z/VM: The PCICC and PCICA cards can be shared and used by any number of Linux guests as shown in Figure 8-7. Each operation is discrete and independent of those that precede or follow it. z/VM manages the queue of requests so that a guest can see only its own request, as with a shared processor or a shared channel.

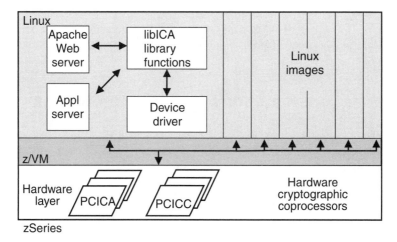

Figure   8-7. Virtualized cryptographic functions

ISPCompany example: secure networking

In a service bureau situation such as at ISPCompany, where there are physical farms of machines in separate caged areas, there is sometimes a LAN that connects all the customer machines. Assuming a client were to exchange the standard network adapter for one that allows all the network traffic to be read, the client could read not only his or her own traffic but also everybody else's.

To prevent this, ISPCompany has point-to-point connections from the incoming data source to the different machines. This costs more, but is more secure than a LAN.

When ISPCompany virtualizes the adapters by putting its customers into z/VM, there is no physical adapter for intruders to sniff. z/VM does not let guests see any traffic other than their own when they share an adapter.

By using HiperSockets, ISPCompany can eliminate the physical risk of someone tapping into the network. Other benefits of HiperSockets include high speed of transfer and close to zero latency. Some savings can be made on not having actual cables and other hardware needed for the physical network.

8.5 Preventing attacks

To detect and prevent attacks on your system, you need to use firewalls, intrusion detection tools, and anti-virus tools.

Firewalls block certain traffic from entering your environment and examine network traffic. Intrusion detection tools examine network behavior behind the firewall for abnormal patterns. Anti-virus tools examine data content for suspicious modifications and virus signatures.

8.5.1 Firewall considerations for Linux on the mainframe

One of the threats you need to assess in any environment, including a Linux-on-the-mainframe environment, is the denial-of-service attack. One part of the defense against denial-of-service attacks is using firewall techniques.

A firewall is a secure and trusted system that acts as a barrier between private and public networks. A firewall, when combined with a VPN, can provide secure, encrypted communications with sites outside the firewall.

Firewall techniques include:

- Establishing a demilitarized zone (DMZ), illustrated in Figure 8-8.

- IP packet filtering, static and dynamic (state-dependent)

   IP datagrams are inspected; the filter decides if a datagram needs to be processed or discarded. Filtering can be done on protocol type, port, datagram type, IP address, and so on.

- Application gateway (or proxy)

   The proxy understands the application protocol, performs logging, and can provide authentication and caching capabilities. An example of a proxy caching server is squid (http://www.squid-cache.org/), which provides access control lists for ports, URLs, and subnets.

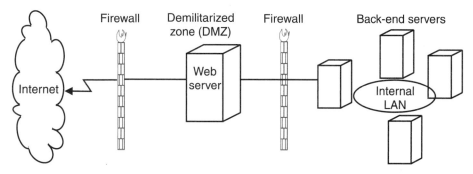

Figure 8-8. Standard firewall implementation with demilitarized zone. The Web server is protected first by one firewall that has connectivity to the Internet. If users are legitimate, they are redirected by a proxy server through the second firewall.

DMZ considerations

Where does your Web server reside within the infrastructure? Traditionally, a Web server is located between filtering devices, such as firewalls and routers. This places it in a "demilitarized" zone (DMZ), which offers some protection from Internet intrusions, as illustrated in Figure 8-8.

The internal network receives protection from the Web server. Outbound filtering devices permit, for example, only ports 80 and 443 to reach the Web server; other potentially dangerous traffic is inhibited. The inside filtering device is important, because the Web server itself should not rely on other hosts within the secure LAN. Although you must allow potentially dangerous parties access to your Web server, careful measures should be taken to prevent unwanted entry. (There are many reference books that address the different DMZ methods in more detail, such as *Building Internet Firewalls* by D. Brent Chapman and Elizabeth D. Zwicky and *Linux Firewalls* by Robert L. Ziegler.)

An example of when a DMZ is needed is to separate Web applications from the Web server, as StoreCompany does for its Web catalog.

With Linux on the mainframe, it is possible to consolidate firewalls on the mainframe. The network firewall can be outside the mainframe to save mainframe resources and the other DMZ firewall can be on a separate image. A firewall can be implemented either on an LPAR or under z/VM (Figure 8-9). This consolidation makes administration of the firewall easier and eliminates the need for separate hardware.

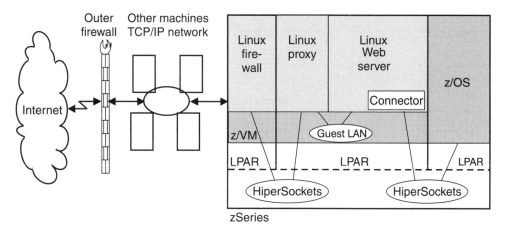

Figure 8-9. Using a firewall in a Linux-on-the-mainframe environment

Linux firewall capabilities

Some firewall capabilities have been integrated into the Linux kernel. These include:

- IP packet filtering, which either accepts or rejects network packets based on the information in the packet header. Packet filtering can be used through the newer iptable tool (kernel version 2.4).

  In a Linux-on-the-mainframe environment, you can use IP filtering. On the mainframe, data that never go outside the machine can never be physically compromised.

- Network address translation (NAT), which modifies the network address in a datagram, thus "hiding" the internal network addresses.

- IP masquerading, which is a special form of NAT, can be used in a hot standby takeover process. When a hot standby image takes over a failing image, it can also take over the IP address. The standby server thus masquerades as the server it replaces.

Using only these capabilities and Open Source tools, you can implement firewalls on Linux. Most distributions deliver some sort of firewall support.

You can also turn to commercial firewalls. For information about firewalls for Linux on the mainframe, refer to IBM's *ISV support for mainframe servers* Web site:
http://www.ibm.com/servers/eserver/zseries/solutions/s390da/.

While a firewall blocks certain traffic from entering the company network, intrusion detection recognizes strange behavior within the network.

8.5.2 Intrusion detection

The goal of intrusion detection is to detect malicious attacks on your infrastructure, such as denial-of-service attacks.

Denial-of-service attacks can occur in different ways. For example, a compromised image could try to use all the CPU resources or all the network resources. Although the damage that a compromised Linux image can cause could be limited by z/VM definitions, the better solution is to detect an intrusion before damage is caused.

Intrusion detection systems (IDS) can be designed for network-based and host-based systems.

- Network-based IDS are attached to the network. They detect attacks by analyzing the content of network packets sent over the wire. An unusually high number of TCP, UDP, or ICMP packets sent to a single destination can easily be detected. IDS are configured to determine if these packets should be considered attacks or normal traffic.

- Host-based IDS are software components that attempt to detect attacks against the computers on which the IDS is installed. Host-based IDS can analyze the network packets received on the network interface, as well as the log files written by the operating system or by applications running on the computer. Typically, a host-based IDS can detect denial-of-service attacks against a Web server by analyzing its log in real-time.

Sites should install both network-based and host-based detection systems. Network analyzers should be available to help determine the nature of an incident and to help formulate possible filtering and rate-limiting responses in the event of an actual denial-of-service attack.

The Linux community and ISVs have developed some sophisticated, useful tools for Linux that work on Linux on the mainframe as well. The leading Open Source intrusion detection solutions include Tripwire and Snort. It is important to note, however, that IDS systems come in different flavors. For instance, Snort (available with SuSE SLES8) is more of a network IDS, while Linux Intrusion Detection System (LIDS) is targeted more to the protection of, and the intrusion detection in, the Linux image.

Tripwire detects and reports file and directory modifications. This can help to detect Trojan horses[11] and modified software (for example, for sniffing out passwords).

IBM offers a Tivoli IDS solution. Tivoli Risk Manager is a network-based IDS that can recognize basic attacks and prevent denial-of-service incidents.

8.5.3 Anti-virus protection

With access control in place and isolation of power between root and user, Linux is not so susceptible to common viruses. (A virus is a program that actively operates, independently of a user, to attack various system resources.) It is reportedly unusual for UNIX-based operating systems to suffer system-level damage from a virus, because most viral code cannot get access to low-level system functions. However, it is possible for a Linux server to host an infected file or e-mail and send it to a Windows user. For this reason, it is still a good idea to routinely check incoming e-mail and downloaded files for viruses.

It is important to note that the commercial definition of "anti-virus" includes not only viruses, but also Trojan horses, worms, and other similar threats. Although it is not technically or semantically accurate, this discussion includes these other threats as part of the "virus" context. The threat of virus can be broken down into three basic areas:

- Viruses targeted at other platforms stored on Linux on the mainframe in an e-mail server.

  The application of most interest to hackers is e-mail clients running on popular software on common platforms. This type of threat can be neutralized by anti-virus applications running on the target platform. A filtering anti-virus tool to neutralize these types of threats while stored in a mainframe e-mail server would be a plus.

- Viruses written in interpretative languages (like Java, HTML, and PERL).

  These are dangerous because they can be executed on any platform that has an interpreter.

- Linux viruses that run on the mainframe.

  Viruses that actually execute on a zSeries server could be a concern. This type of threat would require that the code be placed on an image and be executed, either manually or through some misdirection. This type of exposure would be contained by developing and managing good security policy, limiting the access to production images via a firewall, and monitoring the network access with current intrusion detection techniques.

---

[11] A Trojan horse is a program that cannot operate unless it is invoked (unintentionally) by a user.

Careful use of standard Linux features can reduce the risk of virus attacks. If a system is serving static files (non-writeable), the file system can be mounted as read-only.

When considering anti-virus protection on a server platform, you need to identify the work that is going to be done and what needs to be protected. If the customer is running a mail server on Linux on zSeries, his or her definition of anti-virus protection is likely to be a mail-scanning anti-virus tool that can be integrated with his or her mail server of choice. The mail clients are likely to be PC-based, so the security manager should check for viruses in the customer's stored mail prior to distribution or delivery. This would be necessary to prevent the zSeries server from spreading a virus.

Commercial anti-virus tools are available for Linux on the mainframe. For information about anti-virus tools, refer to IBM's *ISV support for mainframe servers* Web site:
`http://www.ibm.com/servers/eserver/zseries/solutions/s390da/`.

8.6 Keeping up to date on security issues

Distributors maintain mailing lists and sites for fixes that relate to their Linux distributions. Here are some useful addresses for general information on security alerts:

SecurityFocus
Visit `http://www.securityfocus.com/` for general security issues. From this site, you can also link to the BugTraq mailing list for the discussion and announcement of computer security vulnerabilities.

CERT Coordination Center
Visit `http://www.cert.org/` for general information, and `http://www.cert.org/contact_cert/certmaillist.html` for a mailing list with current security fixes.

SecuriTeam
Visit `http://www.securiteam.com/` for a mailing list with news on current security issues and tools.

SecurityTracker
Visit `http://www.securitytracker.com/` for news on security. You can list the issues according to vendors, impacts, and other categories.

SANS/FBI list
Visit `http://www.sans.org/top20/` for a list of the top vulnerabilities of computers.

8.7 Summary

When considering security for Linux on the mainframe, remember that:

- The hardware itself enjoys a higher level of physical security than the average server farm through virtualization and reduced physical resources.

- z/VM can help by using:

  - Defined roles that scope authority

  - Guest definitions to diversify types of guests and their authorizations

  - Virtual communications that eliminate the risk of wire-tapping

The use of a mainframe and z/VM can lower the total cost of ownership:

- Because fewer people need access to the physical machine, the cost of repairing damages caused by intentional or unintentional tampering with the system console, cables, and other hardware is lowered.

- z/VM ensures consistency and speed when defining the secure environment and making copies of a known secure environment. Thus, z/VM can reduce the time spent by administrators identifying, applying, and supporting security patches.

- z/VM ensures the isolation of images you require, in most cases without the need to buy and set up individual machines. Individual machines bring with them costs and interconnection complexity, resulting in additional risks in the configuration that would not be present in a z/VM environment. Corporate rules sometimes state that a specific piece of work must run on a physically separate piece of real hardware. Recall, however, that LPAR, having a certified level of isolation, should be considered as separate, isolated hardware and can make Linux on the mainframe a real option.

Chapter 9.
Setting Up Linux on the Mainframe

In this chapter, we discuss considerations when setting up Linux on the mainframe. These considerations cover obtaining a distribution, installing it, and customizing it. The customization section discusses options for creating Linux images for different purposes in an efficient way using z/VM. Customization also covers I/O considerations when setting up the environment.

In general, installing the Linux operating system on the mainframe is no different from other platforms. Setting up the hardware for Linux on the mainframe is different because of virtualization technology. Setting up virtual hardware can be easier (and potentially less costly) than setting up real hardware.

Installing Linux itself on the mainframe is relatively easy, as was demonstrated by the "Install Fests" (see 3.2.2, "Spreading the word—the Linux install fest"). The initial installation is described in the respective distributor's documentation and is not repeated here. Instead, we focus on configuration choices that can give you some value from Linux on the mainframe.

With Linux on the mainframe, you have an interesting opportunity during the configuration process to address the key areas of availability, security, and management. You can set up for availability early when creating your images. You can also set up for security to a certain degree, and Linux on the mainframe can make it easier to manage both software change and operations. For example, operation management can be simplified if z/VM is set up to be the health monitor. These are choices that you can make when configuring z/VM and the Linux guests.

In this chapter we explore these questions:

- Where can you obtain a Linux distribution for the mainframe, and what are your criteria for choosing one over another?

- What are the runtime environment options for Linux on the mainframe?

- What should you consider when customizing the environment for availability?

9.1 Distribution considerations

The fact that there are several distributions gives you options. The distributions include Open Source packages; it is possible to modify, exchange one distribution for another, and upgrade at your own pace.

How do you choose a distribution? You may already have criteria for selection. In this section, we present some criteria that may be of use. We have found that companies tend to consider the amount of modification they need to make in order for a distribution to fit their needs. The amount of modification needed depends on how well the base distribution fills your needs, what device drivers it comes with, and so forth.

The Linux distributions for the mainframe all come with the unique extra functions for mainframe device drivers and communications features such as HiperSockets. You can choose between 31-bit distributions (Linux for S/390) and 64-bit distributions (Linux for zSeries). Table 9-1 lists some commercial mainframe distributions.

Table   9-1. Mainframe Linux distributions

Company	Web site
Red Hat, Inc.	http://www.redhat.com/
SuSE Linux AG	http://www.suse.com/
Turbolinux, Inc.	http://www.turbolinux.com/

While other mainframe distributions may be available, those listed in Table 9-1 have been tested, not only by the suppliers but by IBM as well.

Any revision of a distribution may at any given time exploit more or less of the full Linux for S/390 or zSeries capabilities. IBM first released its new S/390 or zSeries technology patches to IBM's DeveloperWorks Web site. From there, distributors can download the code.

The distributors each have their own schedule for building new versions of Linux on the mainframe. Distributors "leap frog" each other with the software version they include. For example, Red Hat might have a newer version of glibc, but SuSE might have a newer kernel.

9.1.1 Choosing the right distribution

The price of the distribution will be part of your TCO equation. Contributing factors to the cost of a commercial Linux distribution are the charge for the support and maintenance as well as the rights to future upgrades

A goal of the Free Standards Group workgroup Linux Standard Base (LSB)[12] is to promote compatibility among Linux distributions and thereby enable software applications to run on different Linux systems. The LSB defines a standard against which both the distribution and the middleware/application products can be certified. Ensuring compliance of any distribution (and application) you use with the LSB helps you avoid problems when you change distributions or need to move an application to run on another distribution.

Documentation can be another important aspect of your choice of distribution. Inspect it for coverage in those areas where you have the greatest need for clear information.

9.1.2 Modifying a Linux distribution

As explained in Chapter 1, "Introducing Linux," Linux consists of numerous Open Source packages. Different distributions bundle different versions of various packages. Together with specific installation and administration tools, configuration files, documentation, and so on, this bundle of packages makes up your Linux system. At some point, you may need to make a change to your Linux distribution. You probably already have a change management policy in place for most of your other operating system images, and maybe even for Linux. This section presents a few things unique to Linux that you might want to ensure are addressed.

You might want to change your chosen distributor's basic installation in order to:

- Set up specialized systems for specific tasks.

- Improve security by reducing the number of services on the system.

- Reduce the size of the system.

- Do performance and tuning.

- Include certain patches for enhanced functionality.

- Address dependencies of middleware or applications on certain versions of packages.

---

[12] http://www.linuxbase.org

Some changes, such as installing kernel patches, may invalidate the support contract. It is important that any changes made (for example, to the kernel, to the distribution, to the middleware, to third party applications, and so forth) are acceptable under the terms of the respective maintenance and support contract. Methods of change that usually are acceptable include:

- Changing parameters in configuration files (adding or removing modules, changing module parameters)

- Adding or removing packages

- Choosing different versions of packages (that is, updating the kernel or runtime environment)

Starting with a distribution that is closest to your desired system helps you minimize changes. If you do need to make changes, the preferred method is to use the specific configuration tools of the distribution.

Change management as a discipline is discussed in 16.2, "Change management."

9.2 Running Linux on the mainframe

On the mainframe, there are three options for running Linux:

- Natively on the mainframe hardware

- In a logical partition (LPAR)

- As a guest operating system under z/VM

Of these, the most interesting for the server consolidation case is the z/VM option.

Using LPARs, you can define up to 15 partitions (with the S/390 and zSeries machines), each of which hosts a separate server. If an LPAR contains CPUs that can run any operating system (so called *general purpose engines*), any mainframe operating system can run in that partition. The hardware resources of the mainframe (CPU, I/O, and memory) are divided according to the definition of each LPAR. zSeries and S/390 hardware have the computing power coupled with adequate memory and I/O to support hosting multiple operating-system images at one time.

Using z/VM, virtualization goes further than with LPAR to allow you dynamic definition of CPU, memory, and I/O channels as well as real sharing of memory, channels, and disks. Hundreds of images can run as guest operating systems under VM, as illustrated by consolidating entire server farms to Linux under z/VM by ISPCompany.

Software pricing for operating systems such as z/OS, z/VM, or VSE/ESA is generally based on the processing power of the machine. Adding CPUs normally increases this processing capability and, therefore, software prices. This was an early inhibitor to using Linux on the mainframe. IBM introduced Integrated Facility for Linux (IFL) to allow you to add processing power for Linux without increasing software pricing for traditional operating systems and other software. IFL features are managed by PR/SM as one or more logical partitions with dedicated CPUs. In IFL LPARs, you can have Linux images only or Linux and z/VM. Using the IFL, you can provide capacity dedicated to Linux workloads, as shown in Figure 9-1.

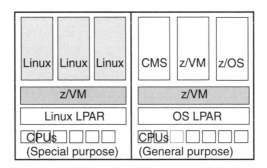

Figure   9-1. An IFL feature can be used to run Linux workloads

9.3 Creating images

As a server farm grows, day-to-day administration can become cumbersome. With Linux on the mainframe, you can plan your installation with a view to ease installation and administration of new servers. z/VM gives you unique possibilities to create virtual Linux servers in a matter of minutes.

Before you install Linux, you can benefit from planning ahead. List your Linux images and decide what categories they fit in, and think about whether you want to take advantage of code sharing. Code sharing can be direct, by having a read-only disk that all images can access, or by copying from one *golden image*. z/VM can support all these choices.

Creating a virtual Linux server is a two-stage affair. You first create a virtual machine, then you can install a Linux image to run in it.

Normally, the system administrator logs on to a CMS guest console and uses the control program functions to configure the virtual hardware for the new virtual machine (guest). Each virtual machine, or guest, in z/VM is known by a unique ID that is used as part of the logon process. In the Linux usage of z/VM, we refer to this logon ID as the *guest name*. The software and data that reside on disks are then made available to the new guest.

These disks are typically of two types: *system disks* that contain the system executable libraries and system parameters and *data disks* that contain the unique data to be used by the Linux image while it is running its applications.

Then the administrator can boot the Linux image that resides on a disk defined to the new guest. (The booting of the Linux image is called *Initial Program Load (IPL)* in the mainframe world.) z/VM isolates the guests from each other (see 8.2.4, "Virtual security") so that if one guest should crash, the others are not impacted.

You can create the virtual machine and define disk or minidisks with z/VM's DirMaint or a similar program product. DirMaint allows you to use profiles and prototype files, so you can create hundreds of virtual servers quickly and easily with no conflicts of resources. (See *Linux on IBM zSeries and S/390: ISP/ASP Solutions* for detailed instructions.)

Having created a virtual machine, you can proceed to install a Linux image in it. For a small number of images, you could install each Linux guest from scratch, as you would with a set of CDs from one physical server to the next. If you require a large number of images, then some Linux distributions offer a means of repeated installs (such as the YaST shortcuts in SuSE and the *mkkickstart* utility in Red Hat). However, using z/VM, there is another simple way to avoid such repeated installs.

Without even having a single Linux image running, the z/VM utilities allow you to copy and duplicate a guest's disks. Companies can install and configure one Linux image; and when they are satisfied with that image, they use the z/VM copy utilities to create a master copy, called the *golden image*. The golden image is then copied to produce the next Linux image. This process of copying is often referred to as *cloning* Linux images. See Figure 9-2.

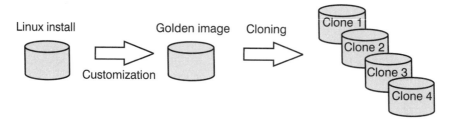

Figure 9-2. Cloning Linux images

When cloning Linux images, a small number of modifications must be made in order for the new image to be useful. For example, the host name and IP address must be changed. An efficient cloning scheme keeps these changes to a minimum. Even if more changes are needed, it can simplify setup to use the golden image as a base. However, an image with many modifications, for example, a different application suite or a different level of glibc, is not strictly a clone, but a new unique image. Each unique image requires separate adminis-tration effort. Keeping the number of unique images down saves administration cost.

When cloning z/VM Linux images, you need to copy the virtual machine definition and the disks. Typically, the disks that contain the system executable libraries and much of the system parameters are cloned, while the local data disks are just defined and initialized. The new guest must have a unique identity. Hence z/VM unique items (such as the guest name and local disks, on the one hand) and Linux items (such as the host name, IP address and root password, on the other hand) need to be changed.

Figure 9-3 shows a guest being cloned into another guest. The first ("golden") guest has two disks with system data and one disk with image-specific data. For example, A000 could contain the kernel and glib, A001 could contain data that needs customizing (such as the IP address) and A002 could contain the applications or databases. In the copy process, the system data are copied over. The second disk will need some customization pertaining to the new image. The third will be filled by the owner of the guest and is separate from the cloning process.

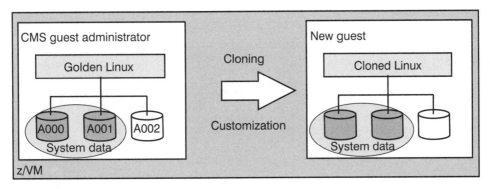

Figure   9-3. Cloning Linux images by using VM guests

Cloning with z/VM gives you a unique opportunity to save disk space. When you create Linux images by copying minidisks, if you were to place the system data on one minidisk and then for each image simply define a read-only link to it, you in effect have only one real instance. This is shown in Figure 9-4. Hundreds of users can then share the disk. In addi-tion to saving disk space, having a read-only disk makes it easier to administer the environ-ment and control change. You must, however, check your particular distribution for what parts of the file system can easily be shared.

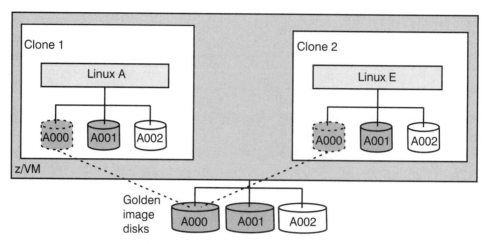

Figure 9-4. Saving disk space by linking read-only disks

9.3.1 Disk space requirements and file system layout

Almost all currently available Open Source executable programs fit in less than 4 GB of disk space. The file system is usually organized into a hierarchy, depending on the files. Concentrating files that need read-only access in one file system makes it possible to save disk space by sharing the file system among Linux guests. Some typical directories found in a Linux file system are:

/usr   The /usr directory contains commands and applications. This directory is a candidate for sharing among Linux guests.

/opt   The /opt directory typically contains additional software packages, such as KDE3 or gnome. The benefit of installing applications under a separate file system is that you can upgrade Linux without re-installing the applications, and vice versa. This directory is a candidate for sharing among Linux guests.

/var   The /var directory is often allocated as a separate file system (not under /). A separate /var file system can help avoid a system halt due to overflowing log, spool, or mail files. Such problems are easier to track and take corrective action when /var is a separate file system. Also, it is possible to set certain file system parameters for the /var file system in order to speed up creation and deletion of file blocks. This directory cannot be shared among Linux guests.

A planned code hierarchy simplifies setup of servers and helps simplify both a cloning process and software maintenance. A more detailed description of the Linux directory structure is in 20.2, "Overview of Linux directory structure."

9.3.2 Example Linux guest directory

The example Linux guest directory below shows the standard definition used by ISPCompany. The standard guest has 256 MB of storage, a Guest LAN, a HiperSockets connection, links one read-only disk, and defines two read-write minidisks. Customization for this directory is limited to changing the user ID (or guest name) and passwords. For ISPCompany, these changes can easily be done (for example, over the phone, while the customer is waiting).

```
USER LINUXE XXXXXX 256M 1024M G
    INCLUDE LINDFLT                         /Links standard DIRMAINT definitions
    SPECIAL EE00 QDIO 3 SYSTEM LINQDIO      /Adapter for QDIO Guest LAN
    SPECIAL FF00 HIPER 3 SYSTEM LINHIPER    /Adapter for Hipersocket Guest LAN
    LINK LINUX0 A000 A000 RR                /Link the read-only common disk
    MDISK A001 3390 1 2000 LIN008 MR RXXX WXXX MXXXX      /Define minidisk A001
    MDISK A002 3390 1 2000 LIN009 MR RXXX WXXX MXXXX      /Define minidisk A002
```

Standard settings that are common across all the Linux guest directory entries can be made available through the INCLUDE command.

9.4 Purpose of Linux images

You may not want to have all identical Linux servers. A typical server farm needs several kinds of servers. Each instance of the Linux operating system we call an *image*. As you customize a Linux image for its particular function, it becomes a specific server. For example, you can have an image that is configured to be a domain name server (DNS) serving the internal local area network, or an Apache HTTP or https server, or a firewall. Before implementing a server farm on Linux, it is advantageous to think about what kinds of servers are needed. Code sharing across servers might be possible, thus making software management easier.

Let us look at ISPCompany for an example of code sharing and easier software management. ISPCompany offers clients a standard Linux image. A custom contract gives clients the right to change the standard image, but a normal contract states that the image should remain unchanged. The standard image contains code on a read-only disk, where ISPCompany can easily support and manage the software. Client programs are on other, read-write disks. For example, if ISPCompany needs to apply a security patch, sometimes it can put the patch on a new read-only copy of the golden image disk. Each Linux image that boots from this disk will pick up the change. You can use z/VM to mark disks as read-only and to share one set of real disks among multiple Linux images as read-only.

If you are moving images from an existing server farm, you probably already know how many images you need, what they do, and which ones are similar. For security reasons, a Linux image should have only the operating system functions needed by the application it supports. Dividing up your servers according to the type of application they run gives you a rough view of what sets of images you need to create. Then, as you consider the dependencies which the applications have on distributions and other software, you can refine your view of what your images need.

Once you have determined how many unique images you need, you can construct them, create the unique golden copies, and then, with DirMaint, create the guests you need.

You can add resources such as processors, memory, minidisks, and so forth, to an existing Linux image by simple configuration changes which you can make dynamically. The initial guest definition can always be changed later.

The cost equation for doing hot standby can be drastically improved by using z/VM. One type of Linux image you are likely to consider in you design are low-cost hot-standby images. These images are redundant images that can share the file system, as shown in Figure 9-5.

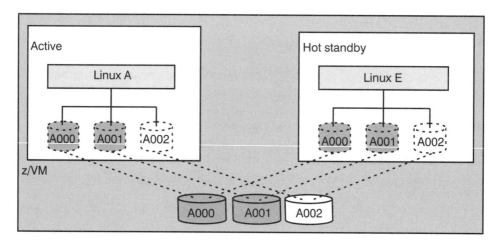

Figure   9-5. Hot-standby Linux image under z/VM

If an image fails and has a hot-standby image, shared disks allow the hot standby to take over quickly. (If data are read-only, such as static Web pages, there is no need for data duplication or RAID-type storage.) You must decide on your particular schemes so that you can configure your system accordingly at the time you are setting up. Availability is discussed in detail in Chapter 11, "Achieving Higher Availability."

9.5 Setting up for secure and efficient I/O

A Linux image needs all three resources of a computer system: CPU, memory, and I/O. Let us present a couple of methods that can give you value in your setup. Resource sharing for Linux guests under z/VM is one of the strong points of the Linux-on-the-mainframe solution. For a guest, you can define the number of CPUs or parts of CPUs it should have, as well as how much memory it should have. In contrast to other solutions (based on individual real processors), a decision to give a guest more CPU capacity does not have to be expensive. Using the guest directory definition, administrators can change resources allocated to a guest in a matter of minutes.

Compared to over-configuring real hardware (such as CPUs), z/VM allows you to simply change the definition to either add more or take some away. Resources taken from one guest can easily be made available to others.

The third resource, I/O, can also be set up to be shared in different ways. I/O on the mainframe is set up by defining the paths, the devices, and the relationship of devices to paths to the mainframe hardware, to z/VM, and to Linux.

The mainframe accesses devices by means of channel paths. The hardware looks only for those devices that are defined to it in a configuration file called *IOCDS (I/O configuration data set)*. The definitions for all LPARs and the number of LPARs are defined in the IOCDS file. If a device and its path are not defined in the IOCDS, the device is invisible and inaccessible to the hardware and all operating systems and programs that run on the LPAR, even if there is an actual, physical cable connection. If a device is defined in the IOCDS, it will be visible and usable as long as it is physically present. A device can be defined in the IOCDS file and not be physically present without causing any errors. In fact, it is common practice to overconfigure the I/O paths to support availability and future growth. For example, you can define a fiber channel with a new set of ESS storage in the IOCDS. You can then later "hot-plug" the ESS without having to change the configuration file.

z/VM can see the devices on all channel paths known to its LPAR (or the machine, if z/VM runs natively). A z/VM guest can see only those devices that z/VM defines to it. These definitions can be changed dynamically from z/VM. z/VM can also split the real devices into smaller virtual devices and control the guest's access at the level of the virtual devices.

On Linux, you have two possibilities. One alternative is to use the auto-detect capability. Linux attempts to access all devices it can find. Thus, if there is an actual cable connection to a device, and Linux has a channel path that can access it, the device will be accessed. In an environment where resources are heavily shared, you might want to avoid this. For instance, you can use the z/VM guest setup to rule out what Linux should not access.

The alternative is to instruct a Linux image to look only for specific devices. Linux is then unable to see any other devices, even if the hardware definitions and z/VM have made them available.

It is possible to overconfigure the paths for the hardware, overconfigure z/VM, and (in the guest definition) restrict Linux' access to devices. By constraining each of the guest's definitions to only the devices actually needed, you effectively protect the data on the devices from misuse by other guests. I/O definitions for a guest can be changed dynamically.

9.5.1 Booting and automatic find

While Linux on the mainframe gives you great flexibility when configuring channels and devices, it may be helpful to know something about how Linux assigns devices so that you can use the flexibility to your advantage.

Unless the kernel parameter file contains an entry for disk or minidisks, Linux on the mainframe assigns disk devices (disks and minidisks) based on the order in which the disks are found at boot time. If there is no such entry, the disks are ordered according to the subchannel number allocation that takes place at boot. To be on the safe side, it is strongly recommended that you list the disk and minidisks that you want Linux to use in the kernel parameter file. This assures a well-known naming convention that commands and applications can safely assume. Here is an example of a disk entry in the kernel parameter file:

```
dasd=200 mdisk=201,202,203 root=/dev/mndc ro
```

This entry ensures that dasda maps to disk 200, mnda maps to minidisk 201, mndb to 202 and mndc to 203. Also, mndc (203) is where the root file system will be mounted. With this entry in the kernel parameter file, these allocations are assured at every boot. Without it, you could have unpredictable allocations, especially if you (or someone else) change the I/O configurations in Linux.

9.5.2 Network considerations

The network setup is central to the design of the solution. Linux on the mainframe offers two unique values for network setup.

- You can share the network interface card. z/VM lets you share the adapter across virtual servers. For example, an OSA-Express card with the Gigabit Ethernet feature allows up to 15 LPARs in a z900 to share one physical port.

- Alternatively, you can easily set up a unique Linux virtual router. A virtual router avoids the cost of a real router. Details on configuring networks in a box and internal LANs is covered in Chapter 10, "Communicating in a Virtual Environment."

9.5.3 File system considerations

Availability of a system involves two key aspects: avoiding system failures and if the system does fail, ensuring a quick recovery from the outage. The file system recovery can add a significant amount of time to the recovery process.

Several different file systems are available on Linux. Broadly speaking, file systems fall into two distinct categories: *conventional* and *journaled*.

Conventional file systems

A conventional file system must be contained within one physical device. This type of file system uses a delayed write protocol which implies that recovering the file system after an outage requires scanning the disk and reconstructing the file system. The advantage of conventional file systems is that these are relatively fast in I/O processing. One down side is that these file systems typically limit the file size to the device capacity. Additionally, if a check or repair of a conventional file system were necessary, the process can take a very long time if it is on a large disk. ext2 is an example of a conventional file system. With the Linux 2.4 kernel, it is the *de facto* standard Linux file system. (Some distributors are now changing the default file system from ext2 to the journaled file system ext3.)

Journaled file systems

A journaled file system keeps a record of all changes that are made to data held on the file. In the event of a software failure or any data integrity problems, recovery and repair can be completed quickly using the journal instead of restoring by hand. For example, restoring a file system to a consistent state takes seconds or minutes, rather than the hours or days it can take with a large non-journaled file system. However, journaled file systems do incur a performance hit because all changes to the data must be recorded. Examples of journaled file systems are:

- ext3 is a journaled follow-on of the ext2 file system. It is compatible with the ext2 file system and requires kernel 2.4.
  (http://www.ibm.com/developerworks/linux/library/l-fs7.html)

- The Journaled File System (JFS).
  (http://oss.software.ibm.com/developerworks/opensource/jfs/)

- The Reiser file system (reiserfs). (http://www.namesys.com/)

Other file systems

There are a great many other types of file systems available. Some of the more common are:

- *nfs*, the network file system, is used for accessing remote file systems over the network.

- *swap*, the swap file system, is not mounted. It is used to page out any unused memory pages.

- *procfs* is a virtual file system that exists in memory. The kernel uses this file system to make certain that key system information is available to programs through standard file operations.

- *smbfs* is the Samba file system, which allows file sharing with Windows clients.

9.6 Summary

In most cases, setting up Linux images on the mainframe hardware means setting up virtual hardware. In many cases, setting up virtual hardware is easier, more flexible, and cheaper than working with real hardware; for example, network setup can be easier because there is no need to install physical machines and cables. You can add and remove resources to meet your needs without having to commit new, extra hardware resources. Additionally, virtual over-configuration makes the environment flexible.

Redundancy can be configured into the LPAR and z/VM guests to allow for recovery from most hardware single points of failure. Hot-standby configurations are economically attractive.

If your company doesn't already have a predisposition toward a distributor, you will have the luxury of choosing the distributor based on what minimizes your need for making changes and getting the types of additional support you might need. The service contract should allow for the changes you plan to make.

The configuration capabilities of the mainframe, z/VM and Linux give you enormous advantage when you need to add extra virtual servers or resources, or if you need to try out new things. You can do so quickly, easily, and at no extra hardware cost. For example, you can create a new Linux server within minutes to try out some new software or idea.

Chapter 10.
Communicating in a Virtual Environment

In a large server farm environment, server-to-server communication is crucial. In stand-alone server environments, this is done with a physical network, real cabling, routers, and associated hardware. Acquisition and operational costs are involved, and as the size of the environment grows, so does its complexity.

A unique communication method available in z/VM involves using the memory bus to implement the communication paths. The memory bus replaces hardware cables, and memory-to-memory transfer replaces hardware adapters.

In this chapter, we explore these questions:

- What communication methods are there for Linux on the mainframe?

- How can a virtual network reduce complexity and cost for server farms?

- How is security improved by using virtual networks for Linux servers?

10.1 Communication methods under z/VM

One advantage of consolidating servers on the mainframe is the elimination of physical network interconnections between virtual servers. Replacing the physical cabling with memory buses inside the machine also improves the data rate and lowers the latency. In zSeries servers, a high-speed interconnection for TCP/IP communication (HiperSockets) enables TCP/IP traffic to flow directly between partitions. HiperSockets exploit the "network in a box" concept that transmits LAN-type data at near memory speeds.

The z/VM computing model, with multiple operating systems each running applications as separate guests, yet with a need to communicate among themselves, naturally led to thinking of a mainframe system as an extensive network of cooperating virtual nodes. This was the springboard to the early development of mechanisms for communicating between virtual machines, managing such communications, and ensuring the integrity of the system's data in such an environment. In fact, because this computing model required an architecture where one virtual machine requested some system service of another virtual machine, VM could be considered the first implementation of a client/server architecture. This natural affinity between the virtual machine computing model and today's network computing model makes z/VM an ideal infrastructure for network-connected Linux systems.

z/VM offers options for communication among virtual servers that greatly reduce complexity. A "virtual network cable" is nothing more than a Control Program service that transfers data from one memory location to another, making the communicating virtual server images believe that they are sending and receiving data over a real network connection. Memory-to-memory data transfers are fast, and they get faster as processor speeds increase. Upgrade to a faster real processor, and the data transfer rate of your virtual network automatically increases in speed.

z/VM provides several types of communication. However, the ones you will probably use in a Linux-on-the-mainframe environment, besides the real connection to the Internet or intranet, are virtual channel-to-channel adapter (CTCA), virtual Network Interface Cards (NICs), and Guest LANs.

10.1.1 Virtual CTCA

Channel-to-channel (CTC) communication was developed before today's high-speed networks. Originally, CTC simply enabled two S/360 or S/370 processors to communicate using a special protocol called CTCA. The processors used channel paths for the connection to replace, for example, communication over a telephone line. In other words, CTC is a point-to-point connection. A CTC connection is considered a secure communication path, because it involves only two parties directly connected only to each other through a channel path that is entirely on the secure raised floor.

Today, a real channel-to-channel adapter is a common method used to interconnect pairs of mainframe systems. z/VM has virtualized this connection. z/VM provides the ability to define virtual channel-to-channel adapters, which can be useful in connecting virtual machines running the CTCA protocol without requiring real CTCA hardware. The virtualization makes a CTC faster. In a Linux-on-the-mainframe environment, this is useful in connecting Linux guests to other guests, such as VSE/ESA, or z/OS. Virtual CTCAs can also be used to connect Linux guests to each other.

Although virtual CTC lets you establish point-to-point connections between pairs of images, it might be more practical to use Guest LANs when many images need to communicate.

10.1.2 Network in a box: NIC and Guest LANs

z/VM Version 4 includes support for virtual NICs. NICs are used to connect to a local area network (LAN). Specific NIC protocols supported by z/VM include HiperSockets and OSA-Express QDIO mode. Real HiperSockets are used to connect server images in separate LPARs on a HiperSockets LAN. z/OS, VSE/ESA, Linux on zSeries, and z/VM all support the HiperSockets protocol. Like a real HiperSockets connection, virtual

HiperSockets are used to connect server images in virtual machines, but data are trans-ferred at near memory speeds. The same is true for virtual QDIO connections. Virtual HiperSockets and virtual QDIO NICs are used to connect a guest to a "virtual LAN"—a LAN totally inside z/VM.

In z/VM Version 4, these virtual LANs are referred to as *Guest LANs*. A server image running on z/VM can connect to a Guest LAN using virtual HiperSockets or queued direct I/O (QDIO) NIC. Virtual HiperSockets and QDIO connections look just like the "real thing" to a Linux server or to any other software that supports the real connections. Unlike the real thing, however, there is no limit on the number of virtual HiperSockets or QDIO connections that can be defined in a z/VM environment. And there is no predefined limit on the number of Guest LANs that can be created.

Guest LAN support eliminates some of the point-to-point network management challenges that exist when using virtual CTCA while providing almost all the value. A Linux server con-nected to a Guest LAN can communicate with other virtual machines connected to that LAN (see Figure 10-1). Unicast, multicast, and broadcast communications are possible with a Guest LAN. (OSA Express Guest LANs support unicast, multicast, and broadcast. HiperSockets Guest LANs support unicast and multicast.)

z/VM is designed to enable virtual NICs and Guest LANs on mainframes that do not support real HiperSockets, such as the IBM 9672 G5/G6 models and the Multiprise 3000. This enhances the virtual networking environment on those machines, while letting compa-nies prepare for a real HiperSockets environment before moving to a zSeries server.

There can be "system" Guest LANs and Guest LANs that are associated with a specific z/VM guest (for example, a Linux image). System Guest LANs exist independently of any active, logged-on guest, while Guest LANs associated with a guest exist only as long as the guest is active.

For example, assume ISPCompany (as an ISP and outsourcing provider) has a client that has six servers. ISPCompany can host these six servers on a mainframe and map the real LAN that connected the servers to a Guest LAN on the mainframe (see Figure 10-1).

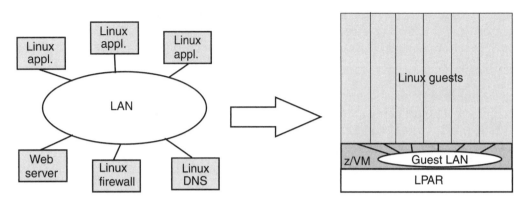

Figure 10-1. A Guest LAN connects z/VM guests

While connected to a Guest LAN, a Linux server can also connect to a real HiperSocket connection and communicate with other servers in a different LPAR on the same mainframe. This offers companies a way to route Guest LAN traffic to another LPAR without requiring each Linux image on the Guest LAN to access a real HiperSockets connection. For example, in order to let one Linux server communicate with the back-end z/OS, StoreCompany uses a real HiperSockets connection (Figure 10-2).

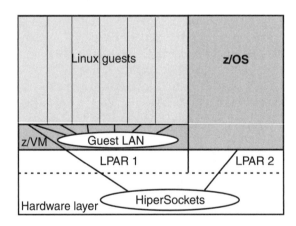

Figure 10-2. HiperSockets connect a Linux server to an image on another LPAR

10.1.3 The value of HiperSockets for Linux

Many data-center environments today have multitiered server applications that include middle-tier servers surrounding a zSeries data and transaction server. Connecting this multitude of servers requires the complexity and cost of many networking components. Furthermore, the performance and availability of interserver communication depend on the performance and stability of this set of connections.

Consolidating this middle-tier workload as multiple Linux virtual servers on a zSeries machine requires a very reliable, high-speed network over which these servers can communicate. zSeries HiperSockets provide this. In addition, these consolidated servers also have direct high-speed access to database or transaction servers running under z/OS on the same zSeries machine.

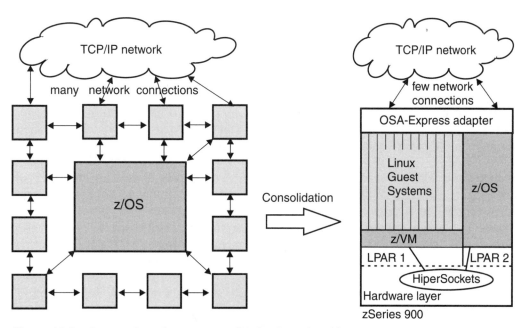

Figure 10-3. An overview of server consolidation based on Linux

The left side of Figure 10-3 shows a server farm surrounding a zSeries machine with its corporate data and transaction servers on z/OS.

The right side of Figure 10-3 shows a Linux-based server consolidation on a zSeries machine. Servers can communicate on the zSeries machine via HiperSockets. In addition, the network connection for all servers is concentrated over a few high-speed OSA-Express interfaces.

10.2 Scenario: networking in a virtual environment

The following scenario illustrates how useful z/VM virtual networking can be:

Figure 10-4 shows a typical multi-tier application infrastructure that many companies have deployed using discrete, real server hardware and networking equipment. StoreCompany deploys this configuration on its mainframe for its online catalog business. The significant difference in this configuration is that the server images shown are actually running on a single IBM zSeries machine. Two logical partitions (LPARs) are configured on the zSeries machine. One is running z/OS and hosts StoreCompany's regular business applications unchanged, including the DB2 database server, the CICS transaction server, and the Websphere Application Server (WAS). The other LPAR runs fifteen Linux images as guests under z/VM, hosting a mix of application and networking software.

A real HiperSockets connection (HLAN1) passes network traffic between the Linux images on z/VM and the z/OS database server. Linux firewall servers control access to the real HiperSockets LAN that connects to the z/OS LPAR. Two z/VM Guest LANs (GLAN1 and GLAN2) are high-speed, easy-to-use virtual LANs that isolate and control network traffic among the various applications that are running in the Linux images. Two of the Linux images running on z/VM function as network routers. They are connected to real network adapters (OSA cards) and route traffic between the "outside world" (XLAN1) and the virtual server environment being hosted on z/VM.

Let us follow the flow of traffic into this virtual server environment from an end-user perspective. This scenario could be deployed as an intranet or Internet solution. In either case, users access the StoreCompany environment by specifying a Web address (URL) on their browsers. The switch passes connection requests to one of the z/VM Linux routers attached to the external LAN (XLAN1). Several physical Internet connections come in through the switch, providing redundant external access possibilities. Having two Linux routers configured for this environment provides a level of availability for the services offered. If one of the routers fails (or, more likely, requires service or a software upgrade), the other Linux router then distributes the requests over the HTTP servers. A second Linux server running on z/VM does not require the duplication of hardware expense normally incurred when deploying this environment on real servers.

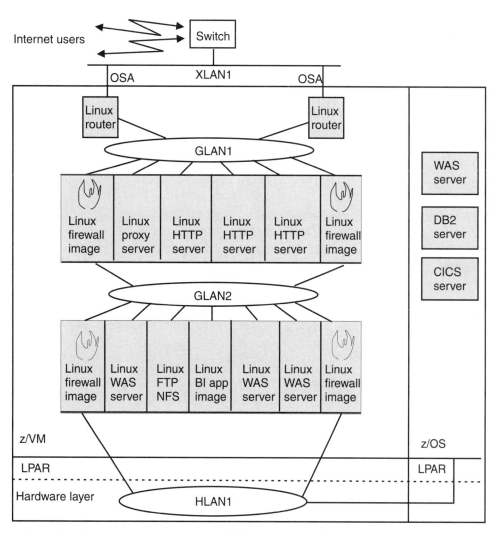

Figure 10-4. StoreCompany virtual network (z/OS network not shown)

The Linux routers are connected to z/VM Guest LAN number 1 (GLAN1). Also attached to GLAN1 are the HTTP servers that process Web requests and perform load balancing of the requests. The Linux router that receives an HTTP call passes the request to one of the Web servers connected to GLAN1. Assuming this is a user's first access to the services offered by this environment, the Web server probably sends back a home page to be displayed on the browser, reversing the flow of network traffic that connected the user to the Web server. When a user clicks on a link that requests a service, the HTTP call is returned to one of the HTTP servers. If the request requires access to one of the Linux WebSphere

Application Servers (WAS) running in the virtual environment, the HTTP server calls the WAS server, which processes the request.

The Linux WAS servers in our scenario are connected to a second z/VM Guest LAN (GLAN2). Communication between the HTTP servers and the WAS servers is controlled by the two Linux firewall servers that are connected to both Guest LANs. Once again, system availability is ensured with a redundant set of Linux images providing firewall services between the LANs.

Once the request has reached the WAS server, it accesses additional server images as needed, depending on the function it is going to perform.

If a WAS server needs to access data found in the z/OS DB2 database, it connects to one of the Linux firewall servers for GLAN2, then accesses the real HiperSockets LAN in order to pass the data request to the DB2 server on z/OS, which is also connected to the real HiperSockets LAN. This connection is also used when an CICS request comes in through WAS that requires processing by the z/OS CICS server. Firewall redundancy has been configured for the HiperSockets LAN as well.

This environment provides a number of benefits:

- Hosting multiple, independent server images on a single machine reduces complexity.
- Redundant servers can increase availability, improve the quality of service, and simplify the maintenance of a virtual server environment.
- Virtual networking saves the expense of real networking equipment, while achieving high-speed communications and easing configuration and reconfiguration.
- Standard networking skills can create a virtual server environment on z/VM. A virtual network looks just like a real network on paper but does not have the cost of a real network.

10.3 Virtual failover solutions

Another consideration for server farm operations is failover. Because z/VM controls the hardware, it can be seen as a single point of failure. Therefore, you might want a failover system in case z/VM suffers an outage.

Depending on company policy, there are three possibilities for a backup system: a duplicate image, a duplicate z/VM on another LPAR, or duplicate machines.

To maintain service during a system failure, company policy might state that a duplicate server must be available to back up the primary server. A physical hot-standby configuration duplicates acquisition and environmental costs for a server that you hope will never have to be online. With z/VM, the costs associated with a backup Linux virtual machine waiting to become active are minimal. If a hot-standby server in the form of a duplicate image is activated, it simply uses the system capacity relinquished by the primary server that just failed.

zSeries 800 or 900 machines can be partitioned into up to 15 logical partitions using the PR/SM feature. One partition can contain a z/VM that acts as a hot standby for the z/VM system in another logical partition. This may require some custom programming (for example, developing a "heartbeat" monitor to verify the operational status of the systems, and programmable operator scripts to initiate procedures on the standby system). Linux-based failover solutions can also incorporate a secondary z/VM system as part of the approach. See Chapter 11, "Achieving Higher Availability," for more information.

10.4 Communicating with the outside world

We have covered communications inside the mainframe; let us now look at communications with the outside world. High-speed communications between the mainframe and external networks are primarily supported through these communication adapters:

- Open Systems Adapter-Express (OSA-Express)

  This TCP/IP-based adapter is important for server consolidation, because it is designed to communicate between a consolidated server environment (that uses virtual adapters and IP addressing) and the "outside world." The OSA-Express adapter can use the QDIO architecture to provide direct connectivity between applications running in a Linux guest or Linux LPAR, and the other platforms on the attached network. The OSA-Express adapter consists of different features: Gigabit Ethernet, Fast Ethernet, ATM (asynchronous transfer mode), and Token Ring.

- Channel-to-channel (CTC) adapters (ESCON and FICON)

  A CTC connection is the typical point-to-point high-speed connection between mainframes. The Linux on zSeries CTC device drivers can be used to establish a point-to-point TCP/IP connection between two mainframe Linux systems, or between a Linux system and another operating system such as z/VM, VSE/ESA, or z/OS.

For a description of the features and adapters, see 20.4.8, "Network device drivers and adapters."

10.5 Summary

This chapter talked about internal communication and communication with the outside world. There are several ways of communicating in a Linux-on-the-mainframe environment. z/VM provides high-performance communication among guests running Linux and other operating systems. Point-to-point connections can be implemented with real or virtual CTC connections. LAN-type connections can be created with real or virtual HiperSockets, or by using virtual Guest LANs. Virtual LANs are cheaper, easier to set up, faster, and more flexible than real LANs. The benefits of virtual networks for your business include:

- Decreased hardware cost of hubs, switches, and cables.

- Improved performance from latency and bandwidth of memory-to-memory transfers.

- Improved security due to the lack of hardware cables to "tap."

- Simplified administration. The logical administration is the same (nothing new for the network administrator to learn to get the value) and the physical administration practically disappears.

- Reduced network outages due to failures of physical components.

An important communication adapter for the communication with the world outside the mainframe is the Gigabit Ethernet OSA-Express adapter.

Chapter 11.
Achieving Higher Availability

The mainframe enjoys the reputation as the most reliable server hardware on the market. One of your reasons for considering Linux on the mainframe might be the outlook of deploying highly available Linux application servers.

In contrast to what many people believe, high availability is not a matter of all or nothing. High availability is driven by trade-offs between business needs and costs. Before working towards high availability, it is important to have a clear idea of what exactly is required. For example, high-availability solutions are often not meant to cover disaster scenarios. In this chapter we examine some availability requirements in relation to what we mean by high availability.

This chapter builds on the other chapters in this part of the book. It describes configuration considerations that might help you to improve the availability characteristics of your Linux servers. We look at various configuration options of the zSeries hardware and the z/VM virtualization that can decrease the probability of an outage and speed up the recovery of a failed Linux image. The corresponding management tasks for keeping an already-running Linux server available are covered in the next part of the book.

We use examples to show how the methods that are available today allow some of the Linux on the mainframe server farms to be configured for specific application workloads, such that any likely failures would not affect the users' access to the services.

There is a rapid evolution of tools for creating and managing highly available Linux servers. In the last topic of this chapter we point to some promising developments that are in under way as we write this book.

We will explore questions such as:

- What is meant by high availability?

- How does z/VM help with configuring for higher availability?

- What types of availability configurations are the easiest to implement with Linux on the mainframe?

- What will be coming next for Linux high availability?

11.1 What is high availability?

Availability is an attribute of an entire system, and is always measured from the user's perspective. High availability is a complex term to define. Most people agree that high availability is an attribute of a system, whereby the system is available to its target users almost all the time. High availability starts with a minimum of 99.99% availability. That is, a particular server configuration is said to be "highly available" if the combination of both planned and unplanned outages in a year is less than one hour. All the pieces of a high-availability solution need to be simultaneously available, as shown in Figure 11-1.

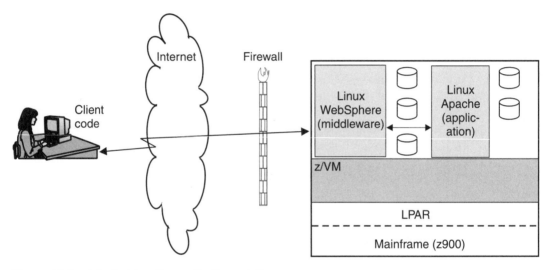

Figure 11-1. A typical two-tier application solution

High availability does not imply that there are never any failures within the system. Instead, the design of a high-availability system accepts that failures occur and focuses the effort on providing continuing service in spite of the failure. So, besides a focus on preventing failures by having robust components, a design for high availability also requires that recovery from failures is so fast as to not allow the failure be visible to the user as an outage.

Building a high-availability application server is a complex process that starts with the definition of the level of service required. Typically, the analysis includes a list of the sources for potential solution failure, and evaluates cost/benefit trade-offs of various recovery designs for potential failures. The higher the availability required, the more it is likely to cost in terms of development, deployment and keeping the solution running. Starting with the right components improves the likelihood of success at an acceptable cost.

A system is only as good as its weakest part. Linux and the mainframe are only a strong foundation to aid in the construction of a high-availability solution. Much of the effort in building such a solution will go into the application software, the middleware, and the management tools that are parts of the system. Here we will focus on what Linux and the mainframe can contribute to an overall high-availability solution.

zSeries and z/VM, having evolved over decades, are both inherently reliable and come with a rich set of tools. Linux, despite being only about a decade old, has earned a reputation for availability and is vigorously growing its tool-set that aids the rest of the software stack in constructing the environment for high availability. The current "state of the art" with Linux is still a distance away from allowing the easy configuration of application servers that meet such a stringent requirement as less than one hour of downtime a year. Even with a less-than-complete Linux tool-set, the existing tool-set, together with the capabilities of zSeries and z/VM, allow you to create application servers where users will not perceive a service outage even if a processor, disk, or Linux image itself, were to fail.

The cost of configuring for high availability is directly related to which risks of failure you want your system to be able to survive. As you can well imagine, it is a lot harder to ensure availability across an earthquake, explosion, or other such major catastrophe, than across a hardware or application failure. Is it enough to have two independent connections to the Internet backbone? Our example ISPCompany did not think so. They installed four separate backbone connections from four different suppliers. They also saw two independent potentials for failure: the bankruptcy of a supplier, and a potential for off-site damage to the fiber connection. Furthermore, they needed to ensure that they had the required bandwidth in case of failure.

To provide a high-availability solution, your design team needs to clearly understand the risks-versus-cost trade-offs that are important to your business. An application solution design is complex, and highly dependent on the particular situation. This chapter focuses on unique opportunities that Linux on the mainframe can contribute to your high-availability design.

11.2 The zSeries hardware availability

At the turn of the century when IBM reorganized its disparate processor divisions into the eServer brand, each of the four server teams got to choose a letter to precede the word "Series." The old S/390 division chose the letter "z" for near-zero downtime, to reflect its focus on a design for continuous availability of the processors.

The design of the zSeries processor takes into account single points of failure in many ways. All levels of memory have a type of ECC (error correction code) that ensures that single-bit (often multiple-bit) failures are corrected "on the fly." The instruction processing unit itself has two identical sets of logic executing every instruction. If the results do not agree, then the instruction is retried. If the processor itself fails, a spare CPU is automatically "configured in" to replace it. In fact a number of types of CPU failures, for example the "adder logic" fails, are completely transparent to the software. The replacement processor simply receives a copy of all the current registers and begins executing again at the point where the other processor had failed.

There are times when an almost-perfectly running system simply needs additional hardware resources to avoid impacting availability. The zSeries family also has some interesting solutions in this arena. In 17.2, "Simple server hardware consolidation," there was a brief discussion of Capacity Upgrade on Demand and the ability to "configure in" additional main storage. The I/O adapters are hot pluggable.

In other words, Linux on the mainframe gets to inherit all these mainframe availability characteristics that come with zSeries. Some find the risks of hardware failure in the zSeries machine so low that having a redundant zSeries machine is only considered during disaster recovery discussions.

11.3 Redundancy and single points of failure

The typical application solution, which consists of hardware and software, has a multitude of parts that all have some failure rate. A single point of failure (SPOF) is that part of a solution, that if it fails, makes the entire solution no longer available. A typical high-availability design focuses on both the availability characteristics of its parts, as well as assuring the continuous availability the face of individual part failures.

Redundancy, having appropriate spare parts available for use, is one design technique used to address single points of failure.[13] Of course, only those with extremely large budgets can afford to have one or more instances of every resource. So the challenge in any high-availability design is determining the single points of failure within the proposed solution, and finding a way at reasonable cost to ensure a quick recovery from the failure of those parts that are important.

Given the definition of 99.99% solution availability, system owners are forced to deal with an exponentially rising costs as various design alternative look to cover more of the poten-

---

[13] Systems that are responsible for controlling human life-support usually have a backup system with a completely unique design, just in case the "failure mechanism" is in the original design! Redundancy is not the only way to handle single points of failure.

tial failure scenarios. High availability is really the business practice of "good enough, and no more." One common approach to high availability is to ignore the catastrophic scenarios. Many find that addressing the set of highly probable single points of failure is their cost-effective answer. This approach can be simplified even further with the assumption that one only needs to deal with one failure at a time. In other words, single failure is used during the design phase to understand failure problems, and as a design assumption to control the complexity and cost of solution development.

Interestingly, redundancy can occur at many levels. You might be surprised to know that the internals of a processor contain many redundancies. Starting with redundancy at the "processor" level, there are further levels of redundancy all the way up to completely redundant application servers. At this higher level for recovery from failures, such a design chooses to disregard which part of an application server failed and simply replaces the entire server with another one of similar capabilities. A set of redundant application servers, interconnected in a redundant way sharing the data on disk is called a cluster. In 11.4, "High availability for the ISPCompany example" we explore how ISPCompany uses a load balancing cluster to provide a high-availability, static, Web-page serving solution.

11.3.1 Linux image redundancy

It is also possible to configure redundant Linux guest images, where availability is achieved by having another Linux image take over work from the failing image. There are two different approaches taken, one called *hot standby* and the other *clustering*.

The hot-standby approach to availability has an alternate, already-booted but idle, Linux image just waiting to take over the workload if the primary image fails. With z/VM, a hot-standby image is simply an idle Linux image that z/VM will have swapped out, not consuming real resources until the point of failure of the primary server. But at that precise time of failure, the primary server stops using z/VM resources. Those resources will begin to be used by the hot standby. The z/VM approach to hot-standby images has an extremely low cost, since the hot standby does not require additional computing resources. This is especially true if you compare this to a discrete server farm implementation, where the hot-standby image is a completely-configured duplicate hardware box. Figure 11-2 is a simplified drawing of this approach on z/VM.

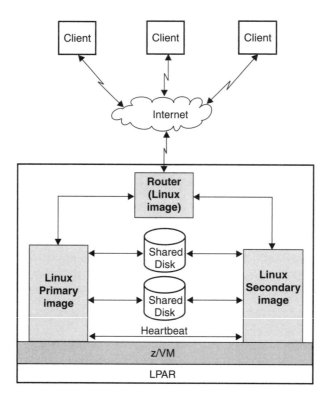

Figure 11-2. A simplified Linux hot-standby environment

It is important to recognize that this hot-standby approach is a special case where read/write file sharing is safe. The hot standby never writes while it is idle, so there is only one "writer" at any one time. Writing only begins when it is driven to recover. After the recovery takeover process, it is safe to write to these shared disks because part of the process is ensuring that the failed primary image can no longer write to disk.

With z/VM, this approach to Linux image redundancy has a number of significant advantages over a discrete server farm implementation. First, there is no need for additional server hardware or cabling which can be a significant cost savings. When we discussed the various types of server consolidation in Chapter 7, "The Value of Virtualization," we emphasized the efficiency with which z/VM managed the logical resources for the hundreds of guests. Here, because an idle guests put almost no resource load on z/VM, the low cost factor makes it reasonable to consider having more production images each having their own unique hot-standby image.

Configuring for hot standby with Linux on the mainframe is also easy. One uses a cloning process to configure the hot-standby image. In this case, the clone will also have the identical set of disks for the data as the primary server. The heartbeat process is a simple communication path between the two images exchanging an "I am well" message. Ensuring that the failed image is in fact no longer able to do I/O is as simple as requesting z/VM CP to "stop" and not reboot the particular virtual machine. The speed for recovery comes down to how fast the application data can be returned to a safe state. The implementation of the data recovery depends upon the application and the specific Linux file system.

There is a very similar story for the cluster approach to Linux image redundancy. This design is based on there being a significant number of equally capable application servers. A few, typically two, servers in the configuration are unique in that they act as workload managers, receiving the incoming work and sending it to one of the many application servers. The cluster approach has two unique advantages. First, an individual server failure does not affect the application availability, so there is zero recovery time. Only the active units of work in that server are lost. The workload manager will no longer send incoming work to a failed server. The cluster just has a little less capacity. The second advantage is that the overall capacity of the cluster can be increased with no availability impact by simply adding yet another application server which, once identified to the workload manager, becomes a candidate for its share of the incoming work.

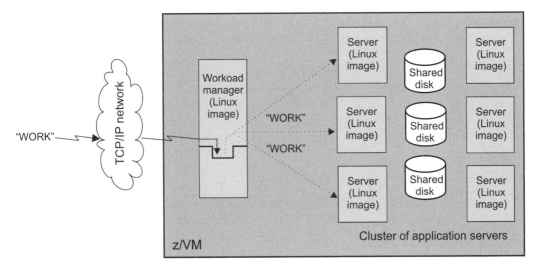

Figure 11-3. A simplified Linux cluster environment

A Linux cluster is fairly simple to implement on z/VM, and there is a related Open Source project called Linux Virtual Server (LVS).[14] The workload manager is actually likely to be

---

14 Table 25-6 provides a pointer to further information about this project.

implemented as two Linux images, one as a hot standby (Figure 11-3). The Open Source module, FAKE, is used to handle taking over the failed workload manager's IP address so that users do not notice that the application server has moved to a new Linux image. The cluster is a set of cloned Linux images, with a Linux file system that allows them to share a common set of disks. The connectivity among the cluster elements would be a z/VM Guest LAN. Only the two workload managers would have redundant connections to real network adapters.

When it is required to increase the work capacity of the cluster, an additional interesting option exists with this type of z/VM Linux cluster. As with a real server farm implementation, one could define yet another Linux image. However, one has the new option to just increase the CPU shares for each of the cluster members. And if the environment was already "maxed out" on the available real CPU capacity, one could use the zSeries feature of Capacity Upgrade on Demand to dynamically add the real CPU capacity to z/VM, and thus to the cluster. See 11.4, "High availability for the ISPCompany example" for details of how ISPCompany uses LVS.

11.3.2 z/VM: Redundancy and recovery time

First we will discuss how z/VM itself uses redundancy, and also lets its guests use redundancy. Then we will discuss having a redundant z/VM.

z/VM inherits the zSeries hardware availability advantages (as described in 11.2, "The zSeries hardware availability") and can be configured to pass them on to its guests. In the case where the hardware is architecturally required to notify the software about a failure, z/VM will process that information. Most of the time it completely hides the failure event from the Linux guest, or, in some worst case scenarios, z/VM will fail the Linux guest. z/VM can then have its own automation control for a recovery of the Linux guest (which usually involves a re-IPL of the Linux guest).

The hardware configuration file (IOCDS), which controls the environment where z/VM executes, should always contain definitions for at least two of every hardware resource:

- There should be at least two CPUs defined.
- Every disk should have at least two paths defined.
- There should be at least two LAN connections.

Similarly, if the intent is to have a Linux guest able to recover from single points of virtual hardware failure, each Linux guest will have the same generic list of redundancy needs as z/VM itself.

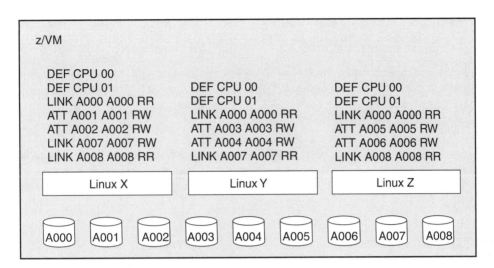

Figure 11-4. Sample statements that show the CPU redundancy for the Linux guests

Figure 11-4 shows how the three Linux guests (Linux X, Linux Y, and Linux Z) have been defined. Each Linux guest has two virtual CPUs that it can use (CPU 00 and CPU 01). Since none of these Linux guests has dedicated real paths and devices, there is no need to specify the path redundancy. z/VM automatically handles that aspect of recovery for the Linux guest.

As with any part of a solution, there is the possibility that z/VM becomes unavailable. z/VM is a very stable operating system, and although it is possible that z/VM itself crashes, it is more likely that factors such as human error or z/VM maintenance or software upgrade might cause an interruption. The same schemes as for Linux image redundancy, hot standby and clusters, can be implemented at the z/VM level.

The first item to identify with a z/VM availability discussion is the source of the risk of z/VM failure. Almost equally important is the speed for recovery from the failure. For example, if it was human error that stopped a z/VM image, it is possible to immediately restart the z/VM and then all the Linux images, and so on. While this approach is simple and inexpensive, it is so lengthy as to not fit any high-availability scenario. If a more timely recovery process is required, then a second z/VM image is needed.

The secondary z/VM image could be in another LPAR on the same machine. This approach is effective providing the zSeries hardware itself was not the cause of the outage. If you need to include the risk of the hardware failure, then the secondary z/VM must be in another zSeries machine, and possibly even at another site, all depending upon which causes of outage you want to survive.

The hot-standby choice for z/VM redundancy makes a lot of sense in the situation where all the lost Linux images can be brought up fast enough to meet the recovery time requirements. A hot-standby z/VM can even share all the disks with the primary z/VM. By using the two LPARs on the same machine approach and sharing the identical set of resources with both the primary and hot-standby LPARs, the failed primary LPAR's resources can be used by the hot standby. The same set of resources adequately serves both LPARs because of the serial nature of the requirements.

The cluster approach of two z/VM images sharing the workload is another approach for z/VM image redundancy. It is going to be required if the recovery time is tight. However, clusters imply a certain amount of actively-shared data across the z/VM cluster and are more challenging to implement.

11.3.3 Data redundancy and recovery time

The data constitute another component of the solution whose high availability must also be assured. There are two levels that need to be addressed: the hardware (the physical layer), and the Linux file systems (the logical layer) that provide access to the data. Having highly available data brings with it the need to address how quickly the data (the logical, consistent view they represent) can be recovered following the interruption of access.

Access to data on the zSeries has two hardware components: the channel path to the device and the device itself where the data resides. Simply assuring that the hardware (and virtual machine) configuration includes multiple paths to each device will assure the appropriate recovery from a channel path failure.

There are a number of approaches used with disk devices based on the concept of redundancy. By eliminating the single point of failure at the hardware level, redundancy ensures continued data availability in face of the loss of a single disk. One such approach is the Redundant Array of Independent Disks, better known as RAID. For example, with disks configured for RAID 5, one adds an extra disk to the set of data disks and keeps a type of error-correcting code for each unit of data stored across the array of data disks. If any single disk in the array fails, there is sufficient information on the other disks to rebuild "on the fly" all the data within the array. The recovery time in this implementation is zero.

Another common, but slightly more expensive, scheme goes by the names of "mirroring" or "dual copy." The concept is that every write-to-disk operation causes the data to be placed on two disks. This dual placement assures that if any single disk fails, there is an up-to-date copy available on the mirror disk. Depending upon the specific implementation when there is a failure of the primary copy, the data may be immediately available, or some specific action, usually automated, needs to be taken to make the second copy available to the running system. This duplication scheme can be extended over significant distances. This latter type of remote dual copy is typically used for availability across a single site disaster.[15]

There is another way that access to the data might be lost to the application. What if the software fails, leaving the data on disk inconsistent? Having a RAID cluster or a dual copy of the data will not help. What additional considerations are needed for a highly available application where the data on disk are damaged?

The typical Linux file systems are byte-stream oriented file systems that have the characteristic that the data from individual files are interleaved throughout the entire disk space managed by the file system. The allocation map as to where the data for each file reside is critical to being able to use any file. The Linux ext2 file system, in the interest of high-speed performance, does not always have this allocation map (that correctly represents that data) actually on the disk with the file system data. If Linux crashes, crucial information about each of the open ext2 file systems can be lost. In the boot process, Linux checks each file system to see if it had been closed properly and if not, then it runs a special file-check program which attempts to rebuild the allocation map. The larger the file system and the more writing done to the file system, the longer it will take to recover access to the data. And some data or files may be non-recoverable!

The Open Source community has developed a number of unique file systems,[16] each addressing some aspects of delivering both high performance while in normal use, and reasonable speed for data recovery in the event of a Linux system crash. The latest emphasis has been on journaled file systems, like JFS, ext3 and ReiserFS. These newer file systems are now showing up in the Linux distributions that support the mainframe. If you consider there to be an availability risk from a Linux crash, then when you install your Linux on the mainframe you should consider exploiting one of these journaled file systems.

---

15 There also is a Linux Open Source project related to data redundancy that might be of use in certain types of solution design. rsync is a tool that can be used to create and manage mirror data across two remote sites. The tool is run periodically to resynchronize the two instances of the data. This approach might prove useful for a disaster recovery design, but would not handle a timely recovery of the data that would meet high-availability requirements.

16 http://www.linuxgazette.com/issue55/florido.html is a good tutorial on various Linux file systems.

11.4 High availability for the ISPCompany example

ISPCompany's ISP division offers its small company clients a very successful static Web-page-serving service, by using the marketing slogan "Anyone in the world, day or night, can find out about your company and its services." By guaranteeing the 24x7 availability, they have differentiated themselves from the competition and have been able to attract a number of smaller businesses to using this service. The real value to ISPCompany is that these clients become excellent candidates for outsourcing a dynamic Web-page-serving environment that is even more profitable.

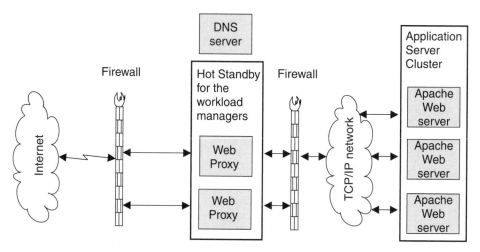

Figure 11-5. Implementing high availability for ISPCompany

The design in Figure 11-5 is their implementation of the Linux virtual server (LVS) cluster technology. Most of this design is a pretty obvious cluster implementation with a workload balancer front-end (in its own hot-standby configuration). In the simple discussion in 11.3.1, "Linux image redundancy" we glossed over a rather interesting challenge. When the primary workload balancer image fails, how do users who already know its IP address manage to connect to the hot-standby image?

Many users of LVS use the program FAKE to connect users to the hot-standby image. In Figure 11-5 you probably noticed the existence of an extra server, called the DNS (Domain Name Server). Among its functions is helping others to locate a specific machine by giving a translation from the IP address to the corresponding hardware LAN adapter address. The DNS can be primed with a lookup table, or dynamically learn the relationship from machines as they become active. There is a type of IP message, an address resolution protocol (ARP), that lets a machine "shout" to the local world: "I'm IP address x.y.z and my physical adapter LAN address is 123456789" (actually it is a large hex number).

FAKE relies on the fact that the DNS will listen to the latest "shout" and use it to further route messages. So, in our particular case, both the primary and secondary workload servers have two IP adapters (for symmetry, both have two.) The normal adapter on the hot standby is the address by which anyone can talk to it, in its standby role. However, once the primary image fails, the secondary image starts broadcasting ARPs, using the primary image's IP address and substituting the hardware address of its own backup LAN adapter. In fact, all the new workload manager's traffic will be done in this "fake" mode.

The Linux Primary image of Figure 11-6 uses the service's IP name as its normal attachment to the LAN. The backup attachment to the LAN is not really needed.

The Linux Secondary image of Figure 11-6 uses its unique real name as its normal attachment to the LAN. Therefore, it is possible to perform a heartbeat and communicate with this Linux Secondary image via this LAN attachment. The backup attachment to the LAN is used to ARP-out the Linux Primary image's IP address, claiming that it should be resolved to this backup LAN MAC address.

A source for additional information on the FAKE process can be found by looking for the LVS tool in Table 25-6 in Chapter 25, "Systems Management Tools."

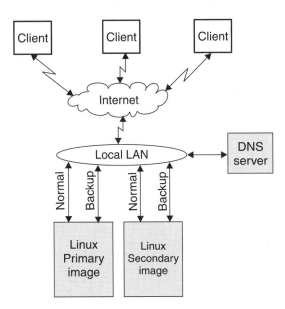

Figure 11-6. Performing a FAKE failover for ISPCompany

There is another, more elegant and effective approach for IP takeover available on the zSeries, called VIPA (Virtual IP Address). For a source of more information on VIPA, see Table 25-6 in Chapter 25, "Systems Management Tools."

11.5 High availability for the StoreCompany OaK example

The purpose of this example is to stress that application design is a crucial part of choosing what types of availability issues need addressing when creating a design for high availability.

The One-of-A-Kind (OaK) StoreCompany project was conceived to validate a marketing idea. It costs StoreCompany little to enter special art items into its standard catalog structure and have the items drop-shipped by the artist. The proposal made by marketing was that by using business intelligence (BI) schemes they could identify, in real time, those customers likely to buy expensive OaK items. They could also identify those types of items that would be of interest by comparing the customers' buying habits with those of other customers. The approach chosen was to give the market development team a few Linux images of their own: the datamart and business intelligence images in Figure 11-7.

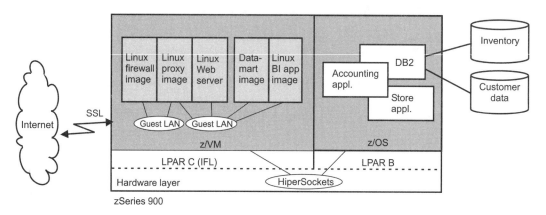

Figure 11-7. Implementing high availability for StoreCompany

StoreCompany considers the availability of its online catalog store to be important to its corporate image. So the design of even the OaK prototype needed to consider high availability. Since the art items are kept in the online catalog, that aspect of this prototype inherited the existing high-availability characteristics of the catalog-ordering system, as described in Appendix B, "StoreCompany."

One of the key items being investigated with the prototype was whether this datamart/BI scheme would work at all. And if it did work, could the real-time BI query be done fast enough in most cases? The purpose of the query was to produce a pop-up window to the customer. This window contained the results of a unique catalog search of the OaK items, based on the "mined" prior preferences of this and similar customers.

The availability consideration netted down to the following conclusion: there was no special treatment for availability needed in the prototype. If the BI query produced its intended results (a catalog search results page), then the customer was directed to the search facility of the catalog ordering system. Therefore, availability from that point onwards was already taken care of. If the new Linux image failed before producing the page, the result was no different, from the customer's perspective, from the query's not returning fast enough.

A restart of the prototype's Linux images would be quite fast because the two Linux images reference only static data in the datamart.

11.6 A quick look at the future

At the time of writing this book, there is already a fair amount of capabilities for building some highly available application solutions using Linux on the mainframe. This chapter has laid out some of the key areas where implementation is both feasible and cost-effective. In the dynamic world of Linux on the mainframe, there is still much going on.

The Open Source community has two major projects dedicated to high availability. This chapter has already discussed the LVS approach from the Linux Virtual Server project. The other key project is the High-Availability Linux project that is building key infrastructure for peer cluster environments. IBM, through its Linux Technology Center, is a very active participant in this latter project, as are some other companies.

The area of high availability has attracted significant attention from both small and large companies, as you can easily see from a Web search such as: Linux + "high availability." Each of the major Linux distributors is also addressing aspects of high availability as part of its mainframe offering.

The IBM Tivoli System Automation (ITSA) for Linux provides the high-level tools that make it much easier to build high-availability clusters from Linux images. These tools are particularly helpful for a cluster built on z/VM virtualization. ITSA for Linux uses the abstractions of: resource types, resource managers, grouping services, and automation policies. There is one resource manager for one or more resource types. Resource types are, for example, network adapters or file systems and disks. ITSA for Linux monitors changes to the resources contained in resource groups, and provides complex proactive and reactive management beyond simple failover capabilities. It moves beyond simple scripts to create policies that can be implemented throughout a cluster. These policies can be used to implement processes in which complex environments are described and automated.

11.7 Summary

High availability begins with defining the failure types for the application solution for which recovery is required, the speed with which the recovery should happen, and the various hardware, middleware, and application parts that constitute the high-availability solution.

The mainframe already has multiple levels of built-in hardware redundancy that contribute to its intrinsic high availability. You can configure the hardware so that the software can directly exploit various levels of hardware redundancy, such as the CPUs and channel paths to devices. Using z/VM virtualization, you can create various types of Linux configurations that provide software redundancy to an application. For example, you can configure hot-standby Linux images without investing in additional hardware.

It is possible today to implement some high-availability solutions with the existing Linux-on-the-mainframe tools. Besides developing their own high-availability products, IBM and other vendors are also supporting several Open Source projects that are working to further improve the high-availability tool set. Additional full-blown products are likely to become available during the year 2003.

Part 4.
Making the Most of
Linux on the Mainframe

This part addresses the ongoing effort that is essential to maintaining the value of a Linux-on-the-mainframe environment. We call this effort *systems management*. What does it take to keep a system containing potentially more than one hundred servers running smoothly, and how can you accomplish this with Linux on the mainframe?

In all likelihood, you already have a systems management scheme in place. In this part, we explore how introducing Linux on the mainframe can affect your existing systems management. How are you going to manage Linux on the mainframe? Should you continue with your existing scheme? Should you treat Linux according to the tight controls of a typical mainframe environment?

We suggest that your Linux projects might call for changes in your systems management style and possibly lead to a review of your systems management policies. We believe that Linux can be a catalyst for change that can benefit your business beyond the scope of a particular Linux project. The driving forces for this change are the requirements of your Linux projects and the key systems administrators in charge of implementing the projects.

The first chapter of this part outlines what we mean by systems management in the context of this book. It then covers general issues, such as policies and tools, that permeate all areas of systems management. Each chapter that follows examines one particular area of systems management in more detail.

An exhaustive treatment of systems management is beyond the scope of this book. We restrict ourselves to specific themes that highlight interesting decision points in the context of Linux on the mainframe.

Chapter 12.
Systems Management

Systems management[17] aims at controlling an IT infrastructure in order to meet given business objectives. This chapter outlines in more detail what we mean by systems management in the context of this book. It discusses the main strategies and principles of systems management and how you might get additional value from Linux on the mainframe.

With today's environments, which are growing both in complexity and in the number of systems to be managed, systems management becomes increasingly challenging. Accordingly, systems management takes a greater share of the TCO of IT infrastructures. Also, because system administration skill is sometimes difficult to find, overworked IT staff is a common phenomenon.

Most operating systems are designed to run alone, on dedicated hardware. Thus, the scope of management functions that come with them tends to be a single system. On the other hand, mainframes with their virtualization technology have been running multiple operating system images concurrently for decades. Consequently, tools for multi-system administration have been growing around the mainframe operating systems for a long time.

In recognition of the difficulties that systems managers encounter today, IBM announced that it would further develop its existing management functions. Through IBM's Autonomic Computing initiative, the vision is to deliver *self-managing technologies* across the entire IBM product line, including the IBM eServer zSeries platform. Autonomic technologies are self-optimizing, self-configuring, self-protecting, and self-healing. Once set up, they are envisaged to run with little to no human intervention while still managing work according to business-level objectives. All operating systems that run on IBM eServer machines benefit, including Linux on the mainframe. For more information on autonomic computing visit: `http://www.research.ibm.com/autonomic/index_nf.html`.

In this and the following chapters, we will look at how to manage IT infrastructures that include Linux on the mainframe to meet given business objectives. We will see how policies, procedures, and tools define the orderly scheme of how people and tools work together to achieve system availability. In this chapter, we will explore:

---

[17] In the UNIX world, systems management is more commonly referred to as *network management*. This reflects the paradigm of an environment with many physical hardware machines that are connected via a network of cables. The mainframe paradigm is that of a small number of machines that contain the critical components or systems.

- Can virtual Linux images on the mainframe be controlled effectively?

- What can you gain from policies?

- What tool options are available?

- Which systems management frameworks embrace Linux on the mainframe?

- Where does the unique manageability of Linux on the mainframe give additional value to your business?

12.1 Controlling the cost of systems administration

Systems management, like all other aspects of a business, is subject to economic constraints. A significant contribution to the TCO of an IT infrastructure is the number of people required to manage it. The number of FTE (Full Time Equivalent) employees required not only depends on the size of the installation, but also on the diversity of the hardware and software and on the desired characteristics, such as security and availability.

For example, ISPCompany runs hundreds of Linux images and expects more images as its business grows. It is inconceivable to manage all of them without the use of tools. Generally, the more numerous and uniform the systems to be managed, the more beneficial it is to use tools.

Let's make the absurd assumption that a large number of systems are managed individually and that all interventions take place through a command line at the respective system's console. Assuming that one FTE can handle a given number of systems, the cost of maintaining the systems is roughly proportional to the number of systems to be maintained. This would mean that administrators would have to be hired and trained at the rate at which the systems increase. Consequently, the potential for growth would be capped by the number of available administrators.

Tools increase the efficiency of administrators and thus keep the number of FTEs down, but are themselves associated with cost. The cost of a new tool is not only the purchase or development cost but includes more hidden aspects like deployment, training, and maintenance. Typically, the expenditure for a tool is high at the time of introduction[18] and comparatively low while it is in use. Applying the same tool to an increased number of systems might mean higher license fees, but it usually means a less than proportional increase in overall costs.

---

[18] A rule of thumb for the cost of deploying a sophisticated tool solution is to plan for three times the purchase cost.

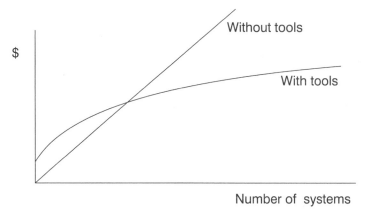

Figure 12-1. Cost of system administration for a growing number of systems

Figure 12-1 illustrates the cost characteristics of people-dominated system administration versus tool-dominated administration. Introducing zSeries hardware and Linux as new elements into an IT environment is likely to mean that either existing tools must be adapted or alternative tools must be acquired to handle the new environment. Tools that accommodate Linux on the mainframe are already available. Linux has been designed as a simple system to manage; that is, it does not come with too many control points that you have to take care of. On the other hand, you can apply system or kernel patches to include any additional controls you need.

Looking for new tools implies the chance to build in the capability for handling a growing number of systems. For example, our hypothetical StoreCompany initially introduces only a few experimental Linux images. As StoreCompany gains confidence and experience with Linux, implementing the departmental servers across the company on Linux could be an attractive option. If the tooling put in place for the first experimental Linux images is chosen with that in mind, moving 50 or 100 departmental servers to Linux images can be an easy exercise. Moving to Linux on the mainframe is also an opportunity to examine whether the tools you are using can be replaced by something that is more suitable for what you want to attain.

Because systems management must be driven by business needs and not by the capabilities of a tool or set of tools, it is essential to know exactly how the business needs translate to management tasks. We argue that this is best achieved by first mapping the business objectives to policies and then to procedures. With procedures at hand, you can then assess how suitable a particular tool is for your purpose. Before we do that, we will map out the territory of systems management.

12.2 Systems management disciplines

In contrast to what you may be used to on a UNIX system, systems management on the mainframe goes far beyond just managing a few users. Systems management covers an extensive range of policies, procedures, and tools. We will divide systems management into essentially arbitrary disciplines that, nonetheless, reflect the division of responsibilities in many large IT installations. Furthermore, the disciplines we are going to use also map to the areas in which many tool providers specialize.

We will distinguish these disciplines:

- Availability management
- Data management
- Security management
- Performance and capacity planning
- System administrator tasks

The following subsections provide an overview of these disciplines. For each discipline, there is a reference to a chapter with more detailed information.

12.2.1 Availability management

Availability management covers all the strategies and activities that have the prime objective of ensuring that systems and applications are available to the target end users for their intended use. The more central your systems are to your ability to do any business at all, the greater are the demands on availability.

Running applications on zSeries gives you hardware for which the mean time between failures (MTBF) of a machine is currently measured in decades, and Linux is itself widely valued as a solid operating system. Linux on the mainframe has the potential for excellent availability and we argue that it can be managed to leverage that potential.

With that foundation, the risks involved in quickly deploying a new application are centered on what you have most control of: the application itself.

Availability is always a high priority, but it is not the only issue in systems management. There are other aspects, such as security and performance, that compete for importance which might require trade-offs with availability. How to rank these aspects and where to strike the inevitable compromises for a particular installation can be inferred from the business objectives that the installation has been set up to serve.

While StoreCompany also benefits from good availability of a new Internet sales project, its prime concern is to ensure that the new project does not compromise existing procedures and the integrity of its database. Security issues and isolation requirements for the new project thus override the new project's availability considerations.

Chapter 13, "Availability Management," addresses the question of which level of availability is appropriate for a given project or application. It also points to some common availability management procedures that have unique considerations in an environment with Linux on the mainframe.

12.2.2 Data management

Data management covers all efforts to have the data available that are to be processed by systems and applications. In a Linux-on-the-mainframe environment, the z/VM virtualization technology can help you to share data between Linux images. In particular, both an image and a hot standby that are ready for failover can share access to data.

A company's business data are a major and vital asset that often cannot readily be recreated. Consequently, many firms have substantial procedures in place to ensure that backups are kept in safe places in case of damage to the currently active set of data. Many governments also have laid down rules on privacy and on record-keeping that have to be covered by the data management procedures.

Our focus is on the logical aspects of managing the data, rather than the physical aspects. We discuss the physical devices only to show what is there for you to use and what consequences the choice of physical devices might have on your options for handling the data. Some of what we discuss under data management is also classified as *storage management.*

Data management activities typically include planning for space requirements for increasing amounts of data. It also involves aspects of security management in ensuring that data are visible and accessible only to programs and persons with specific authorization to the data.

Data management needs to address the interrelationships of sets of data. Sometimes it is critical to have sets of files backed up with the content they had at the same point in time. Such backups require significant coordination with application availability.

Data management is tightly coupled to availability management. If the processor is up and the application is ready to do work, yet the data to be processed are inaccessible, then the end user sees a broken system. The mainframe allows you to attain high data availability, for example, through redundant data access paths and efficient backup tools.

Chapter 14, "Data Management," explores this discipline with respect to Linux on the mainframe.

12.2.3 Security management

The challenge of security management is to make a system as secure as possible without unduly affecting the legitimate user.

Security management protects systems from intended or accidental damage and thus supports availability. Security, however, often also conflicts with availability because it restricts accessibility and deploys barriers that only intended users and applications can overcome. Forgotten passwords can mean that StoreCompany customers temporarily cannot access their accounts with the StoreCompany Internet sales application. Trade-offs have to be made, depending on the overriding concern.

Security issues must be considered when conceiving the layout of a system, so we covered much of the security management discussion in Part 3, "Is Linux on the Mainframe for Me?," which includes Chapter 8, "Security Considerations," and Chapter 9, "Setting Up Linux on the Mainframe." Because that discussion also includes operational issues, there is no separate chapter on security in this part.

12.2.4 Performance and capacity planning

For the sake of discussions in this book, those aspects of "performance" that are used to determine system health are covered under availability management. The performance management and capacity planning chapter addresses those activities that are less directly associated with running systems.

Performance management aims to understand the behavior of the IT infrastructure (such as hardware, software, networks, etc.) to assure that resources are used in an effective way and SLAs (Service Level Agreements) are complied with. Where the results of performance analysis call for changes to the system structure, the running and the availability of the system are affected. Here, performance management intersects with availability management.

Capacity planning takes the analysis of performance data one step further. The objective in capacity planning is to anticipate the impact of changes to workload and resources in the system. The first three disciplines focus on activities that work together to keep everything running smoothly under stable conditions. Capacity planning is about predicting the behavior of the system if something were to change. It is used to answer challenging questions such as, "What happens to response time if we put this new product marketing campaign up on System 3?"

Chapter 15, "Performance and Capacity Planning," explores this discipline with respect to Linux on the mainframe.

12.2.5 System administrator tasks

Rather than introducing a multitude of additional disciplines, we have grouped all activities that do not fall into the above four disciplines into a single fifth category. It includes various activities typically focused on the underlying software infrastructure and the hardware, performed by the most skilled members of the IT staff.[19]

Time-to-market for new ideas is one good reason for having Linux on the mainframe. How this potential is leveraged depends on your key staff of administrators and the tasks that they perform.

Chapter 16, "System Administrator Tasks," delves into some of the cultural (organizational) challenges that occur when marrying the tightly controlled mainframe environment with the Linux mentality of exploiting the latest and greatest. The issue of change management is the common thread across Part 4, "Making the Most of Linux on the Mainframe," in general and Chapter 16 in particular. With Linux on the mainframe, we are now dealing with a large number of Linux images sharing resources where change and control are both key to success.

12.2.6 Putting it all together

The ultimate goal of systems management is to have an IT infrastructure available to support a business. Figure 12-2 illustrates how we see the different disciplines help to support this goal.

---

[19] For those with a mainframe background, this is the system programmer we are talking about. In a small UNIX shop, typically one person, rather than an entire department or division, is responsible for all the activities associated with the care and feeding of one or maybe even ten UNIX systems. Even though the focus in this book is on the mainframe environment where there will be potentially hundreds of Linux images and possibly separate departments handling the other disciplines, we chose to stay with the UNIX terminology for this specialized work.

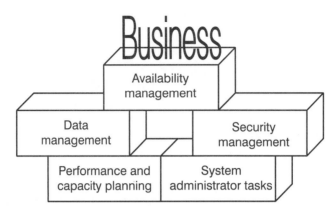

Figure 12-2. Systems management disciplines

Data management and security management directly support availability by providing meaningful content for processing and by protecting the system from damage. These three disciplines are basically operational and require constant attention.

Performance and capacity planning and the set of tasks that have been summarized under system administrator tasks provide the foundation to assure that the system will also be available in the future. These tasks can typically be done at scheduled times and do not require a person to be on call continuously.

12.3 Policies

System administrators cannot operate with just the business objectives as guidelines. There is no setting on Linux or any other operating system where you can adjust a company's revenue or market share and business strategies. After all, market analysis is not the expected expertise of the system administrator.

System administrators need a set of guidelines that are derived from business goals and represent implementation of these goals in more technical terms. Management usually communicates such guidelines in the form of policies. To keep the focus on the key requirements, policies are most effective if they are few.

12.3.1 How to phrase a policy?

In practice, all system administrators follow policies, written or unwritten. The more exten-sive an installation is, the more obvious becomes the need to have formal, written, and agreed-to policies. Like laws in society, policies are needed as a guideline for potentially contentious issues within an organization. And like laws, policies can be phrased in very general terms and remain so, if they express a commonly agreed principle. Where there is less agreement, the policy is refined to a more specific statement.

For example, a common issue of contention is that of storage space usage. While avail-able space, no matter how much there is, tends to get filled up as if by a law of nature, it is the job of the storage administrator to make sure that the company's key applications do not run out of storage. The goal of keeping storage available must be achieved within the limits of a budget. What could a policy look like that is to contain storage requirements?

A general policy could state that "All users must use space economically." This is flawed in two ways. For one, it implies that users are doing something wrong. Thus, it is likely to antagonize the very people who are being asked to cooperate—not a good approach.[20] Secondly, it does not account for application data or for the gray zone where users are consuming space through applications they use.

Assuming that we are in an environment where users access mainframe storage through the Linux images that they use and through the applications that run on these images, a more diplomatically phrased policy could state: "All Linux images are assigned to storage groups. At the end of each month, any group approaching 90% of its storage limit is reviewed to see if it is appropriate to raise the ceiling." This raises the awareness that there is a ceiling for what can be used at any time without pointing an accusing finger at anyone. Which image is allocated to which storage group is negotiable. For storage issues, this is probably still too general. z/VM could add a refinement of this policy, since it pro-vides the possibility to balance the relative usage of space within a group and prevent a single image from seizing most of the available space.

A more specific policy could state that there are fixed quotas for the amount of space for each Linux image. ISPCompany provides Linux images to its clients and must be very spe-cific with what a client is entitled to. Policies are normally intended to be long-lived, so the actual quotas are usually recorded elsewhere, for example, in a service level agreement (SLA). An SLA is an agreement between two parties, for example, the IT division and the

---

[20] At the following URL, a white paper explores the psychology of policies and provides a detailed example for a storage policy and a matching SLA:
http://www.ntpsoftware.com/WhitePapers/docs/DoYouNeedAStoragePolicy.pdf.

sales division of a company or between a company and its clients. It states, in explicit terms, what one party commits to deliver to the other. In our example, this could include the space quotas for users.

To manage its space requirements, ISPCompany sets space quotas in the SLAs for the standard Linux images which it offers to clients. For example, under the terms of its standard contract, ISPCompany allows 100 megabytes of storage for a Web-hosting image that is intended for static content. Linux can be installed to include the function for assigning quotas to users and groups, and most distributions includes this function.

12.3.2 Why use policies with your Linux projects?

Why do we discuss policies in a book on Linux on the mainframe? Using Linux on the mainframe means change and might call for adaptations in your policies. Especially for companies that have been operating successfully with established procedures, change can be seen as a threat to the company's success. New policies are a means of enabling the required change and at the same time confining it to where it is necessary. Thus, those in charge of the Linux project have the freedom they need without everybody else feeling that all rules are being overturned.

We asserted that Linux could provide a platform for rapidly deploying new applications in mainframe shops. StoreCompany might well have policies in place that require lengthy test runs before a system can go into production. While this is perfectly appropriate for a z/OS system that processes financial transactions, it could defeat the purpose for having Linux as a fast deployment platform. Rather than scrapping the policy for z/OS systems, the policy can be altered. It could apply different rules, depending on what kind of system and application is to run. An acceptable solution to this simplified problem could be to continue with utmost care for transactions but to add a fast path for other applications, such as new Web interfaces, to be run on Linux.

ISPCompany has a business objective of being able to quickly respond to client requests for setting up one of three types of standard Linux images. To ensure that this goal can be attained, a ISPCompany policy states that there is a fixed set of services and an SLA for each of these types. No alterations or special provisions, no matter how simple, can be made to the three low-cost types. Otherwise, staff might get carried away with accommodating minor requests for customization and affect the speed of deployment as well as maintenance. After all, ISPCompany offers a separate category where both the fee and delivery time depend on the extent of the requested customization.

Let's assume that the SLA for one of the types also states the following: "Since we do the availability management for you, you are eligible for a rebate on your monthly bill if your server is unavailable for more than a one hour period." We will build on this example in the following sections on procedures and tools.

12.4 Procedures

A procedure outlines what is to be done, under which conditions, by whom, and when, to satisfy policies and SLAs. With the example of the SLA statement in the previous section, a procedure could look like this:

1. If an image goes down as seen by z/VM, z/VM initiates a restart, and, if successful, logs that a successful automatic restart has taken place for the image.

2. If the automatic restart is not successful, the operations staff is notified through the health monitor GUI, and an e-mail is sent to the client contact.

3. If the recovery is not completed after 30 minutes, a page and an e-mail are sent to the responsible system administrator.

An obvious next step to increase productivity is to automate those parts of a procedure that follow a fixed repetitive pattern. For example, you could write a script that issues a set series of commands. A more elaborate piece of code might handle more complex parts of a procedure. Step one of our example is already automated through z/VM.

12.5 Using tools

This section covers considerations and decision points about tools in general terms. There are hundreds of tools available. To preserve the flow of our discussion, we will restrict ourselves to only occasionally mentioning a specific tool. Chapter 25, "Systems Management Tools," provides a more extensive table of individual tools for each systems management discipline.

With procedures in place for the different systems management disciplines, the decisions on how to proceed in all anticipated situations are laid out. The person who follows a procedure need not be as experienced as the person who devised it. Parts of a procedure might be so well-defined that they leave no room for variation. Normally, system administrators identify such parts and write a tool that takes care of a fixed part of a procedure.

Environments with a large number of images cannot be administered at a reasonable cost without the use of tools. Using tools has other advantages, too. A suitable tool can perform a procedure faster, more consistently, and be less error-prone than a human. Hence, the question is not whether to use tools but rather where to get them and how to deploy them in a heterogeneous environment, which Linux on the mainframe necessarily is.

An example of such an environment is that of StoreCompany as represented by Figure 12-3. It does not need many Linux images and runs other operating systems in some LPARs on the same zSeries machine. On z/VM where it runs its Linux images as guests, there is also a CMS (Conversational Monitor System)[21] guest.

The zSeries hardware is controlled by an HMC (Hardware Management Console). z/VM is controlled from a CP console. Both run on workstations in a control room.

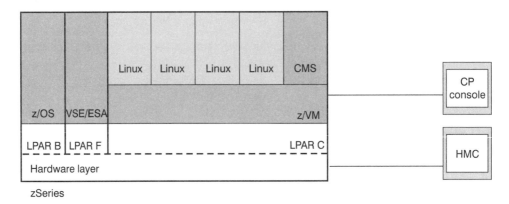

Figure 12-3. StoreCompany environment

The need for systems management tools has given rise to a number of small companies that offer excellent solutions for specific systems management tasks. There are also larger companies that offer suites of integrated tools. Linux, mainframe or not, has long been on their agenda, and the number of available tools for Linux is growing rapidly. If what you are looking for is not available today, it is worth checking again in a few months, not years. It is also worthwhile to check out the Open Source community. Someone else might have come across the same problem already and may have built a solution that is available for you to use.

---

[21] If z/VM runs on an IFL (Integrated Facility for Linux), then CMS is limited to supporting Linux (for example, for systems management).

Generally, you have these options for acquiring tools:

- Use z/VM
- Get your tools from the Open Source community
- Develop your own tools
- Buy your tools

z/VM is listed first because it is an obvious choice for anyone who already has or can acquire z/VM skills and because it is a platform where you can readily deploy scripts that automate other tools. However, you do not have to use z/VM. The most attractive source for tools to you depends entirely on your individual circumstances, preferences, and concerns.

12.5.1 Use z/VM

If you run your Linux images under z/VM, you already have a single point of control for them. The virtual machine control program (CP) is the place where you control the virtual hardware and do much of what you normally do at the hardware level. For example, you can start and stop your systems, assign system resources to your guests, reconfigure real or virtual hardware, or access the guests' consoles. z/VM can serve as a basic availability and performance management tool.

Having a single point of control is a great advantage if you want to monitor numerous Linux images. Instead of gyrating around the raised floor on roller skates and trying to spot red LEDs, your system administrator can check a single screen where all messages on failed images are routed.

Figure 12-4 represents the environment of ISPCompany. It wants as many Linux images as possible and uses a small number of LPARs with z/VM. One LPAR is a hot standby, ready to take over from another LPAR where critical Linux images run, in case z/VM fails.

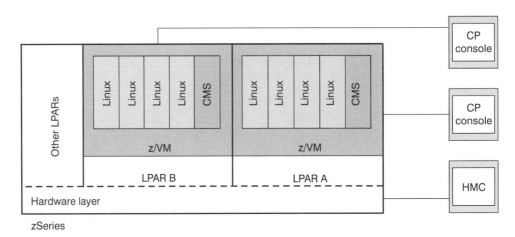

Figure 12-4. ISPCompany environment

Because ISPCompany's main concern is to manage the virtual hardware and its availability to its clients, it chooses to do most of its systems management activities through z/VM. Using z/VM functions saves the expense and overhead of deploying tools on every single Linux image.

12.5.2 Get your tools from the Open Source community

This option carries some of the same advantages that you also get from using Linux. Open Source tools are free and quick to obtain by download. Because they are Open Source, you can tailor them to your needs, and you can exchange ideas and possibly get help from others in the community with similar needs.

You can find a large number of free tools. Some have been around for a long time for UNIX. One example is sar (system analysis report).

Other free tools have been provided for Linux by the Open Source community or contributed by companies that promote Linux. One such contributor is SGI (Silicon Graphics, Inc.)[22] with CSA (Comprehensive System Accounting) and PCP (Performance Co-Pilot).

Generally, you can find good tools for specific tasks. If you have the need and the skill, you can combine these tools into an integrated solution that is tailored to your requirements.

---

[22] For a list of Linux projects by SGI, visit http://oss.sgi.com/projects/.

To assure that you do not have to modify the tools for specific zSeries configurations, use the tools that come with your distribution. One decision point for using or not using a tool might be the degree to which service is available for it.

If you are prepared to compile and possibly make modifications to a tool, here are sites you might want to check:

- `http://www.linux.org/`
- `http://sourceforge.net/`
- `http://freshmeat.net/`

Tools that are available in the Open Source community have mailing lists. You can use the mailing list to get answers for a wide range of questions that are not covered in the tool documentation or that emerge after examining the tool.

If you have to alter a tool, you might have to maintain it yourself. Hence, you are approaching the option of developing your own tools. You could also give your contribution back to the Open Source community by suggesting the alteration to the owner of the tool. If the alterations are accepted, the tool with your alterations can be maintained by the owner.

12.5.3 Develop your own tools

The advantage of a home-grown tool is that it is made specifically for your needs, and you decide what is developed and when.

ISPCompany, as a service provider, has people with the skills to develop tools. It also expects a competitive advantage from having tools in place that are not available on the market.

Some of ISPCompany's clients outsource their infrastructure to ISPCompany but want to stay in control of some aspects of their images. For example, they want to be able to do health monitoring, user management, back up and restore data, and, if needed, reboot their images. The current process starts with a client request, by note or a phone call to the responsible ISPCompany operations person. That person then acts on behalf of the client and performs the requested action from z/VM. ISPCompany is developing a tool that will enable it to automate this process. The tool includes a Web interface through which the client can pass a request to the tool on a Linux image. The tools first does a security check and then passes the request to z/VM for execution.

It is important to remember that tools not only need to be developed but also maintained and constantly adapted to a changing context. For example, new hardware and software need to be integrated as they become relevant to the procedure that the tool covers. Generally, this approach is most useful where fast deployment of specialized tools is critical and where the skill to develop tools is present in the company.

12.5.4 Buy your tools

Buying the tools you need allows you to focus on your core competence (unless tools are your business). Along with a tool, you can also purchase support for its deployment and maintenance. On the other hand, you also create dependencies on the tools you buy, since you cannot easily detach yourself from release cycles and the costs associated with installing new releases.

StoreCompany, for example, established an IT infrastructure not because it specializes in computing, but because it is the most efficient means for most administrative aspects of its business. Later StoreCompany embraced the opportunities of the Internet to gain new customers and boost sales, and the role of its IT expanded beyond administration. Because StoreCompany does not intend to be in the systems management tools business, it turns to a vendor who sells integrated systems management solutions. StoreCompany puts much stress on security, and it chose Tivoli because of the way security control had been implemented within the management structure.

12.5.5 Tool options summary

The following table summarizes the options you have for tools:

Use z/VM	... to manage the virtual hardware and do accounting at the image level.
Get tools from the Open Source community	... to obtain tools at low cost without having to develop them yourself.
Develop your own tools	... if you need special functions fast and if you can use these tools to a competitive advantage.
Buy tools	... if the functions you need are available on the market and you do not want to diverge into building and maintaining tools development skills.

You guessed it, the options are not exclusive, and there is no virtue in a purist approach. However, it is useful to choose the main source of tools and then other possibilities can be used to fill the gaps. In most cases, the least you will have to do yourself is to customize tools you have bought or obtained from the Open Source community to fit your needs. Also, if you have decided to develop your own tools, you will usually find a useful Open Source project to start with. If need be, you can guide your approach to tools by specific policies that address their role within the IT infrastructure.

12.6 Using a framework

With Linux on the mainframe, you are likely to have a heterogeneous environment with multiple operating systems, including traditional mainframe operating systems such as z/VM, z/OS, and VSE/ESA. Systems management frameworks address the question of how to accomplish an integrated management of such heterogeneous environments. This section first provides a general introduction to frameworks and then gives examples for frameworks that are suitable for a Linux-on-the-mainframe environment and encompass Linux and the traditional mainframe operating systems.

During the late 1980s and early 1990s, major vendors of systems management tools began to develop substructures for integrating tools and handling the diversity of heterogeneous environments. Initially, the goal was to make the vendor's own disparate tools work together in a single, integrated, monolithic solution and to provide a single point of control from where an administrator could monitor and control all systems.

Monolithic solutions soon proved too rigid to meet the demands of highly dynamic and diverse customer environments. As a response, the major providers separated the substructure from their tools. With its interfaces published, the substructure became a framework that allowed other vendors and customers to plug in their own tools.

An open framework provides the basis for suitable plug-ins to be assembled into a set of tools that spans all systems management disciplines and all systems in a heterogeneous environment. The framework/plug-in model not only allows tool integration but also the selection of only those tools that are needed in a particular environment.

To a framework provider, the framework is a selling point for the systems management tools that come with it. The suite of tools that the framework provider offers is more attractive to customers if the framework allows other tools to be integrated. Framework providers, therefore, tend to publish their interfaces to enable other vendors and home-grown tools to plug in.

12.6.1 What is in a framework?

A systems management framework is an architecture that allows a user interface, managers, and agents to work together. Managers and agents are plug-ins that communicate with the framework through APIs (Application Programming Interfaces). Managers provide platform-independent management functions and use the agents to run system-specific code on the systems to be managed. For example, a manager that runs a system health monitor could send a request to the agents on each system to find out about free space in the file system. As a response, the agents could use a method that is specific to a particular operating system to get the data. For example:

- Issue a command (such as df on Linux)
- Call an API
- Pass a control block (on z/OS)

In all cases, the agent then sends the results back to the manager. On each image, multiple agents can plug into the framework.

A framework usually includes:

Common services

> that are available on all platforms, such as task management, memory management, or an interface to a security manager.

> Extending a framework to support Linux merely means writing the code to map the common services to the ones provided by Linux. And then, in most cases, all one needs to do is retarget the compile to the respective hardware platform.

Connectivity

> among the plug-ins. The communication is typically based on TCP/IP. It can include encryption and usually provides secure communication across systems.

A data repository

> for information that is shared across the framework. For example, this could be an LDAP-based directory with an underlying SQL database. The database contains common definitions and information about the state of managed objects (for example, processors or applications).

A user interface

> that provides the user with a view of the data in the management data repository and through which the user interacts with other plug-ins. The interface usually runs on a PC or laptop away from the machine room (for example, in a control room or in the system administrator's office). The user interface also connects to the framework through an API, so alternatives are possible. User interfaces are often graphical interfaces but can also be command interfaces.

APIs

for getting to common services and communication with other user interfaces, managers, agents, and the data repository.

Figure 12-5 illustrates how a framework spans the StoreCompany infrastructure.

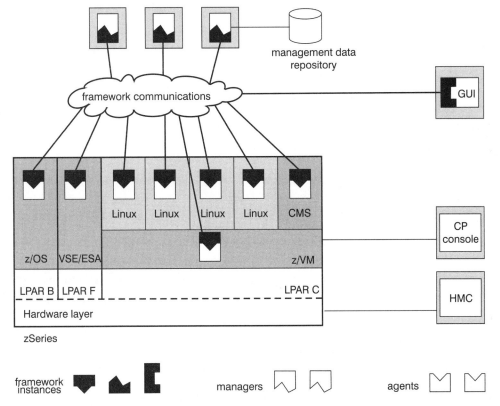

Figure 12-5. Framework for StoreCompany

The framework is installed on all managed systems and the systems where the managers run. It offers interfaces to agents and managers and connectivity with other systems that run the framework. The managers can run on any system for which the system requirements for the framework and the manager are fulfilled. Potentially, a manager could run on one of the systems being managed, but it could just as well be on a different continent.

12.6.2 Frameworks and standards

Systems management vendors with frameworks usually provide a suite of managing functions that plug into the framework. You can usually get plug-ins by vendors other than the framework provider, and there is room for you to plug in your own management tools if you have functions to complement what is provided.

To allow other vendors to use a framework and to enable you to plug in your own functions, framework owners publish the APIs that define their architecture. The architecture describes the behavior of the framework.

There is an interaction between architectures and standards. An architecture can be raised to a standard by approval through a standards body. Framework architects, on the other hand, look to existing standards to make their frameworks compatible with tools that adhere to the same standards.

It is no surprise that different vendors often use competing standards. Some vendor APIs are proprietary, others are open standards like SNMP (Simple Network Management Protocol) or the Distributed Management Task Force (DMTF) CIM (Common Information Model). See `http://www.dmtf.org` for details.

The DMTF is the industry organization that is leading the development, adoption, and unification of management standards and initiatives for desktop, enterprise, and Internet environments. CIM is a common data model of an implementation-neutral schema for describing overall management information in a network/enterprise environment. It includes specifications that define details for integration with other management models, while the schema provides the actual model descriptions.

SNMP is a standard for a systems management protocol that is not only supported by many management tools but also by many "dumb" devices like printers, where the framework cannot be installed. If a tool or framework supports SNMP, it can manage these devices. The Web site for the SNMP standards body is at `http://www.ietf.org`.

12.6.3 Existing frameworks

Examples of frameworks that cover Linux today are:

IBM Tivoli Management Framework

> The Tivoli Management Framework implementation is object-oriented. Earlier implementations were based on the Object Management Group / Common Object Request Broker Architecture (OMG/CORBA) specification (http://www.omg.org/). Its APIs were adopted by DMTF and the Open Group.

More recent development shows a shift to Java, Java Beans, and the CIM data model.

The Tivoli Management Framework has a 3-tier architecture with a TMR (Tivoli Management Region) server at the top. The TMR server can support up to about 200 gateways, each of which can connect to thousands of endpoints. This design provides scalability to a large number of systems and keeps the framework code to be installed on the managed endpoints very small.

Tivoli Management Framework comes with a base set of management functions. There are additional functions that you can optionally plug in, including a plug-in for SAP R3 support. In addition, Tivoli provides a toolkit that helps you to write your own plug-ins.

An administrator with sufficient rights can add a new endpoint to a Tivoli controlled environment by instructing a Tivoli manager or gateway to install the framework code on the new machine. The new machine then communicates with its assigned gateway or registers with a suitable gateway by means of a broadcast.

The Tivoli Management Framework includes a security concept that is based on user roles. These user roles are mapped to regions that are managed by policies.

For the Tivoli Management Framework, Linux has been given increasing attention as a platform for running mainframe managers. For example, IBM Tivoli Storage Manager runs on Linux.

For more information on Tivoli Management Framework visit:
`http://www.ibm.com/software/tivoli/products/mgt-framework/`.

CA Unicenter TNG Framework

The Unicenter TNG Framework provides a base set of management tools, plus optional management tools that you can buy. Optional tools are offered by several vendors, including Computer Associates International, Inc. The Unicenter TNG Framework also provides the Unicenter TNG Software Developer Kit for integrating home-grown tools. Several major system vendors ship systems with the Unicenter.

TNG provides "auto discovery" when an image with a TNG agent registers with the corresponding managers. Unicenter plug-ins can use policies and correlation techniques to attain a degree of autonomous behavior and to reduce network traffic.

The Unicenter GUI and the manager functions run on Linux, so you can control your entire enterprise from a Linux image.

For more information on Unicenter TNG Framework visit:
`http://www3.ca.com/press/PressRelease.asp?CID=37246`.

Other organizations that are worth following in this context are:

BMC PATROL

PATROL does not claim to be a framework but fits our definition of 12.6.1, "What is in a framework?." It takes a more decentralized approach than the other frameworks we have discussed.

It combines what we have called managers and agents into "knowledge modules." These plug into what we would call the framework, but BMC calls an agent. The agent/framework provides, for example, for cross-system communication.

The knowledge modules are platform- and function-specific. Because they act fairly autonomously, once they are set up on a machine, PATROL creates less data traffic than some other frameworks. Knowledge modules take a set of parameters that can be specified in a plain text configuration file.

PATROL comes with a basic set of knowledge modules. There is also a toolkit that allows customers and vendors to write their own knowledge modules. PATROL knowledge modules identify themselves by listening at a specific port.

PATROL does not have knowledge modules for the mainframe operating systems. Instead, there is a separate product, MainView, that provides administrative functions for these systems.

Because the knowledge modules can act independently, PATROL does not provide a GUI. However, PATROL provides knowledge modules that can send messages to the MainView interface, the TNG console, or the Tivoli GUI. Thus, either of these can be a control point, if needed.

For more information on BMC PATROL visit:
`http://www.bmc.com/homepage_elements/ii/idc/ema_bmc_patrol_brief.pdf`.

OpenNMS

OpenNMS is an Open Source group that started from the network view of the world and based much of its work on SNMP.

Its code is based on today's state-of-the art open standard technologies XML (Extensible Markup Language), SML (Simple Markup Language),[23] Java, Perl, and a PostgreSQL object-based relational database.

---

[23] SML: http://www.xml.com/pub/a/1999/11/sml/

For more information on OpenNMS visit: `http://opennms.org`.

We refrain from a detailed comparison of the merits of the various systems management frameworks that can work in a Linux-on-the-mainframe environment because they are subject to rapid change. Which framework is best suited to your environment depends on how well it addresses your current business and operational needs, and on the ease with which you can integrate plug-ins to cover future needs.

12.7 Summary

We have seen that tools are available to cover the systems management disciplines of Linux on the mainframe. We have stressed that managing hundreds of Linux images calls for tools. We have argued that business objectives come first and that the suitability of tools can be assessed only once the business objectives have been translated into policies and procedures.

The systems management disciplines we have introduced are essentially arbitrary, but they still reflect the division of responsibilities in many larger IT installations. The borders between them are not sharply defined, and there are considerable overlaps and interdependencies.

Security, as one of the disciplines, has already been covered to a large extent in Part 3, "Is Linux on the Mainframe for Me?," because it must be designed into an environment from the outset. Because there is no separate chapter on Security in this part of the book, Figure 12-6 summarizes the security tasks here.

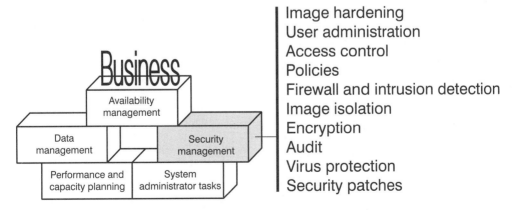

Figure 12-6. Security discipline

The following chapters each focus on one of the disciplines and point to some important decision points to consider when working out policies and procedures to govern Linux on the mainframe.

Chapter 13.
Availability Management

Availability management starts with configuring the various hardware and software components with their individual reliability characteristics into a system that meets the availability requirements of the end user. It covers all the tasks associated with the delivery of service to the end users.

You might expect that Linux on the mainframe enables you to provide a higher available service at reduced cost when compared to alternative server farm configurations. In this chapter, we will cover some of the areas where we believe you will find key leverage points for this value potential.

We will regard a server as available if the end user can perform the desired functions. This definition of availability spans a wide range of failure points, from power to the hardware, the processors running, the disks spinning, and the network running to the operating system, the middleware, and applications all running and functioning together.

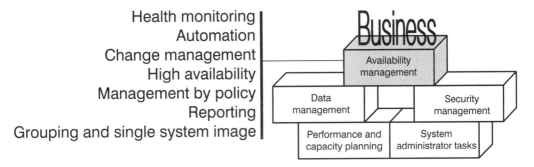

Health monitoring
Automation
Change management
High availability
Management by policy
Reporting
Grouping and single system image

Figure 13-1. Availability management tasks

We will discuss all tasks listed in Figure 13-1 to some degree, but we will primarily focus on the following three availability tasks because they potentially have some unique value for you in a Linux-on-the-mainframe environment:

- Monitoring the individual components and end user experiences. This monitoring is frequently called *health monitoring.*

- Running automatic procedures to recover from various forms of failure. These automatic procedures are usually called *automation.*

- Defined policies and procedures for handling changes to the system. This area of effort is called *change management.*

We will focus on how Linux, the mainframe, and z/VM can all contribute to the management tasks of keeping the system available according to your policies. We will explore questions such as:

- Are there simple ways to determine the health of hundreds of Linux images on a mainframe?

- Can Linux-on-the-mainframe applications provide a 99.9% level of availability?

- What tools are available to manage a high-availability set of Linux images?

- If the required level of availability is greater than what comes with Linux, what options are there?

13.1 Availability policy

Most organizations have a service level agreement (SLA) with their end users, often in the form of an explicit contract. The intent of an SLA is to define what system resources will be provided, on what schedules and, possibly, even at what level of performance. For example, StoreCompany has the following SLA for its internal mail servers:

StoreCompany SLA

The mail server will be available from 7 a.m. to midnight, and no outage should last longer than 10 minutes.

These service level agreements become the availability policy that drives the availability management decisions for the various services.

However, given that availability is now usually defined from the end users' perspectives, there are some very interesting secondary effects that can aid in a system design based on Linux, z/VM, and the mainframe. Here are some examples that show the valuable benefits that both end users and the IT shop can have from properly crafted policy statements.

Based on the simple SLA for StoreCompany's mail server, even if that server is down between 3 a.m. and 5 a.m., service could still be considered 100% available because the scope of the availability is 7 a.m. to midnight. The system administrator can use the non-production time for change activities such as applying preventive maintenance to forestall problems. Not needing to apply changes during the defined system available times permits a less complicated system design, which in turn tends to improve the overall system reliability. Currently, most servers do not need to provide their service 100% of the time in order to meet the requirements of end users.

How often have you entered a URL, seen some activity occurring at the bottom of the Web browser, and then the activity seemed to stall? Most of us just simply try it again. We do not say that the server is unavailable if we manage to connect after a few tries. In truth, during that brief period the Web server might have been down. Then the proxy server, noticing that one server was down, routed all new requests (for example, our second attempt) to other servers that were still functioning properly. Because the user does not require the service from a particular server, the IT shop can use this less expensive design involving the proxy server to meet availability (see also 11.4, "High availability for the ISPCompany example").

Managing availability is a juggling act of providing service to end users in a way that they are satisfied, based on the SLA. Providing higher levels of availability than what is required may, in fact, be a waste of valuable corporate resources.

13.2 Health monitoring

Most IT organizations try to anticipate and avert system problems before calls come into the help desk. The larger the organization and number of servers, the more likely it is that the organization has one or more display windows whose colored icons represent the health of components of various services provided to end users. These health monitors usually come with two functions:

- Agents that reside close to the service to be monitored and that send out either regular status or exception status

- A presentation manager that collects status information from various agents and aggregates that data into a meaningful presentation format (including, perhaps, a page or e-mail to the staff alerting them that a problem needs to be fixed)

What is unique with Linux on the mainframe is that due to virtualization, z/VM has some very useful data about both the individual guests and the aggregate usage of the real and virtual hardware resources. z/VM needs this data in order to manage the guests. Thus, no significant additional cycles are needed to share this data with a health monitoring tool. To the extent that most outages of service can be seen with hardware level performance metrics (for example, the CPU is no longer busy or the outbound LAN traffic has gone to zero), the operations staff can use this easily available data as a first level indicator of potential problems. While some other servers do have some rudimentary hardware monitoring capabilities, it is usually quite expensive to tie that information into the health monitor.

Most organizations also include two other crucial functions that move health monitoring into true health management:

- A manager that collects and logs data about availability

- A presentation manager that allows both a global and specific drill-down control of the managed environment

A tool that includes all four functions of health management becomes a single point of control for the system with all of its disparate images. Some installations have built their Linux systems' health management tool on top of z/VM because z/VM covers all four functions quite well.

In the following section, we will expand on the "control" aspect of health management.

13.3 Automation

Availability management aims at responding to anomalous events fast enough that the damage is contained and repaired before the SLA criteria are missed. Typically, humans take at least a few seconds to observe, analyze, and react to a situation.[24] With the speed of modern processors, a lot of damage can occur in a few seconds.

Automation refers to a program suite that performs the "observe, analyze, and react" processes at machine speeds. At the heart of the automation tool is the automation engine that gathers events, correlates information from various sources, and manages the system state changes with scripts. The key value of an automation tool is the speed at which a new system state (for example, the database manager is down) is recognized and at which it causes the predefined transition policies[25] to be executed. At the time of the writing of this book, automation tools cannot provide recovery itself. Instead, they provide a framework where you can plug in your recovery (state change) processes, typically in the form of a program script.

Linux on the mainframe has an ideal environment for managing availability because a number of automation tools exist. For example:

---

[24] As today's systems continue to improve, these anomalous events happen less and less frequently—a good thing. As a result, we tend to forget what the proper procedure is to respond to the event—a bad thing. Typically, there is a written procedure on how to recover. But a site is almost guaranteed to have a lengthy outage if the operator first has to read up on what to do.

[25] *Policy* is one of those overused words today. So far in the book we have used it exclusively to refer to a set of corporate directives that guide how IT is practiced in the company. Here we are using *policy* to mean one or more scripts that implement a set of procedures that respond to an event. The concept here is that someone has thought through what procedures need to be followed when some event occurs. Loosely speaking, a *policy* on how to respond was developed.

- In z/VM, both CP and CMS have a broad range of commands to control one, all, or a subset of the guests.

- REXX is a very powerful scripting language that runs in the CP and CMS environments.

- A programmed operator interface (called PROP in z/VM) to each guest's console facilitates direct (not over a LAN interface) interaction by REXX with a guest.

A number of automation tools are also available from system management vendors. See Chapter 25, "Systems Management Tools," for some other options.

13.4 Change management

Those in the computer business who are responsible for availability often see system behavior as: *"If the system ran yesterday and no one made a change to it, that system will probably keep running today."* Sometimes this same understanding of change gets expressed by: *"If the system fails today, the probable cause of the failure is the latest change made to the system."*

While change poses a threat to availability, it is critical for continued existence in business. It is, in fact, the acceleration of change that is the hallmark of business today and one of the key drivers for deploying a Linux-on-the-mainframe environment.

Change management in most IT organizations is typically handled by some of the most skilled persons on the staff: the system administrators. We cover this topic in more detail in Chapter 16, "System Administrator Tasks."

With Linux on the mainframe, you typically apply changes to more than one image at a given time. The scripting capability of automation tools, and especially of z/VM, is one of the ways that provides significant control for the orderly introduction of complex changes into a large number of active systems. The use of automation is important for managing change in the Linux-on-the-mainframe environment.

13.5 Key factors to consider in availability

Reliability is an attribute of a component or system and is typically defined as a probability of that component or system being up and running when it should be. It does not include the time when something is planned to be down. Availability focuses on the end user's perspective, which tends to be an "all or nothing" attitude. The system is either up and usable, or it is considered not available.

Most IT organizations include only unplanned outages (system crash) as part of their availability computations. High-availability systems usually have such stringent availability requirements that there is no distinguishing between planned (system administrator time) and unplanned outages. Some end user groups are beginning to require systems that are continuously available, that is, no outage of service ever, for any reason.

Availability management always uses a dual strategy:

- Avoiding an outage in the first place

- Rapid recovery once an outage does occur

As part of any TCO analysis for a new IT project, you should consider the tangible (for example, lost productivity, lost business) and hidden (for example, loss of reputation, bad press) costs of an outage.[26] When these costs are compared with the cost of avoiding various potential outages and the probability of such an outage, you have the basis to build a plan for availability management. The technical team is then able to focus its efforts on both failure avoidance and time to recover in an order defined by business requirements.

13.5.1 Levels of availability

The costs associated with making a service more available can grow exponentially. That cost explosion leads IT directors to examine closely the availability requirements statement and the cost of achieving that goal. Table 13-1 lists various levels of availability.

Table 13-1. Levels of availability

Level of availability	Time of outage allowed
90%	2 shifts per week
95%	1 shift per week
99%	1 shift per month
99.5%	6 shifts per year
99.9%	1 shift per year
99.99%	1 shift per decade (less than one hour per year)
99.999%	1 shift per century

---

[26] See Gartner Research Note, "24x7 is a Management Thing," at http://www.availability.com/resource/pdfs/in4.pdf.

The built-in availability functions in each system component make a significant difference in how costly it is to provide a given level of availability. This aspect of the cost of improved availability is not often discussed. When deciding where to host the various parts of a new application, it is as important to understand what the system components offer for availability functions as it is to have a clear idea about what availability is required. If a system component falls short of what is required, you must expect additional costs in the implementation of your solution.

The system functions required for building an application with a given level of availability also depend heavily on the needs of the application. Most systems today provide at least a 90% availability right out of the box for any application they support. With all the lament about the reliability of our PC hardware and software, most of us do not experience 8 hours of downtime per month when working with a typical PC application, which translates to a respectable 99% availability.

Today's Linux comes with enough features to allow you to build a highly available static Web page server without undue effort. But building a 99.99% available e-business application with a 100-gigabyte relational database would be a significant challenge with Linux. Linux today lacks the built-in capabilities of z/OS parallel sysplex for shared read/write access to large databases. It will cost you to derive your own substitute for those functions that come already built-in with z/OS. Figure 13-2 illustrates how the cost of an availability solution rises steeply as you go beyond what the operating system provides.

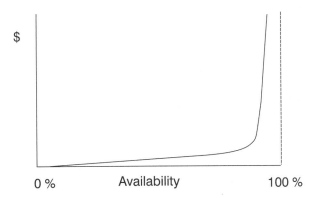

Figure 13-2. The cost of an availability solution

Depending on what level of availability your end users require and on the application you intend to host, Linux might provide what you need.

While the current Linux distributions for zSeries are missing some of the more advanced functions for constructing and managing high-availability servers, numerous tool sets are available from various vendors. For pointers to some of these tools, see Chapter 25,

"Systems Management Tools." A number of Open Source projects in this area are expected to culminate in significant functional improvements in future Linux kernel releases.

StoreCompany with its new Internet sales project specifically chose to leave the parts of the application with complex availability requirements on z/OS and keep on Linux only those parts suited to the Linux availability functions.

13.5.2 Outage avoidance

Outages are typically caused by:

- Deficiencies in the system components
- System complexity
- Human error
- Acts of God (such as storms or earthquakes)

The last two items are fairly independent of the system choices you make, especially if you take significant advantage of automation. We are going to ignore them here.[27] How does Linux on the mainframe help for the first two items? Let's look at some of the key components in a server farm:

- The hardware: CPU, disks, cables, network
- The operating system
- The middleware
- The application

The mainframe has a well-earned reputation for its availability. In Chapter 2, "Introducing the Mainframe," we explained the architectural and design basis that leads to exceeding IBM's 2002 design point for the IBM z900 of greater than 30 years mean time between failures. For those who have experienced life with a server farm of 200 machines, a farm built with z/VM guests on zSeries hardware will be a pleasant experience. The mainframe hardware can almost be ignored as a source of outage.[28]

The operating system is at the core of the software environment. Contrasting factors are involved here:

---

[27] Most systems use automation to minimize the possibilities for operator errors. Linux on the mainframe lends itself to that type of automation.

[28] A component failure that brings down a mainframe machine unexpectedly is a low probability source of outage and for many planning purposes can be ignored. Other hardware-related sources of problems (for example, power grid problems) are still there.

- The more function the operating system provides, the less complex the middleware and applications tend to be. Hence, these higher layers are less prone to failure.

- The larger and more complex the operating system, the more likely that there are cases in which the operating system still has hidden bugs.

By choosing Linux as the core of your available system, you pick up some very strong characteristics that complement the zSeries hardware. Linux is an interesting operating system in that it has robust function yet remains relatively small (as compared to z/OS or Windows XP) in size. It also has a huge user base that is using the system, maybe two orders of magnitude more installed instances than z/OS and rapidly approaching the latest install levels of Windows. The unique aspect of Linux that is important to its availability is the size of the community working at fixing problems found and the speed at which these changes get rolled into the base code.

If you find that the latest levels released by one of the main distributors (Turbolinux, Red Hat, and SuSE) meet your functional requirements, you will have a stable operating system. If you want to have the added security of an organization *guaranteeing* to fix your Linux problems, then you should investigate signing a service contract with either your distributor or IBM's Global Services.

If some new function that is still in the developmental stages (for example, code from one of the Linux high-availability projects), then you have a choice. In your case, Linux might not be *ready* for your needs. Or you will need to analyze and accept the various risks with being on the leading edge. Probably you will find that such functional needs can be isolated to only a few Linux images, and that the rest of the images fall under the stable and contractually supported release levels.

13.5.3 Rapid recovery

Table 13-2 shows typical recovery times for some failure types.

Table 13-2. Recovery times

Failing component	Approximate recovery time
Hardware	hours to repair; 5 or more minutes to restart
Linux (boot)	1 minute
Middleware startup (for example, WebSphere Application Server)	3 minutes
Database manager	5 minutes
Application	depending on the application, 1 minute or more

A typical Service Level Agreement (SLA) that specifies the maximum permitted outage time goes a long way to dictating the availability management strategy for a given server.

In large server farms of PCs (say, more than 200), it is not unusual to experience a hardware failure on the average of once a week. Typically, end users would not be satisfied with a strategy built on repairing or replacing the failed server, since that might take hours.

Based on the numbers in Table 13-2 it would be difficult to meet an SLA of recovery under five minutes with reboot as the recovery strategy. Starting all components adds up to more than five minutes, even if the recovery action is driven by an automation tool! The restart figures can differ for different setups, but there is always a limit to the degree of availability you can achieve with restart as the sole means of recovery.

Similarly, if the SLA calls for 24x7 service with 99.9% availability, the system administrator is going to find it more difficult to apply maintenance and changes than on a server that requires only 99% availability.

A critical decision that you must make in availability discussions is what failures you intend to recover from. For example, if your customers can accept, and do not hold you responsible for, power grid failures that last for more than one day, you can configure for a combination of battery and generator backup. In this case, you do not have to plan recovery actions for an area-wide flood and keep only a day's supply of diesel fuel at your site.

The more failure scenarios you want to cover and the more 9's you need, the harder and more costly it is going to be to accomplish a high level of availability, even with a superb suite of availability management tools.

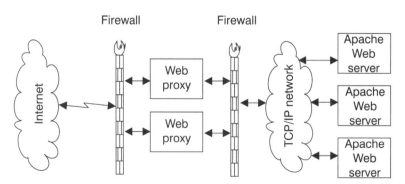

Figure 13-3. ISPCompany high-availability setup for static Web serving

ISPCompany, based on its established procedures and tested systems, is able to guarantee a 99.99% availability to clients doing static Web page serving. It is relatively easy to configure a number of Linux images where two images act as proxy servers (Figure 13-3).

The proxies spray incoming requests to a number of Linux Apache servers that share, read-only, the files with the static Web pages. Any single image failure will be transparent to the end user.[29]

z/VM is a great aid in this environment. First, it provides a highly optimized path, HiperSockets, for the traffic from the proxy servers to the Apache servers. Second, it also has, through the use of REXX scripts, the ability to add a new Apache server instance to take over the lost capacity from a failing Web server. With z/VM, there is no need to have excess capacity in this case because the failing server no longer consumes its portion of the zSeries cycles. They will just be picked up by the replacement image.

13.5.4 High availability

In general, providing availability greater than two 9's, or specifying outages taking less than five minutes, is going to require significant planning and will probably result in more levels of redundancy. The costs of providing such levels of service also typically grow exponentially with the complexity.

As already stated, it is fairly straightforward to provide a high-availability solution for static Web page serving. On the other hand, if you had a read/write database application, the middleware and Linux file systems are still relatively restrictive on sharing a multi-write environment. It is this added state information that complicates the system design and makes it much harder with today's levels of Linux and middleware to achieve a 99.99% availability.

A failure of a database manager that has some state information not yet completely written to the database is going to take more than a few minutes (and maybe even hours) to recover. Much of the design of this type of high availability in Linux is still left to you to analyze and to implement. This is not to say it is impossible; rather, such a solution is likely to be time-intensive for your staff.

Linux has many parameters and install options that can be used to allow for speedy recovery. For example, journaled file systems provide for speedier recovery than other types of file systems. The penalty is a small but noticeable performance degradation.

You normally start from a given availability that you require for a particular application. Figure 13-4 illustrates how the cost for attaining this availability varies with different operating systems (OS_i, OS_{ii}, and OS_{iii}). OS_i represents an operating system with the weakest and OS_{iii} with the strongest availability features. The curve shows how the cost explodes for

---

[29] Redbooks publication, *Linux on IBM zSeries and S/390: High Availability for z/VM and Linux,* REDP0220, defines a number of high-availability configurations.

operating systems that offer too little availability functions to support the application. For operating systems that fall in the middle section of the curve, solutions can be devised at a reasonable cost. If the operating system provides all you need, like OS_{iii} in our example, the solution will cost you next to nothing. Note that the curve would change for a different level of availability, a different application, and different hardware. As operating systems evolve, they generally provide better availability features so that a comparison is also valid only for a particular point in time.

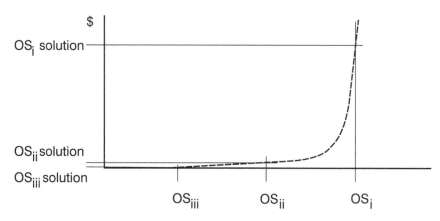

Figure 13-4. The cost of availability solutions depending on the operating system

An operating system like z/OS (an example of an OS_{iii} type operating system) has many availability features built into it. z/OS can also work with a Coupling Facility that makes it significantly easier to build even 99.999% available systems with a geographically dispersed cluster of images. At the time of this writing, if you had a need for such high levels of availability for systems with shared write to data, you would probably be better off basing the design on z/OS than on Linux on the mainframe. Many organizations are actively pursuing high-availability solutions for Linux, and most of these would make good sense if deployed on z/VM and zSeries hardware.

13.6 Summary

What you want for availability from your Linux images is up to you to define in conjunction with your end users' requirements. System availability is not free. It will take effort, and that effort starts with a clear definition of the availability requirements, for example, the various service level agreements with the end users.

Linux as distributed by one of the large distributors with zSeries support is a highly stable operating system benefiting from being both relatively small and having an enthusiastic and skilled group of people dedicated to making it better.

z/VM is a fantastic base on which to run a farm of Linux images. In the first place, you automatically inherit the reliability of the zSeries hardware. z/VM contributes availability tools (such as REXX scripting capabilities) to ensure real time response to events showing up in one or more Linux images. Since z/VM is aware of all the Linux images, it is much easier to build recovery scripts involving related Linux images using z/VM and REXX than it is on most other platforms.

A number of availability management tools from software vendors and the Open Source community also can help you build the level of available Linux servers you need.

At the time of this writing, Linux on the mainframe is not a panacea for all availability problems. However, it is continuously improving and there are many areas where Linux and z/VM are a great pair for delivering the desired levels of availability.

Chapter 14.
Data Management

Data are crucial to a business and the mainframe enjoys the reputation as the best keeper of corporate data. In this chapter, we will turn to examples of ISPCompany and StoreCompany to show how Linux on the mainframe can use that mainframe potential and what Linux provides for managing data. But before going into details, let's summarize the scope of data management.

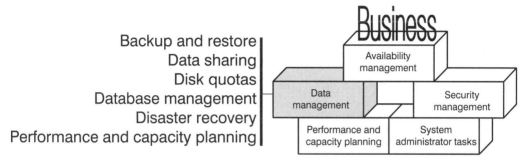

Backup and restore
Data sharing
Disk quotas
Database management
Disaster recovery
Performance and capacity planning

Figure 14-1. Data management discipline

Ultimately, data management ensures that data are available to legitimate users and applications when they need them, while protecting them from misuse or damage through unauthorized access. Data management governs the entire life cycle, from creating new data to archiving or destroying obsolete data.

Data management also covers the physical aspects of storage, including devices, cabling, and floor space. Data for a mainframe Linux image can reside on a variety of devices, including traditional mainframe devices. The mainframe also provides flexibility in the way devices can be attached, the possibility for access path redundancy, and capabilities for dynamic reconfiguration.

In this chapter, we will first discuss some important technical concepts about storing data on the mainframe. Building on this discussion, we will then explore what Linux on the mainframe has to offer to data management. Along with the key data management tasks of Figure 14-1, we will address these questions:

- How can I ensure that data are available only to legitimate users?

- Can I use SCSI devices?

- Do I have to acquire new devices, or can I use devices I already have?

- How can I protect my data from loss or damage from user, application, or hardware errors?

- How do I attain satisfactory performance when disks and channel paths are shared?

14.1 Keeping data on the mainframe

In this section, we introduce the devices that can be used by Linux on the mainframe. Then, we discuss some technical aspects of keeping data on the mainframe. This technical information can help you decide what to bring to Linux on the mainframe. The sections on the data management tasks that follow build on these technical concepts.

14.1.1 Which devices are there for you to use?

Because Linux on the mainframe supports both traditional mainframe devices and Open Standard storage devices, you have much freedom to choose where to place your data.

Traditional mainframe devices

The basic functions of mainframe devices tend to be covered by generic device drivers. However, because manufacturers generally treat their device interfaces as proprietary, special device features and full error recovery are usually not supported by generic drivers. To close this gap, some manufacturers provide device specific drivers as Object Code Only (OCO) modules.

With the exception of some older devices, mainframe shops can continue to use the devices they already have with Linux.

Disk devices: Table 14-1 shows some of the disk devices (DASD, in mainframe language) you can use with Linux on the mainframe (the '*****' signifies any specification):

Table 14-1. Supported IBM disk devices		
Control unit type/model	**Device type/model**	**Restrictions**
3990(2105)/**	3380/**	
3990(2105)/**	3390/**	
9343/**	9345/**	Basic error recovery only
6310/**	9336/**	VM virtual disk in storage only
3880/**	3370/**	Basic error recovery only

Also, Linux on the mainframe supports more recent devices such as the IBM TotalStorage Enterprise Storage Server (ESS).[30]

Because operating systems and their file systems tend to have unique data formats, Linux has its own special formatting of zSeries disks. As of the writing of this book, there is no common data format for Linux and mainframe operating systems such as z/OS or z/VM that allows both operating systems to read or write common files.

There is a disk format (Compatible Disk Layout) that allows Linux file systems to be managed by zSeries storage management products, for example, DFSMS (Data Facility Storage Management Subsystem) for backup and restore, or GDPS (Geographically Dispersed Parallel Sysplex) for disaster recovery. However, this disk format does not allow Linux data to be processed from operating systems other than Linux.

Tape drives: You can use tape drives that are compatible with IBM 3480, 3490, and 3590 magnetic tape subsystems.

FCP attached devices

Beginning in late 2002, Open Systems devices can be attached to a zSeries machine through a Fibre Channel Protocol (FCP) link. The generic SCSI device drivers provide basic support for most devices such as tape drives and libraries, or fiber-attached SCSI disks. However, the generic drivers are subject to restrictions with regard to functionality and reliability. Such restrictions can be overcome by using vendor supplied device drivers (for example, "ibmtape" provided by IBM for tape devices).

The immense test effort involved in confirming the scores of SCSI-compliant devices that this FCP attachment opens up to Linux on the mainframe is the limiting factor for "official" support. Many devices are known to run, but have not been tested exhaustively. On the other hand, there is also a small number of devices with limited SCSI compliance that are not suitable for Linux on the mainframe.

At the time of writing, we are anticipating an increasing number of "official" support statements by IBM and other vendors to be issued as qualification tests are completed for specific devices.

---

[30] IBM TotalStorage Enterprise Storage Server is also known as "Shark."

SAN

You can also attach a Storage Area Network (SAN) through an FCP link. However, operating system images, even on the mainframe, inherit the open security and management issues that SANs suffer on other platforms.

SANs are considered enterprise-ready in environments where a single operating system controls the entire SAN. As of the writing of this book, SANs are still subject to data isolation problems in heterogeneous environments and for usage across security domains. Intense work is under way to address these problems. In anticipation of a breakthrough on these management issues, Linux on the mainframe already supports SANs.

14.1.2 Data sharing

Here, we are not using *sharing* to mean a particular technical implementation, but rather to describe the logical instances in which multiple users need access to a common set of data.

With Linux on the mainframe, it is likely that you are not dealing with a single Linux image and its data, but with data that are needed by multiple Linux images and maybe even a z/OS image. This sharing can be through NFS, by getting a point-in-time copy of the file of interest, or by making a program call to another application for the required data. It is not only possible but sometimes also desirable to keep data on z/OS. The mainframe provides the communication methods and there are numerous connectors (see 19.3, "Connectors to back-end systems") that facilitate the use of data in z/OS resources from Linux on the mainframe.

Sharing data raises questions about who owns which data and who is responsible for managing them. Data could be owned and controlled by an individual user, but also by a Linux image or by an application.

Where data are created by an application, it is usually the application that owns them. Especially where interrelated data are created and used in multiple locations, the application is best suited to determine what constitutes a consistent set of data (for example, for backup purposes). If the Linux image shares the use of data with a z/OS image, the data are probably directly attached to z/OS by a channel path so that you can exploit z/OS data management capabilities.

For data management, it is important that all parties are aware of who owns the data, who uses the data, and who is responsible for which aspects of their management.

Data sharing reduces the amount of required storage, both for the original data and for backup copies. It can, however, introduce latency for getting data from the owner, which might lead to unacceptable response times.

Data sharing need not be the best solution for providing the same data to multiple applications or users. Where sharing is advantageous, Linux on the mainframe can exploit the mainframe technology with its fast internal communication methods for accessing the data of other operating systems on the same machine. The next section is about the opposite of sharing: privacy.

14.1.3 Data isolation in a virtualized environment

Multiple operating systems have been running on the mainframe long before the emergence of Linux and Linux on the mainframe. Consequently, the question of isolating data and protecting each operating system's data from other operating systems is not a new concern. It has long been addressed and robust isolation mechanisms are at hand.

Channel paths

To understand data isolation and access control on the mainframe, we need to know a few things about *channel paths*. Channel paths are the physical access paths with their associated logic and controls that the mainframe machines use to access data (see Figure 2-13). The zSeries architecture supports 256 channel paths.

The number of devices you can attach to a channel path depends on the path type. In total, a maximum of 64 K devices can be attached to a single hardware machine. Even in the old days of 3 gigabyte-sized disks, you could directly attach close to 200 terabytes of data on disk. In Open System environments, comparable capacities can be provided by using a smaller number of large disks, rather than a large number of small disks, as typical for the mainframe.

You can share channel paths among operating systems. Path sharing is a necessity if you intend to run hundreds of Linux images. Path sharing is also a means to save on cabling and adapters (channel cards). Conversely, it is common practice to provide more than one channel path for accessing a particular device (multipathing). This redundancy eliminates cabling as a single point of failure and can boost performance.

Controlling access to devices

With a zSeries machine running numerous Linux images, you might ask how one image's data could possibly be kept safe from the other images. There are several lines of defense:

- The hardware definitions
- z/VM
- The Linux images

The combination of these control mechanisms provides flexibility for addressing the individual data isolation and sharing needs of different installations.

The hardware definitions: The mainframe accesses devices by means of channel paths, that is, the work queue, the involved system assist processor, and the cabling. A channel path constitutes the hardware logic and processing required to access a device through a particular communication line (for example, a parallel link or a serial ESCON or FICON link). The hardware looks only for channel paths and devices that are defined to it in a special file, the *IOCDS (I/O configuration data set)*. Devices must be defined in the IOCDS to be detected by the zSeries hardware. Undefined devices are inaccessible to the hardware and all software that runs on it.

To isolate data, you can dedicate a device, that is, define it in the IOCDS only to a particular LPAR. As a result, programs or operating systems that run in other LPARs cannot access the isolated data.

You also can dedicate a channel path with all of its devices to a particular LPAR. Channel path dedication is often used for allocating bandwidth to one LPAR in favor of others. For data isolation, all possible paths to a device would have to be dedicated.

z/VM: z/VM can detect the defined devices on all channel paths that are defined to its LPAR (or the machine, if z/VM runs natively). A guest can use only the devices that z/VM defines to it. These definitions can be changed dynamically from z/VM. z/VM also can split the real devices into smaller virtual devices (minidisks) and control the guest's access at the granularity of the virtual devices.

The Linux images: With root access to Linux, you have two more ways to control data access: at the device level and at the user level. Both can be suitable control mechanisms if only trusted personnel or applications have root access.

You can instruct a Linux image to look only for specific devices. As a result, Linux will not be able to detect any other devices, even if the hardware definitions and z/VM have made them available.

In addition, Linux can restrict the access rights of individual users to the data in Linux file systems.

Example: Using z/VM for access control

One widely-used method is to over-define the relatively static hardware definitions and the Linux definitions and then use the dynamic z/VM definitions as the effective control. Over-defining means defining devices that do currently not exist but may be added in the future. A newly added device that has already been defined to the hardware can be brought online without taking the machine down.

Figure 14-2 illustrates a z/VM that knows nine devices (A000 through A008) and has three Linux guests (Lx, Ly, and Lz). Figure 14-2 also shows the statements that z/VM uses to selectively make devices available to the guests.

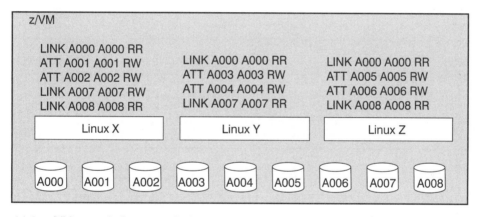

Figure 14-2. z/VM control of storage devices

z/VM can give a guest exclusive access (ATTach) or shared access (LINK) to a device. Figure 14-3 shows the logical views of the devices that the guest systems have according to the statements of Figure 14-2.

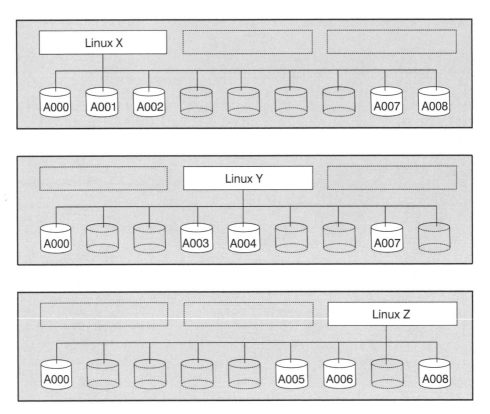

Figure 14-3. Linux guests' view of devices

z/VM assures that each guest can detect only the devices that are defined to it.

14.2 Introduction to backup and restore

Companies establish backup and restore procedures against loss of data if:

- Users unintentionally delete or damage data.[31]
- An operating system or application crashes.
- Hardware fails (for example, a disk head crash).

---

[31] Loss of data due to erroneously hitting a key is also known as a "finger check." In an early version of the S/360 Time Sharing Option (TSO), the command for editing a file was the single character E, while the command for deleting a file was a D. A glance at your keyboard will tell you why this short command for deletion was soon abandoned for the three-character command DEL.

Linux on the mainframe allows for the usual schemes, including tape libraries and dual copy facilities, that are used for backup, restore, and disaster recovery. z/VM's data management tools can help you to physically isolate critical data on particular disks that can then be handled by z/VM disk copy tools.

The standard backup method is to copy data to tape at regular intervals. Tape allows you to recover an earlier version of data that have been lost by accidental deletion or damaged by a failing application. However, with this method, you lose all changes that have occurred since the time the last backup was made.

Maintaining two synchronized copies of current data (for example, by dual copy) is a backup method that always assures a current copy of your data. This protects you against a head crash, but not against accidental deletion or damage through a malfunctioning application.

Because backup activities can be disruptive and consume processing power, communication, and media resources, backup rarely covers all of a company's data. Backup is often limited to important data, which cannot readily be recreated. Generally, the more critical and dynamic the data, the more frequent the backups.

For a selection of tools to handle your backup and restore procedures, your choices range from developing your own solution, to leveraging the Open Source community or buying a solution. Amanda is one of the better-known examples of Open Source tools.

tar and ftp from Linux can supplement the formal backup and restore process for smaller amounts of data that are controlled by single or small groups of individuals.

14.2.1 Tape versus disks

In the past, backup meant tape. With disk space becoming cheaper, backups on disk are becoming a viable alternative to tape for some types of data.

Backups on disk can be restored with less latency than backups on tape. In addition, the mainframe allows you to connect an enormous number of storage devices, so that disk as a backup medium becomes an option.

Tape prevails where backups must be taken off-site and where floor space is limited.

14.2.2 Layout of backup infrastructure

Most backups are still written to tape. Because highly reliable tape devices can be costly, the typical server farm approach is to have a LAN-attached backup server with an attached tape device or library (Figure 14-4).

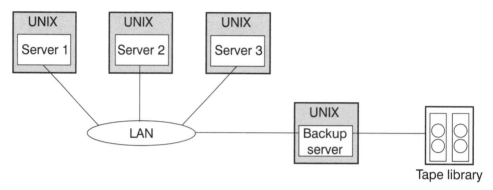

Figure 14-4. Backup server in a distributed server farm environment

If you have consolidated a server farm using Linux on the mainframe, you can continue to use the backup server on the LAN with its tape library (Figure 14-5).

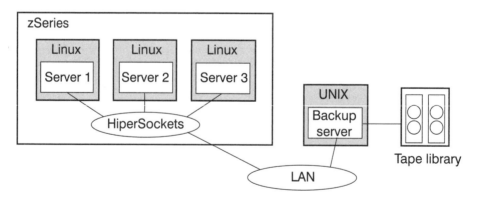

Figure 14-5. Consolidated server farm with the backup server on the LAN

However, a LAN-attached backup server has disadvantages, including:

- Backup activities can overload a LAN and sometimes necessitate a separate LAN.[32]

---

[32] With Gigabit Ethernet, you are less likely to experience LAN overloads from the backup data.

- Moving backup data across the LAN is a potential security exposure.

With a consolidated server farm on a zSeries machine, you can also have directly attached tape devices (Figure 14-6). You can move data to the backup server through HiperSockets, which are secure, provide high bandwidth, and, being virtual, require no cabling.

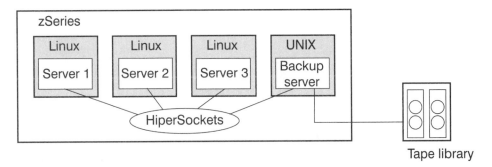

Figure 14-6. Backup server on the mainframe

You can attach multiple tape devices to the same zSeries machine and perform multiple backup operations concurrently.

14.2.3 Restore

An important decision point for selecting a backup/restore tool is whether it satisfies your security requirements (for example, to control who can retrieve backed-up data). Before buying a tool, be sure that it can be integrated with your security checks.

Restoring a single file usually takes longer than backing it up, especially when the restore medium is a tape. The tape must be mounted, and the required data must be located by winding the tape to the correct position. The greater the tape capacity, the longer is the expected response time.

You can have faster response times by keeping the backed-up files on disk. By keeping the disk available to a Linux guest image or by making it accessible through z/VM, you can provide rapid access to a backed-up file system.

14.2.4 Disaster recovery

Disaster recovery is a business survival scheme that is used in the event that an installation is partially or totally destroyed. Disaster recovery includes contingency plans for a range of possible disaster scenarios. These plans involve physical aspects, such as the location from where to operate and the machines and devices to be used.

z/VM tools and hardware facilities such as FlashCopy for Enterprise Storage Server allow rapid copying at the device level. If you ensure that all critical applications keep their data on a specific set of physical devices, you can create your data copies for disaster recovery at the physical level and take advantage of these facilities.

For most disaster scenarios you must keep data copies off-site, usually on tape. If the initial copy is on disk at the primary site, a slower but non-disruptive secondary copy to tape should follow the initial fast copy. If you are using a remote dual copy, you might not need to go to tape. ESS, for example, provides the remote dual copy features Peer-to-Peer Remote Copy (PPRC) and eXtended Remote Copy (XRC).

This section and the disaster recovery examples of our hypothetical companies are not a full discussion of disaster recovery. Our view is limited to aspects of data management in which special considerations apply to Linux or to the mainframe.

With z/OS Parallel Sysplex,[33] the mainframe offers an unsurpassed availability scheme for z/OS images. You cannot build sysplexes with Linux images; but if you already run a Parallel Sysplex, you might be able to exploit the sysplex capabilities to protect critical data.

At StoreCompany, for example, Linux works with data that are copied from z/OS. The z/OS copy is the master copy (see 14.4.2, "StoreCompany data management") and is included in the disaster recovery scheme. No additional precaution is required to safeguard the survival of data on the Linux side of its operations.

14.2.5 Backup tools summary

Table 14-2 summarizes some of the tool options you have when taking backups:

---

[33] A Parallel Sysplex is a mainframe clustering technology that can also involve geographically distant systems. One or more Coupling Facilities assure integrity as data are shared among constituent systems. If a shared storage device fails, the data can be reconstructed from the Coupling Facilities' log streams in conjunction with the application and the middleware that owns the data.

Table 14-2. Entities to be backed up	
Backup level	**Tool**
Disk	DASD dump restore
Minidisks	DASD dump restore
CMS files	CMS copy command
Linux files	Tivoli Storage Manager
Incremental database backups	Database utility
Cross-resource increments	Application that owns the resources

z/VM can take care of entities that it knows, for example, the physical disks. Where the entities are of a more logical nature, such as a Linux file system, you need tools that operate at the same abstraction level as the entities to be backed up. See also 25.2, "Data management tools."

14.3 Quota

In this section, we use *quota* as any way of constraining the use of disk storage by operating system images, applications, or users. Constraints can be applied for the available disk capacity at different levels: the machine level, the z/VM level, or within a Linux image.

Potentially, there is a large number of individual devices attached to a mainframe machine. The hardware definitions limit what is available to each LPAR, for example, an LPAR with a z/VM.

z/VM can allocate logical portions of its available storage to individual guests. In z/VM, such logical portions of storage are referred to as *z/VM minidisks.* Access to a minidisk can be restricted to a single image, or the minidisk can be shared by multiple images. Usually only one image has write access to a particular minidisk. Within the constraints that result from the physical devices, you can also allocate a minidisk of a moderate size and increase it on demand. Thus, you can divide the available real disk space into well-known portions, and you can keep some portions inaccessible as a reserve that no one can use without your active intervention.

If you place all the spare disk space into a single pool that the storage administrator can use for any of the systems, you can realize some significant disk storage savings. In a server farm where each system has its own discrete devices, each system must also have its own excess capacity that allows for unexpected storage needs. Because it is highly unlikely that unexpected needs arise on all systems in a server farm simultaneously, much less overall excess capacity is required if spare storage can be made available wherever it is needed. Attaching an extra physical disk to a small machine means a reboot. Adding a z/VM minidisk to a guest system does not disrupt operations.

Users who perceive storage as an inexhaustible commodity for which they are not accountable are unlikely to use it economically. In a multi-user environment where storage is provided centrally, containing the erratic behavior of individuals is an important aspect of storage administration. User quotas are one way of returning a sense of responsibility for the consumed storage resources to the individual user. Linux images can be installed with the capability to have any Linux system administrator assign quotas to users and groups in that image.

Linux quota and disk allocation schemes must give special attention to the various Linux system logs and temporary files. These two file categories have a tendency to grow relentlessly over time and a housekeeping strategy is essential for them. Often the cron daemon is used for an automated approach where tasks scheduled at intervals redirect the log streams to new files, archive current logs, and discard obsolete files.

A log file that has filled all available space can cause a Linux image to crash. Therefore, managing log files is typically part of availability management schemes. Availability schemes usually have tools in place that intercept warning messages indicating that the available space has fallen below a critical mark and either automatically assign new storage, or inform the storage administrator, or both.

14.4 Data, policies, and tools

Enterprises know how vital their business data are to them. Accordingly, most companies use policies (and an SLA) to control how its data are handled.

Because there is no universally valid answer to the question of which policy and SLA are suited to the data that are required and generated by an application on Linux, let us turn to our hypothetical companies to explore some interesting possibilities for Linux on the mainframe.

14.4.1 ISPCompany data management

ISPCompany, as an ISP and outsourcing partner, is the keeper of the corporate and personal data of a large number of clients. ISPCompany faces the challenge of isolating different clients' data and of catering to a wide spectrum of needs for backup, disaster recovery, and space management.

As the guiding principles for its data management, ISPCompany follows these policies:

ISPCompany data management policies

- The client's privacy is paramount. This applies to all clients.

- Mail on ISPCompany mail servers is managed uniformly for all ISP mail customers.

- Clients of ISPCompany's outsourcing services have a choice of multiple service levels for each of the following: backup and restore, disaster recovery, and storage.

ISPCompany maintains two geographically distant sites, each with a zSeries machine. Our discussion focuses on the primary site, where ISPCompany manages a total of 14 terabytes of data. The primary site is illustrated in Figure 14-7. By far, most of the data is client data (Web content, mail, applications, and various business data). A much smaller amount is ISPCompany's own data. This includes its production capital (master copies of its z/VM and Linux operating systems, configuration files, the middleware and applications it offers to clients, and the Linux images it uses to manage itself). The rest is ISPCompany's business data (accounts receivable, payable, in-house developed code, the log files it uses for accounting, and other minor proprietary items).

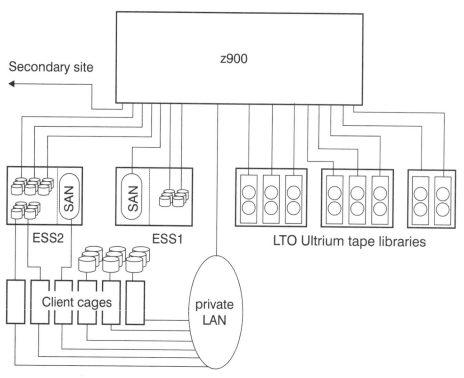

Figure 14-7. ISPCompany storage devices and connections at its primary site

ISPCompany devices

As illustrated in Figure 14-7, ISPCompany uses two IBM TotalStorage Enterprise Storage Server (ESS),[34] ESS1 and ESS2, to store 14 terabytes of data at its primary site. Approximately 8 terabytes reside on ESS1 with 6 terabytes on ESS2. Each ESS has about 500 gigabytes of empty disk space. There is redundancy for all critical parts (such as control units) to eliminate single points of failure.

To cope with the massive amount of data for archiving and backup and restore purposes, three IBM TotalStorage LTO Ultrium tape libraries are available.

Each ESS is divided into two sections: one that acts as a SAN and another with direct-attached virtual 3390 disk devices. The SAN on ESS1 is owned by the mail servers. Only

---

[34] At the time of writing of this book, a single ESS can be fitted with a maximum capacity of 55.9 terabytes.

the mail servers and a trusted ISPCompany Linux image that handles backups can access this SAN.

The SAN on ESS2 provides storage for a client of ISPCompany's outsourcing section. The client has made special arrangements with ISPCompany to be able to experiment with a SAN. No one but this client's images have access to the SAN. All further security aspects are left to the discretion of the client.

Some clients of the outsourcing section have their own devices that are accommodated in their respective client cages. Clients can also include in their contract the ability to attach to devices in the ESS2.

ISPCompany data security

ISPCompany has to meet the challenge of protecting its many clients from each other, while assuring that all clients have access to their own data. To isolate data for medium and large client accounts, ISPCompany uses dedicated disks that can be accessed only from the owners' Linux images.

ISPCompany uses z/VM as the place from which to do the physical data security management. No client has access to z/VM. This means that accounts which control their own Linux images cannot boot them directly. Instead, such clients send a message to a z/VM tool. The tool checks if the request originates from an authorized source. If so, the tool performs the requested IPL and logs it for auditing purposes.

The thousands of e-mail accounts do not get pre-allocated dedicated disk space. These customers access their data through the mail server instead of directly. ISPCompany uses the mail server's security to protect the data.

In keeping with its privacy policy for client data, ISPCompany logs each occasion in which an ISPCompany employee accesses client data. Accessing client data is permissible only when necessary for debugging and is mostly restricted to viewing diagnostic data. Breach of these rules is seen as serious enough by ISPCompany to warrant dismissal.

ISPCompany data sharing

The large accounts in the outsourcing business have their data on dedicated disks that can be accessed only by a client's own images. ISPCompany's tools see only disks and partitions, not file systems and files, unless the tools actually log in to the client's image.

Medium-sized accounts in the outsourcing business use standard Linux images and share (read-only) the respective disk with Linux code libraries. The same rules apply to some of the standard applications. The unique data of these accounts are kept on dedicated disks.

ISPCompany backup and restore

The clients of ISPCompany's outsourcing services have an enormous amount of data to back up. To minimize disruptions to these clients' businesses and stay within acceptable backup windows, ISPCompany uses a carefully devised scheme:

- Full backups are taken only at agreed times when minimal impact is expected for a particular client.

- Incremental backups are taken at more frequent intervals. Linux provides this capability for the changed files in Linux file systems, for example, through GNU-tar.

- Peer-to-Peer Remote Copy reduces the backup window for the most critical data to almost nothing and protects against outages due to device failure. Peer-to-Peer Remote Copy is an IBM TotalStorage Enterprise Storage Server advanced feature.

- Fast backups to disk are used as a first backup level. zSeries hardware with its enormous number of directly attachable devices makes this a viable option. These backups to disks provide an interim backup until the subsequent slower backup to tape.

ISPCompany divides the data into three regions, each attended to by an IBM Tivoli Storage Manager on a Linux image. Agents on the clients' Linux images determine which files to back up. Each manager schedules and coordinates the different backup operations across the ISPCompany clients within its region. To cope with the workload—backups for the three regions—ISPCompany usually performs backups simultaneously.

The mail server's data are backed up only to protect the mail that has not been replicated to the users' mail clients. The responsibility for backing up mail that has been replicated to a user client is transferred to the user. Backups are taken every day and kept for a month.

The medium and large business accounts can directly request a restore from the responsible Tivoli Storage Manager. The manager performs an authentication and an authority check to determine if a request is legitimate before it routes the request to the tape library.

ISPCompany data handling for disaster recovery

Every month, ISPCompany uses a z/VM tool, *DASD Dump/Restore (DDR)*, to dump to tape all of the data that it has earmarked for disaster recovery. The tape device is a high-speed IBM LTO Ultrium. DDR is invoked from a REXX script on z/VM, where the script defines which disks are to be copied. Incremental backups of the disaster recovery data are taken daily. Because these increments do not map to complete devices, DDR is not used.

After the data are written to tape, the tapes are removed and sent to the second ISPCompany site for safekeeping. The secondary site acts as a recovery site. Disaster recovery tapes are exchanged between the sites so that each site keeps the recovery tapes of the other site.

Each z900 has an idle LPAR that is ready to be IPLed with a z/VM system laid out on disks. At the expense of a mere three 3390 devices' worth of storage for the z/VM system data and with no extra hardware, a z/VM for the most essential ISPCompany and client Linux images has been deployed, ready for IPL, at the recovery site.

Resumption of full services depends on the scale of the disaster. Resumption also involves special agreements for fast delivery of replacement machines and devices to a contracted site.

ISPCompany database management

ISPCompany uses DB2 databases, both for its own purposes and on behalf of its clients. ISPCompany performs backup for all databases that it controls. It uses Tivoli Storage Manager to drive the backups. Clients who have opted to manage their databases themselves can schedule these activities from their Linux images (for example, using the cron daemon).

ISPCompany space quotas

ISPCompany can control disk space usage at the image level and at the Linux user level.

At the image level, ISPCompany uses z/VM disk storage virtualization as a means of providing storage to clients who use the company's outsourcing facilities. A Linux image under z/VM is given access to the amount of storage agreed to in the respective SLA. Space can be allocated as full disks or as z/VM minidisks.

To limit the storage of individual Linux users, the Linux kernel can be installed with a quota function. Most of the Linux images which ISPCompany provides to its clients and the Linux images which ISPCompany maintains for its ISP clients use the Linux quota facility.

14.4.2 StoreCompany data management

StoreCompany has been running its department store chain with the support of a z/OS Parallel Sysplex at each of its major sites. At the site we are going to examine, StoreCompany had been using hundreds of 3390 disks for storing its data. StoreCompany has also recently purchased an IBM TotalStorage Enterprise Storage Server (ESS) with a capacity of 1.25 terabytes.

The challenge for StoreCompany is to experiment with its new Linux project without endangering the integrity of its corporate data. StoreCompany responds to this challenge (and largely sidesteps the overhead for managing data for its new Linux project) by adopting a policy that uses existing procedures and tools.

> **StoreCompany data management policy**
>
> A Linux image owns no critical business data. All business data remain under the ownership of a z/OS image, and no alterations are made to managing these data.

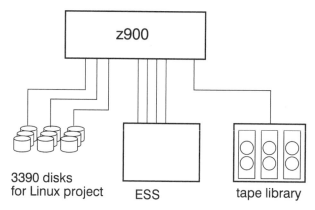

Figure 14-8. StoreCompany storage devices

StoreCompany devices

StoreCompany has approximately 900 gigabytes of data, most of which is owned by its z/OS sysplex. There is enough spare capacity for operations, plus some room for future expansion. Besides the ESS, there are the older 3390 disks and a tape library for backup and restore (Figure 14-8).

StoreCompany keeps the z/OS data on the ESS. To conveniently provide a separate space for the new Linux project, StoreCompany places the system data for these Linux images and the local data for the new Linux application on some of the spare 3390s.

StoreCompany data integrity

Through its policy that the new Linux application must not be responsible for business data, StoreCompany eliminates any new risk of losing data. The application on Linux does not generate new data. The application can feed data back to the online sales application on z/OS only through the existing order entry process and, hence, is protected by the existing order entry's management of these data. If the new application fails, no data are lost. In the worst-case scenario, an order does not make it to the sales application and would have to be re-entered by the end user.

StoreCompany data sharing

Store inventory and client accounts data are located in the z/OS DB2 and are shared across the sysplex. Linux accesses (shares) these data only through interaction with applications that run on the sysplex, using connectors to CICS and DB2.

StoreCompany backup and restore

Because the new Linux images own no business data, the impact on the existing StoreCompany backup and restore processes is minimal.

The 3390 disks with Linux system data and the new application are backed up at the file level as part of the scheduled weekly Linux backup. As the need arises, important intermittent changes to configuration files or the application are handled by the Linux development team and are backed up with the help of the tar and ftp commands to a remote system.

The new application requests a data extract from the corporate data warehouse once a week. The query is performed by the database manager on z/OS. The extract is written to a separate tablespace on z/OS and is then sent to the Linux image by ftp. If the data get lost or damaged on the Linux side, it can easily be restored from the original on z/OS.

StoreCompany disaster recovery

StoreCompany covers its disaster recovery needs by maintaining a similar infrastructure at both its two major sites, including similar sysplexes and storage devices.

The Linux project is not part of the immediate disaster recovery plan, but could be recreated from the backups that are compressed with tar and then transmitted to a remote system with ftp.

14.5 Database management

In the context of an application, backups must present consistent records across all of the data repositories that are used by the application. For example, a transaction must either be reflected in all of the affected data repositories or in none. This can be ensured by driving the backup from the application and relying on the intelligence of the application, or by quiescing the application and all associated data repositories during the backup.

General-purpose backup tools usually provide backup capability at the volume level or at the file level. For example, FlashCopy for Enterprise Storage Server, with a subsequent copy to tape, can back up a volume from z/VM, or a Tivoli Storage Manager agent can back up single files in a file system. Both the storage manager and the agent can reside on a Linux image. To the agent, a database looks just like any file. However, taking a full backup of a database is time-consuming and, if taken at close intervals, can also be wasteful of storage space.

Industry standard databases come with tools or APIs, or both, to facilitate data backup and recovery. These tools and APIs can be integrated with standard backup/recovery storage management products to support a rich set of backup/recovery storage services for relational database data. For example, DB2 has an API for incremental backups at the tablespace level. DB2 also includes a backup utility for non-disruptive DB2 backup that is integrated as a Tivoli Storage Manager client. Hence, you can run both full backups and incremental non-disruptive backups from Tivoli Storage Manager on a Linux image's databases.

A UNIX application that is to be consolidated on Linux on the mainframe might include databases on UNIX. For an application that has been set up properly, it can be assumed that a management solution for full and possibly incremental backups of the database is in place. When porting the application to Linux, it can be useful to port the entire application, including the database, in one stride. However, depending on your priorities and goals, different scenarios are conceivable. For example, you can migrate the application only and use a connector (for example, IBM DB2 Connect) to connect to an existing database on UNIX.

14.6 Performance tuning and capacity planning

Performance tuning aims to alleviate imbalances in system resources where one resource is underutilized because of constraints introduced by other resources. This section discusses I/O as one of the resources to be balanced. Although the diagnostics that reveal I/O shortcomings belong to the performance management discipline, I/O is discussed here because any corrective measures are usually the responsibility of the data administrator. For a more general discussion, see Chapter 15, "Performance and Capacity Planning."

In the mainframe tradition, the CPU is regarded as the most important part of the system, which must be kept busy whenever work is to be done. The mainframe's I/O subsystem has, therefore, evolved to live up to this demand. On the mainframe, providing paths is inexpensive compared to adding memory or processor capacity, and a skilled mainframe system architect will tend to deliberately overconfigure I/O.

It is also common practice to provide redundant data paths to ensure availability in case a path fails. A welcome side effect of multipathing is an improvement in the average response time for I/O. At the customary path utilization,[35] the probability of finding multiple paths occupied simultaneously is low. z/VM manages the available paths to provide more effective bandwidth to the Linux images. Multipathing can also compensate for a possible performance degradation that might result when multiple images share data.

For newly established systems, you should not need to worry about I/O bottlenecks that are rooted in your system layout. For example, if you consolidate a server farm on a zSeries machine, you will have an idea of the required bandwidth for different components, and multipathing gives you the means of removing bottlenecks you might have had in the server farm.

However, I/O bottlenecks can develop if the load profile of a system changes over time, for example, as you add new Linux images. You will have to discern trend lines on the utilization of your I/O resources. Both z/VM and Linux provide the means to gather the required data. Which operating system is more useful depends on the scope of what you want to assess.

z/VM is better suited for getting summary data on all of the Linux images that run under it, or for summary data for an entire image. From Linux, you can gather data on the absolute I/O usage of individual Linux users in the image, which might be required for accounting purposes. Where a breakdown for individual users is not required but, for example,

---

[35] 20% utilization is a common rate.

summary data on an application that runs on the Linux image is of interest, z/VM provides the simpler means of getting the data.

Linux allows you to gather the performance data that you expect from UNIX. In particular, you can use the iostat facility (see Chapter 25, "Systems Management Tools") to gather I/O data for the scope of a particular Linux image. However, while a Linux image can give you useful data for the resources that are dedicated to it, its limited view of shared virtualized resources can be misleading. For example, Linux might indicate a low utilization for a channel path that is actually heavily used by other images.

z/VM is designed to pool and allocate resources. To do so efficiently, z/VM gathers performance data at the virtual and real hardware levels for devices and channel paths. Without incurring a great performance penalty, you can write these data to a log stream for analysis. Getting a comprehensive report on all of the systems in a distributed server farm would require some special software and probably even hardware. A typical Linux-on-the-mainframe environment already includes z/VM with its diagnostic capabilities.

Moreover, z/VM provides the means to take corrective action. Not only can you identify potential bottlenecks, you also can re-allocate resources to alleviate them. For example, you can dedicate a path to a particular image that suffers I/O delays. You can do this from a z/VM terminal without having to go to the machine room to physically make changes to the cabling and even without having to restart any Linux images.

14.7 Summary

Linux on the mainframe can use all supported mainframe devices, such as IBM TotalStorage Enterprise Storage Server (ESS), or the more traditional 3390. Also, support for fiber SCSI over an FCP link will allow Linux images to reach SCSI devices that are common in the UNIX world.

At the end of 2002, it became possible to use SANs in the context of Linux on the mainframe. However, until current security and management issues are resolved, the use of SANs should be restricted to constrained environments.

The mainframe with its channel paths allows an enormous number of directly attached devices. Because your Linux images run in the same physical machine, you can share physical access paths. The large number of configurable paths also provides for multiple channel paths leading to the same device. Multipathing can increase availability and bandwidth.

Although physical connections might be in place, a Linux image cannot access a device unless the mainframe's hardware definition and z/VM definitions permit it. z/VM definitions can be changed dynamically without the need to restart any images or to change any cabling on the machine floor.

Chapter 15.
Performance and Capacity Planning

The decision to run a particular set of work on the mainframe entails many factors, one of which is the performance of the environment. Part of the value you can get from the Linux-on-the-mainframe environment is the efficiency of the mainframe to support the diverse workload of a server hardware consolidation environment. Since we expect the majority of the Linux-on-the-mainframe deployments to be on z/VM, this chapter focuses on performance and capacity planning in this environment.

Sometimes, performance and capacity planning on a physical server farm means watching for response time problems. When response times reach the limit of acceptability, one solution might be to split the workload and buy a new machine, complete with more CPU, memory, I/O, and cables.

Linux on the mainframe allows you to rethink your methods for performance and capacity planning. The tasks included in the performance and capacity planning discipline are listed in Figure 15-1. Tools are available on the mainframe for these tasks, both with z/VM and the Linux mainframe distributions.

Data collection
Software tuning
Hardware tuning
Data visualization
Capacity modeling/planning

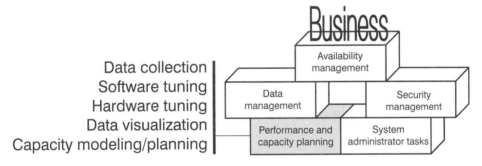

Figure 15-1. What performance covers

For the simpler Linux-on-the-mainframe start-up projects such as domain name server (DNS) or static Web page serving, the focus is primarily on getting familiar with the Linux-on-the-mainframe environment. Performance issues will typically be of secondary importance in a server farm environment. When consolidating servers on the mainframe, planning for performance enables you to make efficient use of the mainframe resources. For more complex projects, for example, a business intelligence application like StoreCompany's OaK (Appendix B, "StoreCompany"), you might want to put in the necessary effort when you set up your system to ensure that you meet your performance goals.

The tools and techniques that performance experts need are readily available, and z/VM gives you great flexibility in achieving performance objectives.

In this chapter, we explore the following questions about Linux on the mainframe:

- How are performance data collected?
- How are hardware tuning and software tuning performed?
- How is capacity planning performed?
- What is unique about performance in this environment?

15.1 Day-to-day performance

Performance tuning aims to satisfy service level agreements that reflect users' requirements pertaining to performance.

A key advantage of running Linux on the mainframe is the decades of experience developing the right knobs and meters for performance tuning. These well-documented knobs and meters are equally valuable for providing the insight for performance tuning in the new server consolidation Linux-on-the-mainframe world. The knobs are the parameters that the analyst changes and the meters are the reports by which the analyst can observe the effects of the parameter changes. These knobs and meters are realized with the various performance management tools.

Performance measurement and tuning are costly. Why would you do it, and when is a good time to do it? In a server farm environment, when the cost of purchasing a new system is often less than the cost of measurement, it might not be necessary to take any measurements. However, in a Linux-on-the-mainframe environment, it might be a good idea for the following reasons:

- To maintain and demonstrate compliance with the service level agreements.

  Where there are service level agreements, performance monitoring becomes essential to ensure that the agreements are met and service does not degrade over time. For example, StoreCompany might decide to monitor the new OaK application to learn what to expect on resource consumption with its first application.

- To prevent surprise resource shortages and to plan capacity for the future.

  If changes in your workload cause over-utilization of a real resource, it might indicate that the application does not scale and needs to be modified. Under these circumstances, routinely monitoring performance and gathering historical data are essential tasks if you are to anticipate problems and deal with them before they reach crisis proportions. For example, StoreCompany might decide to monitor the new OaK application to gather the data during the beta phase and use that understanding to project the resources required if OaK matures.

- To ensure that adequate resources are kept in reserve. Reserve resources are needed to handle the various peaks of the guests or even the introduction of new workloads.

  Like ISPCompany, if your installation has several different clients, you might want to monitor each server to ensure that resources are not wasted in the local Linux image (and hence are not consuming unneeded resources in z/VM). Or you might want to measure only the aggregate use across all of a client's servers to ensure that the SLA is being met. ISPCompany wants to closely monitor resources because it gets market share by charging lower fees than the competition for similar levels of service. To maximize profits, it is important to optimize the use of assets, whether human or machine.

For these and other reasons, a mainframe installation requires both real-time monitoring and analysis as well as a structured methodology for capacity planning. z/VM has the built-in tools to monitor and collect performance data and other data that you can use for billing, input to capacity planning, analyzing bottlenecks, and tuning purposes.

See Chapter 26, "Performance Reference," for more details about the available tools.

15.1.1 Performance metrics

Many metrics are used for performance tuning and capacity planning. The following metrics are easily available with Linux on the mainframe and might help you to manage your SLA in accordance with agreement:

Response time
> This is a measure of the time taken to perform a certain task, such as running a specific job. Response time is related to external throughput rate (ETR).

CPU utilization
> This is a measure of how busy the processor is over any given period of time, for example, 24 hours. To obtain maximum return on investment, it is usual to purchase a system whose capacity matches the requirements as closely as possible plus whatever near-term growth is expected during this budget cycle. CPU utilization is a factor in the internal throughput rate (ITR).

Memory utilization
> This is a measure of how the real memory and the individual guest virtual memory are used, and is typically derived from page usage rates.

I/O utilization

I/O utilization covers two areas: the utilization rates of paths and devices and the amount of disk space currently in use. High I/O rates are usually symptomatic of a fixable problem. For a discussion of I/O aspects of performance, see 14.6, "Performance tuning and capacity planning."

Interactive users

The number of users that are supported in a unit of time. One use of this number is to cap the number of users allowed to be logged into the systems at the same time in order to guarantee an agreed-to ETR.

Consistency

Erratic system behavior can cause considerable user dissatisfaction. Thus consistency of response time, I/O service time, and so forth are important considerations for most installations.

Throughput

This is work that is done per unit time, and you can measure it in different ways:

- External Throughput Rate (ETR) can be defined as work completed per second. For example, a Web server serving 30 pages per second can be said to have an ETR of 30 pages per second.

- Internal Throughput Rate (ITR) can be defined as units of work completed per unit of processor busy time. For example, if a Web server serves 30 pages per second and thereby shows the CPU as 50% busy, then its ITR is 60 pages per second.

If you are trying to understand the experience of your end user, you look at the ETR. If you are planning capacity, or looking at rehosting an application, you would look at ITR numbers. You might also want to have the supporting data that show how CPU, memory, and I/O utilization influence throughput.

15.1.2 Data collection

Gathering the right amount of data has always been a key challenge to any service provider. With Linux on the mainframe, one of the "knobs" that can be adjusted is the set of data to be captured and logged. Data collection provides the facts that many decisions in performance management rely on. Collected data are used in the following activities:

- Tuning

- Visualization of the data

- Debugging of performance problems

- Capacity planning

Data collection typically presents two questions for administrators: what data to collect and how much data to collect. Each question can impact the running of the environment unfavorably.

Collecting data costs machine cycles, extra I/O operations, and disk and tape space. The only thing worse that not collecting performance data is collecting too much. With Linux on the mainframe, there are two places where you can collect data: within each Linux image itself and in z/VM. The least expensive place to collect data, from a resources and management view, is z/VM because it already has significant data on each guest.

The typical Linux image is running only one function. So whether you gather usage data, such as memory or CPU behavior, from the Linux image itself or from the virtual machine, the information is effectively the same and will give a correct picture for most cases. Thus z/VM provides the "meters" for resource consumption. z/VM also has immediately available the "knobs" for making adjustments to either the runtime image itself for immediate effect or the guest definitions to take effect at later boots.

In a typical server farm environment, you might set up the performance tool to have clients in each application server and a separate server for the performance tool itself. The clients run in each Linux image, thus adding to the workload of that image. The client is responsible for forwarding data to the server for logging and other uses. Alternatively, the client or operating system image does its own local logging.

Using z/VM as your primary performance data collecting tool, you avoid adding a performance tool client in every image. z/VM allows you to monitor the performance and collect data for each guest (Figure 15-2). The measurement does not add to the load of the guest, and thus you get more correct data about the load of the guest when you use z/VM. You also save the additional LAN traffic out of each of the guests.

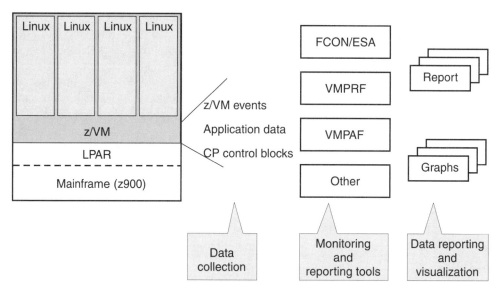

Figure 15-2. Data collection in a Linux-on-the-mainframe environment with the help of z/VM

VM has been enhanced over the years to support, manage, and monitor hundreds, even thousands, of guests. VM tools available for data collection and monitoring include the *VM Performance Reporting Facility (VMPRF)*, *VM RealTime Monitor (RTM)*, and the *VM/ESA Full Screen Operator Console and Graphical Real Time Performance Monitor (FCON/ESA)*. For short descriptions of these tools, see 26.3.3, "Monitoring tools."

If there is a need to monitor performance or collect data inside the Linux guest, you can still use Linux tools, as described in 26.3, "Performance tools."

15.1.3 Hardware tuning and software tuning

Hardware and software tuning is about extracting even more value from the Linux-on-the-mainframe consolidated environment.

Hardware tuning in a Linux-on-the-mainframe environment means tuning the virtual hardware on which the Linux images reside. This tuning mainly consists of giving the Linux images the virtual resources they need, such as a larger CPU share or more memory. This type of tuning is more flexible than tuning real hardware, because there is no need to take the machine down, for example, to add more memory to an image.

A benefit of collecting data in z/VM is that the means for adjusting the resources are also in z/VM. Were you to collect data in Linux itself, some analysis would have to take place to correctly remap that data into z/VM terms.

Figure 15-3 shows performance monitoring and tuning schematically. The monitoring tool moves the data to a log stream. The log stream, depending upon current settings, provides the data to any registered "listener" and to a file for permanent record. Report applications can be run off the real-time stream, but most often read the log file. Visualization most often looks at the real-time stream. Automation tools subscribe to the log stream for some of their data. Reporting applications create the user reports. A system administrator can change parameters depending on the data.

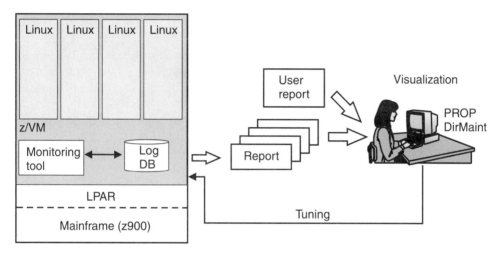

Figure 15-3. Performance tuning

While hardware tuning gets you better use of resources, by fine tuning z/VM you might get even more effective resource use out of the virtual hardware, for example, allow for more guests. Software tuning in a Linux-on-the-mainframe environment can generally be summarized as: first do standard z/VM tuning, then do standard Linux tuning. z/VM presents the architecture very effectively to the guest. In general, this means the guest does not need to know that it is running on virtual hardware.

Only if you have done standard tuning and want to improve performance further should you look at the potential interactions between guest tuning and virtualization tuning. The best starting area for analysis would be where the same ideas and techniques are used by both z/VM and Linux, such as paging and memory usage or I/O buffering. Consider data buffering as an example. What part of the system owns which buffer and how the various buffers interact is important to system tuning. In Linux on the mainframe, you can specify the buffer management to be at a layer closer to the data store, and that saves Linux and its applications from having to be specifically configured to manage I/O performance.

Using z/VM tools (a preferred tool is DirMaint), a system administrator can make changes to the virtual hardware configuration in a matter of minutes, validate solutions, and visualize results.

For some tuning tips for this environment, refer to 26.1, "Tuning Linux guests under VM."

15.1.4 Data visualization

Performance data lend themselves to presentation schemes varying from the simple red-green status displays of health monitors to some very complex graphing. Graphic displays often make it easier to get insight than when reading a table of numbers. System administrators will probably want to use visualization tools to analyze real-time performance problems as well as to review collected data.

Tools from the Open Source community, IBM, and other vendors provide the real-time visualization capabilities that allow a skilled administrator to track down the root cause of a performance problem. And with z/VM the analyst could even make dynamic changes to a given guest's environment to attempt an immediate "repair."

15.2 Relative capacity and capacity planning

Capacity planning is the process of estimating the computer resources necessary to meet IT needs, not just for now, but also in the future when the business expands.

With a Linux-on-the-mainframe environment, you will want to do capacity planning to ensure that new business projects do not get ahead of implementation capabilities. If you are looking to use Linux on the mainframe to introduce IT changes faster for your business than you have in the past, you may need to enhance the frequency with which you do capacity planning. A benefit from the Linux-on-the-mainframe environment is that the raw data you need to do capacity planning can be captured by z/VM and used as input to your (or your consultant's) capacity planning model.

For example, StoreCompany has a new workload that it is adding to its system. It asks, "What will happen to the production system if OaK goes well and we get 500 hits a day and 75 purchases? Is it possible to get by with just adding more disks? Or is more memory or more CPU needed?" Acceptable response times are a key measurement that StoreCompany considers for its Web application. What if the regular catalog response time went from 0.5 seconds to 0.75 seconds? This is the kind of information that will help StoreCompany justify buying additional capacity sooner than planned.

Capacity planning is often done through modeling. The models help in identifying the key system interactions that impact throughput and capacity. As with any model, there are a number of variables that you can manipulate. With z/VM it is quite easy to obtain the input data, even for the most detailed models.

15.2.1 What makes mainframe performance different?

Real throughput in a system depends on many factors; the primary ones are processor power (processor design and clock speed), scheduling capability, and internal bandwidth for memory and I/O. Therefore, the capacity of two systems can be effectively compared only by taking all these factors into account.

If you ask a performance expert, "What is performance?" you might get the answer, "It depends." The mainframe approach to performance is, in a sense, based on efficient use of its resources. The mainframe aims to make sure there is the right balance of resources (CPU, memory, and I/O) needed for the type of work typically done by businesses.

In a balanced system, all computer resources (CPU, storage, I/O, operating system) work together without workloads causing a bottleneck or conflict for any one resource. Such a system accomplishes more than just being simply busy. It provides service to all its users within the required response time and meets throughput objectives, even when the business grows or when unexpected load conditions arise. A balanced system optimizes system capacity and achieves the best performance and throughput in accordance with the goals that were set (for example, throughput, response times, number of users).

Figure 15-4 and Figure 15-5 show a graphical representation of the balance concept for a given workload. In the figures, the CPU's axis is related to CPU speed times the number of CPUs per system. Bandwidth is a measure of data rate from all sources to memory, both CPU and I/O. Scheduler capability is the ability of the operating system to schedule work in a way that utilizes the system resources in the most efficient manner (with the objective of avoiding conflicts and bottlenecks).

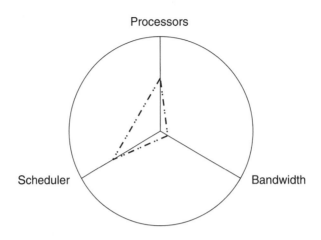

— ·· — Non-IBM vendor: 16-way machine

Figure 15-4. Servers optimized for different workloads

Figure 15-4 shows an example of a server optimized for many users who do not process much data. This might be a support center with many people who accept calls and must be able to work on the problems when they come in. Only a small number are active at a time. The system in the figure is balanced for this workload; however, this workload is not typical for a commercial system.

What happens to a small Web server run by StoreCompany if the number of users increases from tens to hundreds? For example, let us say you need to support static Web serving at 60,000 hits during an eight-hour working day. That is 125 hits per second involving numerous I/O operations if all the users want to look up books or CDs on a catalog. An increase in CPU does not automatically mean an increase in bandwidth, as is shown Figure 15-4. A mainframe traditionally has been extended in all dimensions, as is shown in Figure 15-5.

The mainframe CPU, memory hierarchy, and I/O are primarily designed for resource sharing. That does not mean that one design is right and the other is wrong. What is undeniable is the fact that they are different, and this is what creates difficulty in assessing relative capacity. If, for example, you used a benchmark of one single user running a C program with very little I/O to compare the mainframe with other machines, the mainframe would not fare well. This is because such a benchmark does not make use of the memory hierarchy, the I/O structure, the context switching capability, or the work scheduling capabilities of the mainframe. Relative system capacity is heavily dependent upon the workload. IBM measures performance on the mainframe with the use of special workloads designed to represent real, commercial workloads of different types.

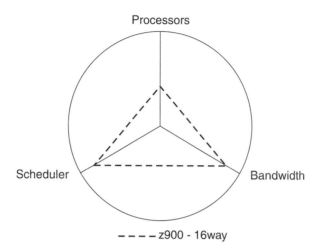

Figure 15-5. The mainframe is balanced for commercial workloads

Conceptually, the way performance is measured on the mainframe is similar to how it is done on other platforms: Data are collected, logged, and analyzed. However, the workload used for measuring performance is different from other platforms because of the long mainframe history. It may be useful to you to know something about how the IBM laboratories measure and publish the results of mainframe performance measurements, not least when you need to compare the capabilities of two processors. You need to have numbers that represent the aspects of the new processors that your work will use—not the typical MHz-type rating that is always available.

How you define performance depends on what kind of workload you run (for example, whether you have many interactive users or more batch-like workloads). The IBM mainframe performance group has defined a family of workloads that emulates varied, real-world workloads. Throughput measurements done with these workloads are known as *Large Systems Performance Ratio (LSPR)* measurements.

One common mainframe processor performance measurement is internal throughput rate (ITR). Why the ITR and not the external throughput rate (ETR)? ETR depends on factors external to the processors, such as the network configuration. These factors vary depending on company setup. However, when deciding on the better machine to purchase, the focus is on the performance contribution of the machine, that is, its ITR.

Reliable mainframe performance for varied workloads is due to the balanced design of the internal bus bandwidth, I/O, processor speed, context switching, and scheduling capability. You can track how well your Linux-on-the-mainframe environment is working for you by gathering statistics for ITR and ETR calculations. By creating your own ITR and ETR numbers for your workload and comparing them with IBM's suite of workloads, you might find some combination of IBM workloads that have characteristics similar to yours. With that information, you can better predict how your workloads might behave on a new machine.

An LSPR ITR ratio for comparing two IBM mainframe processors is obtained by dividing the ITR for one processor running a certain workload with the ITR of another processor running the same workload. IBM labs started measuring these ratios with the IBM Model 158 in 1972. For more details including a list of the workloads, see *Large Systems Performance Reference for IBM zSeries and S/390*
(http://www.ibm.com/servers/eserver/zseries/lspr/).

15.3 Summary

Linux on the mainframe provides an excellent opportunity for hosting many mixed work-loads due to its balanced design of CPU, memory, and I/O bandwidth. The design balance will help you meet the expectations of the end users of these differing workloads, as codi-fied in the SLAs. Should you wish to tune, find anomalies in application behavior, or plan capacity for the future, you can do so relatively easily.

In a Linux-on-the-mainframe environment using z/VM, abundant data are available for anal-ysis. z/VM also provides tools for tuning. There are tools for gathering and analyzing data.

Since z/VM functions as the means to adjust guest resources and is a good data gatherer and analyzer, in many cases no further interpretation of the data is needed. The collected data are in a format that directly corresponds to the means of resource adjustment. While it is possible to build an entire performance management scheme entirely out of the z/VM environment, there is no need to limit yourself to that approach. There are many tools avail-able from both software vendors and the Open Source community, so that any company can feel at home in doing Linux-on-the-mainframe performance management.

The mainframe has a different architecture and design from most other computer systems. Its resources, CPU, memory hierarchy, and I/O are primarily designed for resource sharing in mixed workload environments.

Chapter 16.
System Administrator Tasks

This chapter covers administration tasks that require the skill of a senior system administrator. These tasks (see Figure 16-1) are usually difficult to automate or cast into well-defined procedures that can be blindly followed by a less skilled colleague. Some tasks (for example, debugging and troubleshooting) defy automation because they deal with the unexpected. Others, such as system design, are performed too infrequently for an automated approach, or require the judgment of a human.

This is not to say that tools cannot be employed. We will give some attention to tools that can assist the system administrator in a Linux-on-the-mainframe environment.

The system administrator is instrumental for turning the potential of Linux on the mainframe into profitable operations.

With Linux on the mainframe being a new option, where do you obtain the required Linux and z/VM skill? Linux skill is abundant among young professionals, and Linux on the mainframe has the same feel as any Linux. Because Linux is UNIX-like, a good UNIX administrator will also feel reasonably at home with Linux.

An administrator with a UNIX or Linux background who works with Linux on the mainframe will face the challenges of handling the mainframe hardware, working with z/VM, the potentially large number of Linux images, and possibly, organizationally fitting into an existing mainframe shop with established structures and procedures.

A Linux system administrator needs skill for the hardware platform where the Linux instances are running. For Linux on the mainframe, the hardware is virtual, and the required hardware skill is z/VM skill. While the key z/VM concepts and the z/VM command language may be new for many administrators, they are by no means difficult to learn. In this chapter, we will point out sources of information on z/VM training.

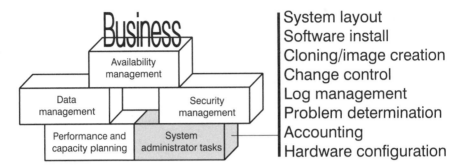

Figure 16-1. System administrator tasks

Usually, an IT division that works with a zSeries machine is large. We are probably talking about a team responsible for the systems administration, not a single person. In 5.1, "Building a team," we discussed the mix of skills you require for Linux on the mainframe. When we talk about the system administrator, we mean the team leader or representative as a personification of the combined skill of the team.

In this chapter, we will explore questions such as:

- Which roles does the system administrator have for a Linux project?
- What does Linux mean for change management?
- How can you keep track of hundreds of Linux images without dozens of administrators?
- Why do tools for the system administrator require special consideration?

16.1 Expanding the system administrator's role in your organization

Linux on the mainframe will change your IT environment, and you will have to acquire new skill, either by training or by hiring. Both the requirements of the changed environment and the changed roles of staff members will change the balances within your IT team. The early adopters of Linux on the mainframe stress that success hinges on a well-functioning systems administration team who's members are ready to learn while implementing the projects. This section summarizes some points that have turned out to be crucial to success.

IT infrastructures in commercial enterprises justify their existence by supporting the company's business goals and opportunities. As organizational divisions, they have deliverables—probably services—that they provide. System administrators have to balance the business demands on an IT infrastructure with the technical possibilities that this infrastructure can offer. To perform this bridging function, the administrator needs an insight into both worlds.

It is important that lead system administrators are prepared to look beyond their purely technical passions and take an interest in the business objectives of their companies. They are in the best position to understand the implications that a business strategy has for IT and can understand the costs and trade-offs that a decision might mean for IT. It is the system administrator who must translate the policies into suitable procedures (see 12.4, "Procedures") and implements or leads the implementation of these procedures. This role makes the system administrator a key member of your decision-making team.

System administrators are specialists in their field and usually take pride in their skill. A business manager who interferes with the technical decisions of a system administrator is as likely to cause offense as a patient is who tells his medical doctor what cure to prescribe. As a patient, you have to trust in your doctor's judgment and give up some control over yourself. Similarly, for the working relationship to be fruitful, the business manager must have confidence in the professional capabilities of the system administrator.

This confidence in the administrator must translate into freedom to make technical decisions. Problems can be avoided if the expectations of what the IT division is to deliver and the constraints within which the system administrator must operate are clearly communicated. The customary language for this communication is policy and SLA. For individuals who have been cooperating well for some time, this formal communication is less important than for new teams or projects, such as Linux on the mainframe, where the working relationship might have to be negotiated.

On the technical side, a good Linux administrator takes an interest in the activities of the Open Source community. Staying in touch with new developments is essential in this very dynamic field. Permitting or encouraging a Linux administrator's involvement in the Open Source community is the equivalent of permitting or encouraging an administrator to attend courses or join user groups for other operating systems. An active member of the Open Source community is likely to be more resourceful as a Linux administrator.

In the tradition of Open Source, participation is centered on communication through the Internet. The main expense is probably the administrator's time invested with much lower travel expenses and course fees than you might expect for active involvement with other operating systems.

16.2 Change management

Companies that intend to survive in today's rapidly changing world must constantly adapt to these changes. It is important to remember that unregulated change can be just as disastrous as a reluctance or refusal to undergo change. Controlled change is a change toward a well-defined destination, with a clear idea of the cost and risks involved. In a Linux-on-the-mainframe environment with numerous Linux images and possibly traditional operating systems all on one machine, there are both challenges and opportunities for change management. In this section, we describe in some detail our hypothetical companies' change management strategies to represent the diverse successful approaches to change management in real-world Linux-on-the-mainframe environments.

Our StoreCompany example (see 16.2.1, "StoreCompany change management policies") shows how Linux images can be used to isolate risks in a mainframe environment. Risk isolation provides the opportunity for rapid deployment of new applications and projects. This does not mean that all Linux projects depend on rapid change for value. You obviously do not need to apply the same change management policy to all of your Linux images, especially those images associated with high risk.

We use the examples of ISPCompany and StoreCompany to illustrate which policies can govern change in different environments. We will see that both companies apply the most conservative rules and restraints to changing assets that are associated with the greatest overall risk, while applying less stringent rules to assets that are not associated with great risk.

The reasons for making changes fall into three broad categories, which are often covered by separate policies:

- Some changes introduce new functions. These changes can open up new opportunities for your business.

- Some changes fix or prevent problems. These changes are also referred to as *maintenance.*

- Security patches, because of their sensitivity, are usually treated as a third category. (See 8.6, "Keeping up to date on security issues," for sources of information on current security issues.)

    After a security patch has been applied to an image, you have to verify that your image is still hardened to the extent that you intended. 8.3, "Before opening the doors: hardening," addresses this issue and also includes a brief discussion of security patch policies.

16.2.1 StoreCompany change management policies

StoreCompany is using Linux as an opportunity to rethink its conservative change management policies. StoreCompany's aim is to facilitate fast deployment of new applications where this opens up significant business opportunities.

StoreCompany has a set of change management policies that is typical for mainframe shops. These policies have served well by keeping individual system outages to an absolute minimum in their sysplex environment.

Existing StoreCompany change management policies

- There are no planned sysplex-wide IPLs. No more than one production z/OS image is ever changed at a time.

- All changes follow the IT division's production change management rules:
  - The proposal goes to the change management review board for initial approval and scheduling.
  - An interim review is held when the impact is assessed, and the schedules are built.
  - A final review follows after stress test results are completed, including the entire install and back-out process validation tests.
  - The change is scheduled for the next change window, which minimizes the risk of interacting with other changes going in at the same time.

- After three months of successful execution on one image, the change is eligible to be moved to the other z/OS images in the sysplex.

- The change management review board meets once a month.

These change management policies have also impeded the speed at which new concepts can mature into changed operations. To overcome this obstacle, StoreCompany is experimenting with a set of Linux images that it provides to the business manager in charge of exploring new opportunities. At the same time, StoreCompany introduces a set of policies that permits fast deployment of Linux-based projects.

```
┌── New StoreCompany change management policies for Linux projects ──────────┐
│                                                                            │
│   •  The base IT organization makes weekly backups, but the team members can install │
│      changes and boot their own Linux images on whatever schedule they need — pro- │
│      vided that any such outages do not create a negative customer impression of the │
│      overall e-business.                                                    │
│                                                                            │
│   •  New workloads should not require changes to the z/OS images or procedures │
│      unless absolutely necessary. All such changes will have to be scheduled and must │
│      follow the IT division's production change management rules.           │
│                                                                            │
│   •  When a Linux image project has proven successful and is to be owned by the IT │
│      Division's production control, normal change management rules will be followed. │
│                                                                            │
└────────────────────────────────────────────────────────────────────────────┘
```

The last of the new StoreCompany policies constitutes a concession toward the established ways. The policy limits the fast path to only the experimental phase of a project. StoreCompany intends to review this policy when the approach of isolating new applications and processing in Linux images has proven successful. A policy that permanently opens the fast path for Linux images would provide a space for projects that are not only quickly deployable, but also can be rapidly adapted to a changing market when the need arises.

In contrast to a z/OS image that is designed to efficiently run multiple applications concurrently, a Linux image typically runs a single application. This limits to an extent the scope of failures that might occur. However, more constraints are needed to contain the potential damage that a malfunctioning Linux application could do. StoreCompany makes the applicability of the new policies conditional on the following constraints:

- The Linux image must not own corporate data.

- No two Linux-based functions may run in the same Linux image.

- IBM WebSphere Application Server must be used as the basic programming model. Where possible, functions running on z/OS are exploited by Linux.

The first constraint ensures that applications on the Linux image do not endanger the integrity of corporate data. The second constraint isolates functions and applications within a Linux image and thus eliminates the risk of a failing function or application damaging an unrelated capability.

The last constraint is not a means of risk isolation; instead, it demands adherence to the corporate object-oriented data model. It saves costs by ensuring that existing skill is applied and that successful projects can later be integrated into the production environment without the overhead of a complex port. See B.3, "Programming model and middleware platform."

The combination of Linux technology, constraints, and policies provides a safe arena for experimentation. StoreCompany envisions benefits beyond this isolated experiment. Establishing a group that generates revenue by bypassing the old established policies puts these old policies into question, but it does not overthrow them. After all, the old policies have proven useful for a long time. It does, however, open up the discussion of where the established policies are helpful and where they do not further the business, but endanger it by preventing useful and profitable changes. With Linux, you can introduce an advocate for change that brings new ideas into an IT organization with established ways.

16.2.2 ISPCompany change management policies

Linux, per se, does not require change management policies that are conducive to rapid and frequent change. Change is not an end in itself and still only belongs where the expected benefits outweigh the associated risks. ISPCompany has a well-established ISP business section that operates satisfactorily and currently sees no advantage in making changes to the services it offers. The main concerns of the ISP section are to maintain availability for its customers and to continue generating revenue. Consequently, the ISP section follows a conservative change management scheme that allows fast changes only where inaction might endanger the availability of its services.

ISPCompany change management policies for the ISP section

- Security exposure fixes that impact the delivery of mail service will be applied as soon as they are verified. If possible, the fix should be applied within 24 hours of being released.

- Changes to introduce new function in the system that are to be featured in marketing or save us costs in providing the service (for example, changes to improve availability) follow the normal review cycle and become candidates during the quarterly update window.

- Everything else will be considered if there is an unused time slot in the quarterly change window.

As shown in this example, Linux can be used in a tightly controlled environment. Of course, ISPCompany cannot expect Linux to deliver benefits from fast deployment if it applies policies that impede change. Here, it uses Linux not as an agent for change, but as a low-cost and stable operating system that is suited to the task at hand.

In ISPCompany's outsourcing section, the readiness to change means a competitive advantage because it enables ISPCompany to offer new technologies and functions faster to its clients. ISPCompany maintains a small number of *golden* Linux images that it replicates when clients request a standard Linux image. While changes to a golden image affect a large number of clients, changes applied to a custom-made image have a narrow scope, usually only a single client. The damage that could result from a harmful change to a golden image is so widespread that ISPCompany applies stringent controls to any changes.

Tight controls that involve lengthy procedures are neither possible nor necessary for the customized images offered to clients with special requirements. Lengthy change procedures would nullify the flexibility that is the essence of this business opportunity. The small scope of the change makes assessing the likelihood of problems and the associated potential losses easier than it is for the golden images. Here, the rules can be more relaxed.

ISPCompany change management policies for the outsourcing section

- Controlling our costs in providing "standard" service is crucial. Limit the number of golden copies for the "standard" systems to five.

- Excluding the category of changes for security exposures, a golden image's code libraries and parameter settings will be changed only once a year, in the summer.

- Other changes to golden images must be reviewed by the change board and systems fully load tested for at least a month before being cut over to production.

- For those clients with special system contracts, all changes will be managed according to the terms specified in the contract, including at a minimum, final sign-off by both the client and our client satisfaction team.

For the golden images, ISPCompany strikes a balance between the benefits and the risks that are implied in a change. The custom-made images and the contexts to which they are applied by clients are too diverse for a generic benefit/risk assessment. Instead, the policy stipulates that an agreement on how to handle change must be part of the contract with the client. A risk assessment is then conducted for each individual case.

Linux can be managed to be rigid or flexible. ISPCompany applies Linux to a full spectrum of risk scenarios and corresponding change management. The same IT staff that handles the fast deployment end of the spectrum also handles the tightly controlled images. Whatever the software risks, the mainframe adds improved availability and makes the overall risk of outages lower and easier to assess.

16.3 Tasks that are unique to Linux on the mainframe

The mainframe environment offers a number of opportunities to the system administrator for becoming more efficient in dealing with numerous Linux images, thus lowering operational costs.

16.3.1 System layout

In a Linux-on-the-mainframe environment, the system administrator might have to manage hundreds of Linux images. One way of making this multitude manageable is to curb the variety by using a small number of standard images, as ISPCompany does. The aim is to cover most needs with these standard images and have as few as possible unique images for special purposes. While standard images also can be used in distributed server farms, they are particularly advantageous in a Linux-on-the-mainframe environment.

When creating a new image from a standard image, the binaries from the golden image typically are copied over. With Linux on the mainframe, you can share code for standard images more directly.

Linux allows you to map parts of its file systems to individual disks, and z/VM can provide these disks in the form of read-only shareable z/VM minidisks. Because Linux images on the mainframe can share disks, instances of the same standard image can actually use the same physical file system, or parts of it, for their kernel and application code. Considering the multitude of images, code sharing can amount to substantial disk storage savings.

Code sharing requires careful planning from the outset. There are always data that make an image unique and, therefore, not all files can be shared. Code sharing puts some constraints on how freely you can make alterations to the derived images. The system administrator needs to judge what is the most advantageous strategy for sharing code in an individual installation.

For the system administrator, code sharing can simplify maintaining the Linux images that share the code. In a distributed environment with no disk sharing, a code fix has to be applied to every instance of a standard image. If disks are shared and a fix is applied to a shared file system, all images that share the file systems inherit the fix.

Code changes are usually applied to a copy of the shared code. An image then can pick up the change by being booted from the changed copy. This approach saves you from having to simultaneously take down all Linux images that share the code. The penalty is that you have to keep track of which Linux image runs from which copy.

While booting a Linux image, there is a lot of I/O from the system disks. If a disk is shared by many images, booting the images might have to be spaced over some time to avoid contention. If time is critical, more than a single disk might be desirable. Typically, there would be at least two copies of the shared system libraries on disk, with one disk as a backup and a further copy on tape.

Sharing code allows rapid creation of a new instance of a standard image. All that is needed for a new Linux image is a new guest definition in the z/VM directory. Only a small amount of data that includes the image's unique parameters (for example, TCP/IP parameters) needs to be copied for the new image.

ISPCompany, for example, physically shares most of the code for each of its standard images. Each standard image is used by tens of clients. To quickly create a new image for a client, ISPCompany uses a scripted procedure that makes the required entry in the z/VM directory, points to the shared file system, inserts the unique parameters on the image-specific disks, and starts the new image.

16.3.2 Handling a diversity of Linux images

Using standard images can reduce the number of diverse Linux images that system administrators have to manage. Even with z/VM, for large server farms, it can be a challenge to keep track of which golden image is running where, and there are always a number of images with special requirements. Does attending to these Linux images mean a proportional growth in the number of system administrators, each specializing in a number of variations of Linux images? The answer is no, but you will probably need tools to make your system administrator more productive in change management tasks.

Depending on your requirements, there might not be a single tool that covers your tasks sufficiently. We will use an example to show how a combination of two tools can allow a company to implement a robust Linux change management that supports both central control and image owner control. Aduva and Linuxcare are two young companies that are pioneering Linux change management and already offer products. Each represents a different approach to software change management.

Linuxcare is based on a push model where the system administrator uses a central control point to apply common changes to groups of similar images. The push model puts the responsibility for changes into the hands of its most skilled staff.

Aduva uses a pull model where image owners can decide when to apply specific changes to their individual images. The pull model gives a degree of freedom and responsibility to image owners.

Aduva approach

Aduva assumes that a primary challenge of putting together a Linux image is handling the dependencies among the Linux components. Aduva provides a central OnStage server and an OnStage agent on each of the controlled Linux images. The OnStage server has a software component repository and an associated knowledge database (KnowledgeBase). The software component repository contains certified software modules, and the knowledge database describes the dependencies between these modules. Users interact with OnStage either from the OnStage agent or through an OnStage console. Environments where the OnStage server is remote from the Linux images have an OnStage local rules lab that has the local rules and interacts with the remote OnStage server (Figure 16-2).

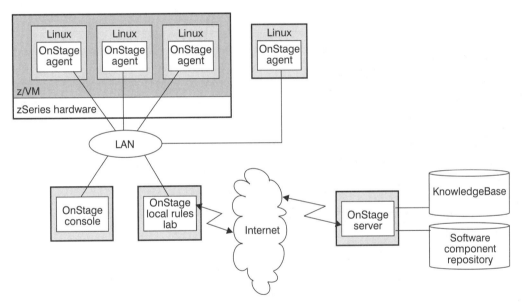

Figure 16-2. OnStage structure

The OnStage agent is the component that adds, changes, or removes software components of a Linux image. It communicates with the OnStage server to draw on the information in the knowledge database and assesses what a modification means for the other components on the Linux image, that is, which other components must be upgraded, downgraded, installed, and so on, to support the proposed modification.

Changes can be initiated from the OnStage console or an OnStage agent. From the manager, the system administrator can enforce changes (for example, apply security fixes) for a set of Linux images. From an OnStage agent, the owner of a Linux image can request changes for that particular image. The content of the OnStage component repository gives the image owner a well-defined degree of freedom to make changes.

See http://www.aduva.com/ for more information on Aduva OnStage.

Linuxcare approach

Linuxcare Levanta uses a golden image model in which a customized Linux image is built and thoroughly tested before it is to be copied to locations where it is needed. Fixes or additions are first applied to a copy of the golden image and tested. When the tests are successful, the change is propagated to all images that descend from the particular golden image.

The Levanta components run on a z/VM that also contains the managed Linux images. The central component is the Linuxcare Configuration Manager (LCM). LCM communicates with an agent, the Linuxcare Instance Manager (LIM), that runs on each managed Linux image. A file server gives the LCM write access to each image's system disks. A CP agent plugs into z/VM, for example, to boot Linux instances, or to create or make changes to the directory entries of the Linux guests (Figure 16-3).

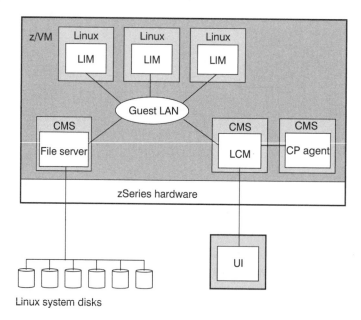

Figure 16-3. Levanta structure

In the Linuxcare model, all changes to the Linux images are made by the system administrator who ensures that each change is first tested. The administrator interacts with the LCM from a Linux, CMS, or Web-based user interface.

See `http://www.linuxcare.com/products/index.epl` for more information on Linuxcare Levanta.

A mixed approach

The two approaches can be complementary. The Linuxcare model focuses on scenarios where the risk of putting a malfunctioning Linux image into production must be minimized. The Aduva model caters to scenarios where a degree of control and responsibility for changes is delegated to image owners who are not highly experienced Linux administrators.

A company might want to manage both risk scenarios with tools. It is possible to combine both approaches and use Linuxcare Levanta to manage a set of well-tested standard images as a stable basis for further customization, which can be performed by the IT staff or the image owner using the OnStage agent and console. The IT staff can control the list of OnStage-managed components that is available to the image owners, and it is at the discretion of the IT division which amount of customization is permissible before renewed testing and management through Levanta are required.

Figure 16-4 illustrates how OnStage and Levanta can interleave.

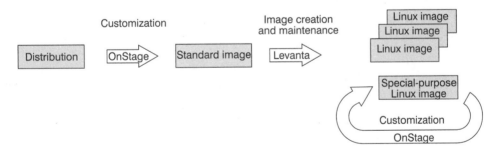

Figure 16-4. Using both OnStage and Levanta

An initial standard image is created with the help of OnStage. OnStage could also be used to upgrade an existing standard image even to the extent of migrating to a new release of a distribution. The standard image is then tested and verified by the IT division. When testing is completed, Levanta is used to deploy and maintain multiple copies of the standard image. Individual Linux images that need to be adapted for special purposes can then be further customized with OnStage by either the IT division or the individual image owners.

ISPCompany change management practices

Within its outsourcing section, ISPCompany has different business segments with different needs. ISPCompany uses both OnStage and Levanta.

The majority of ISPCompany's outsourcing clients use the standard images under a standard contract. ISPCompany uses Levanta to build, distribute, and maintain clones of these standard images. Clients with special needs can either have full control of and responsibility for their image, or they can have ISPCompany experts build the images according to their specification and have it maintained under a special SLA.

ISPCompany uses the Aduva model to cater to clients who want some control of their Linux images without losing ISPCompany maintenance support. The OnStage software component repository defines a set of program packages that clients can use to modify their own images. Changes made through OnStage are covered within the support contract.

StoreCompany change management practices

StoreCompany's IT division provides a number of Linux images to various departments. It uses OnStage and Levanta in combination to optimize its change management.

Because the requirements of the various departments differ significantly, the standard image approach is not applicable. Instead of creating a standard image, the IT division uses Levanta to build a Linux image that constitutes the greatest common denominator of all requirements and provides these images to the departments. The departments can then build on the tested foundation of the Levanta-built image and make their alterations from an OnStage software component repository.

The expertise of the IT division is used for building the basic system and for defining the possible alterations through the OnStage software component repository. The IT division delegates making small, relatively safe alterations to the image owners. This saves time for the image owners as they can apply the changes without first consulting the IT division. It also saves time for the system administrators because they do not have to attend to every change in individual images.

StoreCompany uses OnStage and Levanta as tools that provide the means to safely delegate workload from the system administrator to others with less systems management skill.

16.3.3 Accounting

Depending on your accounting objectives, Linux on the mainframe offers different accounting points and opportunities to accomplish the task. There are two basic reasons why you might want to do accounting: cost recovery or behavior modification. There are tools for Linux on the mainframe to accomplish either.

For cost recovery, you typically provide an infrastructure that can cope with a workload with the terms laid down in an SLA. Billing is then based on the costs associated with the provided resources: hardware cost, floor space, power, license fees, and so on. In a distributed server farm, billing is usually based on the number and types of the machines provided and the software that runs on them. In a Linux-on-the-mainframe environment, the equivalent of machines would be the number of images and the resources (for example, processing power) that have been allocated to them.

In cost-recovery-driven accounting, billing is based on the resources provided, regardless of how these resources are being used. Accounting done to encourage a change in resource-consumption patterns is usually motivated by a resource shortage and an attempt to discourage usage of this critical resource. For example, if a company is running short of CPU power and there is no budget to acquire more CPU power, an IT division can charge more for CPU usage and, thus, encourage economic use of CPU resources.

If the goal of accounting is behavior modification, you must gather data on the critical resource and on the accounting group (for example, user, user group, or application) that consumes the resource. The accounting point has to be chosen so that the resource consumption can be measured at the granularity of the consuming group. Accounting as an agent for behavior modification is controversial because users tend to find workarounds that lead to other resource shortages. If achieving behavior modification through accounting makes sense in your environment, Linux on the mainframe allows you to do it.

The resource consumption of a Linux application can conveniently be measured from z/VM if the rule of having a single application per Linux image is adhered to and the image is used by only one accounting group.

z/VM cannot measure resource consumption at the level of individual Linux users. For accounting at the user level there are tools you can install on Linux (see 25.5, "System administrator tools").

Accounting can be difficult where an application acts as a server that consumes resources on behalf of different accounting groups. Measurements would then show that the application is using resources but not indicate on behalf of which accounting group. Linux on the mainframe offers a unique solution for this accounting problem. On the mainframe, it is possible to set up a separate Linux image with an instance of the application for each accounting group without having to buy additional hardware. The resources consumed on a zSeries machine by the sum of these instances are not significantly more than the resources used by a single Linux image that does all the work.

16.3.4 Debugging

For its Linux guests, z/VM offers an answer to a well-known dilemma in debugging.

On the one hand, debugging uncovers the underlying reasons for system failures and thus provides the basis for corrective action to avoid similar failures. On the other hand, the demands on availability in many production environments simply do not allow for real-time debugging or even for taking a dump. Immediate reIPLs are often the rule, and this means loss of the data for debugging.

z/VM offers the opportunity for hot standbys as backup images that consume almost no resources. On failure, a failover to the backup image occurs. The failed image remains in place and can now be analyzed without impacting the downtime as seen by the user.

Part of the system administrator's work is calling maintenance personnel (vendor support) with problems. Techniques for finding the root of problems are described in Chapter 22, "Debugging and Dump Analysis."

16.4 Tools policies

The tools for the system administrator tasks are unique in some aspects. Thus, you might want to create policies for these tools that are different from the policies you apply to other disciplines.

16.4.1 Tools strategy

In an environment with a large number of images to be managed, disciplines such as data management or availability management are hardly conceivable without tooling. Where many administrators are frequently impacted, you can easily calculate the cost benefits of using tools, and a budget for buying tools is easily justifiable.

Tools for the system administrator are used by fewer people and the tools' impact is sometimes much harder to assess. In days of economic constraints, system administrator tools can easily become the target for cuts. Yet these tools can help to avoid costs (for example, of downtime). If there is no explicit agreement for tools, the unspoken assumption by the system administrator is likely to be that there is no tools budget.

Why would you want to buy tools for these tasks? A purchased tool can to some extent limit the freedom of your administrator. An administrator who develops a tool actively defines its scope and procedure. The decision in favor of purchased tools versus in-house developed tools, therefore, is also a decision on how decisive a role the administrator is to play in establishing and enforcing procedures. Be aware that a vendor-supplied tool limits the degree of change that you can apply to the corresponding procedures in the future, even if it matches your needs at a particular moment in time.

Also, a tool is never for free. If you do not pay for purchasing it, you pay with the time of the administrator who develops it. While developing a tool can help to keep up the administrator's programming skills and Open Source contacts, you might not want to afford the time spent away from tasks more directly related to running your installation.

16.4.2 Corporate standards

To the extent that tools implement procedures, they are an embodiment of policies. For example, installing a particular antivirus program on the workstations of a company's employees implements a security policy.

Within your enterprise, Linux on the mainframe is unlikely to operate in isolation. To prevent your administration of Linux on the mainframe from diverging from the rest of your infrastructure in an uncontrolled manner, it is useful to define the boundaries with suitable policies. An important aspect for choosing your Linux-on-the-mainframe tooling is whether it supports your corporate standards and conventions, in other words, whether it operates within the boundaries of your policies.

You might have a corporate security database, for example, an LDAP (Lightweight Directory Access Protocol) directory, for your entire enterprise. A possible requirement for your tools could be that all security-related aspects of the tool are based on the corporate security database.

Another standard could be a corporate data model, for example, an object-oriented model. Requirements for your tools could be that they use an object-oriented approach and that the objects they work with can be integrated into the corporate data model.

When it comes to the system administrator's tools, you might want to relax your rules. If your Linux administrator suggests a tool for an administration task and the tool is not compatible with your policies, this could mean one of two things: either the administrator does not appreciate the existing policies and the tool is really not suitable in the context of your enterprise, or it is an indication that your policies are too tight or undifferentiated.

This is not to suggest that the Linux administrator should be allowed to violate policies at will. Rather, the Linux administrator should be in a position to negotiate the policies. This is especially true where Linux is used to induce change. The relative isolation of the system administrator tasks is a good environment for experimentation with standards. It is a chance to discover new standards that you can later extend to other segments of your enterprise.

16.4.3 Sources for tools

You are not alone. Even if an administration problem is not frequent enough to have sparked a commercially available tool on the marketplace, similar problems are likely to occur in other locations. There are numerous specialist Web sites where Linux programmers exchange ideas, tools, experience, and advice. A good system administrator uses the entire spectrum of these sites.

`http://freshmeat.net/` is a popular site for information on newly available tools. The actual tool projects are available from other sites, for example `http://sourceforge.net/` is a major one.

Almost by definition, Open Source tools have Web sites associated with them. Usually, there is at least one site with the tool code and a discussion site with a mailing list.

16.5 Becoming familiar with the mainframe

Any new hardware needs specific skill. In this respect, zSeries machines are no different from other platforms. Setting up Linux on the mainframe requires zSeries skill and probably also z/VM skill. If you do not have sufficient skill in your IT division, you will have to acquire it. A zSeries machine has too much potential not to invest in optimizing its operations. Your system administrator's mainframe skill is instrumental in this effort.

You can find a roadmap of training courses that are relevant to Linux on the mainframe, z/VM, and zSeries hardware at the IBM Global Services site:
`http://www.ibm.com/services/learning/us/roadmaps/`

For more general information on IBM Global Services training, visit:

- `http://www.ibm.com/services/`
- `http://www.ibm.com/services/learning/`

16.6 Summary

Linux on the mainframe can be a platform for isolating the risks that are associated with changing applications in your production environment. This makes your business more responsive to the market place and allows you to rapidly follow up opportunities that you might otherwise lose. Where rapid deployment is not a part of the business opportunity, Linux can benefit from more conservative change management policies, just like any other platform.

The Linux system administrator requires a clear statement of requirements and constraints. Beyond that, the freedom to operate is a necessity. This works best if the Linux system administrator is a trusted member of the decision-making team.

Tools exist to make the system administrator more efficient in performing many system administrator tasks. Like the tasks themselves, selecting the best tools for a given environment requires skill. Because these tools are subject to special considerations, you might want to apply policies to them that are different from those you apply to general tooling.

Part 5.
Running Applications

This part is intended to give an overview of the many options that Linux on the mainframe provides for setting up server environments. It is of particular interest to system architects.

First, we look at alternatives for obtaining Linux applications and the benefits of running those applications on the mainframe. We then describe what it means to port an application to Linux on the mainframe. Finally, we look at the advantages that the mainframe's internal communication methods provide to consolidated integrated server environments. We describe *connectors*, middleware components that allow you to closely integrate the traditional mainframe operating systems with virtual Linux servers in a heterogeneous environment.

Depending on their point of view, different people use the terms *applications, middleware*, and *tools* with slightly different, often overlapping, meanings.

Sometimes the term *applications* is used exclusively for programs that directly serve an end user. We use applications with a broader meaning that includes middleware and tools. Where we want to differentiate, we use *end user applications*. An application covers all program modules that cooperate to provide a function. Parts of a single application can be spread across multiple operating system images on different machines.

We use *middleware* for software that provides a framework or service that end user applications can exploit to accomplish their tasks. For example, middleware can provide programming interfaces, security, workload management, database services, or administration capabilities.

We use *tools* for programs that help in developing code and maintaining IT infrastructures. For example, tools can be editors, compilers, or programs that facilitate systems management.

Chapter 17.
Deploying Linux Servers

The ease at which Linux applications can be ported to the mainframe has given rise to a rapidly growing number of tools, middleware, and end user applications for Linux on the mainframe.

Because Linux is UNIX-like, it is relatively easy to port software from UNIX operating systems to Linux. Increasingly, software vendors are providing Linux versions of their commercial UNIX applications.

The effort for porting an application from another Linux platform to Linux on the mainframe is generally minor, because Linux is designed to be platform-independent. For a given level, the Linux kernel has almost the identical capabilities and characteristics across all its architectural implementations. The small amount of platform-dependent code is normally not directly invoked by applications and, therefore, is transparent to most of them.

In this chapter, we explore questions such as:

- Where can you find applications for Linux on the mainframe?
- What do suppliers of applications for Linux on the mainframe offer to your enterprise?
- What are the advantages of running application servers on the mainframe?
- What value does Linux give for running applications on the mainframe?

17.1 Where can you find applications for Linux on the mainframe?

It is not difficult to find applications for Linux on the mainframe. Here are some sources:

- Applications that come with your Linux distribution
- Open Source applications that are not shipped by distributors
- Commercial applications from independent software vendors

The following sections cover general considerations for sources of applications. For specific examples of Linux-on-the-mainframe applications, see Chapter 27, "Examples for Applications."

17.1.1 What comes with a distribution?

While some companies might have the skill to build their own Linux systems, most of them turn to commercial Linux distributions as the source for well-defined and stable foundations for their production systems. Distributions for Linux on the mainframe, like all major Linux distributions, contain hundreds of program packages.

The large number of available Linux applications and the broad spectrum of user require-ments make it impossible for a single distribution to serve all needs. Many of the applica-tions included in distributions, therefore, serve general needs that are common to most IT installations, and you are likely to find an interesting set of applications that is useful to you.

All current mainframe distributions include Samba for file and print serving, Sendmail for e-mail services, Apache and Tomcat for Web serving, MySQL as a database server, Network File System (NFS) for file serving, openLDAP for directory access, and openSSL for implementing secure connections.

Typically, distributions also include tools that help you to manage the applications on your Linux system. These tools cover, for example, installation, packaging, problem manage-ment, and version control. In addition, there are some basic utilities such as editors, com-pilers, and debuggers that you might need for porting or developing code on Linux.

A distributor assures the compatibility of the software packages within a distribution. Hence, you do not need to worry about the compatibility of an included application with the Linux kernel and the interoperability of included applications. Applications from your distribution are available on the installation medium. The distribution might also provide service and maintenance support for the applications.

17.1.2 Open Source applications

The Internet offers a spectrum of applications that goes far beyond what any distribution may offer. The following three Web sites are good starting points for finding Open Source applications:

- http://www.linux.org/
- http://sourceforge.net/
- http://freshmeat.net/

With Open Source applications that are not included in a distribution, it is up to you to ensure the compatibility with your base Linux system and any other software you run on it.

Open Source applications are maintained by the Open Source community. Usually, there are no contractual guarantees of service and accountability. Often, this lack of contractual commitments is an inhibitor to businesses for deploying Open Source applications from the Internet in mission-critical functions. In response to that, commercial versions have been provided for some of the Open Source software. For example, for Samba and MySQL there are commercial versions as well as Open Source versions available under the GPL license.

The value of obtaining Open Source applications from the Internet is the great degree of choice and freedom it gives you, including the option to modify the code, and the low cost of acquisition. If you are looking for an application to cover very specific requirements in your installation, you are likely to find Open Source code that you can tailor to your needs.

17.1.3 Commercial applications

Many useful applications for Linux on the mainframe are commercial applications. These applications are usually subject to regular release cycles, which means better predictability in planning your systems.

For information on the commercial IBM software that is available for Linux on the mainframe visit:

```
http://www.ibm.com/software/is/mp/linux/software/
```

IBM maintains a separate site with information on the hundreds of commercial program packages for Linux on the mainframe that are offered by other independent software vendors:

```
http://www.ibm.com/servers/eserver/zseries/solutions/s390da/linuxproduct.html
```

With commercial applications, you incur license fees and you might also incur dependencies on supporting software, specific distributions, and release cycles. What you gain is maintenance and service support for the product.

17.1.4 What if the application you want is not available?

If an existing application you want to run is not available for Linux on the mainframe, you might want to ask its provider if a port is planned in the near future and register your requirement for such a port.

You might also want to check for alternative applications. There might be suitable solutions available that are already supported. Moving applications to Linux on the mainframe is an opportunity to upgrade the technologies you are using. Linux applications generally have a reputation for being up to date on new standards.

You might also have your own proprietary applications that you want to bring to Linux on the mainframe (see Chapter 18, "Porting Applications to Linux on the Mainframe").

17.2 Simple server hardware consolidation

Server hardware consolidation can deliver advantages beyond hardware savings. For example, application servers that run on the mainframe derive advantages from the outstanding Reliability, Availability, and Serviceability (RAS) of the mainframe hardware.

Figure 17-1 illustrates simple consolidation, where discrete servers on multiple machines are mapped to the same number of Linux images on a single mainframe. The z/VM virtualization allows you to run numerous Linux images concurrently.

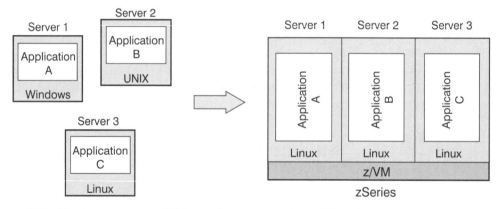

Figure 17-1. Simple server consolidation to the same number of Linux images

The number of installed images remains the same, but you might be able to reduce hardware administration and maintenance costs. You can also bring the images under the control of the mainframe environment's tools.

Virtualization leads to further advantages. Machines that run single applications often have a low average utilization. Applications that run in z/VM guests consume significant resources only when there is work for them to do. Figure 17-2 shows the consolidated servers of Figure 17-1 at a single point in time when the load is different for each application. In the diagrams, the sizes of the boxes indicate the relative resource consumption at a particular time.

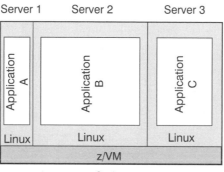

Figure 17-2. Linux images can scale with the work load

In effect, z/VM dynamically scales the Linux images' CPU resources according to their load. This scaling is based on z/VM's virtualization. Adding CPU in a distributed environment involves hardware changes. Scaling the virtual CPU resources in a Linux-on-the-mainframe environment is transparent to the application and does not even require rebooting Linux. The z/VM guest definition determines the range within which this dynamic scaling is possible and permissible.

If you want to make more resources available to an application, you can scale it vertically by changing the respective z/VM guest definition. When you do this, you enable z/VM to assign more resources to it. You can also scale it horizontally by deploying additional Linux images to run more instances of the application. Deployment of new Linux images is very fast, because under z/VM images are logical definitions and can share the already available hardware resources.

What if your mainframe machine runs short of processing power for all the scaling that is going on? There is yet another level of scaling. You can also scale the capacity of a mainframe machine. Visit `http://www.ibm.com/servers/eserver/vertcap.html` for information on the Capacity Upgrade on Demand options.

Server hardware consolidation is likely to be profitable in environments such as that of ISPCompany where there is a large number of servers to be consolidated.

StoreCompany also takes advantage of server hardware consolidation by moving its departmental servers onto the mainframe. For example, it plans to consolidate all its Samba print and file servers on the mainframe. Figure 17-3 illustrates the consolidation scenario.

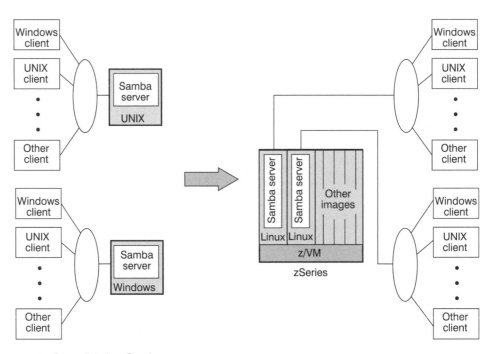

Figure 17-3. Consolidating Samba servers

StoreCompany not only gains flexibility from Linux on the mainframe through consolidation. It also uses Linux to quickly bring additional applications to its mainframe environment, while assuring close integration with applications on the traditional mainframe operating systems. This translates into improved time-to-market for new projects. We look at integrated server environments with Linux applications and applications on traditional mainframe operating systems in Chapter 19, "Building Integrated Server Environments."

Simple server hardware consolidation is an opportunity for implementing a successful Linux-on-the-mainframe project and to realize some savings. It is also an opportunity to gain experience and confidence with Linux on the mainframe and to pave the way for future more complex and profitable projects.

The final answer on whether a hardware consolidation makes sense for a particular environment can be given only after a TCO analysis. It typically examines various options for providing the hardware. For low-utilized infrastructure servers (for example, DNS servers or archive file servers), there might be enough spare capacity on an existing machine. Where significant workload is moved to Linux on the mainframe, you might need extra processing capacity. Often it is advantageous to purchase dedicated IFL features for the migrated workload. See 21.4, "Integrated Facility for Linux (IFL)."

17.3 Summary

There is a wealth of applications and middleware available for Linux on the mainframe, both from Open Source and software vendors. Sometimes a new application is available for Linux on the mainframe before it becomes available for the traditional mainframe operating systems.

Linux can improve your time-to-market for new projects. Application servers running on the mainframe inherit the RAS characteristics of the mainframe hardware and can take advantage of the mainframe's virtualization technology.

In the next chapter, we look at how you can bring existing applications to Linux on the mainframe. In the chapter that follows, we discuss the additional benefits you can get if application servers perform functions that are tightly related to other servers in a consolidated environment.

Chapter 18.
Porting Applications to Linux on the Mainframe

As a general rule, it is easy to port UNIX applications (including Linux applications on other hardware architectures) to Linux on the mainframe. Some software vendors were surprised to discover that their application ran after just recompiling their source.[36] Of course, it is not always that easy. This chapter gives guidance on how to decide if a port is feasible for a particular application.

We address questions such as:

- Why port an application to Linux on the mainframe?
- What is required for porting an application?
- How much effort will the port take?
- Where to get more information?

18.1 What you can gain by porting an application to Linux on the mainframe

As with any project, assessing the Return of Investment for porting an application must balance the expected advantages against the cost. There are two different cases where porting promises to be profitable:

- Porting the application is very simple and means a small investment that can easily be recovered.
- The expected advantages of having the application on Linux on the mainframe are significant enough to justify the required investment.

If your company uses its own proprietary applications in production, it might be able to capitalize on the quality and flexibility of the mainframe hardware. It can also take advantage of zSeries features like virtualization, HiperSockets, the cryptographic facilities, or the 64-bit architecture. It might also be able to use the mainframe's virtual communication methods to achieve a closer integration of the application in an integrated server environment. See Chapter 19, "Building Integrated Server Environments."

---

[36] For a sample of reports on porting experiences, visit `http://www.ibm.com/servers/enable/linux/quotes.html`.

There is a growing demand for Linux applications for the mainframe. If you are a software vendor, having a Linux-on-the-mainframe version of your application can be a decisive competitive advantage. A number of major software vendors already have ported some of their strategic software to Linux on the mainframe.

18.2 Before you decide to port

This section discusses some key considerations for porting applications to Linux on the mainframe. Before choosing an application as a candidate for porting, you need to be aware of the application's dependencies on other software, decide which mainframe architecture to target (31-bit or 64-bit), and determine whether you want to provide support for different distribution levels and distributions.

18.2.1 Third-party dependencies

Whether porting an application is feasible also depends on the context in which the application is to run. The application might depend on supporting software. A port would then imply also porting that software. If the required supporting software is a proprietary application or middleware of a third party, the port becomes dependent on the willingness of that third party to port its software. StoreCompany, for example, required DB2 Connect (see 19.3, "Connectors to back-end systems") for its online sales project.

18.2.2 Distribution dependencies

Companies or software vendors might want to build a distribution-neutral application. The effort for ensuring support by different distributions depends on how strongly the code depends on specifics of a distribution and on how different the distributions are. The additional effort is likely to be restricted to tests for each distribution where the application is intended to run.

18.2.3 31-bit versus 64-bit

Linux on the mainframe applications can be for the 31-bit or for the 64-bit architecture. In keeping with the mainframe principles, zSeries architecture supports all software that ran on its 31-bit predecessor. Applications that are built for 31-bit run on both zSeries and S/390 machines.

If an application requires any new capabilities of the zSeries architecture (for example, 64-bit addressing), it can be built only for 64-bit distributions. It is possible to run 31-bit applications on a 64-bit distribution. However, a 31-bit application cannot use 64-bit shared libraries. All libraries required by the application must be provided in 31-bit format.

18.2.4 Architecture-dependent code

If application code makes implicit or explicit assumptions about the underlying hardware or software platform, the code will probably have to be adapted before it can run on Linux on the mainframe. This section points to some sources where interfaces are documented.

How Linux on the mainframe differs from Linux on other platforms is described in the ELF Application Binary Interface Supplement available on:
`http://www10.software.ibm.com/developerworks/opensource/linux390/index.shtml`.

zSeries assembler code for Linux follows the syntax conventions of the GNU assembler but uses zSeries (S/390) machine code. For reference information on zSeries machine code, see *z/Architecture Principles of Operation*.

Because zSeries is a big endian system application code that processes byte-oriented data that originated on a little endian system may need to be adapted.

For details, refer to

`http://www.ibm.com/servers/esdd/articles/linux_s390/`

and to

`http://www.ibm.com/servers/eserver/zseries/library/techpapers/pdf/gm130115.pdf`.

The effort for handling architecture-dependent code depends on how the application is structured. A well-designed application might have such code in only a few specific modules. In this case, the code sections to be adapted are isolated and easily located.

The architectural differences between the mainframe and other platforms are documented. If it is required, the documentation can be found and accessed on the Internet.

18.3 What effort to expect

The effort for porting an application strongly depends on the language it is written in and the platform it has been written for. It can be very simple, but in the worst case, it can amount to a rewrite.

If an application is entirely written in Java, it will run unchanged on any platform where the required Java environment is available. For applications or modules written in high-level languages that are not compiled at runtime (such as C and C++), a recompile to the zSeries architecture is required. Applications or modules with operating system or hardware dependencies need to be adapted to account for the different interfaces.

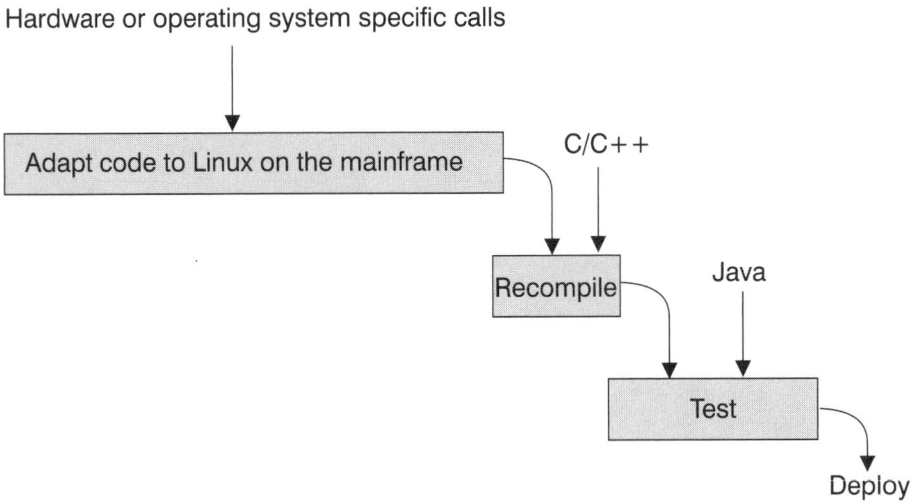

Hardware or operating system specific calls

Adapt code to Linux on the mainframe   C/C++

Recompile   Java

Test

Deploy

Figure 18-1. The effort for porting an application depends on the language in which it is written

In general, the lower the level of the program language and the more platform-specific features that are used by the code, the more porting effort is to be expected (Figure 18-1). In some cases, it can be advisable not to port but instead rewrite in a higher-level portable language, for example, C or Java.

18.4 What you need

This section summarizes which resources you will need for a porting project.

The skills required for porting an application to Linux on the mainframe are common software development skills. Your development team also needs the skills to use the Linux application development tools required to build your application. The standard Linux development tool chain (for example, compilers and editors) is included in the mainframe Linux distributions.

The GNU compiler and binary utilities can be configured to support a cross-compile environment. In cross-compiling, the target platform of the compilation is not the platform where the compilation runs. Application code can be compiled on a PC or low-end server but targeted to the zSeries platform. Many companies do a significant portion of the porting effort on a workstation.

Naturally, the final test of the ported application needs to run in the target mainframe environment. Operating a zSeries test environment requires some zSeries and probably also z/VM skills.

If you already have a mainframe machine, an LPAR or z/VM guest can easily be set up as a test environment. If you do not have a mainframe, you might be able to get assistance from IBM. Visit IBM's Linux Community Development System Web site at `http://www.ibm.com/servers/eserver/zseries/os/linux/lcds/` to find out the terms and conditions for gaining access to IBM mainframes for testing your port.

18.5 Where to get more information

Visit the following site for technical documentation:
`http://www10.software.ibm.com/developerworks/opensource/linux390/index.shtml`.

Visit this site for links to useful tools: `http://www.ibm.com/developerworks/oss/linux/`.

For help, you can also contact one of IBM's porting centers, IBM Global Services, or a distributor.

18.6 Summary

Porting an application from UNIX to Linux can be a small effort, especially for Java or C/C++ applications. The ported application can take advantage of the mainframe hardware. For example, it can use HiperSockets or cryptographic facilities. As we will explore further in the next section, you can also use virtual networks to achieve a close integration with other applications on the same machine.

Most of the porting work can be done in your developers' favorite Linux environment. The final test requires access to the target Linux-on-the-mainframe environment. Given that sufficient resources are available, this means a z/VM test image that can easily be created.

The Linux distributions include much of what you need for porting an application. There are Web sites with tools, documentation, and other resources you might find helpful for porting. There is a possibility for gaining access to a Linux-on-the-mainframe test environment so you do not necessarily need your own mainframe machine to port an application to Linux on the mainframe.

Chapter 19.
Building Integrated Server Environments

Servers often cooperate with other servers in an integrated environment. The foundation for this cooperation is server-to-server communication. In this chapter, we will show how the mainframe not only facilitates communication between the Linux images that run on it, but also provides additional benefits for such integrated environments.

A Linux image can use the mainframe's internal communication methods to communicate with other Linux images or with any traditional operating system images on the same machine. You can, therefore, build e-business environments with the latest Linux application as a middle-tier server and a traditional z/OS or VSE/ESA application as a back-end server.

In this chapter, we address these questions:

- What advantages does inter-image communication offer above the communication between discrete servers?

- How can Linux on the mainframe exploit existing z/OS or VSE/ESA resources?

- How can traditional mainframe operating systems exploit Linux resources?

19.1 Inter-image communications

The communicating applications or application parts can be located within one hardware machine or on separate machines that are connected by physical network components. Your choice of communication methods depends on where the applications to be connected run. Table 19-1 lists some of the more interesting options that are used today:

Table 19-1. Recommended inter-image communications among applications

Applications on different hardware machines	• Gigabit Ethernet
Applications on the same machine but in different LPARs	• HiperSockets
	• Gigabit Ethernet
	• Channel to Channel (CTC)
Applications in guests of the same z/VM	• Guest LAN
	• Virtual CTC

At the time of the writing of this book, Gigabit Ethernet is the mainframe's high-speed LAN adapter for connecting to the outside world (other machines).

The machine's internal LPAR and z/VM-based virtual networks are even faster than Gigabit Ethernet. They work at near memory bus speed and reduce the typical network latency. They replace physical cables with *virtual cables*, which reduces the cost of the external cabling, control panels, switches, routers, and other physical components.

Virtual cables improve security, since they defy physical attacks. This immunity to physical attacks can eliminate the need for data encryption. Virtual cables do not protect from harmful content. Firewalls might still be required.

Guest LAN and Virtual CTC are unique to z/VM and can be used only among guests of the same z/VM. Guest LANs are virtual LANs that can be based on a physical LAN protocol (Gigabit Ethernet) or on the HiperSockets protocol. Apart from these recommended means of communication, applications in guests of the same z/VM can also communicate via LPAR's real HiperSockets, a real CTC, or a physical Gigabit Ethernet connection.

Normally, the communication technology is transparent to an application. This transparency allows you to relocate an application's communication partner without having to change the application.

Figure 19-1 illustrates two scenarios of how a Linux application uses a TCP/IP socket to communicate with an application elsewhere.

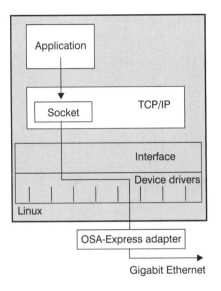
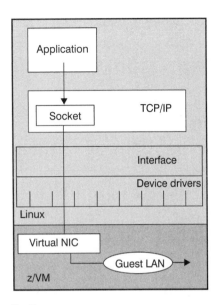

Figure 19-1. Communications are transparent to the application

In the left part of the diagram, the Linux application communicates with a partner on another machine. The Linux configuration assigns the TCP/IP socket to an OSA-Express adapter card, and the communication goes through a Gigabit Ethernet LAN.

In the right part of the diagram, both the Linux application and its communication partner run in guests of the same z/VM. The application talks to the same socket as before. Now the Linux configuration assigns this socket to a virtual Network Interface Card (NIC), and the communication is through a Guest LAN.

19.2 Example for an integrated environment

The following example describes an integrated environment where several servers are functionally interacting. This environment is consolidated onto a single zSeries machine. As part of the consolidation, the functional relationship between the servers with the required inter-server communications is implemented with the virtual communication methods of the zSeries environment.

One of ISPCompany's outsourcing clients has been running four small servers that made up the environment for their static Web serving. The machines were located in one of the cages that ISPCompany maintains for its clients' hardware. When an increasing workload necessitated an upgrade of the client's infrastructure, a TCO analysis showed that with the expected growth rate for the next three years, it was advantageous to rehost the servers in

Linux images on a ISPCompany zSeries machine (Figure 19-2). The TCO considerations also included savings on network components, flexibility due to virtualization, and simplified administration.

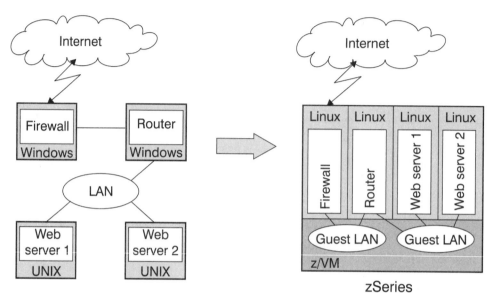

Figure 19-2. Integrated Web-serving environment using z/VM communications

The rehosting is transparent to everyone accessing the Web pages. ISPCompany can easily scale this environment on behalf of its client either horizontally by running more Web server images or vertically by assigning more resources to the existing images.

19.3 Connectors to back-end systems

Connectors are middleware components that simplify moving parts of an integrated environment between platforms and operating systems. This gives you flexibility to set up and restructure heterogeneous environments. Connectors make it easy for an application on one operating system to use a resource that runs remotely on another instance of the same operating system or on a different operating system altogether.

Figure 19-3 shows an application that uses an API (Application Programming Interface) to communicate with a database server on the same operating system instance.

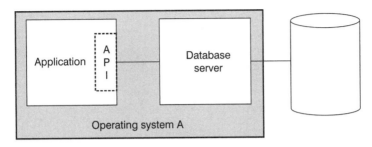

Figure 19-3. Application and database on one operating system

Figure 19-4 shows how a connector permits the database server to be moved to another operating system.

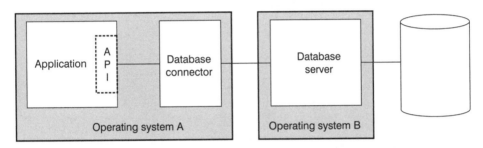

Figure 19-4. Application and database server on separate operating systems

The two operating systems need not be the same. Operating system B could be any operating system that supports the database server, and Operating system A could be any operating system for which there is a connector to that database server. For example, Operating system A could be Linux and Operating system B could be another Linux or a UNIX system with DB2 UDB. Operating system B could also be a traditional mainframe operating system, for example, z/OS with DB2 as the database server. The application is not aware that it is talking through the database connector to the database server.

Connectors handle the complexities of the higher- and lower-level protocols for communicating with the remote resource. To the application, it is transparent that the resource is not running under the same operating system. Connecting to back-end servers is especially attractive when using HiperSockets or Guest LANs.

Many software vendors provide connector technology for their applications, although the term *connector* is not always used. The following sections give an overview of the IBM connectors.

19.3.1 Connector examples

Connectors give you a lot of freedom for the layout of application environments. The following examples all exploit connectors:

- Set up an application in a Linux (Operating system A) image that uses a traditional mainframe operating system (Operating system B) as a back-end.

- Consolidate an integrated server environment in stages, where some resources are moved to the mainframe and other resources temporarily remain on their initial platform.

- Use a Linux system (Operating system B) as a back-end for a traditional mainframe operating system (Operating system A).

Example: Linux with a traditional mainframe operating system

An application on Linux can use a traditional mainframe operating system as a back-end. Figure 19-5 illustrates this possibility.

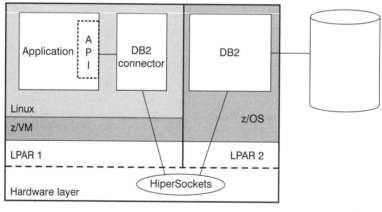

Figure 19-5. Example: Linux application with a database server on z/OS

Connecting to a traditional back-end can be a strategic decision for an integrated environment that draws on the strengths of both Linux and the traditional mainframe operating system. This is essentially the setup that StoreCompany has implemented for its Internet sales project.

Example: Linux with a non-mainframe back-end

Linux on the mainframe can also use a database server on a non-mainframe system. Figure 19-6 illustrates this possibility.

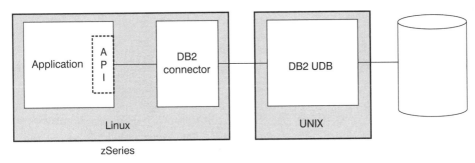

Figure 19-6. Example: Linux application with a database server on UNIX

Using a UNIX back-end with Linux on the mainframe can be an intermediate solution in a staged consolidation where the DB2 UDB database server is migrated later to a Linux image on the mainframe.

Example: Traditional mainframe operating system with a Linux back-end

Linux can be the back-end for an application on a traditional mainframe operating system. Figure 19-7 illustrates this possibility.

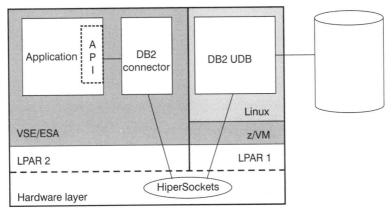

Figure 19-7. Example: Linux as a back-end system for VSE/ESA

If the data is created by an application on the Linux system, it can be advantageous to maintain it on that system.

19.3.2 Java connectors to z/OS and VSE/ESA

There are connectors for different environments, including connectors that connect applications on different Linux images and connectors that are based on languages other than Java.

This section describes some of the connectors that apply to our context of Linux on the mainframe: connectors that connect Java applications on Linux to resources on traditional mainframe operating systems. Because of their portability, Java applications are of particular significance in heterogeneous environments. The Java applications can easily be moved between platforms that support a Java virtual machine, and the connectors provide the integration with other operating systems in the environment.

Table 19-2 summarizes the IBM connectors to mainframe operating systems that can run in Java environments on Linux.

Table 19-2. Connectors to mainframe operating systems

Connector	Connect to
IBM IMS Connector for Java	z/OS
IBM CICS Transaction Gateway	z/OS or VSE
IBM DB2 Connect (JDBC)	z/OS, VSE/ESA, or Linux
IBM WebSphere MQ	z/OS, VSE/ESA, or Linux
VSE/ESA e-business connectors	VSE/ESA

Connectors to z/OS

The connectors to z/OS enable applications on Linux on the mainframe to exploit z/OS resources. Figure 19-8 summarizes the available IBM connectors.

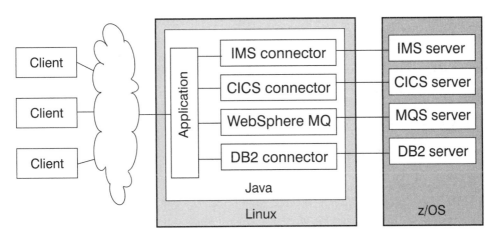

Figure 19-8. Connectors to z/OS

The Linux and z/OS images could be, but do not need to be, on the same machine.

Figure 19-9 illustrates how StoreCompany connects a Linux Web application server to its z/OS DB2 server to implement an online catalog.

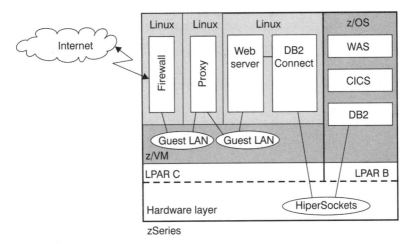

Figure 19-9. StoreCompany example for using a DB2 connector

An online sale would also trigger a communication from the Web application via the CICS connector to a CICS server on z/OS. This communication has been omitted from the diagram.

In a consolidated environment, you can take advantage of the virtual communication methods. For example, on z/VM, you can define multiple separate Guest LANs without having to invest in additional hardware. Figure 19-9 shows two separate Guest LANs.

Connectors to VSE/ESA

Connectors to VSE/ESA enable applications on Linux on the mainframe to exploit VSE/ESA resources, including native VSE/ESA resources, such as VSAM files, the VSE/ESA libraries, or the VSE/ESA spooler (VSE/POWER).

Conversely, applications for Linux on the mainframe enrich existing VSE/ESA environments. VSE/ESA does not provide a Java environment. With Linux on the mainframe, you can run Java-based applications or Java-based application servers, such as the IBM WebSphere Application Server (WAS), in close integration with VSE/ESA applications. Figure 19-10 summarizes the available IBM connectors.

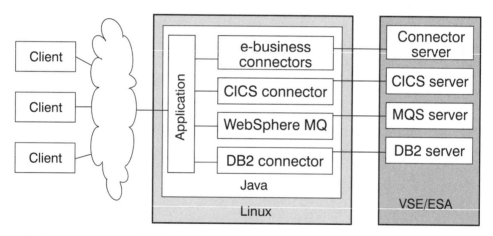

Figure 19-10. Connectors to VSE/ESA

The Linux and VSE/ESA images in Figure 19-10 could be, but do not need to be, on the same machine.

Figure 19-11 shows an example of an integrated server environment where a number of Linux images run on z/VM. The environment includes several firewalls in Linux images and an initial firewall server outside the mainframe. One Linux image runs a WAS that provides dynamic Web content from data in a VSE/ESA VSAM back-end.

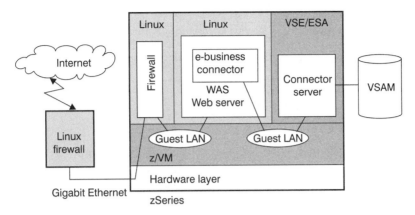

Figure 19-11. Example for using e-business connectors

The Linux images are connected through several Guest LANs that provide point-to-point connections between each firewall and the image drawn adjacent to it. WAS supports an e-business connector that connects to a connector server with access to VSAM on the VSE/ESA back-end.

19.4 Consolidating a 3-tier environment

Integrated server environments are often implemented as 3-tier environments, for example, consisting of (1) Web browsers, (2) Web application servers, and (3) back-end servers. A common physical implementation of such a 3-tier environment is shown in Figure 19-12. The Web browsers run on workstations, the applications servers on UNIX servers, and the back-end server on a mainframe. The examples show VSE/ESA as the traditional mainframe operating system, but it could also be a z/OS system.

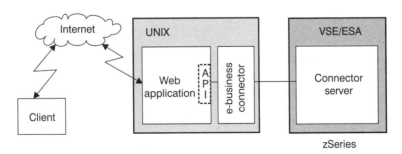

Figure 19-12. 3-tier server environment

Linux on the mainframe allows you to implement a logical 3-tier environment on a physical 2-tier. Figure 19-13 shows how the physically distinct application server has been moved to a Linux image on the mainframe.

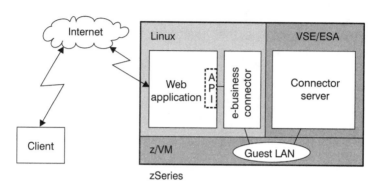

Figure 19-13. Physical 2-tier implementation for a logical 3-tier server environment

This consolidation can provide the benefits of hosting applications on the mainframe. The benefits possibly include cost savings due to reduced hardware acquisition and mainte-nance cost, simplified systems administration, and improved availability. For applications running on the mainframe, you can achieve a better operational integration into existing traditional mainframe application environments. For example, you can bring your Web appli-cations closer to your data via virtual communication methods (HiperSockets or Guest LAN). Virtual communication can improve security and performance.

19.5 Enriching your mainframe environment with new applications

Adding a new application as a middle-tier to an existing mainframe environment can be an attractive proposition for a new business opportunity.

On the mainframe, it is easy to create an additional image for a new application. The mainframe's virtualization technology provides isolation that prevents the new operating system from interfering with the other operating systems on the machine.

Deploying a new application on Linux on the mainframe does not necessarily require addi-tional hardware. The resources needed for starting a project can sometimes be covered by spare mainframe capacity. If a successful project's success requires more resources, its profitability can justify the purchase of the extra capacity.

As seen frequently in our discussion of StoreCompany, it uses this opportunity of easily adding additional images to great advantage for its online sales application and later for its business intelligence application.

19.6 Summary

The mainframe provides virtual inter-image communications that allow you to deploy integrated Linux server environments on a single mainframe machine. In this chapter, we have used mainly examples based on z/VM. For environments with a small number of images, many of the opportunities that we have described for z/VM can also be provided by LPARs and HiperSockets.

Connectors allow applications on Linux images to exploit resources on the traditional mainframe operating systems or vice versa. This means that it is possible to set up a heterogeneous server environment with a middle-tier based on Linux on the mainframe and a z/OS or VSE/ESA back-end.

Conversely, you can set up environments where applications on the traditional mainframe operating systems use Linux back-end servers.

You can implement a logical 3-tier application environment (non-zSeries clients, application servers, and back-end servers) within a physically consolidated 2-tier environment, where only the client is not on zSeries.

Linux on the mainframe can provide a fast deployment platform for new applications. While z/VM and LPAR provide isolation, connectors ease functional integration with an existing traditional mainframe environment.

Part 6.
Reference

In the process of gathering information for the book, we found material too good to not pass on. When we found that adding the detailed explanations of an idea detracted from the flow of a chapter, yet still thought the information was important, we moved that additional material to the reference section. The reference chapters offer additional breadth and depth of technical details and point to some of the key software that is available to your Linux-on-the-mainframe solution, including applications, middleware, systems management, and performance tools.

Each subsection in the reference chapters can be considered a separate topic that does not necessarily fit in any particular way with the other topics. Unless stated otherwise, the architecture discussed is the 64-bit z/Architecture.

Chapter 20.
Linux-on-the-Mainframe Reference

This chapter provides additional detail about Linux on the mainframe, including:

- Linux distributions for the mainframe

- An overview of the Linux directory structure

- A discussion of the differences between Linux on the mainframe and Linux on other platforms

- A list of available device drivers

20.1 Linux distributions for the mainframe

At the time of writing, there were three distributions available for Linux on the mainframe from distributors Red Hat, SuSE, and Turbolinux, as shown in Table 20-1.

Table 20-1. Mainframe Linux distributions

Distributor	Version	Web site
Red Hat, Inc.	• Red Hat Linux 7.1 for zSeries (64-bit) • Red Hat Linux 7.2 for S/390 (31-bit)	http://www.redhat.com/
SuSE Linux AG	• SuSE Linux Enterprise Server (SLES) 7 for S/390 and zSeries (31-bit) • SLES 7 for IBM zSeries (64-bit) • SLES 8 powered by UnitedLinux	http://www.suse.com/
Turbolinux, Inc.	Turbolinux 6.5 for zSeries and S/390	http://www.turbolinux.com/

In May 2002, Connectiva S. A., the SCO group, SuSE Linux AG, and Turbolinux, Inc., created an initiative called UnitedLinux. This initiative will work to streamline Linux development and certification around a global, uniform distribution of Linux designed for business.

The initiative hopes that UnitedLinux will address enterprise customers' need for a standard, business-focused Linux distribution that is certified to work across hardware and software platforms, accelerating the adoption of Linux in the enterprise. Under the terms of the agreement, the four companies will collaborate on the development of one common core Linux operating environment, called *UnitedLinux software*. The four companies will each bundle value-added products and services with the UnitedLinux operating system, and the resulting offering will be marketed and sold by each of the four partners under their own brands.

UnitedLinux is available for the mainframe through SuSE SLES 8 Powered by UnitedLinux.

For more information, white paper, and strategy documents about UnitedLinux, see `http://www.unitedlinux.com/`.

20.2 Overview of Linux directory structure

Earlier in the book, we talked about disk sharing using read-only files. Table 20-2 contains a more complete directory listing. Directories where content could potentially be read-only shared are marked in gray.

Note: Directory structures vary with distribution.

Table 20-2 (Page 1 of 2). Typical Linux directory structure

Directory	Description
/	Referred to as the "root" directory. The root directory normally contains all other directories. When a directory structure is displayed as a tree, the root directory is at the top. It is generally considered a bad idea to store single files in this directory.
/bin, /usr/bin	Contains many important Linux commands such as the shells (ash, bash, and csh) and essential utilities such as grep, gzip, ping, and su. /usr/bin generally contains applications for system users. The distribution of programs between /bin and /usr/bin depends on the distribution.
/boot	Contains information needed at boot time, such as the Linux kernel.
/dev	Contains device definitions. In Linux, devices are treated as a file. Files in /dev/ serve as gateways to physical computer components such as a printer, modem hard disk, and so forth. Even your terminal is treated as a device file. A popular device is /dev/null, which is useful for sending output to be deleted.
/etc	Contains the configuration files for the Linux system. Most of these are text files and therefore are easy to edit. Although Linux distributions ship with configuration tools, editing the files manually in /etc is often necessary.

Table 20-2 (Page 2 of 2). Typical Linux directory structure

Directory	Description
/home	The top-level directory for users' home directories. For each user there is a separate directory within /home. If your user name is JOHN your home directory will be /home/john. You can always return to your home directory by typing "cd" at the shell prompt.
/lib	Contains shared libraries for programs that are dynamically linked.
/lost+found	Where Linux keeps any files it restores after a system crash or when a partition has not been unmounted before a system shutdown. It provides a means of recovering files that otherwise would have been lost.
/opt	Contains additional software. /opt is home for many large packages such as StarOffice, KDE, and Oracle.
/proc	Contains the process file system. /proc contains all the "virtual files" representing different aspects of your system such as your CPU, RAM, and so forth.
/sbin	Contains programs that are reserved for the superuser and are needed to start the system.
/sbin/init.d	Contains scripts used to start the system. These scripts are executed directly or indirectly by /sbin/init, the father of all processes.
/tmp	Contains temporary files. Many applications use this directory to hold some information.
/usr	Contains user commands and applications. Also their source code, pictures, and documentation. /usr can be the largest directory on a Linux system. It can be useful to have this directory in a separate partition.
/var	Contains files that change constantly when the system is running, such as log files and mail spools.

20.3 Exploiting mainframe processor architecture

A unique feature of the mainframe is its processor architecture.

On the mainframe, you can address up to 2G in the 31-bit architecture. This is less than on other architectures. However, you do not have the kernel included in the user address space as you might have on other architectures (see Figure 20-1).

The separation of the kernel from the user space results in additional security for the kernel. It is impossible for the user to access the kernel address space other than by system calls.

282   **20.3 Exploiting mainframe processor architecture**

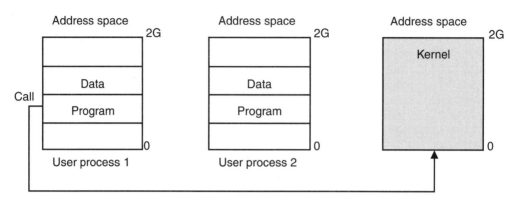

Figure 20-1. On the mainframe architecture, with 31-bit addressing, the kernel is in its own address space

20.4 Linux-on-the-mainframe device drivers

Earlier in the book, we mentioned the I/O subsystem and the fact that you can attach a variety of devices to Linux on the mainframe. This section details how the Linux I/O approach was accommodated on the mainframe as well as lists the various device drivers available. For more detailed descriptions of the device drivers, see the *Device Drivers and Installation Commands* book from IBM.[37]

20.4.1 Common I/O layer

Linux was originally designed for the Intel-based PC architecture, which uses two cascaded programmable interrupt controllers (PIC) that allow a maximum of 15 different interrupt lines. All devices attached to that type of system share those 15 interrupt levels (or IRQs). In addition, the bus systems (ISA, MCA, EISA, PCI, and so forth) might allow shared interrupts, different polling methods, or DMA processing.

Unlike most other hardware designs, the mainframe implements a channel subsystem that provides a unified view of the devices attached to the system (Figure 20-2). Although a large variety of peripheral attachments are defined for the mainframe architecture, they are all accessed in the same manner using I/O interrupts. Each device attached to the system is uniquely identified by a subchannel, and the mainframe architecture allows up to 64 K (65,536) devices to be attached.

---

[37] Available from `http://www.ibm.com/developerworks/opensource/linux390/index.shtml`

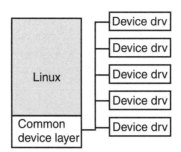

Figure 20-2. Linux device uses the common I/O layer to connect to device drivers

To avoid the introduction of a new I/O concept to the common Linux code, mainframe Linux developers decided to preserve the IRQ concept and systematically map the mainframe subchannels to Linux as IRQs. This allows Linux for zSeries and S/390 to support up to 65,536 different IRQs, each representing a unique device.

In the following pages, we list some of the important devices that are supported in a Linux-on-the-mainframe environment. For network device drivers, see Chapter 24, "Communications Reference."

20.4.2 System console support

The intended use of the console device drivers is solely to launch Linux. The following consoles are supported:

- Integrated Console at the Support Element (SE)

- Hardware Management Console (HMC)

- 3215 console (VM)

20.4.3 SCSI device support

Linux on the mainframe can make use of all SCSI device types currently supported by Linux on other platforms. These include SCSI disks, tapes, CD-ROMs, and DVDs.

SCSI-over-Fiber Channel support through the zfcp device driver requires a zSeries z900, z800, or later mainframe. zSeries FCP adapters do not work with older S/390 models. Both 31-bit Linux and 64-bit Linux are supported.

20.4.4 Disk support

The following disk types are supported through the DASD device driver:

- ECKD (see Table 14-1)
- VM minidisks (CKD, ECKD, FBA)

20.4.5 Tape support

The Linux-on-the-mainframe tape device driver manages channel-attached tape drives which are compatible with IBM 3480, 3490, and 3590 magnetic tape subsystems. Various models of these devices are handled (for example, the 3490E). The device driver supports a maximum of 128 tape devices.

20.4.6 Cryptographic device support

The Linux device driver z90crypt is a generic character device driver for a cryptographic device. This virtual device will route work to the physical cryptographic devices, such as PCI Cryptographic Coprocessor (PCICC) or PCI Cryptographic Accelerator (PCICA), installed on the system.

There are two interfaces to the device driver: through the OpenSSL engine or through the Public Key Cryptography Standards (PKCS) 11 interface.

The device driver controls the PCICC or PCICA features in a Linux environment. Its current function is RSA-PKCS 1.2 decryption using a private key. The owner of the key can decrypt messages that were encrypted using the corresponding public key.

20.4.7 Expanded memory support

The XPRAM device driver is a block device driver that enables Linux for zSeries and S/390 to access the expanded storage. Thus XPRAM can be used as a basis for fast swap devices and/or fast file systems.

The zSeries architecture in 31-bit mode and the S/390 architecture support the access of only 2 GB (gigabytes) of main memory. To overcome this limitation, additional memory can be declared and accessed as expanded memory. For compatibility reasons, this expanded memory can also be declared in the 64-bit mode of zSeries. The zSeries and S/390 architectures allow applications to access up to 18 EB (exabytes) and 16 TB (terabytes) of expanded storage, respectively (although the current hardware can be equipped with at most 64 GB of real memory). The memory in the expanded storage range can be swapped in or out of the main memory in 4-KB blocks.

20.4.8 Network device drivers and adapters

This section introduces the most important drivers and network adapters that are used in a consolidated server environment based on Linux. It lists device drivers supported by Linux on the mainframe and the adapters supported by the drivers.

The *channel device layer* provides a common interface to Linux for S/390 or Linux for zSeries channel devices. You can use this interface to configure the devices and to handle machine checks (devices appearing and disappearing).

The drivers using the channel device layer at the time of writing are:

1. LCS—supports OSA-2 Ethernet Token Ring and OSA-Express Fast Ethernet in non-QDIO mode

2. CTC/ESCON—high-speed serial link

3. QETH—supports OSA-Express feature in QDIO mode and HiperSockets

The QETH device driver

The QETH device driver supports Linux for zSeries (64-bit mode) and Linux for S/390 (31-bit mode), and is important for server consolidation. Version 2.4 of the Linux Kernel is required.

The QETH Linux network driver supports these features in *QDIO mode*:

- OSA-Express Fast Ethernet
- Gigabit Ethernet
- zSeries 900 High Speed Token Ring
- ATM (running Ethernet LAN emulation)

These additional functions are supported:

- HiperSockets
- Virtual IP addresses (VIPA) and IP Address Takeover
- Auto-detection of devices
- Primary and secondary routers
- Priority queueing
- Individual device configuration. It is possible to configure different triples of channels on the same CHPID differently

The channel-to-channel device driver

A CTC connection or an ESCON connection is the typical high-speed connection between mainframes. The data packages and the protocol of both connections are the same. The difference between them is the physical channel used to transfer the data.

Both types of connection may be used to connect a mainframe, an LPAR, or a z/VM guest to another mainframe, LPAR, or z/VM guest, where the peer LPAR or z/VM guest may reside on the same or on a different system.

A third type of connection is virtual CTC, which is a software connection between two z/VM guests on the same z/VM system and which is faster than a physical connection.

CTC can be used to establish a point-to-point TCP/IP connection between two Linux for zSeries systems or between a Linux for zSeries system and another operating system such as VM/ESA, VSE/ESA, Linux for S/390, OS/390, or z/OS.

The Linux for zSeries CTC device driver supports all three types of connection and can be used to establish a point-to-point TCP/IP connection between two Linux on zSeries systems or between a Linux on zSeries system and another operating system such as VM/ESA, VSE/ESA, or z/OS.

The LCS device driver

This Linux network driver supports OSA-2 Ethernet/Token Ring and OSA-Express Fast Ethernet in non-QDIO mode. To configure this device driver, you use the channel device layer. This device driver is available in source code.

The LAN Channel Station (LCS) network interface has two channels: one read channel and one write channel. This is very similar to the zSeries and S/390 CTC interface.

The OSA-Express network adapter

The OSA-Express network adapter is a TCP/IP-based adapter that is important for server consolidation, since it is designed to communicate between a consolidated server environment that uses virtual adapters and IP addressing, and the "outside world." OSA is an abbreviation for *Open Systems Adapter*. The OSA-Express adapter is based on the QDIO (Queued Direct I/O) architecture and provides direct connectivity between applications running in a Linux Guest or Linux LPAR, and the other platforms on the attached network. The QDIO architecture allows a highly efficient data transfer, since it eliminates the need for conventional I/O and interrupt processing, which are instead virtualized.

The OSA-Express is identified in the hardware I/O configuration by its channel path identifier (CHPID). The CHPID is assigned when the OSA is installed and is based on the number of features already installed in the mainframe. The OSA-Express channel can be shared among all Linux LPARs within the mainframe. This is also referred to as *port sharing*. If a Linux system is running in an LPAR, an OSA channel path can be defined to be shared among those LPARs to which it is defined in the system hardware I/O configuration (IOCDS). This allows a network port on the OSA to be shared by as many as 15 Linux LPARs.

The OSA-Express adapter consists of these *features* which support the QDIO architecture:

The OSA-Express Gigabit Ethernet feature

The Gigabit Ethernet feature supports direct attachment through two separate channels to Gigabit Ethernet (GbE) LANs, where clients communicate using TCP/IP. The OSA-Express Gigabit Ethernet feature is available as short and long wavelength features, and supports full duplex data transmission.

The OSA-Express FENET feature

The FENET feature provides direct attachment through two separate channels to 100 Mbps or 10 Mbps Ethernet LANs running in either half- or full-duplex mode. The OSA-Express FENET supports *auto-negotiation* with its attached Ethernet hub, router, or switch. Auto-negotiation is a process that takes control of the cable when a connection to a network device is established. It detects the various modes that exist in the device on the other end of the wire and advertises its own abilities in order to automatically configure the highest common performance mode of interoperation.

The OSA-Express ATM feature

The ATM feature supports 155 Mbps over single-mode or multi-mode fiber-optic connection. When set up for QDIO, the ATM feature can be configured for Ethernet LAN emulation. When set up for non-QDIO, it can be configured for ATM Native or LAN emulation (Ethernet and Token Ring).

The OSA-Express Token Ring feature

The Token Ring (TR) feature provides direct attachment through two separate channels to 100-, 16-, or 4-Mbps LANs running in either half- or full-duplex mode. The OSA-Express TR also supports autosensing.

Communication between Linux LPARs is supported when the destination IP address is the same as the IP address for the target LPAR, and the port is enabled. Otherwise the packet is sent out on the network.

The OSA-2 network adapter

The OSA-2 network adapter enables an S/390 or zSeries mainframe to have a multipurpose and integrated open systems network interface, connecting to an Ethernet, Fast Ethernet, Token-Ring, and FDDI LANs and ATM networks. Both native and LAN-emulation ATM implementations are supported.

OSA-2 also supports concurrent channel upgrade and maintenance (*hot-plug*): that is, OSA-2 *features* can be added or updated as desired. Using the *Open Systems Adapter Support Facility* (OSA/SF), the OSA-2 adapter can also be configured to allow sharing among logical partitions (LPAR support).

ESCON channel adapter

ESCON (Enterprise System Connection) channels use fiber-optic cables, which transmit light pulses. They are *serial channels*, that is, they transfer information 1 bit at a time over the cable. They are used in zSeries or S/390 computers in LPAR mode, and ESCON channels can be shared *across* LPARs. This reduces the number of channels required to add new partitions or applications.

By sharing ESCON channels, Linux LPARs can connect to I/O devices using far fewer cables and are therefore *an important part of server consolidation*.

ESCON can be used to connect a mainframe, a Linux LPAR, or a Linux Guest to another mainframe, Linux LPAR, or Linux Guest, where the peer LPAR or VM Guest may reside on the same or on a different system.

FICON channel adapter

FICON (Fiber Connection) channels are similar to ESCON, except that whereas ESCON operates in half-duplex mode (data move in one direction only at any point in time), FICON operates in full-duplex mode (data move in both directions at any point in time). This means that under FICON the distance between the channel and the control unit can be 43 km and under ESCON only 23 km.

In addition, FICON can handle up to eight simultaneous I/O operations and ESCON only one. It increases the maximum throughput rate from 500 to 4000 I/Os per channel per second. FICON can also be used to connect a mainframe, a Linux LPAR, or a Linux Guest to another mainframe, Linux LPAR, or Linux Guest, where the peer LPAR or VM Guest may reside on the same or on a different system. It also allows Linux LPARs to share channels and use far fewer cables.

Chapter 21.
Mainframe Reference

This chapter provides technical details about the mainframe, beyond the short introduction given in Chapter 2, "Introducing the Mainframe." This chapter contains:

- A discussion of the mainframe architecture

- An overview of the (architecture-dependent) mainframe register set

- An introduction to the program status word (PSW)

- An introduction to the Integrated Facility for Linux (IFL)

21.1 The mainframe architecture

The mainframe architecture is a long-lived architecture that is designed to excel at business computing. This section is for readers looking for a quick understanding of what an explicit architecture can do for them, as well as an understanding of the key architectural components in z/Architecture that contribute to the mainframe's robustness. This section discusses what architecture is, the mainframe instruction set, mainframe recoverability, storage, and the interrupt structure. The full mainframe architecture is described in *z/Architecture Principles of Operation*, SA22-7832.

The mainframe is based on the von Neumann computer model illustrated in Figure 21-1. While most computers are based on this model, the mainframe is different from most other implementations of it. The mainframe has always allowed parallelism in all three components, which allows the mainframe to perform large amounts of I/O without adversely affecting the other components.

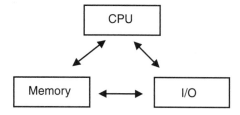

Figure 21-1. The von Neumann model of computing

We talked about the fundamental resources of a computer—CPU, memory, and I/O—in Chapter 2, "Introducing the Mainframe." In this section, we discuss the following architectural topics:

- Instruction set. The mainframe is a complex instruction set computer (CISC).

- Interrupts. The mainframe architecture is interrupt driven.

- The program status word (PSW). The PSW contains information required for the execution of the currently active program.

The mainframe architecture is still evolving from modest beginnings with the S/360 systems to parallel processing and clusters of today. Table 21-1 shows some important milestones and their impact on storage and virtual storage development. The current zSeries architecture has evolved from S/360 in an upwardly compatible way so that your applications continue to run, without modifications, when you upgrade your mainframe.

Table 21-1. Summary of mainframe architecture development

Time	System announced, features
1964	System/360
1970	System/370 EC mode
1972	Virtual memory, multiprocessing, and multiple address spaces
1983	System/370 Extended Architecture, extends addressing from 24 to 31 bits, real and virtual
1988	Enterprise Systems Architecture/370, access registers, data spaces
1990	Enterprise System Architecture/390
1994	S/390 Parallel Enterprise Server, CMOS technology, and sysplex clusters with Coupling Facility as cluster-aware shared read-write storage
2000	zSeries, z/Architecture, 64-bit addressing, real and virtual
2003	Architecture extension to allow attachment of SCSI devices to a mainframe

21.1.1 Architecture versus design

Architecture, in the context of this book, is an explicit, formal definition that states the *behavior* and *results* from a set of valid and, in some cases, invalid, inputs. An architecture will usually refrain from specifying the technology and design for any implementation.

The zSeries architecture specifies the structure of a computing machine (CPU, memory, and I/O) of the class called symmetric multiprocessors. This particular architecture specifies attributes of the components.

The CPU definition specifies: The number of CPUs allowed, the interaction of the CPUs, the interrupt structure, and the interaction of CPUs with memory and I/O.

The memory definition specifies: The atomicity of stores and loads of storage, real and virtual storage, and some of the behavior for dynamic address translation.

The I/O definition specifies: The behavior of the I/O subsystem, the channel programming instructions for communicating with external devices, the paths to the devices, and the response to normal and abnormal conditions that might surface from either a CPU or a device with respect to I/O operations.

In contrast, the *design* is a set of engineering specifications from which the actual computing machine will be built. The design of a zSeries machine that implements the zSeries architecture specifies how the symmetric multiprocessing capability is implemented so as to preserve the behavior defined in the architecture.

For example, the architecture specifies that only one instruction is executed at a time. The design of the zSeries machine allows for partial execution of multiple instructions during a machine cycle. The design preserves the "one and only one" restriction by ensuring that multiple partial executions are not detectable. If the machine were put into a "stop state," there would be no evidence of multiple partial executions. For example, if a page fault was needed during a partial execution, that condition would not be surfaced until the architecturally correct time.

Similarly, the architecture specifies only the data input and output behavior for an instruction. The architecture assumes that the physical implementation itself does not fail and fully implements what is specified. According to the architecture, if an instruction fails to produce the correct result, a specific type of machine check interrupt should occur. The zSeries design has special circuitry that assures that either the results are correct or a machine failure is raised for whatever might go wrong.

The architecture defines a single memory structure where all load and store instructions happen atomically. In the zSeries design, there are multiple layers of cache and significant logic circuitry that assure that, even though each processor has its own unique cache, the atomicity of the load and store still behaves architecturally correctly while gaining a significant performance improvement over a design that was built on a single level of store.

21.1.2 The mainframe instruction set

The mainframe is a complex instruction set computer (CISC). CISC instructions aim to minimize the number of instructions that need to be processed. These instructions tend to be relatively complex. Intel-based architectures also use a CISC instruction set.

In contrast, reduced instruction set computers (RISC) aim to reduce the instruction set by getting rid of all but the most necessary instructions and replacing more complex instructions with groups of smaller ones. CISC and RISC represent two different design strategies aimed at reducing processing time.

Most RISC computers excel at CPU-intense computing, for example, simulating microseconds of nuclear explosions or weather forecasting. The mainframe CISC computer excels at commercial computing involving heavy I/O traffic.

21.1.3 Recovery from hardware error

Some knowledge of hardware errors is useful for understanding how the mainframe accomplishes recovery. Hardware failures can be transient, permanent, or intermittent:

- A transient error (also called a soft error) occurs randomly when environmental conditions, noise, or cosmic particles cause an incorrect result but the circuit itself is functioning correctly. Errors in CMOS technology are predominantly environmental and, therefore, transient. A transient error can be recovered by retrying the operation. Of interest is the mainframe's ability to (1) detect the error and (2) recover dynamically and transparently from the error.

- A permanent error (also called a hard error) is an error in a hardware unit, such as a circuit: The circuit no longer gives the correct output, given the same input. A permanent error requires repair or replacement of the failing unit. Again, the mainframe has the ability to (1) detect the error and (2) replace the failed unit without application downtime.

- Intermittent errors sometimes produce an incorrect result, sometimes not. They can be handled as transient errors if recoverable. They become permanent errors if the error recurs beyond a threshold.

In a zSeries machine, each central processor contains dual instruction processing units. The units operate simultaneously and independently of each other. The results of processing an instruction are compared dynamically. If the results do not match, the instruction is retried. This retry capability allows the zSeries to detect and recover from transient errors. zSeries computers achieve the retry with no measurable loss of performance. The recovery is controlled by hardware and is independent of any operating system.

An error that cannot be successfully retried or that exceeds a certain threshold is considered a permanent error that requires repair rather than recovery. The mainframe achieves that repair dynamically with dynamic CPU chip sparing.

Some microprocessors are designated as "spares." If a running CPU chip fails and an instruction retry is unsuccessful, the spare CPU chip begins executing at precisely the instruction where the other CPU chip failed. Activation by the spare is done completely by hardware, with no operating system awareness. The system is restored to full capacity at machine speed as opposed to hours of downtime for swapping in a new card or board. Therefore, Linux, as well as operating systems such as z/OS, benefits.

In addition, the mainframe provides memory chip sparing: An error threshold is maintained for each chip and, when exceeded, a new chip is nondisruptively substituted by the memory subsystem hardware.

Similarly, the mainframe provides cache-line sparing. When an error threshold is exceeded, the defective cache line can be nondisruptively removed and later substituted by hardware. On the mainframe, all data in the cache hierarchy are protected by data redundancy, provided by means of write-through cache design and ECC. Errors are both detected and corrected.

Microcode patches can also be applied nondisruptively.

21.1.4 Storage

Imagine storage as being a long horizontal string of bits. For most operations, accesses to storage proceed in a left-to-right sequence. The string of bits is subdivided into units of eight bits, or bytes. Each byte location is identified by its byte address. Only bytes can be addressed; in other words, the storage is byte-addressable.

There are three basic types of addressing:

- Absolute addressing: the use of actual byte-positions in the main storage.

- Real addressing: like absolute addressing, except that a real address must be *prefixed* by a bit-string to form the absolute address. In a multiprocessor environment, all CPUs share storage. Yet every CPU must have its own unique prefix area from 0 to 8 KB. (Actually, from 0 to 8 KB − 1.) The zSeries architecture solves the problem by giving each CPU a unique prefix. This prevents clashes between CPUs for referencing their own private low core pages. Yet they can address the same storage locations, if necessary.

- Virtual addressing: a virtual address is *translated* into a real address. Virtual addresses may indicate bytes not currently in main storage, but which will be brought in from auxiliary storage by *paging*. A virtual storage address can exceed the maximum address of installed absolute storage.

21.1.5 Interrupts

In order to process the workload and use the processor resources efficiently, a technique is needed to facilitate switching control from one task to another. While one task waits, another can execute. This switching is driven by *interrupts*.

What are interrupts?

The mainframe architecture is interrupt-driven. An interrupt is an event that alters the sequence in which the processor executes instructions. An interrupt can be solicited (specifically requested by the program) or unsolicited (caused by an event that is not related to the executing task).

The interrupt process consists of the hardware recognizing that a special condition has occurred (see list below), storing interrupt information in a well-defined location, and causing the instruction flow to transfer control to the specific interrupt handler which then proceeds to execute. When the interrupt handler finishes, it typically exits back to the system dispatcher. The zSeries architecture's interrupt behavior is quite similar to many other operating systems' interrupt behavior.

Types of interrupt

Mainframe interrupts are grouped into six classes, listed here in order of priority:

- Supervisor call—Caused by the SUPERVISOR CALL instruction.
- Program—Enables the CPU to respond to and report exceptions and events that occur during the execution of programs.
- Machine check—Enables the CPU to respond to malfunctioning equipment.
- External—Enables the CPU to respond to various signals from inside or outside the configuration.
- Input/Output—Enables the CPU to respond to errors in I/O devices and the channel subsystem.

- Restart—Provides a means for the operator or another CPU to invoke the execution of a specified program.

Each interrupt type has an old program status word (PSW) and a new PSW associated with it. The six classes are distinguished by the storage locations at which the old PSW is stored and from which the new PSW is fetched. During an interrupt, the CPU stores the current PSW as an old PSW and fetches a new one. Along with the old PSW, information that identifies the cause of the interrupt is stored. The old PSW contains the address of the instruction that would have been executed next, had the interrupt not occurred, thus permitting resumption of the interrupted program.

For each processor, the old and new PSWs are stored in the real storage area called the *Prefix Save Area* (PSA), as shown in Figure 21-2 for a single processor.

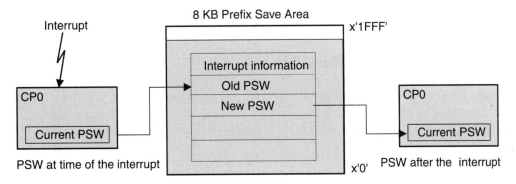

Figure 21-2. Single processor low-storage PSA

Each type of interrupt has a first level interrupt handler (FLIH) in the operating system kernel or nucleus. The new PSWs that are loaded have instruction addresses that point to the corresponding FLIH. A FLIH itself cannot take an interrupt; it runs disabled. The FLIH saves the register state from the interrupted process. It must not be interrupted until at least the raw state information is safely stored.

In this way, the processor can be enabled or disabled for external, I/O, machine check, and certain program interrupts. If an interrupt occurs while the processor is disabled for any of the first three types, the hardware will leave the interrupt pending.

In a tightly coupled multiprocessor, each processor has a unique PSA assigned to it, as shown in Figure 21-3 for a 64-bit system.

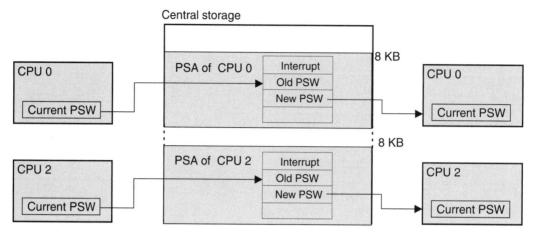

Figure 21-3. Multiprocessor low-storage PSA

21.2 Mainframe registers

If you develop your own applications, it may be of use to know something about the mainframe register sets. A full description is in *S/390 ELF Application Binary Interface Supplement* and *zSeries ELF Application Binary Interface Supplement*, both available at http://www.linuxbase.org/spec/ELF/zSeries/.

21.2.1 zSeries registers

S/390 has 16 general-purpose registers of 32-bit width; with zSeries, the registers are 64-bit wide. The number of floating-point registers depends on the model. Older systems have only four floating-point registers; recent systems come with 16. The 16 registers were introduced together with the IEEE floating-point implementation. All Linux programs are able to use 16 floating-point registers. The missing 12 on older hardware are emulated within the Linux kernel. The use of the registers on z/Architecture is described in Table 21-2.

Table 21-2. Register usage

Register name	Usage	Call effect
r0, r1	General purpose	Volatile[1]
r2	Parameter passing and return values	Volatile
r3, r4, r5	Parameter passing	Volatile
r6	Parameter passing	Saved[2]
r7–r11	Local variables	Saved
r12	Local variable, commonly used as GOT pointer	Saved
r13	Local variable, commonly used as literal pool pointer	Saved
r14	Return address	Volatile
r15	Stack pointer	Saved
f0, f2, f4, f6	Parameter passing and return values	Volatile
f1, f3, f5, f7	General purpose	Volatile
f8–f15	General purpose	Saved
Access registers 0, 1	Reserved for system use	Volatile
Access registers 2–15	General purpose	Volatile

[1]Volatile: These registers are not preserved across function calls.

[2]Saved: These registers belong to the calling function. A called function will save these registers' values before it changes them, restoring their values before it returns.

The registers in Table 21-3 have assigned roles in the standard calling sequence.

Table 21-3. Standard calling sequence roles

r12	Global Offset Table pointer. If a position-independent module uses cross-linking, the compiler *must* point r12 to the GOT. If not, this register may be used locally.
r13	Commonly used as the literal pool pointer. If the literal pool is not required, this register may be used locally.
r14	This register will contain the address to which a called function will normally return. r14 is volatile across function calls.
r15	The stack pointer (stored in r15) will maintain an 8-byte alignment. It will always point to the lowest allocated valid stack frame and will grow toward low addresses. The contents of the word addressed by this register may point to the previously allocated stack frame. If required, it can be decremented by the called function.

Signals can interrupt processes. Functions called during signal handling have no unusual restrictions on their use of registers. Moreover, if a signal-handling function returns, the process will resume its original execution path with all registers restored to their original values. Thus programs and compilers may freely use all registers listed above, except those reserved for system use, without the danger of signal handlers' inadvertently changing their values.

Register usage

With these calling conventions, the following usage of the registers for inline assemblies is recommended:

- General registers r0 and r1 should be used internally whenever possible.
- General registers r2 to r5 should be second choice.
- General registers r12 to r15 should be used only for their standard function.

21.3 The program status word

In a mainframe instruction stream, the next instruction is pointed to by the program status word (PSW). The current instruction is the only instruction according to the architecture. Everything else is considered to be data. Until the current instruction completes and the PSW changes its address, we can never be sure of what the next instruction is.

What is the program status word? The PSW in each CPU contains information required for the execution of the currently active program. In the z/Architecture, it is 128 bits long and includes the instruction address, condition code, and other control fields.

There are different ways that a PSW can get the address of the next instruction:

- If this instruction is not a branch, then add the length of the current instruction to the PSW to get the next address.

- If this instruction is a branch, then the resolved address of the branch is put into the PSW and that instruction is fetched.

The PSW governs more than what the next instruction is. It is also responsible for determining what addressing mode the mainframe should run in, as we explain in the next section.

21.3.1 Mainframe multimodality

The addressing scheme of the mainframe has evolved over the years, beginning with 24-bit real addressing for S/360. Subsequently, as more storage space was needed by applications and operating systems, 31-bit addressing and, more recently, 64-bit addressing were introduced.

The zSeries architecture provides for two schemes of floating-point arithmetic:

- Hexadecimal floating-point arithmetic, which uses the hexadecimal (radix-16).

- Binary Floating Point (BFP), which conforms to the IEEE standard for binary floating-point arithmetic, allows you to use IEEE floating-point instructions and introduces interoperability between zSeries and other platforms. Thus, programs can be migrated to and from workstations and any other platforms with different architectures, provided that they conform to the IEEE floating-point arithmetic standard.

21.3.2 The PSW bits

A zSeries can operate with one of three addressing schemes: 24 bits, 31 bits, or 64 bits. With 24-bit addressing, you have the ability to address 16MB, with 31-bit you can address 2GB, and with 64-bit you can address 16EB. The addressing mode (how many bits to be used for addressing) is governed by bit 31 (the extended addressing mode bit) and bit 32 (the basic addressing mode bit) of the PSW. See Table 21-4.

Table 21-4. The PSW controls addressing mode

PSW bit 31	PSW bit 32	Addressing mode
0	0	24-bit
0	1	31-bit
1	1	64-bit

Addresses computed for 24- and 31-bit addressing mode have 40 or 33 zeroes, respectively, appended to the left to form a 64-bit address. So the resulting logical real and absolute addresses are always 64 bits long on the zSeries.

The other bits in a PSW are described in Table 21-5.

Table 21-5 (Page 1 of 2). Description of the bits in a PSW		
Bit number		Description
S/390	zSeries	
0	0	Reserved (must be 0); otherwise, a specification exception occurs.
1	1	Enables Program Event Recording (PER). PER is used to facilitate debugging, in particular, single stepping.
2–4	2–4	Reserved (must be 0).
5	5	Enables dynamic address translation (DAT).
6	6	Input/Output interrupt mask
7	7	Input/Output interrupt mask
8–11	8–11	PSW key used for complex memory protection mechanism (not used under Linux).
12	12	1 on s/390; 0 on z/Architecture
13	13	Machine Check Mask, enables machine check interrupts.
14	14	Enables wait state. Stops the processor except for interrupts.
15	15	Enables problem state (if set to 1, certain instructions are disabled). All Linux user programs run with this bit on.

Table 21-5 (Page 2 of 2). Description of the bits in a PSW

Bit number		Description
S/390	**zSeries**	
16–17	16–17	Address Space Control • 00 Primary space mode. The Linux kernel currently runs in this mode, CR1 is affiliated with this mode and points to the primary segment table origin. • 01 Access register mode. This mode is used in functions to copy data between kernel and user space. • 10 Secondary space mode. Not used in Linux. • 11 Home Space Mode. All user programs run in this mode.
18–19	18–19	Condition codes (CC)
20	20	Fixed-point overflow mask; if 1=FPU exceptions for this event occur (normally 0)
21	21	Decimal overflow mask; if 1=FPU exceptions for this event occur (normally 0)
22	22	Exponent underflow mask; if 1=FPU exceptions for this event occur (normally 0)
23	23	Significance mask; if 1=FPU exceptions for this event occur (normally 0)
24–31	24–30	Reserved, must be 0.
	31	Extended Addressing Mode
	32	Basic Addressing Mode. Used to set addressing mode.
32		1 = 31-bit addressing mode; 0 = 24-bit addressing mode (for backward compatibility). Linux always runs with this bit set to 1.
33–64		Instruction address
	33–63	Reserved, must be 0.
	64–127	Address • In 24-bit mode, bits 64–103=0, bits 104–127 are the address. • In 31-bit mode, bits 64–96=0, bits 97–127 are the address. **Note:** Unlike 31-bit mode on S/390, bit 96 must be zero when loading the address with LPSWE; otherwise, a specification exception occurs. LPSW is fully backward compatible.

21.4 Integrated Facility for Linux (IFL)

The Integrated Facility for Linux is a feature of the zSeries hardware. When this feature is installed on the machine, a spare processor is moved into a special pool of processors that can be used only for Linux work. Unlike when a processor is added to the general purpose processor pool, the model number of the machine does not change as IFL features are installed. These special IFL processors are usable only in an LPAR that is defined as "Linux Only."

The traditional operating systems such as z/OS, VSE/ESA, and TPF, are not able to access IFL processors. The IFL feature also allows z/VM to be run in the LPAR of type "Linux Only," provided that z/VM is hosting Linux guests. Thus, one is not limited by the LPAR boundary on the number of partitions and can instead run hundreds of Linux guest images on these IFL features.

Chapter 22.
Debugging and Dump Analysis

In a perfect world, computer programs would not have any bugs. Unfortunately, we do not live in this perfect world and normally programs have many errors. New programs tend to be error-prone. Tools exist which help us find and analyze these errors. Probably the most well-known under Linux is the user space debugger, gdb, but there are many others.

Since Linux is Open Source code and everyone can modify and compile his or her own kernel, kernel debugging becomes more and more important. For kernel debugging, other tools exist than for user space debugging. Common symptoms of kernel-related problems are kernel panics, oopses, and deadlocks.

In this chapter, we will concentrate on particulars of mainframe debugging. We will look at basics of the Linux on zSeries design, which are necessary for successful debugging, and we will introduce several tools which can be used. Both user space and kernel debugging will be described.

22.1 What information you need

Let's briefly review the information you need for successful debugging on the mainframe.

22.1.1 User address spaces

You may remember from 20.3, "Exploiting mainframe processor architecture," that there are several kinds of address spaces. In particular, the Linux kernel runs in primary space mode, and all user programs run in home space mode.

Let's have a short look at the virtual address space or user space process. In Figure 22-1 we see the organization of the virtual memory. The stack grows from high addresses to low. The dynamic segments are used, e.g., for shared libraries, and are located above the anonymous mapping base. The code and heap of a user program are located between the program base and the anonymous mapping base.

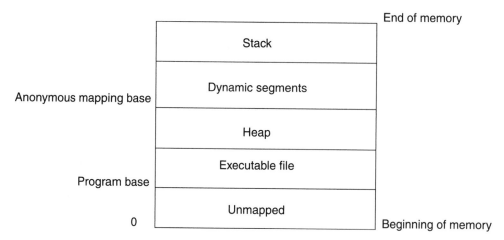

Figure 22-1. Address space organization

The addresses for "end of memory" and "anonymous mapping base" depend on the version of the Linux kernel used. "Program base" depends on the linker script setting. These will change with time, as everything in Linux does. Table 22-1 lists some values of kernel versions current at the time of writing.

Table 22-1. Kernel addresses		
	Linux for S/390 (31-bit hex)	**Linux for zSeries (64-bit)**
End of virtual memory	7fff ffff	2exp(41-1)
Anonymous mapping base	4000 0000	2exp40
Program base (assume normally used linker script setting)	40 0000	2exp31

Knowing these values, it is possible to see, for example, on the address portion of a program PSW whether a program currently is running in a shared library or in program code. We will show examples of this later.

The above scheme is valid only for user space processes. Kernel space addresses can be located beween 0 and "end of virtual memory." If you find an instruction address smaller than "program base," this might indicate that it is a kernel address.

22.1.2 The PSW

A very important piece of information is the PSW. We looked at both the 31-bit PSW and the 64-bit PSW in 21.3, "The program status word." The most relevant bits for problem determination and debugging are the interrupt masks (the input/output mask, bit 6, and the external mask, bit 7; see also 21.1.5, "Interrupts"), the machine check bit (bit 13), the wait state bit (bit 14), the problem state bit (bit 15), and the address space control bits (bits 16 and 17).

A single bit (bit 15) defines the state: the machine runs in problem state if the bit is set to 1. Certain instructions are then disabled. All Linux user programs run with this bit set to 1. Kernel programs run in supervisor state with the bit set to 0. Therefore, the PSW can tell us if the CPU executes kernel or user code.

In some cases, the DAT mode, or virtual addressing bit (bit 15), can be of interest. This bit indicates whether dynamic address translation is enabled. Dynamic addressing is always enabled under Linux. The meanings of the address space control bits are:

00	Primary Space Mode with DAT on. The Linux kernel currently runs in this mode. Control register CR1 is associated with this mode and points to the primary segment table origin.
01	Access register mode. This mode is used in functions to copy data between kernel and user space.
10	Secondary space mode. This is not used in Linux. However, control register CR7, which is associated with this mode, is used in Linux. Normally, CR13=CR7 to allow data to be copied between kernel and user space.
11	Home Space Mode. All user programs run in this mode. This mode is associated with CR13, which points to the home segment table origin.

22.1.3 Registers

Registers were covered in 21.2.1, "zSeries registers." The most important registers for debugging are 14 and 15. Register 14 is the return address, and register 15 is the stack pointer.

22.1.4 The stack frame

Each function normally has an associated stack frame on the runtime stack. This stack grows downward from high addresses. Figure 22-2 shows the stack frame organization. This organization applies to both kernel and user space stacks. SP in the figure denotes the stack pointer. When the function is executed by a CPU, SP is held in general purpose register r15.

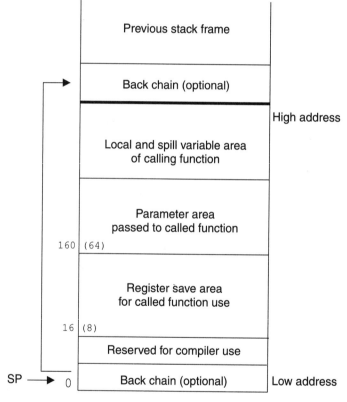

Figure 22-2. Standard stack frame

The register save area (see Figure 22-3) on the stack frame for the currently executed function is for use of the next called function. In the prolog of the called function, the registers of the calling function, which are overwritten, are saved in the register save area of the calling function's stackframe. Therefore, the register save area of the currently executed function does not contain valid register values (they are not yet saved).

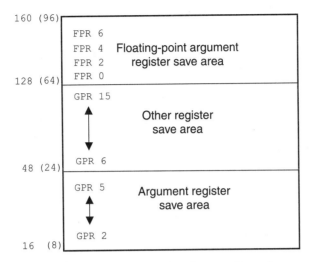

Figure 22-3. Register save area for 64-bit (31-bit values in parentheses)

If the backchain is implemented (which means that the compiler created code for setting up the backchain), it is possible to walk by hand through the stack frames by just following the backchain. The first stack frame on the stack normally has a backchain of 0 (NULL), which indicates the end of the stack.

22.2 Debugging under z/VM

When running Linux under z/VM, the z/VM debugging tools are at your disposal. These include several useful commands such as display and trace.

In order to use these commands, you must be in CP mode. You can usually enter CP mode by pressing the PA1 key. If you want to issue a debug command without halting your virtual machine with the PA1 key, you can prefix the command with #CP; for example:

```
#CP TRACE I PSWA 2000
```

22.2.1 The trace command

The trace command is used to trace the flow of program execution.

To use this command, you need to create a *trace set* containing so-called *trace traps*. A trace trap consists of the trace command and operands. (If you do not specifically name a trace set at the first time you create a trace trap, CP places it in a trace set named INITIAL.)

22.2.2 References

The following books contain more details on the z/VM and VM/ESA commands introduced in this chapter (query, trace, display):

* *z/VM CP Command and Utility Reference*, SC24-5967

* *Virtual Machine/Enterprise Systems Architecture CP Command and Utility Reference*, SC24-5773

22.3 General Linux debugging facilities

As in every Linux system, there are tools you can use to debug the kernel and to debug user space programs on the mainframe. Naturally, a lot of the tools you use on other Linux systems work here too, such as LTT, dprobes, rgbd, and kdb. As the subject of the book is the mainframe, we will concentrate on tools particular to the mainframe, and only skim over the Linux tools, for which there are readily available descriptions.

Table 22-2 lists some tools for Linux debugging. Detailed information about the tools can be found in the corresponding info- and man pages.

Table 22-2 (Page 1 of 3). General Linux debugging facilities		
Tool name	**Where available**	**Purpose**
gdb	`http://www.gnu.org/ software/gdb/gdb.html`	The GNU debugger (gdb) is a user space debugger also available for Linux on zSeries. It can be used to do stack backtraces, set breakpoints, and print out variables.
ldd	Included in Linux base system	The ldd utility can be used to get a list of all shared libraries which an executable uses. It is also possible to see the addresses where the libraries are located. When investigating a given PSW, you can use this information to find out in which shared library a program is currently running.
ltrace	Included in Linux base system	The ltrace utility will output all dynamic library calls of a program. It is possible to see all libc calls of a program such as "printf" or "strcpy." In order to trace the library calls of a program, the program has to be executed under ltrace. ltrace also can attach to an already running process.

Table 22-2 (Page 2 of 3). General Linux debugging facilities

Tool name	Where available	Purpose
nm	GNU binary utilities	The nm tool lists object file symbols, including address, type, and name. The nm tool can be of help if you get an "undefined reference" error when linking a program. Then you can search system libraries and object files and libraries of your software project after the corresponding symbol. The output of nm is also helpful when debugging kernel modules with lcrash.
objdump	GNU binary utilities	The objdump utility displays object file information and can be used to create debug information lists.
OOPS message	Included in base Linux system	In certain situations, for example, when the kernel tries to access a bad page, the kernel generates an Oops message. The Oops message is written to the kernel buffers. Usually the message is written via klogd and syslogd to a syslog file. In the Oops text, you find the following information: • What error occurred • Contents of some architecture-specific registers • A stack backtrace, which shows how the kernel ran into the error situation
proc file system	Included in base Linux system	The /proc file system is a powerful concept that allows you to investigate and modify kernel parameters. It is a virtual file system created by the kernel. Read requests from this file system are fulfilled by the kernel with the current system status. Write requests to this file system are used to modify kernel parameters on the fly.
s390dbf	Included in base Linux system	The Linux on zSeries Debug Feature traces kernel components such as device drivers. It produces trace logs, which can be useful when that specific component shows an error. Not all components produce the logs, however. A component must register with the feature to produce the traces. The /proc directory holds debug logs from the s390dbf tool. Under the path /proc/s390dbf, there is a directory for each registered component. The names of the directory entries correspond to the names under which the components have been registered.

Tool name	Where available	Purpose
strace	`http://sourceforge.net`	Strace is a tool for intercepting calls to the kernel and logging them to a file and on the screen. You could use it, for instance, to find out what files a particular program opens.
SysRq	Included in base Linux system	You can use the "magical key combination" of SysRq to debug on the mainframe. Linux on zSeries supports SysRq. The key combination is directly intercepted by the kernel and can be used to perform an emergency shutdown, to synchronize disks, to unmount, and to reboot if the machine becomes partially hung.
top	Included in base Linux system	Use top to find out where processes are sleeping in the kernel. To do this, copy the System.map from the root directory where the Linux kernel was built to the /boot directory on your Linux machine.

Table 22-2 (Page 3 of 3). General Linux debugging facilities

22.4 Linux kernel debugging tools

Of course, tools exist for Linux (kernel) debugging that we did not introduce here. Some of these tools are already ported to Linux for S/390 or Linux for zSeries; others are not. However, this can change quickly as new tools are developed and proven tools are ported every day. In Table 22-3 we list some of the interesting current Linux projects that may ease (kernel) debugging on Linux now or in the future:

Table 22-3. Linux kernel debugging projects

Project	Where available	Description and location
Linux system RAS	http://systemras.sourceforge.net/	The mission of this project is to expand acceptance of Linux on enterprise-class systems through improved reliability, availability, and serviceability.
LTT	http://www.opersys.com/LTT/	Linux Tracing Toolkit: LTT provides you with all the information required to reconstruct a system's behavior during a certain period of time.
dprobes	http://oss.software.ibm.com/ developerworks/opensource/ linux/projects/dprobes/	Dynamic Probes is a generic and pervasive debugging facility that will operate under the most extreme software conditions, such as debugging a deeply rooted operating system problem in a live environment.
kdb	http://oss.sgi.com/projects/kdb/ http://oss.software.ibm.com/ developer/opensource/linux/ projects/kdb/	The built-in kernel debugger for Linux is part of the Linux kernel and provides a means of examining kernel memory and data structures while the system is operational.
Event logging	http://evlog.sourceforge.net/	Platform-independent event-logging facility for the Linux operating system and applications, which offers capabilities and features comparable to event- and error-logging facilities found in enterprise-class, UNIX-based operating systems.

22.5 Linux system dump tools

Table 22-4 lists tools for deugging Linux system dumps.

Table 22-4. Linux system dump tools		
Tool name	**Where available**	**Description**
SA dump tools	`http://www.software.ibm.com/ developerworks/opensource/ linux390/index.shtml`	Two stand-alone dump tools are shipped with Linux on zSeries for generating system memory dumps: • DASD dump tool for dumps on DASD volumes • Tape dump tool for dumps on tape
lcrash	`http://sourceforge.net/ projects/lkcd`	When your Linux for zSeries completely crashes or hangs, the last thing you can do is to take a system memory dump and afterward inspect the dump to identify the problem. To inspect the dump, you can use lcrash—the Linux crash dump analyzer. lcrash has a command-line interface with simple command-line editing, history mechanism, and command-line completion.

Chapter 23.
Security Reference

This chapter presents background information on the security certification available for LPAR, as well as short descriptions of z/VM tools that can be used for Linux-on-the-mainframe security. For more security tools, see 25.3, "Security management tools."

23.1 Security certification

Over the years, security has become an essential requirement for information technology. Security consists of many measures, including:

- Preventing unauthorized access to information (read and/or write)
- Preventing unauthorized withholding of information or resources (for example, denial-of-service attacks)
- Providing accurate user identification

IT managers need to know if the security of the system they are using, or intend to purchase, meets the security needs of their organization. To answer these questions, first, you need to define a set of criteria. Then, you need to have an appropriate organization certify that your IT system has been adequately tested and meets the designated criteria. The organization that usually performs this certfication is the appropriately qualified and recognized national certification body for each country. See, for example, `http://www.bsi.de/zertifiz/itkrit/itsec-en.pdf`.

Different sets of criteria exist:

- Common Criteria are proposed at an international level for the United States, Canada, and the European Community.
- ITSEC—Information Technology Security Evaluation Criteria. ITSEC is the certification standard traditionally used in the European Community.
- TCSEC—Trusted Computer Security Evaluation Criteria (also called Orange Book). TCSEC is traditionally used in the United States and Canada.

For the future, it is anticipated that Common Criteria will become the *de facto* criteria. All future IBM certification will be to Common Criteria standards. For current information about Common Criteria for Linux on eServer platforms, see `http://www.ibm.com/servers/eserver/zseries/security/certification.html`.

For more information about Common Criteria, see `http://www.commoncriteria.org/`.

Common Criteria are designated by Evaluation Assurance Levels (EALs). Table 23-1 summarizes the different levels that have been defined. For a comprehensive definition, see `http://www.commoncriteria.org/docs/EALs.html`.

Table 23-1. Evaluation assurance levels

EAL1	Functionally tested
EAL2	Structurally tested
EAL3	Methodically tested and checked
EAL4	Methodically designed, tested, and reviewed
EAL5	Semiformally designed and tested
EAL6	Semiformally verified design and tested
EAL7	Formally verified design and tested

Table 23-2 compares different criteria levels for ITSEC and TCSEC.

Table 23-2. ITSEC and TCSEC criteria

TCSEC	ITSEC	Security
D	E0	Inadequate assurance
C1	E1	Vendor assured
C2	E2	Independently tested
B1	E3	Independently assured
B2	E4	Structurally sound
B3	E5	Rigorous design
A1	E6	Assured design

23.1.1 LPAR certification

Logical partitioning on the mainframe, in the form of the underlying Processor Resource/Systems Manager (PR/SM) microcode, received the EAL5 certification level in March 2003. The certification was conducted with the PR/SM for the IBM eServer zSeries 900. Because the certification process is an extremely time-consuming and costly process, it cannot be performed for every single model and product on the mainframe.

EAL5 certification means that an independent body assessed the isolation of workload from one mainframe logical partition to another and determined that the isolation is equivalent to that of separate physical servers. You can be assured that one logical partition running a

Web environment and another logical partition running production work, are truly separate and isolated while sharing common hardware resources on a single physical server.

23.1.2 VM integrity

VM integrity can be captured in the following short form:

VM integrity statement, short form

If you find any way for one guest machine to influence another, we will accept that as an integrity APAR.

There is no official certification of VM/ESA or z/VM comparable to the certification of PR/SM. However, the z/VM guest machine separation uses the same machine facilities that were created for, and are used by, PR/SM. Because of this, the same level of confidence can be placed in the z/VM and VM/ESA guest machine separation as in the PR/SM micro-code. To this end, IBM makes an unequivocal system integrity statement for z/VM (in the publication *z/VM General Information*, GC24-5991), which is as follows:

VM integrity statement

System integrity is an important characteristic of z/VM. This statement extends IBM's previous statements on system integrity to the z/VM environment.

IBM has implemented specific design and coding guidelines for maintaining system integrity in the development of z/VM. Procedures have also been established to make the application of these design and coding guidelines a formal part of the design and development process.

However, because it is not possible to certify that any system has perfect integrity, IBM will accept APARs that describe exposures to the system integrity of z/VM or that describe problems encountered when a program, running in a virtual machine not authorized by a mechanism under the customer's control, introduces an exposure to the system integrity of z/VM, as defined in the following "z/VM System Integrity Definition" section.

IBM will continue its efforts to enhance the integrity of z/VM and to respond promptly when exposures are identified.

In the VM integrity statement, cited below, IBM promises that it will fix every exposure of the system integrity of z/VM.

---

z/VM system integrity definition

The z/VM control program system integrity is the inability of any program, running in a virtual machine not authorized by a z/VM control program mechanism under the customer's control or a guest operating system mechanism under the customer's control, to:

- Circumvent or disable the control program real or auxiliary storage protection.

- Access a resource protected by RACF. Resources protected by RACF include virtual machines, minidisks, and terminals.

- Access a control program password-protected resource.

- Obtain control in real supervisor state or with privilege class authority or directory capabilities greater than those it was assigned.

- Circumvent the system integrity of any guest operating system that itself has system integrity as the result of an operation by any z/VM control program facility.

Real storage protection refers to the isolation of one virtual machine from another. CP accomplishes this by hardware dynamic address translation, start interpretive-execution guest storage extent limitation, and the Set Address Limit facility.

Auxiliary storage protection refers to the disk extent isolation implemented for minidisks/virtual disks through channel program translation.

Password-protected resource refers to a resource protected by CP logon passwords and minidisk passwords.

Guest operating system refers to a control program that operates under the z/VM control program.

Directory capabilities refer to those directory options that control functions intended to be restricted by specific assignment, such as those that permit system integrity controls to be bypassed or those not intended to be generally granted to users.

In short, since z/VM uses the same instructions as previous systems to isolate the different guests, IBM warrants the integrity of the virtual machine interface and will accept integrity APARs and will fix any problem that is exposed.

23.2 General security considerations

This section discusses what to consider before applying patches and other security considerations. For more information on patches and hardening than we can provide here, see `http://www.ibm.com/servers/security/planner`.

23.2.1 Linux patch policy considerations

A typical Linux security attack is based on vulnerabilities in commonly used Open Source software, such as BIND, Sendmail, NFS, and "r"-programs such as rexec, rsh, and rcp. One of the main advantages of Open Source software is the speed at which security vulnerabilities are identified and patched. Because of this, it is important to develop a strategy for upgrading critical server software components. This strategy should include the following processes:

- Subscribing to security-related mailing lists. This includes a vendor's security update mailing list (for example, Red Hat, SuSE, or TurboLinux), as well as security advisory mailing lists from your local incident response team. These mailing lists are typically low-volume and provide invaluable information for system and security administrators.

- Retrieving of the latest patch list from your vendor and retrieving of any recommended security patches not included with your system. Some Linux distributions provide tools (such as SuSE YaST and RedHat Up2Date) for automatically checking the packages on a local system with the latest recommended security patches. Some patches may re-enable default configurations, so it is important to go through this checklist after installing any new patches or packages. Patches for software applications not supplied by the operating system vendor should be obtained directly from the software vendor's Web site.

- Ensuring that software patches and packages are downloaded from a reliable source only (for example, directly from the vendor or a trusted mirror site). Patches are often provided with check sums or PGP signatures to ensure that the patch has not been tampered with once the fix is posted.

- Verifying the cryptographic digital signature of any signed downloaded files to ensure integrity. Never use a file whose signature does not match its contents. Pretty Good Privacy (PGP) (`http://www.pgpi.org`) and GNU Privacy Guard (GnuPG) (`http://www.gnupg.org`) can be used for encryption and authentication and are commonly used by many Open Source software developers to provide digital signatures. To learn how to use GnuPG to verify digital signatures, see: `http://www.dewinter.com/gnupg_howto/english/`.

- Verifying the md5 checksum, when possible, of any downloaded patches with a utility such as md5 or md5sum. Md5sum is a standard utility on all major distributions and is very straightforward to use (`md5sum -c md5-file` will check the integrity of the md5 file). For example, Red Hat includes an md5 file in the same directory as its distribution ISO images. The file contains md5 entries for each file in that directory, which can be used to verify authenticity. For example,
  `ftp://ftp.redhat.com/pub/redhat/redhat-7.2-en/iso/i386/`.
- Using the -K or -checksig options if you are using RPM as your package management system. These options to the rpm command verify the cryptographic signature of the package.

23.2.2 Security considerations at the device driver level

This section discusses security considerations when using network attachment cards.

In a typical low-end server farm environment, for example, each server has a network attachment card that ideally should be plugged into a router with firewall capabilities. This allows you to securely control traffic that flows through the cards to the servers, as shown in Figure 23-1.

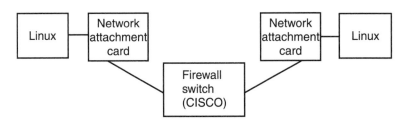

Figure 23-1. Controlling traffic through a card

One of the cards in widespread use on zSeries is the Open Systems Adapter (OSA) card. The OSA card is an adapter for network attachment. The card has several ports that Linux guests can connect to.

Whereas you could connect each Linux guest on the mainframe to its own OSA card, the OSA cards are designed for sharing. Therefore, you can connect several Linux guests to one such card. Security has to be provided with firewall images that control the data flow between Linux guests and between the Linux guests and external network, as shown in Figure 23-2.

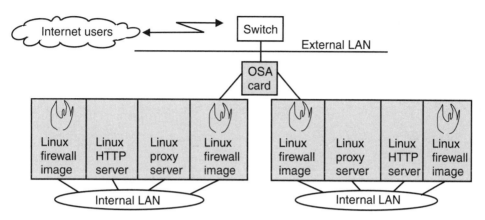

Figure 23-2. OSA cards connect Linux images to an external network

23.3 z/VM tools

Add-on software products exist that can be used to further enhance the integrity and security of a z/VM system. Two of those products from IBM are z/VM Version 4 feature options called IBM Directory Maintenance for z/VM (DirMaint) and IBM Resource Access Control Facility for z/VM (RACF).

23.3.1 DirMaint

DirMaint provides a safe, efficient, and interactive way to maintain the z/VM system directory. Through its command line or full-screen interface, you can quickly and easily add, modify, or delete users from the system directory. DirMaint includes these features:

- Distributed virtual machine management. DirMaint is designed on the assumption that there are multiple system administrators and is implemented so that two administrators cannot change the same directory entry at the same time.
- Automatic minidisk allocation. Instead of requiring you to pore over minidisk map reports to find available slots for new minidisks, DirMaint will automatically locate gaps in any number of DASD pools that you define and assign new minidisks in those gaps. This avoids the accidental definition of overlapping minidisks.
- Automatic minidisk erasure. When a minidisk is deleted, DirMaint asynchronously erases all data content on the minidisk before returning it to the pool of available DASD. No residual data remains.
- Support for end users. A general user has the ability to make limited changes to his or her own system directory entry.
- Auditing of all transactions.

- Automatic backup of the system directory.

In any z/VM installation where large numbers of virtual servers are being deployed, DirMaint is recommended.

23.3.2 RACF

The Resource Access Control Facility (RACF) is an external security manager. It provides comprehensive security capabilities that extend the standard security implemented by the base z/VM product. RACF controls user access to the VM system, checks authorization for use of both system and virtual machine resources, and audits the use of those resources. Like DirMaint, RACF is packaged as a priced feature of z/VM Version 4 and is preinstalled on the system installation media.

RACF helps an installation implement its security policy by identifying and authenticating virtual machine access, controlling each virtual machine's access to sensitive data, and logging and reporting events that are relevant to the system's security.

RACF verifies virtual machine logon passwords (which are stored using a one-way strong-encryption algorithm) and checks access to minidisks, data in spool files, network nodes, shared segments, and some system commands. You can use RACF commands to audit security-relevant events such as:

- Any CP command or DIAGNOSE code (including privileged commands and codes)
- The creation, opening, and deletion of spool files
- The dumping and loading of spool files through the SPXTAPE and SPTAPE commands
- APPC/VM CONNECT and SEVER operations
- The creation and deletion of logical devices

When running a Linux guest, such auditing may provide additional insight into the activities of the Linux guest. For example, an Open Source package is available for Linux on zSeries that provides an interface to some CP functions. One of the components is the hcp command, which uses the DIAGNOSE 8 interface to issue CP commands on behalf of the guest virtual machine running Linux. If desired, RACF can be used to track the execution of specific CP or DIAGNOSE commands.

z/VM provides the ability for users who have not yet authenticated themselves to the system to do two things: send messages to users who are logged on and access (using the CP DIAL command) virtual 3270 devices, other than the virtual console, created by a virtual machine. If your security policy prohibits such anonymous access to VM terminal sessions, RACF provides facilities that can disable these functions.

Chapter 24.
Communications Reference

When planning your network configuration for an efficient and secure configuration, you need to know what network options there are for Linux on the mainframe. 20.4.8, "Network device drivers and adapters" listed all relevant device drivers. This chapter describes the virtual connections that are available, as well as a detailed example of server consolidation using these virtual connections.

24.1 zSeries virtual connections

z/VM provides two major TCP/IP connectivity options for Linux guests: Linux can be given access to a real connection, or to a *virtual* connection. The *virtual* connections are described in this section. They are generally used to connect Linux to another Linux guest on the same z/VM system. The other Linux guest might have access to a real network connection and act as an IP router or gateway.

zSeries virtual connections include HiperSockets, virtual channel-to-channel (CTC), and the Inter-User Communication Vehicle (IUCV).

24.1.1 HiperSockets

The zSeries HiperSockets function (HiperSockets) is a microcode function supported by the operating systems z/OS V1R2, z/VM V4R2, VSE/ESA 2.7, Linux for zSeries (64-bit mode), and Linux for S/390 (31-bit mode). Functions of HiperSockets include the following:

- Provides the fastest TCP/IP communication between consolidated Linux, z/VM, and z/OS virtual servers in a zSeries by allowing virtual machines and logical partitions (LPARs) to communicate internally over the memory bus using the internal-queued-direct (IQD) channel type in the z900.

- Provides a higher level of network availability, security, simplicity, performance, and cost-effectiveness than an external single server solution communicating across an external TCP/IP network.

The HiperSockets (IQDIO) support is an extension to the OSA-Express QDIO support.

Linux supports up to four real HiperSockets, which is the microcode limit. Linux uses the QETH device driver to support HiperSockets, as described in 20.4.8, "Network device drivers and adapters."

HiperSockets advantages

The zSeries HiperSockets function uses an adaption of the Queued-Direct Input/Output (QDIO) high-speed I/O protocol. HiperSockets operates with minimal system and network overhead. It also eliminates the need to utilize I/O subsystem operations and the need to traverse an external network connection to communicate between LPARs. HiperSockets offers significant value in server consolidation by connecting many virtual servers.

HiperSockets is transparent to applications. To an operating system, it looks like any other TCP/IP interface.

Because Hipersockets has no external components (cables or cards), it provides a very secure connection. For security purposes, servers can be connected to different HiperSockets. All security features, such as firewall filtering, are available for HiperSockets interfaces as they are with other TCP/IP network interfaces.

Management and administration cost reductions over existing configurations are possible. Since HiperSockets does not use an external network, it can free up system and network resources, eliminating attachment costs while improving availability and performance.

Implementing the HiperSockets function on Guest LANs

In addition to supporting the HiperSockets microcode function, z/VM also supports the HiperSockets function on Guest LANs, for interconnecting virtual machines. That is, VM simulates the HiperSockets function for communication among virtual machines without the need for HiperSockets microcode supporting IQD (internal-queued-direct) channel path identifiers.

The VM Guest LAN support works similar to the way that VM emulates channel-to-channel adapters for communication among virtual machines without the need for the physical media (such as ESCON, FICON, or other channel-to-channel connections).

Each Guest LAN can be used by a group of virtual machines to communicate among themselves, independent of other groups of virtual machines on other Guest LANs. The z/VM Guests connecting to a Guest LAN must have HiperSockets support. These are currently z/OS V1R2, z/VM V4R2 TCP/IP, VSE/ESA, Linux for zSeries, and Linux for S/390.

VM Guest LAN support is available for zSeries, S/390 G5 and G6, and for S/390 Multiprise 3000.

The VM Guest LAN function performs a complete emulation of HiperSockets hardware, providing connectivity within a single z/VM image.

HiperSockets usage example

There are many possibilities for applying the HiperSockets technology. Figure 24-1 shows the use of both virtual and real HiperSockets with Linux in a zSeries.

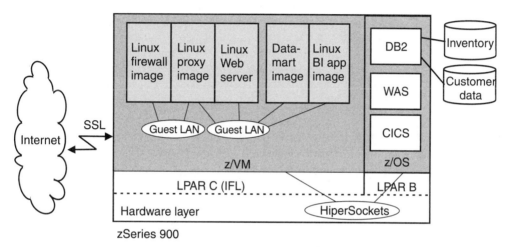

Figure 24-1. An example showing possible uses of HiperSockets

The three HiperSockets illustrated in Figure 24-1 are used as follows:

- Guest LANs: Serves multiple Linux servers running under z/VM in LPAR-C.

- Real HiperSockets: Exclusively serves the z/VM and z/OS systems running in LPAR-C and LPAR-B.

24.1.2 Virtual channel-to-channel

A *virtual channel-to-channel (CTC)* connection is a software connection between two VM guests on the same VM system. In Figure 24-2, a virtual CTC connection is used to connect the first two Linux guests of Mainframe-B, in which Linux for zSeries systems are installed. A virtual CTC connection is much faster than an equivalent physical connection.

Virtual CTC devices are created using the CP DEFINE command and are connected using the COUPLE command.

24.1.3 Inter-user communication vehicle

The *Inter-User Communication Vehicle (IUCV)* is a VM/ESA virtual connection that enables a Linux program running in one VM guest to communicate with another Linux program running in another VM guest, or with a control program, or even with itself. The communication takes place over a predefined linkage called a *path*. IUCV has now largely been replaced by HiperSockets (described in 24.1.1, "HiperSockets").

IUCV provides high-speed cross-memory data transfer without using virtual device I/O functions. CP directory authorization is required if you want to use IUCV to connect two Linux guests. No authorization is required to connect to the VM TCP/IP stack.

IUCV provides functions, through the IUCV macro, to create and dismantle paths, send and reply to messages, receive or reject messages, and control the sequence of IUCV events. Communicators receive information about IUCV events by handling IUCV external interrupts.

The following IUCV features are supported by Linux for S/390:

- Multiple output paths from a Linux guest.
- Multiple input paths to a Linux guest.
- Simultaneous transmission and reception of multiple messages on the same or different paths.
- Network connections via a TCP/IP service machine gateway.

24.2 An example of server consolidation based on Linux

Figure 24-2 shows an example of a consolidated server environment that is based on Linux. There are two mainframes: A and B. Mainframe A is an IBM zSeries 900 machine, in which z/VM runs in an LPAR.

- z/VM is required to manage the three VM guests, one is used to run Linux for zSeries, a second is used to run Linux for S/390, and a third is used to run TCP/IP. The Linux for S/390 guest acts as a router for routing information between the internal network that connects the three z/VM guests and the external Ethernet LAN.

- The Linux guests and TCP/IP guest are connected by means of virtual HiperSockets, ensuring fast and efficient communication among these guests.

- The z/OS and Linux for zSeries that run in LPARs communicate with each other via a hardware HiperSockets function. They can also communicate with each of the Linux guests of Mainframe A through the OSA-Express adapter and the Linux for S/390 guest.

- The OSA-Express adapter, which uses a high-speed I/O protocol called *Queued Direct Input/Output (QDIO)*, enables communication to take place between the 1-Gigabit Ethernet LAN and the:
  - Linux for zSeries operating system running in an LPAR of Mainframe A.
  - z/OS operating system running in an LPAR of Mainframe A.
  - Linux guests of Mainframe A, through the Linux for S/390 guest.

Mainframe B represents a technology that is slightly older than that of Mainframe A. It is either an IBM 9672 G5 or G6 computer, where z/VM runs in native mode.

- z/VM manages the five VM guests, each of which is used to run a Linux for zSeries operating system.

- The VM guests are connected by means of virtual CTC connectors.

- The Linux guest called Linux for zSeries (3) acts as a router between the Gigabit Ethernet LAN and the Token-Ring network.

- Any of Mainframe A's Linux systems, or Mainframe B's Linux systems, can communicate with the Token-Ring through Mainframe B's:
  1. OSA-Express adapter
  2. Linux for zSeries (3) router
  3. OSA-2 adapter

  This assumes, of course, that the routing table of the TCIP/IP guest in Mainframe A contains an appropriate routing entry.

In the "real world," however, companies might configure their mainframe to have a hundred or more Linux guests and LPARS, used for running a wide range of applications. Such configurations are considerably more complex than that shown in Figure 24-2.

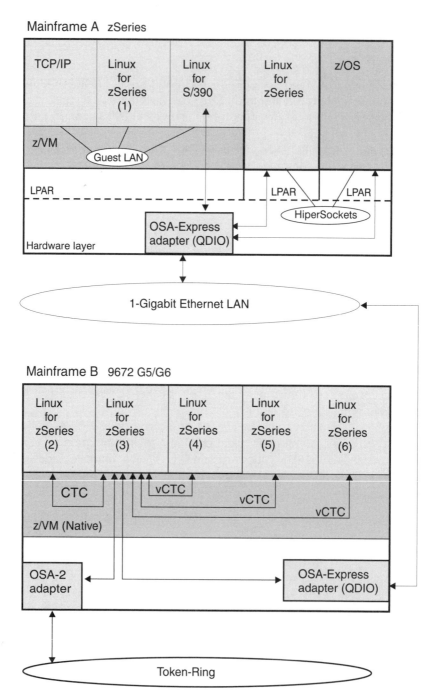

Figure 24-2. An example of server consolidation based on Linux

Chapter 25.
Systems Management Tools

PLEASE NOTE: The set of tools mentioned below may be incomplete. The information provided merely reflects the (potentially limited) knowledge of the authors. Moreover, the authors' classification of the functionality of the discussed tools is based on their own assessment. It should be noted that others might classify the functionality differently. Furthermore, due to the evolution of the tools, their capabilities may undergo additional changes not reflected in the information given below. The reader should form his/her own opinions. If interested in a particular class of tools, the reader is strongly advised to perform his/her own research, and may contact the providers of the various tools directly for further information. The reader may find the list of URLs at the end of the chapter helpful in this respect.

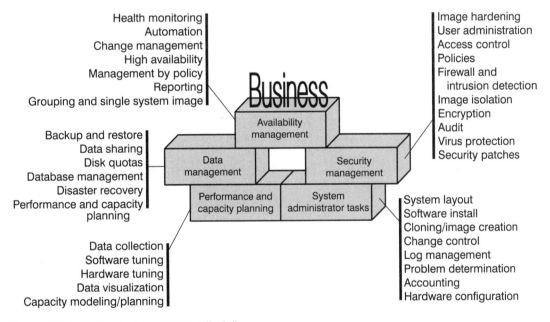

Figure 25-1. Systems management disciplines

This section contains tables of systems management tools and products. The tables are based on a survey of the systems management products offered by three major vendors and of three well-known Web sites with numerous Open Source projects or links to projects. The tables do not include tools or products that at the time of the survey had a release level below 1.0.

All but the final table are dedicated to one of the systems management disciplines as introduced in 12.2, "Systems management disciplines."

The table columns correspond to subdisciplines. Each table row represents a particular tool. For convenience, we are using the term tool in a very broad sense. The spectrum of *tools* ranges from single commands, to Open Source projects, vendor products, suites of products, and technologies, up to the entire hypervisor z/VM and its associated tooling. The tools are listed in alphabetical order. A check mark (√) indicates that the tool addresses some aspects of the subdiscipline.

The tables reflect our view of systems management as outlined in Chapter 12, "Systems Management," the scope of our survey, and our judgment at the time of the survey. We do not claim to have presented the only possible view of systems management, nor do we claim that our list of tools and products is complete. Because the number and scope of the available tools is constantly changing, the tables cannot possibly be complete.

To avoid overloading the tables, the final table summarizes all tools and provides the URL of a site with more information for each tool or, where applicable, to the corresponding vendor site.

We are presenting these tables to you because we want to share our effort with you and to give you a head start for developing your own tables. Your own research can focus on those aspects of systems management that are of the most concern to you and that reflect your own judgment on which concerns are addressed by each tool or product.

25.1 Availability management tools

In Table 25-1, entries for Open Source software are shaded.

Table 25-1 (Page 1 of 2). Availability management tools							
Tools	Health monitoring	Automation	Change management	High availability	Management by policy	Reporting	Grouping and single system image
Aduva OnStage			√				
BMC PATROL	√	√	√		√	√	√
BMC Mainview							√
CA Unicenter	√	√					√
HA Linux				√			
IBM Tivoli Configuration Manager			√		√	√	√
IBM Tivoli Enterprise Console	√	√			√	√	√
IBM Tivoli Monitoring	√	√			√	√	√
IBM Tivoli System Automation for Linux		√		√			
IBM Tivoli Workload Scheduler					√	√	√
Linux Virtual Server				√			
Linuxcare Levanta	√		√		√		√
Linuxconf		√	√		√		
moodss	√						
OpenNMS	√	√			√		√
VA Linux Cluster Manager	√						

Table 25-1 (Page 2 of 2). Availability management tools							
Tools	Health monitoring	Automation	Change management	High availability	Management by policy	Reporting	Grouping and single system image
Virtual IP Address				√			
Wily: Introscope	√						
z/VM	√	√	√		√	√	√

25.2 Data management tools

In Table 25-2, entries for Open Source software are shaded.

Table 25-2. Data management tools						
Tools	**Backup and restore**	**Data sharing**	**Disk quotas**	**Database management**	**Disaster recovery**	**Performance and capacity planning**
Amanda	√					
CA BrightStor ARCserve Backup for Linux	√				√	
GFS		√				
IBM Tivoli Storage Manager	√			√	√	
Innovation FDR/Upstream	√				√	
Linuxconf			√			
Linux DiskQuota			√			
quota			√			
tar	√				√	
UTS Tape Service Suite for Linux	√				√	
z/VM	√	√	√		√	√

25.3 Security management tools

In Table 25-3, entries for Open Source software are shaded.

Table 25-3 (Page 1 of 2). Security management tools

Tools	Image hardening	User administration	Access control	Policies	Firewall and intrusion detection	Image isolation	Encryption	Audit	Virus protection	Security patches
Bastille	√									
BestBits			√							
BMC INCON-TROL		√	√	√				√		
CA eTrust Access Control			√							
CA eTrust IDS					√					
IBM Tivoli Access Manager for e-business		√	√	√			√	√		
IBM Tivoli Risk Manager					√					√
netfilter/iptables					√					
LIDS					√					
LPAR						√				
McAfee E-Business Server							√			
MIMEDefang									√	
OpenSSL							√			

Table 25-3 (Page 2 of 2). Security management tools										
Tools	Image hardening	User administration	Access control	Policies	Firewall and intrusion detection	Image isolation	Encryption	Audit	Virus protection	Security patches
PAM		√								
RAV antivirus									√	
RSBAC			√	√						
Security-Enhanced Linux			√	√						
Snort					√					
StoneGate					√					
TARA	√									
Tripwire					√					
zGuard					√					
z/VM						√				

25.4 Performance and capacity planning tools

In Table 25-4, entries for Open Source software are shaded.

Table 25-4. Performance and capacity planning tools

Tools	Data collection	Software tuning	Hardware tuning	Data visualization	Capacity modeling and planning
Big Brother	√				
BMC PATROL	√	√	√	√	√
IBM Tivoli Monitoring	√	√	√	√	
IBM Tivoli Monitoring for Transaction Performance	√	√	√	√	
moodss		√		√	
OpenNMS	√	√	√	√	
Performance Co-pilot	√			√	
RMF PM	√				
sysstat (sar, iostat)	√		√		
Velocity Software ESAxyz (MAP, MON, TCP, WEB)	√	√			√
z/VM(1)	√	√	√	√	√

(1) For more details on the z/VM tools see Table 26-2.

25.5 System administrator tools

In Table 25-5, entries for Open Source software are shaded.

Table 25-5 (Page 1 of 2). System Administrator Tools

Tools	System layout	Software install	Cloning/ image creation	Change control	Log management	Problem determination	Accounting	Hardware configuration
Aduva OnStage			√	√				
BMC PATROL						√		
CA Unicenter		√						
cfengine			√	√				
HCM								√
IBM Tivoli Configuration Manager		√		√	√			
IBM Tivoli Monitoring						√		
IBM Tivoli Workload Scheduler					√	√		
Linux debugging facilities(1)						√		
Linux dump tools(2)						√		
Linuxcare Levanta	√	√	√	√				√
Linuxconf	√			√				
logconf					√			
moodss						√		
Red Hat kickstart		√						

The debugging reference section contains more information on the Linux debugging tools:

(1) For details on the "Linux debugging facilities" see Table 22-2 and Table 22-3.

(2) For details on "Linux dump tools" see Table 22-4.

Tools	System layout	Software install	Cloning/ image creation	Change control	Log management	Problem determination	Accounting	Hardware configuration
RPM	√	√	√	√				
SAC							√	
SGI CSA (Comprehensive System Accounting)							√	
SGI Rhino	√							√
SuSE YaST	√	√		√				
System Imager	√	√	√					
System Installer	√	√						
Velocity Software ESAxyz (MAP, MON, TCP, WEB)						√		
z900 Input/Output Configuration Program	√							√
z/VM	√	√	√	√	√	√	√	√

Table 25-5 (Page 2 of 2). System Administrator Tools

The debugging reference section contains more information on the Linux debugging tools:

(1) For details on the "Linux debugging facilities" see Table 22-2 and Table 22-3.

(2) For details on "Linux dump tools" see Table 22-4.

25.6 Tools Web sites

Table 25-6 summarizes the tools of the previous sections in this chapter and gives a URL for each tool where you can find more information.

Table 25-6 (Page 1 of 4). Tools Web sites	
Tool	**URL**
Aduva OnStage	http://www.aduva.com/
Amanda	http://www.amanda.org/
Bastille	http://www.bastille-linux.org/
BestBits	http://acl.bestbits.at/
Big Brother	http://bb4.com/
BMC	http://www.bmc.com/
BMC INCONTROL	http://www.bmc.com/products/documents/60/51/6051/6051.pdf
BMC MAINVIEW	http://www.bmc.com/products/proddocview/0,2832,19052_19429_26309_8716,00.html
BMC PATROL	http://www.bmc.com/products/proddocview/0,2832,19052_19429_26321_8978,00.html
CA	http://www3.ca.com/Solutions/SubSolution.asp?ID=3279
CA BrightStor ARCserve Backup for Linux	http://www3.ca.com/Solutions/Product.asp?ID=3370
CA eTrust Access Control	http://www3.ca.com/Solutions/Product.asp?ID=154
CA eTrust IDS	http://www3.ca.com/Solutions/Product.asp?ID=163
CA Unicenter	http://www3.ca.com/press/PressRelease.asp?CID=37246
cfengine	http://www.cfengine.org/
GFS	http://www.sistina.com/products_gfs.htm
HA Linux	http://linux-ha.org/
HCM	http://www.ibm.com/servers/eserver/zseries/zos/hcm/
IBM Tivoli Access Manager for e-Business	http://www.ibm.com/software/tivoli/products/access-mgr-e-bus/

Table 25-6 (Page 2 of 4). Tools Web sites

Tool	URL
IBM Tivoli Configuration Manager	http://www.ibm.com/software/tivoli/products/config-mgr/
IBM Tivoli Enterprise Console	http://www.ibm.com/software/tivoli/products/enterprise-console/
IBM Tivoli Monitoring	http://www.ibm.com/software/tivoli/products/monitor/
IBM Tivoli Monitoring for Trans-action Per-formance	http://www.ibm.com/software/tivoli/products/monitor-transaction/
IBM Tivoli Risk Manager	http://www.ibm.com/software/tivoli/products/risk-mgr/
IBM Tivoli Storage Manager	http://www.ibm.com/software/tivoli/products/storage-mgr/
IBM Tivoli System Auto-mation for Linux	http://www.ibm.com/software/tivoli/products/sys-auto-linux/
IBM Tivoli Workload Scheduler	http://www.ibm.com/software/tivoli/products/scheduler/
Innovation FDR/Upstream	http://www.innovationdp.fdr.com/linux_fdrupstream.cfm
netfilter/iptables	http://www.iptables.org/
LIDS	http://www.lids.org
Linux DiskQuota	http://sourceforge.net/projects/linuxquota/
Linux Virtual Server	http://www.linuxvirtualserver.org
Linuxcare Levanta	http://www.linuxcare.com/products/index.epl
Linuxconf	http://www.solucorp.qc.ca/linuxconf/
logconf	http://sourceforge.net/projects/logconf/
LPAR	http://www.ibm.com/servers/eserver/zseries/library/whitepapers/pdf/gf225174.pdf

Table 25-6 (Page 3 of 4). Tools Web sites	
Tool	**URL**
McAfee E-Business Server	http://www.mcafeeb2b.com/products/ebusiness.asp
MIMEDefang	http://www.roaringpenguin.com/mimedefang/
moodss	http://freshmeat.net/releases/103156/ http://jfontain.free.fr/moodss/
OpenNMS	http://www.opennms.org/
OpenSSL	http://www.openssl.org/
PAM	http://www.kernel.org/pub/linux/libs/pam/index.html
Performance Co-pilot (PCP)	http://oss.sgi.com/projects/pcp/
quota	http://www.asenec.com/quota.html
RAV anti-virus	http://www.ravantivirus.com/pages/isp.php
Red Hat Kickstart	http://www.redhat.com/docs/manuals/linux/RHL-7.3-Manual/custom-guide/ch-ksconfig.html
RMF PM	http://www.ibm.com/servers/eserver/zseries/zos/rmf/rmfhtmls/pmweb/pmlin.htm
RPM	http://www.rpm.org/
RSBAC	http://www.compuniverse.com/rsbac/
SAC	http://mama.indstate.edu/users/ice/sac/
Security-Enhanced Linux	http://www.nsa.gov/selinux/
SGI CSA (Comprehensive System Accounting)	http://oss.sgi.com/projects/csa
SGI Rhino	http://oss.sgi.com/projects/rhino/
Snort	http://www.snort.org/about.html
StoneGate	http://www.stonesoft.com/products/StoneGate/
SuSE YaST	http://www.suse.de/us/whitepapers/yast/
sysstat (sar, iostat)	http://perso.wanadoo.fr/sebastien.godard/
System Imager	http://sourceforge.net/projects/systemimager/
System Installer	http://systeminstaller.sourceforge.net/

Table 25-6 (Page 4 of 4). Tools Web sites

Tool	URL
tar	http://www.gnu.org/software/tar/tar.html
TARA	http://www-arc.com/tara/
Tripwire	http://www.tripwire.org/
UTS Tape Service Suite for Linux	http://www.utsglobal.com/linuxprod.html
VA Linux Cluster Manager	http://vacm.sourceforge.net/
Velocity Software ESAxyz (MAP, MON, TCP, WEB)	http://www.velocitysoftware.com/product.html
Virtual IP Address	http://www.ibm.com/servers/eserver/zseries/networking/vipa.html
Wily: Introscope	http://www.wilytech.com/solutions.html
zGuard	http://www.zguard.de/zGuard-02.01e-Flyer.pdf
z/VM	http://www.vm.ibm.com/
z900 Input/Output Configuration Program	http://publibz.boulder.ibm.com/epubs/pdf/b1070290.pdf

Chapter 26.
Performance Reference

This chapter presents detailed guidelines for tuning guests under z/VM, as well as a selection of performance tools.

26.1 Tuning Linux guests under VM

26.1.1 DASD subsystem

Linux disk support for the traditional zSeries disks is provided by the DASD driver code, dasd.c. It provides support for Count-Key-Data (CKD) and Fixed Block Address (FBA) disk devices, as well as VM minidisks. The DASD driver uses channel I/O to perform read and write operations.

There are currently three ways to format disks used by Linux:

1. dasdfmt

   The DASD driver in Linux for zSeries and S/390 comes with the dasdfmt utility to format the disks. It formats all tracks on the disk with a fixed block size. There is no support for this particular format in existing S/390 software.

2. CMS FORMAT

   The FORMAT program in CMS also formats the disk with fixed block size, but adds a special eye catcher in R3. This format is recognized by CMS and by CP.

3. RESERVE

   With the CMS RESERVE command, a file is created to fill the entire (CMS-formatted) minidisk. The Linux file system is then built into this file so that the original CMS formatting of the disk is retained.

DASD guidelines

1. If you use IBM RAMAC Virtual Array (RVA), there would be a benefit if you use the "Instant format" function. The instant format function is part of the VM SnapShot function; an instant copy of a formatted (empty) disk is made on the extent to be formatted using the SnapShot feature of RVA. This copy is instantaneous and does not occupy back-end storage in the RVA.

2. For DASD (disk) storage, there are options to read-only share some amount of disk between servers. Using VM's minidisk cache to cache shared data once is significantly more effective than having Linux cache the same data.

3. For VM minidisks using the CMS RESERVE format, VM Diagnose I/O can be used to provide better performance. See "VM Diagnose I/O."

4. Linux can also use a disk that was only formatted by CMS. In this case, Linux will use all the blocks on the disk, so that CMS ACCESS will fail on this disk afterwards. Even when you do not need the ability to access the blocks from CMS, there may still be a reason to prefer this format over Linux dasdfmt. VM directory management products such as DirMaint can format the disk before making it available to the user ID.

5. There is no reason to use the dasdfmt command for Linux images on VM, except for the situation where you have a virtual machine running Linux, and you forgot to format the disks. Since Linux does not yet tolerate DETACH and LINK of minidisks very well, you would have no other option than to shut down the Linux system and get back to CMS to format it.

   Note: This would not occur if you do an automatic format with DirMaint.

6. XPRAM (see 20.4.7, "Expanded memory support") enables Linux to use expanded memory as disk space. For data that are used often in a session, using the XPRAM driver may help to enhance your performance. Another way to enhance performance is to use LVM for your DASD containing the Web content. LVM enables you to combine several DASDs on one logical volume. Stripping the logical volume can enhance DASD access times considerably.

Minidisk caching (MDC)

VM provides a feature that can provide a good performance benefit for physical disk access. VM minidisk caching allocates memory in VM to cache guest minidisks to accelerate disk access.

While Linux provides its own buffer cache, it is still advantageous to provide a "second-level" disk cache, because the Linux cache takes lower priority to real user processes in Linux's memory allocation. This means that there may not always be enough free memory available for Linux to provide an effective cache internally. The memory for the minidisk cache is pre-allocated, so there is always at least one level of caching available to the Linux guests.

Minidisk caching has been shown to dramatically improve the performance of Linux guests with file systems on minidisk. There is a trade-off, however, because allocating memory to minidisk cache means that there is less memory available to be allocated to guests. Adding more memory to the processor may be justified in order to be able to take advantage of the available performance gain.

Minidisk caching effectiveness is greater for minidisks that are shared between Linux guests. In those cases, a single copy of the data can reside in the MDC instead of multiple copies of data, a different one in each guest. Minidisk caching can be done at a track level or at a block level.

Minidisk cache guidelines:

1. Configure some real storage for MDC.

   You need some real storage allocated to MDC to keep it from thrashing in real storage. The idea is that MDC must use main storage anyway unless the reads work out perfectly block-aligned. If you do not allocate real storage for MDC, you lose the benefit of those intermediate real storage buffers. MDC picks the amount of real storage for its needs in such a way that the average lifetime of an MDC page equals the average lifetime of a user page in the dynamic paging area (DPA).

2. In general, enable MDC for everything.

3. Disable MDC for:

   * Write-mostly or read-once disks (logs, accounting, and so forth)
   * Backup applications

4. For large storage environments, it is not advisable to use MDC.

   In large storage environments (greater than 2GB) CP tends to overcalculate MDC pages needed. Use SET MDCACHE to apply a scale-down fudge factor to CP's calculation.

5. MDC is a better performer than vdisks for read I/Os.

   "MDC faster than vdisk reads" is a path length statement. vdisk uses system utility address spaces which tend to be accessed via general-purpose (read "slower") macros.

VM Diagnose I/O

The biggest advantage of the CMS RESERVE format is that it is the only disk format for which the current Linux for S/390 DASD driver can use VM Diagnose I/O. Diagnose I/O is a high-level protocol that allows the user ID to access blocks on its minidisks with less overhead than pure S/390 channel programs with Start Subchannel (SSCH). To enable VM diagnose I/O in the DASD driver, you must configure the kernel to enable the "Support for DIAG access to CMS formatted Disks," which is not done in the default SuSE kernel. To enable the option, you first need to disable the "Support for VM minidisk (VM only)" configuration option (also known as the old mdisk driver).

DASD response time

When evaluating DASD response time, the response time value is usually the most significant; it shows how much time an average I/O takes to the device. If this value is large, the components of response are evaluated. Thes DASD components are evaluated as follows:

1. Pend time

   This is the amount of time it takes to start I/O on the channel; normally less than one ms.

2. Disc time

   This is the amount of time it takes for the control unit to access the data. This includes rotational delays, seek delays, and processing time inside the control unit. Disc (for disconnect) time is normally less than 2 to 3 ms on cache controllers.

3. Connect time

   This is the amount of time it takes to transfer the data on the channel, normally less than 2 ms for a 4 KB block of data.

4. Service time

   This is the sum result of pend, disconnect and connect times added together. In some environments, installations may choose to use only the sum of disconnect and connect, but this is not typical.

5. Queue time

   This is the result of many users accessing the same device. If the device is already servicing another user when an I/O is started, the I/O sits in queue. The length of time in queue is queue time. This is the component of response time that, under load, is the most variable and the most serious.

26.1.2 Processor subsystem

Knowing how much processor is used, and by which servers, is information you need to know for efficient performance monitoring and problem analysis. Controlling the rate at which your servers access the processor is done by setting Shares. Share settings have a minimum value and a maximum value, with several options and variations of each. Using the CP monitor, you can capture over 99.9% of the processing power used. Building a processor map showing how much processor is used by LPAR, VM, Linux servers, VM servers, and CMS allows you to project future requirements based on new users or customers.

Processor guidelines

1. A virtual machine should have either all dedicated or all shared processors.

   Dedicating is a bad idea if you are CPU-constrained. However, a dedicated processor gets the wait state assist and the minor time slice becomes 500 milliseconds. Do not mix dedicated and shared processors because it results in VM CPUs of drastically different speeds, which is problematic. Usually a higher absolute share is as good as dedicating a processor.

2. Share settings:

   - Use absolute if you can judge the percentage of resources required.
   - Use relative if it is difficult to judge the percent of resources required and if a lower share is acceptable when the system load increases.
   - Do not use LIMITHARD settings unnecessarily.

   The downside of LIMITHARD is more scheduler overhead. Also, it masks looping users, which means you cannot discern them from legitimate work and debit their accounts.

3. Use a short minor time slice as it keeps CP reactive.

   A long minor time slice blocks master-only work and increases the trivial response time. Additionally, if the minor time slice is long, managing absolute shares is problematic.

Server guidelines

1. Set QUICKDSP ON to avoid eligible list. QUICKDSP ON allows us to overcommit storage. However, you must make sure the paging system can handle it. Maybe the 50% rule should be changed to 33%, and you should ensure that the paging system is ready for concurrency.

2. A higher SHARE setting. Maybe even absolute is appropriate.

3. SET RESERVED in directory option.

4. NOMDCFS in directory option. NOMDCFS suppresses CP's usual attempt to hold the VM back to "its share" of MDC pages. Since we are "eating for two" (or N) here, this is OK. You must be careful, though, as you are giving up your only throttle on MDC for this.

5. Exploit DASD Fast Write for servers that do synchronous writes. In DASD FW, the CPU gives CE and DE as soon as the write is safe in NVS. 3990-3 and early-6 needed this. Knobs are: SET DASDFW ON, SET NVS ON, and SET CACHE ON. Later on, control units will do this entirely under the covers, and you will no longer have any control, not even to turn it off.

Virtual Machine (VM) guidelines

Do not define more virtual CPUs than necessary. Too many virtual CPUs erodes share and increases path length through the dispatcher.

CP command guidelines

Using the CP Indicate command, you can interrogate many items. However, for detailed analysis over long periods, you are probably better off looking at reports from VMPRF or some other tool if you are trying to discern trends via repeated use of these commands.

1. LOAD: shows total system load.

   IND LOAD shows processor utilization, XSTOR, PAGING, MDC summaries, dispatcher queue lengths, and potential load on storage (sum of working set size of virtual machines in the dispatch list divided by size of the DPA). The STORAGE value is unreliable as working set size often includes scheduler fudge factors as well as the QUICKDSP value (which causes storage to become overcommitted anyway).

2. IND USER EXP: more useful than IND USER.

   This command provides a good sketch of one user's consumption history: pages resident, use of paging resources and processor time consumed. It is more useful than the USER command, because it shows every address space (data space) and the fields will not overflow.

3. IND QUEUES EXP: great for scheduler problems and quick state sampling.

   This command shows the contents of the dispatch list and the eligible list, in priority order. It helps to show if an eligible list is forming. (If an eligible list forms, it means some resource is constrained.)

4. IND PAGING: lists users in page wait.

5. IND IO: lists users in I/O wait and the device they are waiting on.

6. IND ACTIVE: displays the number of active users over a given interval.

CP QUERY command:

1. USERS: number and type of users on system.

2. SRM: scheduler/dispatcher settings.

   Using this command, you can look up the settings for the scheduler (DSPBUF, LDUBUF, STORBUF, and so forth). For a description of scheduler knobs, see HELP CPSET SRM.

3. SHARE: type and intensity of system share. Shows relative/absolute and maximum (if applicable).

4. FRAMES: real storage allocation.

   Shows use of real storage frames: V=R, res NUC, DPA, pageable NUC, trace table. However, it does not show contention information; only how the frames are spread among these key areas.

5. PATHS: physical paths to device and status.

6. ALLOC MAP: Shows DASD allocation—what's where on your DASD. Make sure to check to see if you left paging on your respack.

7. XSTORE: assignment of expanded storage.

8. MONITOR: current monitor settings.

9. MDC: MDC usage.

10. VDISK: virtual disk in storage use.

State sampling

Using state sampling, you can record the state of some object (user, device) periodically and then observe the sequence of samples to try to discern a trend. You can take a snap view, a low-frequency view, or a high-frequency view.

1. Snap view:

   INDICATE QUEUES tells you about the whole system's scheduler behavior and RTM. Display User can tell you about a particular user.

   - INDICATE QUEUES gives a snapshot view of the scheduling system. If we see an E-list over a long period, for example, we can suspect a resource contention issue (storage or paging, probably). We can then go to other sources to learn more.

   - RTM Display User: a snapshot of recent consumption history for the specified user. Viewed repeatedly over time, we can discern trends.

2. Low frequency view:

   - RTM Display SRC:

     Over a very long period (hours), we can witness the percentage of time the whole set spent being active, in page wait, I/O wait, running, in E-list, and so forth.

3. High frequency view:

   HF data are very useful for discerning short-lived phenomena. The counters and state variables are sampled every few seconds and are rolled up into the monitor data each time a sample is written. The roll up is a histogram of the sample period or the sum of the samples over the period along with the number of samples taken.

- Monitor: user, processor, and I/O domains:
  - User: The user's state (running, waiting on I/O, waiting on paging, test idle, inst sim wait, scheduler class, for example, Q1, and so forth). Be careful here because a user can be in more than one state at a time (for example, test idle and async I/O, or paging), and the states are interrogated in a certain order (only the first state found is reported). This can cause discrepancies.
  - Processor: Size of PLDV, size of master-only queue.
  - I/O domains: number of items in queue for RDEV.

26.1.3 Storage subsystem

Lack of storage to meet the requirement results in paging, and paging causes delays in service. Monitoring the storage requirements and the impacts of applications provides necessary feedback for capacity planning and performance problem analysis. There are many ways to reduce storage, and on VM there are different types of storage. For storage capacity planning purposes, you should maintain a map of your storage to understand the requirements for VM, minidisk cache, Linux user storage (by customer), VM Servers (TCP/IP, management service machines), and CMS users, if any. This map should be maintained for both Expanded Storage and Real Storage.

For storage (memory), there are several options, each with different impacts on Linux, applications, and your global resources. Coming from a minicomputer or microcomputer environment, administrators have been taught that swapping is undesirable. When swapping to slow SCSI devices, this may be true, but on zSeries and S/390, there are many other options—and these options can reduce your overall (global) resource requirements. For swapping, the alternative options are:

- Use Virtual disk as a swap device. The benefit is a much smaller page space requirement, as well as a smaller requirement for real storage.

- Use RAMdisk as a swap device. The benefit is a smaller requirement for real storage. When sharing storage between many servers, this is important.

Storage guidelines

1. Use SET RESERVE instead of LOCK to keep the user's pages in storage. LOCK is ill advised unless you have a very clear view of what is going on inside the virtual machine. Even locking page 0 of a VM guest is not recommended.

   SET RESERVE holds a count whereas LOCK hits specific pages. Guidelines for SET RESERVE:

   * Working set plus 10%

   * Observe via user state sampling and adjust again.

   * Watch that WS does not run away.

2. Define some processor storage as expanded storage.

   The purpose is to provide paging hierarchy, even when running a 64-bit CPU. Unless you have absolutely no storage constraints (paging=0), leave some expanded storage because it helps even out paging waits. See article in:
   http://www.vm.ibm.com/perf/tips/.

3. Exploit shared segments and SAVEFD where possible.

4. SFS use of VM data spaces saves storage because it shares FSTs.

5. DB/2 use of VM data spaces requires storage.

   DB/2 uses MAPMDISK to improve its DASD performance and creates private spaces for its own purposes (for example, sorting). This trades storage for I/O mostly.

Paging guidelines

1. Keep DASD paging allocations less than or equal to 50%.

   Allocate enough space so that your paging space is never more than 50% full. You can use QUERY ALLOC PAGE to see how full your paging space is. One of the VMPRF reports also shows this.

2. Watch blocks read per paging request (keep > 10).

   If blocks read per page-in is less than 10, you do not have enough paging space allocated. The idea is to make it easy for CP to find large runs of unused slots so that it can do block paging easily.

3. With multiple volumes, remember the rule: *One I/O per subchannel at a time.*

4. With multiple paths, remember the rule: *All paging devices on same string, one channel for whole string is a bad idea.*

5. Do not mix with other data types.

Mixing makes VM stop seldom-ending channel program it runs for paging. However, the system is delivered this way; therefore, at installation time, use stand-alone ICKDSF to get rid of the paging on the SYSRES. At the same, move the spool, if possible.

6. In a RAID environment, enable cache to mitigate write penalty.

The consensus used to be "don't enable cache for paging devices" because it thrashed the caches for non-paging devices behind the controller. However, in RAID, one write can result in two reads (parity and data) and then two writes (parity and data). Enabling cache helps the controller deal with this. Also, recent controllers (3990–6) are much smarter about caching, and they have enormous (GBs) cache, so cache thrashing is less of an issue.

26.2 When to use kernel patches

From time to time, if you need to monitor your Linux Kernel, you will need to install the necessary patches. For example, for the Kernprof (Kernel Profiling) tool, you need patches that implement a number of profiling data collection mechanisms, as well as a device driver for controlling them, plus the user level command kernprof that allows you to configure and control the kernel profiling facilities. Also included is a small gcc patch that is necessary to build correct i386 kernels.

The patches that you need to install are therefore dependent on the tool you are going to use.

Note: If you tweak the code (patch the kernel), you may lose your service contract with SuSE or RedHat or anyone who supplied you with Linux. Therefore, this is typically only an option for test environments, not for production.

26.3 Performance tools

There is a joke that goes something like this:

A drunk is seen falling about on the roadside beside a lamp post, looking for something. A passerby asks him: "What are you looking for?" "My car keys," replies the drunk. "Well," says the passerby, "do you know approximately where you lost them?" "Somewhere over there," says the drunk pointing to the dark side of the road. "So why look for them here?" "Because there is light here," replies the drunk!

The problem with many proprietary operating systems is that you are compelled to expend your energies looking for performance problem solutions, but only in areas where the available tools permit you to do so. Here the zSeries and S/390 are different from other platforms. The S/390 platform has been designed and tuned for more than two decades and there exists a vast array of tools, both from IBM and other vendors, that can be used to find bottlenecks and tune them out. Additionally, with Linux, you have the option to tweak the source code.

26.3.1 Lockmeter

When you have a shared-memory multiprocessor operation, you require a locking mechanism before you access a shared resource, such as shared data structure, and a release mechanism when you are done. Contention occurs if more than one process tries to acquire the lock at the same time. Since only one process can have the lock, the other process has to wait until the lock is released. This wait can be implemented in one of two ways:

1. A tight instruction loop that constantly attempts to acquire the lock until it succeeds. This is referred to as "spinning."

2. The task requiring the lock is suspended and the processor runs some other task.

Locks are therefore classified as either "spin" locks or "suspend" locks.

Symmetric multiprocessor (SMP) system performance is typically determined by two factors:

- Instruction path length

- Lock contention

Lockmeter is an Open Source tool from SGI to monitor the spin lock and read/write lock usage. It reports statistics for all spin locks, summary for each spin lock, and data for each caller of the lock. You can use the data from lockmeter to identify which portions of the kernel code are responsible for lock contention and hence a source of bottlenecks.

The tool consists of a kernel patch that implements the data collection mechanisms and the user level command **lockstat**. Lockmeter is available at:
http://oss.sgi.com/projects/lockmeter/.

A version of a kernel patch for S/390 platform is available for both 31-bit and 64-bit platforms. For more information, see "Lockmeter: Highly-Informative Instrumentation for Spin Locks in the Linux Kernel" at:
http://oss.sgi.com/projects/lockmeter/als2000/als2000lock.html.

26.3.2 Profiling tools

Kernel profiler—kernprof

kernprof is an Open Source tool from SGI. It is a kernel profiler that collects performance-related data in the Linux kernel to help you to identify performance problems. The tool offers various sampling modes which differ in the quality and quantity of the information collected (and in the overhead imposed on execution time):

- The simplest mode merely gathers the program counters at certain intervals.

- The most sophisticated mode constructs a complete call graph containing data for each function that is called and the callers while profiling was on.

The tool consists of a kernel patch and the command, kernprof, that allow a user to configure and control kernel profiling. For more information and downloads, see Kernprof (Kernel Profiling) at: http://oss.sgi.com/projects/kernprof/.

Application profiling

You do profiling if you are trying to understand the performance characteristics of an application such as heavily used areas of an application source code. The goal is to determine problems with a view to making code changes to fix the problem. Three application profilers currently available on Linux on the mainframe are listed in Table 26-1.

Table 26-1. Tools for application profiling		
Tool name	Where available	Description
gprof	Part of the binutils component of Linux for S/390.	gprof is the GNU profiler for single-threaded C programs that is available on Linux for S/390. You can run gprof repeatedly to collect data, then average the results of each run to obtain more accurate statistics.
cprof	Part of the binutils component of Linux for S/390.	cprof is the GNU profiler for multithreaded C and C++ programs that is available on Linux for S/390.
vprof	http://aros.ca.sandia.gov/ ˜cljanss/perf/vprof/	vprof is a visual profiler you can use for single-threaded C and C++ programs. It is available with SuSE Linux Enterprise Server offering.

26.3.3 Monitoring tools

Display processes—the top command

In Linux, any running program is assigned a process ID. The system administrator can list these IDs with the top command. The administrator can use the IDs to stop, restart, or change the priority of a process. The top command gives a relatively complete list of the processes running on the system (Figure 26-1 and Figure 26-2). Especially useful with the wchan option (to enable: "f," "u" and "enter").

Notes:

1. top does not show any LAN activity.

2. Resident set size (RSS) is often incorrect because it simply adds the resident size of the process without taking shared memory into consideration.

```
top output:

   8:59am  up 10:22,  1 user,   load average: 5.00, 5.00, 5.00
38 processes: 36 sleeping, 2 running, 0 zombie, 0 stopped
CPU0 states:  0.0% user,  0.0% system,  0.0% nice, 100.0% idle
CPU1 states:  0.0% user,  0.0% system,  0.0% nice, 100.0% idle
CPU2 states:  0.0% user,  0.0% system,  0.0% nice, 100.0% idle
CPU3 states:  0.0% user,  0.0% system,  0.0% nice, 100.0% idle
Mem:    124020K av,   68792K used,   55228K free,       0K shrd,   16272K buff
Swap: 2047960K av,    3972K used, 2043988K free                    10556K cached
```

Figure 26-1. TOP output

```
PID USER        PRI  NI  SIZE   RSS SHARE WCHAN       STAT %CPU %MEM  TIME COMMAND
  1 root          8   0   316   272   264 do_select   S     0.0  0.2  0:00 init
  2 root          9   0     0     0     0 down_inte   SW    0.0  0.0  0:00 kmcheck
  3 root          9   0     0     0     0 context_t   SW    0.0  0.0  0:00 keventd
  4 root         19  19     0     0     0 ksoftirqd   SWN   0.0  0.0  0:00 ksoftirqd_CPU0
  5 root         19  19     0     0     0 ksoftirqd   SWN   0.0  0.0  0:00 ksoftirqd_CPU1
  6 root         19  19     0     0     0 ksoftirqd   SWN   0.0  0.0  0:00 ksoftirqd_CPU2
  7 root         19  19     0     0     0             RWN   0.0  0.0  0:00 ksoftirqd_CPU3
  8 root          9   0     0     0     0 kswapd      SW    0.0  0.0  0:09 kswapd
  9 root          9   0     0     0     0 bdflush     SW    0.0  0.0  0:01 bdflush
 10 root          9   0     0     0     0 kupdate     SW    0.0  0.0  0:00 kupdated
 66 root         -1 -20     0     0     0 down_inte   SW<   0.0  0.0  0:00 lvm-mpd
 85 root         -1 -20     0     0     0 end         SW<   0.0  0.0  0:00 mdrecoveryd
265 root          9   0     0     0     0 down_inte   SW    0.0  0.0  0:00 qethsoftd14e8
268 root          9   0     0     0     0 down_inte   SW    0.0  0.0  0:00 qethsoftd0bc8
365 rpc           9   0   532   448   448 do_poll     S     0.0  0.3  0:00 portmap
385 rpcuser       9   0   684   584   576 do_select   S     0.0  0.4  0:00 rpc.statd
432 root          8   0  2296  2296  2048 do_select   S     0.0  1.8  0:00 ntpd
443 root          9   0   332   152   148 do_select   S     0.0  0.1  0:00 sshd
459 root          9   0   508   400   360 do_select   S     0.0  0.3  0:00 xinetd
478 root          9   0   900   452   400 do_select   S     0.0  0.3  0:00 sendmail
489 root          8   0   252   212   196 nanosleep   S     0.0  0.1  0:00 crond
533 xfs           9   0  2896   256   216 do_select   S     0.0  0.2  0:00 xfs
571 root          9   0   164   108   108 read_chan   S     0.0  0.0  0:00 mingetty
618 root          9   0     0     0     0 down        DW    0.0  0.0  0:00 zfcp_erp_0x5a02
619 root          9   0     0     0     0 down_inte   SW    0.0  0.0  0:00 scsi_eh_0
624 root          9   0     0     0     0 down        DW    0.0  0.0  0:00 zfcp_erp_0x5b02
625 root          9   0     0     0     0 down_inte   SW    0.0  0.0  0:00 scsi_eh_1
630 root          9   0     0     0     0 down        DW    0.0  0.0  0:00 zfcp_erp_0x5900
631 root          9   0     0     0     0 down_inte   SW    0.0  0.0  0:00 scsi_eh_2
636 root          9   0     0     0     0 down        DW    0.0  0.0  0:00 zfcp_erp_0x5910
637 root          9   0     0     0     0 down_inte   SW    0.0  0.0  0:00 scsi_eh_3
662 root          9   0     0     0     0 kjournald   SW    0.0  0.0  0:07 kjournald
1389 root         9   0   720   720   604 do_select   S     0.0  0.5  0:00 syslogd
1394 root         9   0   476   472   408 do_syslog   S     0.0  0.3  0:00 klogd
1601 root         9   0   748   748   620 do_select   S     0.0  0.6  0:00 in.telnetd
1602 root        10   0  1160  1160   920 wait4       S     0.0  0.9  0:00 login
1603 root        10   0  1352  1352  1012 wait4       S     0.0  1.0  0:00 bash
1631 root        14   0  1252  1252  1064             R     0.0  1.0  0:00 top
```

Figure 26-2. Display of CPU top processes

Display system status—the sysstat package

SYSSTAT is an Open Source statistics gathering package comprising the listed commands:

1. mpstat

   The mpstat command reports processor statistics for each available processor, starting with processor 0. The command can be used for SMP or UP machines. It reports global average activities among all processors. For UP machines, only global average activities are printed. For more information, see the SYSSTAT utilities home page at: http://perso.wanadoo.fr/sebastien.godard/.

2. vmstat (report virtual memory statistics):

   vmstat produces a report that contains information about processes, memory, paging, block I/O, traps, and CPU activity. A sample output is shown in Figure 26-3. See *VMSTAT: Report virtual memory statistics* at: http://nodevice.com/sections/ManIndex/man1908.html for further information.

```
vmstat output:
    procs                     memory      swap          io     system          cpu
  r  b  w   swpd   free   buff   cache  si   so    bi    bo   in    cs  us  sy   id
  0  5  4   4012  13680  12016   61664   0    0    13    92    0    25   0   0  100
  0  5  5   4012  13252  12020   62088   0    0     0 13736    0   276   0   2   98
  0  5  5   4012   4792  12148   70372   0    0     0 15532    0   233   0   5   95
  0  5  5   4088   2548  11164   73860   0   72  1000 18104    0   344   2   6   91
  0  5  5   4088   2236  11176   74148   0    0    72 11476    0   198   0   0  100
  0  5  5   4088   3020  11200   73296   0    0    28 15640    0   207   1   0   99
  0  5  5   4088   2540  11252   73724   0    0    48  5092    0   137   0   0   99
  1  4  4   4088   5740  11280   70496   0    0     0   104    0    84   2   0   98
  4  0  6   4088  25312  12072   50456   0    0  7224     0    0   833  45  21   34
```

Figure 26-3. Sample output of vmstat command

3. iostat (report CPU statistics and input/output statistics for tty devices and disks):

   You can use the iostat command to monitor disk loading. It calculates this by measuring the time the disks are busy in relation to their average transfer rates. You can use reports generated by iostat to change system configuration to balance I/O load between physical disks. For more information, see SYSSTAT utilities home page at:
   http://perso.wanadoo.fr/sebastien.godard/.

4. sar (system activity information):

   The sar command displays selected activity counters in the operating system. The data can be saved in a file you specify as well as being displayed on screen if you specify the –o filename flag. If you omit the filename, /var/log/sa/sadd file is used. The dd parameter indicates the current day. sar is used to look at the historical view of system performance. sar does not show LAN activity or paging, etc. For more information, see SYSSTAT utilities home page at:
   http://perso.wanadoo.fr/sebastien.godard/.

   Other sar related tools are:

   a. sadc (system activity data collector):

      This command reports only local activity and is to be used as a back-end to the sar command. The command samples system data a specified number of times at specified intervals in seconds. The data are written to screen or to a file. If no outfile is specified, sadc saves to /var/log/sa/sadd file, where the dd parameter indicates the current day.

   b. sa1 (collect and store binary data in the system activity daily data file):

      The sa1 command can be started by the cron command. It is a shell procedure variant of the sadc command; therefore, it handles all of the flags and parameters of that command. The command collects and stores binary data in the /var/log/sa/sadd file, where the dd parameter indicates the current day.

   c. sa2 (write a daily report in the /var/log/sa directory):

The sa2 command can be started by the cron command. It is a shell procedure variant of the sar command, so it handles all of the flags and parameters of the sar command. It writes a daily report in the /var/log/sa/sardd file, where the dd parameter indicates the current day.

RMF PM of OS/390—Linux support

Resource Measurement Facility Performance Monitoring of OS/390, or RMF PM, or PM of OS/390 for short, is a workstation-based (any Windows platform or Linux) function that allows you to monitor the various resources in a z/OS, OS/390, or Linux on zSeries system. Using RMF PM, you can analyze Linux on zSeries performance data, together with z/OS performance data in one application from the same workstation. RMF PM provides filtered data in a graphical format, referred to as *DataViews*. This allows you to manage multiple DataViews as one entity by providing the concept of a *PerfDesk*, and it offers the means to make DataView and PerfDesk definitions persistent for re-use at any time.

To gather data on the host system, you need to install the RMF Distributed Data Server (DDS). It is available for Linux for zSeries 64-bit, Linux for zSeries and S/390 31-bit, and for PC-based Linux. The data gatherer must be active on the Linux machine that you want to monitor. You also need client code on the workstation from which you intend to carry out the performance monitoring. The new PM of OS/390 Java Edition is now provided on a product level and runs, in contrast to its predecessor, on any Windows platform, such as Windows 9x/NT, or on Linux.

Both the data gatherer and the client code can be downloaded from the RMF Web site at no charge (and without warranty) under IBM's licensing terms:
http://www.ibm.com/servers/eserver/zseries/zos/rmf/rmfhtmls/pmweb/pmlin.htm

Here, you can also determine the exact requirements for the workstation on which you want to run RMF PM.

Highlights:

- Generate graphical trend reports.
- Store the data in spreadsheet format (*.WK1, supported by Lotus 1-2-3, StarOffice, MS Excel, and so forth).
- Persistently store performance analysis scenarios (Performance Desktops).
- Gather historical performance data.
- Filter the performance data.
- Mix OS/390 and Linux performance data in one screen.
- Use a graphical user client to access performance data in a flexible and well-configured format.

For Linux, the following classes of metrics are available:

- LINUX_SYSTEM: (for example, *My Penguin* in Figure 26-4) general statistics and Apache metrics.

- LINUX_CPU: metrics related to CPU(s).

- LINUX_FILESYSTEM: metrics related to file systems attached or mounted by the Linux image or DASD performance. The DASD performance metrics are available only if running Linux kernel 2.4 on an IBM zSeries or S/390 mainframe.

- LINUX_NETWORK: metrics related to the network devices attached to the Linux image.

- LINUX_MEMORY: memory statistics for the Linux image.

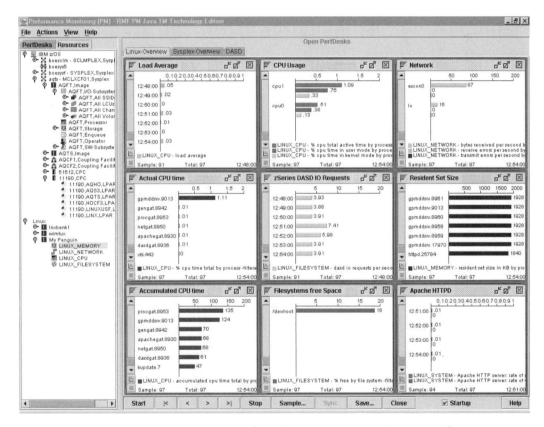

Figure 26-4. With this tool, you can create DataViews that graphically depict different resources. Reprinted with permission from International Business Machines Corporation

Data analysis: The most striking feature of RMF PM is its capability to navigate through a large number of resources or users that are using the resources, or users that are delayed by these resources, in a logical and methodical way.

Commencing data analysis is simple. From the PM of OS/390 main panel, double click any metric of interest. This will bring up the *PM of OS/390 Analysis in <sysplex>* panel. From here, you can use the tool to very quickly and effectively locate the performance bottleneck and to act appropriately before the problem gets severe. For example, if you notice a very high activity rate in PerfDesk, you can ask RMF PM to show the jobs that are using the associated volume most frequently, that is, the jobs that are responsible for the high activity rate. Additionally, RMF PM also shows you the jobs that are most impacted because they are waiting for that volume.

z/VM monitoring tools

Tools that are useful for monitoring z/VM are listed in Table 26-2.

Table 26-2. z/VM monitoring tools

Tool name	Where available	Description
FCON/ESA	`http://www.vm.ibm.com/perf/perfprod.html`	A sophisticated system console and performance monitor. FCON/ESA monitors and displays system performance on a real-time basis. It also stores and can process historical information. You can use FCON/ESA to analyze bottlenecks. The clarity of data presentation enables even casual users to use the tool with ease. Threshold monitoring is provided which allows alerts to be generated so that corrective action can be taken at an early stage. FCON/ESA can be configured to communicate with the RMF Distributed Data Server that is used with RMF PM.
VMPAF	`http://www.vm.ibm.com/perf/perfprod.html`	Use IBM's VMPAF to correlate and chart system performance problems and to perform trend analysis. VMPAF analyzes the relationships between performance variables. Using interactive graphics, it gives you a clear picture of these relationships. The variables analyzed can come from various sources such as VMPRF, RTM, and other data sources.
VMPRF	A priced feature that ships with the z/VM system, for more details, see: `http://www.vm.ibm.com/perf/perfprod.html`	VMPRF uses your system's monitor data to analyze system performance. VMPRF detects and diagnoses performance problems, analyzes system performance, then gives you printed reports and trend data showing performance and usage of your z/VM system. It produces performance reports and history files from the monitor data of your VM system. VMPRF simplifies performance analysis and resource management of z/VM.
RTM VM/ESA	A priced feature that ships with the z/VM system, for more details, see: `http://www.vm.ibm.com/perf/perfprod.html`	RTM VM/ESA is a real-time monitor and diagnostic tool which can be used for short-term monitoring and the installation management of z/VM environments. RTM VM/ESA gives you the current z/VM system performance. You can also use it to validate the system and to establish additional hardware or software requirements when you install extra hardware and/or software.

Chapter 27.
Examples for Applications

This chapter is intended to give you an impression of the wide spectrum of software that is available for Linux on the mainframe today. Because there is already a large number of available program packages and new ones are becoming available frequently, we do not attempt to provide a comprehensive list, but restrict ourselves to listing some examples that we think you might find useful.

In Table 27-1, we have sorted the examples into the following broad categories:

- File and print serving
- Mail serving
- Application platforms
- Web serving
- Database services
- Connectors
- Systems management
- Messaging
- ERP

Table 27-1 (Page 1 of 3). Linux-on-the-mainframe applications	
File and print serving	
Samba	http://samba.org
Application platforms	
IBM Java Development Kit	http://www.ibm.com/developerworks/java/jdk/linux140/
Micro Focus Server Express	http://www.microfocus.com/products/serverexpress/
Mail serving	
Bynari InsightServer	http://www.bynari.net/
Sendmail	http://www.sendmail.org
Sendmail Advanced Message Server	http://www.sendmail.com/products/msmgr_policy.shtml
Samsung Contact	http://www.samsungcontact.com/en/product/
Web serving	
Apache	http://www.apache.org
BEA WebLogic Server	http://www.bea.com/products/weblogic/server/mainframe.shtml
BEA WebLogic Integration	http://www.bea.com/products/weblogic/integration/

Table 27-1 (Page 2 of 3). Linux-on-the-mainframe applications

IBM WebSphere Application Server	http://www.ibm.com/software/webservers/appserv/
IBM WebSphere Commerce Business Edition	http://www.ibm.com/software/webservers/commerce/wc_be/
IBM WebSphere Host on Demand	http://www.ibm.com/software/webservers/hostondemand/
IBM WebSphere Portal	http://www.ibm.com/software/webservers/portal/
Tomcat	http://jakarta.apache.org/tomcat/
Database services	
IBM DB2 Universal Database Enterprise Server Edition	http://www.ibm.com/software/data/db2/
IBM Directory Integrator	http://www.ibm.com/software/network/directory/integrator/
IBM Directory Server	http://www.ibm.com/software/network/directory/server/
MySQL	http://www.mysql.com/products/mysql/
Oracle9i Database	http://www.oracle.com/ip/
Software AG Tamino XML server	http://www.softwareag.com/tamino/
Connectors	
IBM DB2 Connect	http://www.ibm.com/software/data/db2/db2connect/
IBM CICS Transaction Gateway	http://www.ibm.com/software/ts/cics/ctg/
IBM IMS Connector for Java	http://www.ibm.com/software/data/db2imstools/imstools/imsjavcon.html
VSE/ESA e-business connectors	http://www.ibm.com/servers/eserver/zseries/os/vse/
Systems management	
Aduva OnStage	http://www.aduva.com/
BMC MAINVIEW for Linux Servers	http://www.bmc.com/products/proddocview/
BMC PATROL for Linux Enterprise Server	http://www.bmc.com/products/proddocview/
CA BrightStor ARCserve Backup for Linux	http://www3.ca.com/Solutions/Product.asp?ID=3370
CA eTrust Access Control	http://www3.ca.com/Solutions/Product.asp?ID=154
CA eTrust Directory	http://www3.ca.com/Solutions/Product.asp?ID=160
CA Unicenter Software Delivery	http://www3.ca.com/Solutions/Product.asp?ID=234
IBM Tivoli Access Manager for e-business	http://www.ibm.com/software/sysmgmt/products/access-mgr-e-bus.html
IBM Tivoli Access Manager for Operating Systems	http://www.ibm.com/software/tivoli/products/access-mgr-operating-sys/
IBM Tivoli Configuration Manager	http://www.ibm.com/software/tivoli/products/config-mgr/

Table 27-1 (Page 3 of 3). Linux-on-the-mainframe applications	
IBM Tivoli Monitoring	http://www.ibm.com/software/tivoli/products/monitor/
IBM Tivoli Distributed Monitoring	http://www.ibm.com/software/tivoli/products/tds_390/
IBM Tivoli Enterprise Console	http://www.ibm.com/software/tivoli/products/enterprise-console/
IBM Tivoli Identity Manager	http://www.ibm.com/software/tivoli/products/identity-mgr/
IBM Tivoli Risk Manager	http://www.ibm.com/software/tivoli/products/risk-mgr/
IBM Tivoli Software Distribution	http://www.ibm.com/software/tivoli/products/software_dist/
IBM Tivoli Storage Manager	http://www.ibm.com/software/tivoli/products/storage-mgr/
IBM Tivoli Workload Scheduler	http://www.ibm.com/software/tivoli/products/workload_sched/
Legato Systems NetWorker (Server and Client)	http://legato.com/products/networker/
Linuxcare Levanta	http://www.linuxcare.com/products/
RAV AntiVirus for Mail Servers	http://www.raeinternet.com/rav/
Stonesoft StoneGate Firewall/VPN Security Software	http://www.stonesoft.com/products/stonegate/
zGuard	http://www.zguard.de/
Messaging	
IBM WebSphere MQ	http://www.ibm.com/software/ts/mqseries/messaging/
Software AG EntireX Communicator	http://www.softwareag.com/entirex/
ERP	
SAP Web Application Server	http://www.sap.com/solutions/

Part 7.
Appendices

Appendix A.
ISPCompany

ISPCompany is a hypothetical company that we created to show many of the character-istics of real companies. This company and StoreCompany are used in this book to demon-strate issues of security, performance, and system management in a realistic way.

A.1 Corporate profile of ISPCompany

ISPCompany started out as a service bureau. It is now also in the business of outsourcing IT services to companies who do not want to maintain a server themselves. Founded in 1985, ISPCompany is a pioneer in the outsourced IT management business for small and medium-sized companies. Recently, ISPCompany has recognized that companies are moving into the "e-business on demand" space and need variable amounts of computing capacity for certain aspects of their business computing. In the future, ISPCompany also hopes to outsource applications. The company has one site outside the city limits of Pancake City, New Jersey, on the east coast of the United States (Figure A-1) and one site in southwest Germany.

The company's core activity has been providing infrastructure, systems, and managed network services to large and medium-sized enterprises. Due to rapid changes and increasing complexities in information technology, outsourcing is an efficient solution for many businesses.

ISPCompany helps customers bridge the gap between their mainframe/legacy operations and the Internet with a comprehensive suite of IT-managed services that assure the highest levels of availability of mission-critical applications. The company also provides integration expertise to link customers' online businesses and e-commerce functions with existing pro-prietary back office systems. ISPCompany's ability to remotely monitor all aspects of a com-pany's operations greatly reduces the number of people needed to perform the management function. Managed services are offered on an outsourced basis to companies seeking optimal performance, security, reliability, and scalability of their computer systems without the large cash outlays required to maintain this function in-house. In today's chal-lenging business climate, when executives are looking for ways to cut costs and maximize their business potential, ISPCompany offers the expertise and advanced tools to effectively control their entire IT operation.

ISPCompany has two locations, but in this chapter we will concentrate on only one of them.

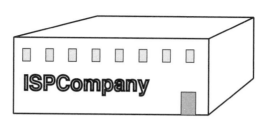

Figure   A-1. ISPCompany's building in Pancake City, New Jersey

The customers of ISPCompany range from Fortune 1000 to Fortune 200-type companies.

A.1.1 Business objectives

The company's objective is to provide a comprehensive alternative to meet all or part of its clients' information technology and mission-critical Internet requirements. Typically, the company enters into contracts with clients providing for automatic renewal unless prior written notice is given. The contracts have varying terms, typically ranging from one to five years. The rates for the company's services vary according to factors such as the volume and types of services used by a particular client. Industry-specific outsourcing applications and services are developed so that the company's in-depth knowledge of a particular industry can be applied to servicing multiple clients in that field. The company currently provides outsourcing services to approximately 500 clients in such diverse fields as financial services, publishing, home health care, apparel, and consumer products.

A.2 Offerings

The company offers a spectrum of services that ranges from supplying the bare iron through applications, helpdesk, and backup/restore services. The company provides data system outsourcing services in the following areas:

1. Internet Data Center and server-hosting services

2. A full suite of automated integrated managed services that assure optimal performance, security, reliability, and scalability of a customer's computer systems operations

3. Information technology (IT) hosting services

4. Systems infrastructure and operations consulting

These offerings correspond to how much the customers might want to do themselves, which ranges from doing everything themselves to having everything, including user management, done by ISPCompany. Examples of offerings are shown in Table A-1.

Table   A-1. Spectrum of ISPCompany offerings

What ISPCompany offers	What the customer can do
Base system	Everything
Base system plus the operating system	Health monitoring, all applications, all user management
Base system, OS, middleware	Install packages
Base system, OS, middleware, applications	User management
Base system, OS, middleware, applications, helpdesk	End-user tasks only
Base system, OS, middleware, applications, helpdesk, backup/restore	End-user tasks only

ISPCompany offers Linux distributions from the following companies:

- Red Hat
- SuSE

ISPCompany offers the following middleware:

- Apache
- IBM WebSphere Application Server (WAS)
- SendMail and Bynari Insight Server
- DB2 UDB

A.2.1 The Internet service offering

The ISP offering is a stable part of ISPCompany's revenue model. It is low-risk with reasonable returns, but offers only moderate growth opportunity. ISPCompany has a few thousand mail customers, some of whom also have some static Web pages to be served. The company has both low-speed and high-speed lines that its clients can use. Its rates are very competitive and it emphasizes the use of the static Web pages to present a company image along with an associated mail account that Web users can contact for additional information. The mail service side of the ISP business allows many of the clients to avoid owning and managing a mail server at their business site.

A.2.2 The data systems outsourcing offering

The outsourcing of data systems services, whereby a client company obtains all or part of its information processing requirements (including systems design, software management and hardware, network communications, training, maintenance, and support) from providers such as ISPCompany, continues to be a growing trend. ISPCompany believes that it is generally 10% to 50% more cost-effective and efficient for its clients to outsource information processing services to the company than it would be to provide equivalent services for themselves by purchasing or leasing in-house systems and hiring or contracting for service and support personnel.

Outsourcing provides clients with the following benefits:

- The refocus of personnel, financial, and technological resources on core business and client-related activities

- Access to highly skilled personnel and newer technology resources

- Access to resources that support technological re-engineering

- Reduction of operating costs

- Reduction of future investment in infrastructure not directly related to the core business activity

A.3 Description of environment

ISPCompany began offering Internet data center (IDC) services in the first quarter of fiscal 2000 by retooling a portion of its state-of-the-art mainframe outsourcing data center into an IDC. Hosting Internet systems demands many of the same skills, procedures, and physical requirements as for mainframe and midrange environments.

The company's IDC features state-of-the-art physical and network infrastructure, including:

- Multi-layered security with 24x7 guard station, video surveillance, and restricted physical (secure equipment cages) and network access

- Redundant power systems with two tiers of backup (two UPSs and two diesel power generators) to ensure continuous operation in the event of a power outage

- Leading edge fire suppression as well as smoke and fire detection systems, and sprinklers

- Redundant climate control systems in a raised floor environment

- Four high bandwidth, network access points with physically diverse connections into the IDC

A.3.1 Physical environment of Pancake City site

The 67,000 square feet (6700 sqm) building at the Pancake City site has two floors. The first floor (shown in Figure A-2) houses the data center, a conference room with one-way windows out to the secured equipment area and into the control room, and the building entrance with a security guard. The second floor houses the offices.

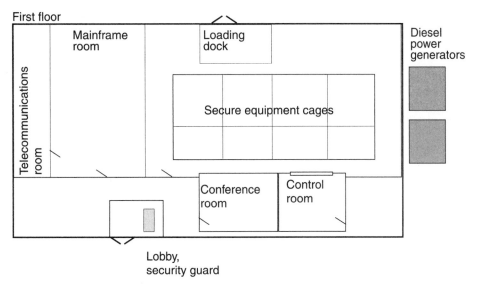

Figure   A-2. Floor plan of Pancake City site

A.3.2 Logical setup of Pancake City site

ISPCompany's logical setup is shown in Figure A-3, and consists of:

- Customer cages containing equipment owned by customers of ISPCompany
- A zSeries box for server consolidation, connected to disk and tape storage
- A private LAN connecting all machines with the control center (remember the HMC of zSeries)
- Entire setup connected through an Internet backbone with fiber (multiple connections)

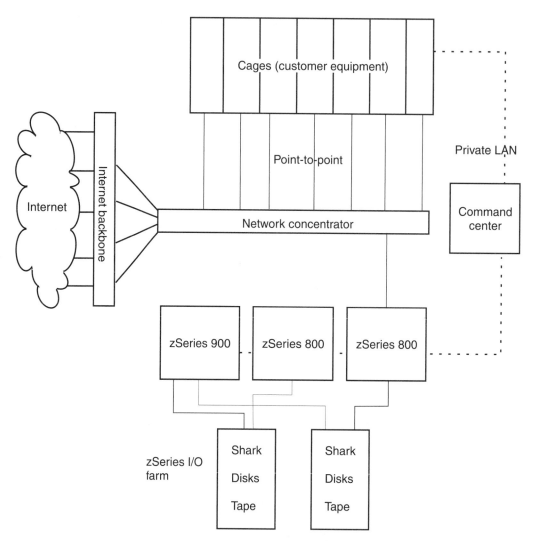

Figure   A-3. Hardware and software logical setup of ISPCompany

ISPCompany handles many different platforms. The company uses IBM Tivoli as a systems management platform.

At the rate that the SAN management technology is improving, ISPCompany's New Jersey site is looking at deploying a shared SAN for a subset of its outsourcing clients in late 2003. The first sets of clients moved to SAN will be those with over 100 GB of data who need their own dedicated channel path.

IBM Tivoli Storage Manager server is running in a Linux image on z900. This is used to back up customer data on tape.

A.4 Example new client

This customer approaches ISPCompany about outsourcing:

- Small server farms that do back-office-type things

- The beginnings of this client's Web business, as it doesn't want to get into Web administration or system administration (they have a business to run).

The client used to have only static Web pages (information about their business) with ISPCompany; but really it wants to go to dynamic page interaction with the rest of its business and is considering a complete outsourcing. But as any conservative business would do, the first step is to move the hardware, then buy some services, and finally, contract it all. This client was into horizontal growth. And ISPCompany, as it adds more clients of this type, is itself into horizontal growth.

Appendix B.
StoreCompany

StoreCompany is used in this book to demonstrate issues of security, performance, and system management. StoreCompany is the larger of the two example companies, being a Fortune 1000 company.

StoreCompany demonstrates different possibilities for using Linux on the mainframe:

- Integration of the middle-tier with the back-end

- Vertical and horizontal growth

- Extending existing applications by using new technologies on Linux

StoreCompany, an upmarket department store chain with 85 stores, has been in business for decades, mostly in large cities in the eastern United States. Its IT organization has been very progressive over the years moving from just back-office and support functions to actively managing sales and inventory in real-time. It also has moved into business-to-business type transactions with its key suppliers. StoreCompany deploys the following:

- WebSphere Application Server (WAS)

- DB2

- CICS

- VSAM

At the end of 2001, StoreCompany decided to expand into making its store items (basically its inventory database) available online to shoppers. As the very first Linux on the mainframe project, a firewall server and a proxy server were created as Linux images. See B.4, "Project 1: Firewall and proxy server."

By extending their use of WebSphere Application Server (WAS) and WebSphere Commerce Suite (WCS), StoreCompany next was able to quickly create a Web store using a few Linux images for the Web front-end part, and leveraging all the CICS, DB2, and VSAM databases on the z/OS side for the critical parts of the new order confirmation and fulfillment system. See B.5, "Project 2: Web application server."

Project 1 and Project 2 are examples of back-end integration.

Given how successful Projects 1 and 2 have been and how quickly they went from pilot to production, it was decided to give the marketing organization an opportunity to explore new opportunities. Any new opportunity would have to isolate the IT-required changes within a small number of Linux images with no changes to the normal production applications on z/OS.

The new business opportunity is to enter the specialized gift category, leveraging the StoreCompany brand name. A new catalog store will be created within the existing online store. It will be called One-of-a-Kind (OaK) and will offer items in the $300 to $10,000 price range from artists specializing in paintings, sculpture (stone and wood), and jewelry. While the items (with full color photos) will appear in the online catalog, StoreCompany will not actually stock the items. Instead, when an item is purchased, the order is electronically routed to the artist for scheduling and shipping. Customer billing is handled by StoreCompany. To the StoreCompany customer, it looks and feels like an order from StoreCompany, including StoreCompany's customer satisfaction guarantee. See B.6, "Project 3: OaK project."

B.1 Corporate profile of StoreCompany

StoreCompany started out as a small western Pennsylvania department store chain in the 1960s. It has since expanded its network of stores over most of the eastern United States.

While merchandising is the heart of StoreCompany's business, it relies on its infrastructure for support. Its management information systems help store clerks, increase accuracy and efficiency of the four distribution centers, and manage the details of product range planning. Figure B-1 shows an overview organization chart.

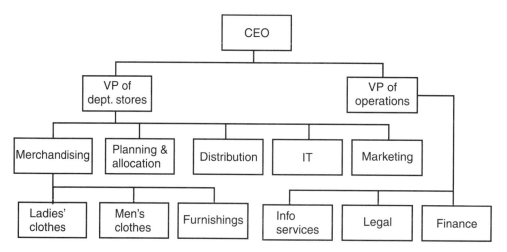

Figure   B-1. Organization chart of StoreCompany

B.2 Description of environment

B.2.1 Logical setup

Figure B-2 shows the logical setup of StoreCompany. StoreCompany has two zSeries 900 Model 105 (with five CPUs) machines configured in a Parallel Sysplex. The Coupling Facility in the second LPAR of the second machine (LPAR-E) uses an Integrated Coupling Facility (ICF). The business applications run under z/OS with DB2, CICS, VSAM and WAS.

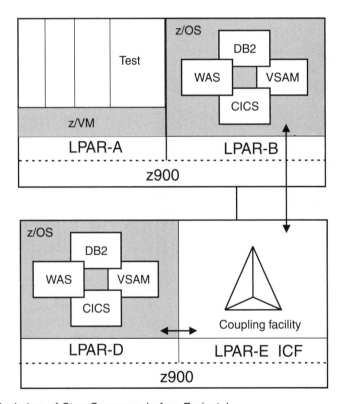

Figure   B-2. Logical view of StoreCompany, before Project 1

B.3 Programming model and middleware platform

StoreCompany made a strategic decision to develop an object-oriented model of its business processes.

The advantage of object-oriented program modules is that their clearly defined interfaces make them easy to reuse. There are also effective tools that support object-oriented programming. Enhancing and changing object-oriented programs is much faster than with traditional programming methods. An object-oriented approach allows for the rapid development and deployment of IT based projects that StoreCompany needs to turn its IT capabilities into a competitive edge.

StoreCompany chose IBM WebSphere Application Server (WAS) as the middleware platform for its object-oriented applications. WAS offers a solid basis with rich security interfaces and transaction capabilities. For StoreCompany it was important that the spectrum of supported operating systems include z/OS and Linux. StoreCompany's vital business data and transaction processing are all on z/OS with its strong availability and recovery features. Mainframe Linux is intended as the initial integration point and rapid deployment platform for new technology ideas.

This dual approach of running some application parts on Linux and others on z/OS is tied together logically by WAS and physically by the mainframe hardware with its LPARs and HiperSockets. As an application evolves and its requirements to the underlying operating system change, StoreCompany can use WAS to redeploy the application or parts of it on a different operating system.

Because Linux and WAS subscribe to open standards, the flexibility and potential for integration that StoreCompany gains goes beyond its current infrastructure. Open standards facilitate assimilation of future additions to its infrastructure. Open standards also pave the way to take advantage of current and future developments, for example, business to business applications or on demand computing.

B.4 Project 1: Firewall and proxy server

StoreCompany's desire to add its catalog to the Internet sparked an audit into security and feasibility of the project. A firewall and demilitarized zone would be needed to separate the zSeries from the Internet. The conclusion was that infrastructure servers could be located as Linux guests under z/VM on the mainframe. This would have three desirable results: a standard setup for all guests, some savings in actual hardware, and a fairly simple project for introducing Linux on the mainframe into the production environment.

The team doing the Linux infrastructure work was composed of both mainframe and UNIX/Linux people. The infrastructure work went well. It was fast (75 days) and it was on budget. After the conclusion of Project 1, security had the structure needed to give the green light to the more complicated online catalog project.

As a follow up from Project 1, StoreCompany then decided to move its departmental Samba servers from UNIX and Windows servers to the mainframe. These servers hold data for the various StoreCompany departments.

B.4.1 Changes needed

- Project 1 needs only 10% or so of an engine, but to prepare for future projects, one IFL is placed on order.

- As soon as the IFL arrives, z/VM is set up on a new LPAR with the IFL, LPAR-C.

- Acquire a Linux distribution, in this case, SuSE.

- Configure firewall and proxy.

- Test firewall and proxy.

- Test IP filtering.

B.4.2 Implementation

Work started out with Linux on z/VM under the test LPAR, LPAR-A. Once that worked, an IFL was ordered as a trial, knowing that it could be sent back if things did not work. While the IFL order process was wending its way through StoreCompany, the project went into production using the test LPAR just before the IFL was to show up to accelerate delivery. Once the IFL was in place and the second z/VM was set up, ISPCompany just moved over the Linux image and the network attachment, and so forth. The final implementation is shown in Figure B-3.

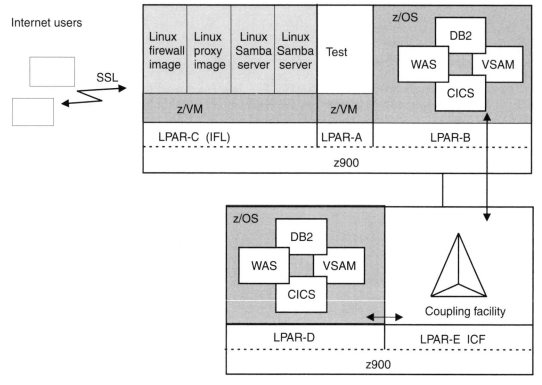

Figure B-3. Logical setup of StoreCompany after locating the firewall and the proxy on the zSeries machine

- The firewall and the proxy server were located on a new LPAR, LPAR-C, which uses an IFL engine.

  The proxy re-addresses requests from the Internet to a machine that can handle requests. That machine is on a network that is not visible to the outside. In other words, the proxy does two things: re-direction, and occasionally workload management.

- As a second line of defense, IP filtering is used between proxy and the application images.

  IP filtering is used to ensure that traffic in and out is only from servers that have business here. For example, only traffic from the proxy is allowed in. This is the minimum needed to define the end of the DMZ.

- Intrusion detection systems (IDS) will be implemented on three levels: Network, host, and Web.

B.5 Project 2: Web application server

The next project StoreCompany undertakes is to implement a Web catalog. The Web catalog project can exploit the work done by the successful team from Project 1.

B.5.1 Changes needed

- WAS and WCS for Linux. WCS provides everything StoreCompany needs to set up an online catalog.

- Three new Linux images: one for development and test, two catalog Web servers.

B.5.2 Implementation

The Web server which StoreCompany uses is Apache. Once the Web business was started, a second IFL was immediately ordered to ensure that there would be no hardware single point of failure for the Linux images. The final implementation is shown in Figure B-4.

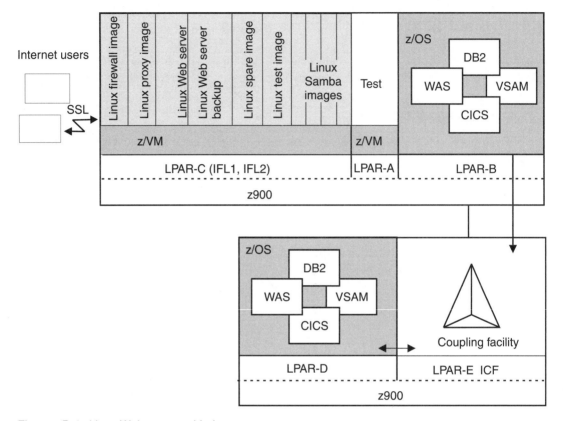

Figure   B-4. Linux Web server added

B.6 Project 3: OaK project

Linux has created a beachhead in StoreCompany through two successful projects. The first was a simple consolidation of some security-related infrastructure images (firewall and proxy servers) onto a few Linux images on one of the z900 machines. The second project, described above, was the use of WCS to create an online store.

The new marketing programs manager at StoreCompany has suggested that it should be a relatively simple thing to offer a new brand of products: a category of exclusive gifts called One-of-a-Kind (OaK). They would be presented on the StoreCompany Web site, but would actually not be in stock at StoreCompany. Instead, third-party vendors (craftspeople, artists) would offer their products for inclusion in the OaK Web catalog. This would give the third parties the advantage of this new marketing channel, as well as the brand recognition of StoreCompany.

A small team consisting of one person familiar with the WAS interfaces to the order entry and inventory systems, one person from the Linux WCS side, one Web-page designer, and the lead marketing person whose idea spawned the project will design and implement these ideas. The intent is to have a first deployment for customers in one month, with three experimental trial periods lasting an aggregate of six months. At the end of the project, a recommendation on how and whether to add this opportunity to the standard portfolio will be made to the management committee.

B.6.1 Concept

Artists supply StoreCompany with information about the articles for sale. StoreCompany presents the articles in its Web catalog. Customers can then browse the catalog and place orders. When an order comes in through the catalog to StoreCompany, it is sent directly through to the third party who creates the item and then ships it to the customer. The process is illustrated in Figure B-5.

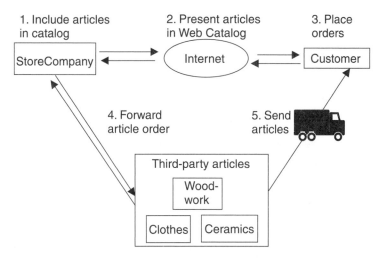

Figure   B-5. Flow of new business opportunity "One-of-a-Kind"

StoreCompany adds the articles into their Web catalog under the existing category of "specialty items." The lead OaK person wants to measure the probability of a purchase when certain types of customers are presented with search results tailored to their known preferences.

Using business intelligence (BI) methods to mine customers' buying patterns it is possible to both determine an appropriate target customer and identify OaK items that are likely to appeal. When a customer from this special set enters their catalog site, a BI query is triggered to create a pseudo search page result from the OaK set of items. The page is presented to the customer in a pop-up window with the heading "a new service for you."

Market opportunity and benefits

For StoreCompany, the following benefits are expected:

- Keep high-end customers and encourage customers to buy more
- Receive a higher profit margin per transaction

For the artists and craftspeople, the following benefits can be expected:

- A new channel to reach clients the company wouldn't normally see
- Benefit from the brand name of "StoreCompany"
- Little interaction with the end client during the business transaction process (more time for art or crafts)

For the customer, the following benefits are expected:

- One-of-a-Kind special items from a trusted, respected retailer
- Ease in finding the perfect present

B.6.2 Business objectives

- Allow the marketing department to rapidly try out new ideas for creating new retail business opportunities by making experimental applications available to customers
- Increase revenue and profit per individual sale.

B.6.3 Policies

- There will be risk management plans in place for all "market trials."
- All changes are to be implemented within new Linux images exploiting only IFL engines. The new Linux images should place less than a 10% peak and a 1% average utilization increase on the z/OS image. Thus it cannot impact normal business commitments.
- No business data should be kept on the new Linux images. That is, the items for sale are part of the sales database on DB2; the transactions for completing a sale will be the standard CICS transactions, and any inventory information for the new opportunities is kept in the inventory database on z/OS.

- The marketing department owns the new Linux images—that is, it owns the availability requirements and any resulting impact to its business experiment. The IT organization will support the operation of those images.

B.6.4 Procedures

The OaK team has established the following:

- All new business data representing the OaK products, customers, and vendors will be managed as part of the standard backup/restore/disaster recovery processes in place on z/OS for the respective databases.

- The OaK catalog starting point will be the only change allowed on the production catalog system. During this trial phase, control and information will be given over to one of the new Linux images.

B.6.5 Changes needed

- New business intelligence (BI) image that coordinates all the activities of OaK, such as order entry and delivery.

- Change to production system: authorizing the new BI image to make certain requests of the production system that result in the customer data being forwarded to the BI image for further processing.

- Customer data to artist or craftsperson for shipping; shipping process data back to customer.

- New code will be required to implement dynamic concatenation of suitable items (such as Amazon.com's "Customers who bought this also bought").

B.6.6 Implementation

A new BI application was written to handle gift offering in connection with the OaK. Some of its functions are:

- Based on shopping history and customer profile, find and display list of gifts in suitable interest area and price range.

- When customer orders, return customer to main application to conclude sales. Send shipping information to third-party vendor for handling.

A datamart is a convenient way to get information from all your data. A datamart approach was chosen to handle the different pieces of information that need to be consolidated into a new Datamart database:

- A batch job will run on z/OS that extracts the information needed for the new OaK query from the various databases, creating a unique database that will be transferred to DB2 UDB on a new Linux image that has all the data optimized for real time queries of customer buying interests.

- Change to production side: Schedule the datamart building job at some "quiet time" on the production machine. Since only a small portion of StoreCompany's business is 24x7 (the catalog) and the larger portion is still store-based, the company does have these quiet times.

The BI application and the datamart were added to StoreCompany's set up, as shown in Figure B-6.

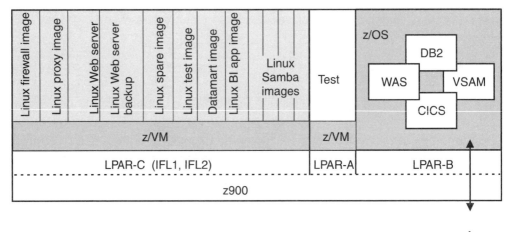

Coupling facility

Figure B-6. The new datamart image and Linux image for business intelligence are added

Other changes include:

- WAS to implement the cross-system interactions between the new Linux images and z/OS.

- BI transactions that finds customer profile will be implemented in new image.

- The BI image will not have an external IP address.

- The existing accounting and ordering applications are not changed and are separated from the BI image (and so is most of the rest of this customer's catalog experience).

- A HiperSockets LAN and Guest LANs are used for the most secure communications, as illustrated in Figure B-7:
  - A HiperSockets LAN connects the z/OS applications with the new business intelligence image, as well as the Web application image, the Web server, and the proxy.
  - One Guest LAN connects the firewall image with the proxy server, and another connects the datamart and business application images with the Web server.
  - Cross-memory services provide communication among the z/OS applications.

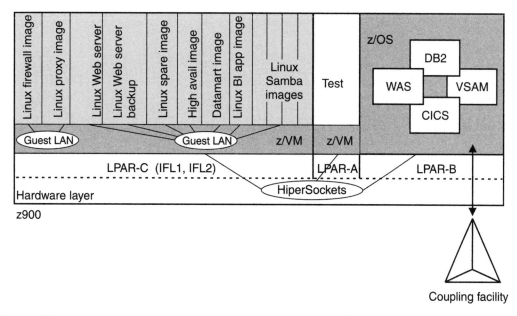

Figure B-7. Logical implementation of new business opportunity, One-of-a-Kind gifts

B.6.7 Opportunity cost

- Development and deployment cost:
  - Excess capacity of the second IFL will be used, as the online catalog needs the first one, and growth is expected
  - Project staff
  - One new DB2 UDB license
- Cost for including articles in catalog: small, just the storage it takes to describe one.
- Cost of finding articles to include: advertising cost and part of the cost of one specialized buyer for selection of appropriate items.
- Cost of failure: Low. Some of the new code will be re-usable for other experiments.

Glossary

This glossary defines technical terms and abbreviations used in this book. If you do not find the term you are looking for, the Web is likely to produce a quick result. One place to check is the IBM Dictionary of Computing, located at: `http://www.ibm.com/networking/nsg/nsgmain.htm`.

ACL. Access control list. (1) In computer security, a collection of all access rights for one object. (2) In computer security, a list associated with an object that identifies all the subjects that can access the object and their access rights; for example, a list associated with a file that identifies users who can access the file and identifies their access rights to that file.

address space. An address space is a range of contiguous virtual storage addresses, unique for each user, that the operating system creates. A small portion of the address space has system data and programs mapped into it, to ensure fast execution of system requests.

API. Application programming interface. A defined software interface that enables programs to communicate with each other. An API is the set of programming language constructs or statements that can be coded in a program to obtain the specific functions and services provided by an underlying operating system or another program.

application. A collection of software components used to perform specific types of user-oriented work on a computer.

ASCII. American Standard Code for Information Interchange. ASCII is widely used outside of the mainframe. It relates to a coding scheme that is used to hold one character of information in one byte (8 bits). For the ASCII coding sheet, see

`http://www.ibm.com/servers/eserver/iseries/software/globalization/pdf/cp00038z.pdf`.

ASP. Application service provider. A company that offers application software to clients on a centrally located (and centrally-managed) host. Businesses gain the benefit of running sophisticated applications while avoiding the cost of deploying the required hardware and software in-house.

autonomic computing. Autonomic computing is a technology that can manage and improve its own operation with minimal human intervention. For further information, see

`http://www.ibm.com/autonomic/index.shtml`

back-end. A part of an application that is the least visible to its user. Typically, the back-end is that part of the application logic that contains the database and transaction manager.

BSD. Berkeley Software Distribution. Pertains to any of the series of UNIX specifications or implementations distributed by the University of California at Berkeley. The abbreviation BSD is usually followed by a number to specify the particular version of UNIX that was distributed (for example, BSD 4.3). Many vendors use BSD specifications as standards for their UNIX products.

CCW. Channel command word. A doubleword at the location in main storage specified by the channel address word. One or more CCWs make up the channel program that directs data channel operations.

channel. Communication link (parallel, ESCON) between system and control unit.

channel-to-channel adapter (CTCA). An adapter that cross-connects a pair of channels between systems to allow for point-to-point communications between two systems.

CHPID. Channel path identifier. In a channel subsystem, a value assigned to each installed channel path of the system that uniquely identifies that path to the system.

CIM. Common information model. An implementation-neutral, object-oriented schema for describing system management information. The Distributed Management Task Force (DMTF) develops and maintains CIM specifications.

CISC. Complex instruction set computer. Such computers have a large number of instructions, typically 100 or more. Instructions are provided for most common programming tasks, for example, there would be one instruction to move hundreds or thousands of bytes, saving the need for a program loop to move the data.

CMOS. Complementary metal-oxide semiconductor. CMOS is the semiconductor technology used in the transistors that are manufactured into most of today's computer microchips.

CMS. Conversational Monitor System. A Virtual Machine operating system that is used for general interactive time-sharing, problem solving, and program development capabilities, and in recent years operates only under control of the VM Control Program.

COBOL. Common Business Oriented Language. COBOL was the first widely used high-level programming language for business applications. Many payroll, accounting, and other business application programs written in

COBOL over the past 35 years are still in use, and it is possible that there are more existing lines of programming code in COBOL than in any other programming language.

connector. A connector provides access to resources of another system image. For example, an application server running on Linux may connect to data of a z/OS or VSE/ESA system distribution.

consolidation. See *server consolidation*.

control unit. I/O controller attached to a channel supporting up to 255 devices.

CP. Control Program. The base component of z/VM that manages the resources of a single computer so that multiple computing systems appear to exist. Each of these apparent systems, or Virtual Machines, is the functional equivalent of an IBM System/370, 370-XA, ESA computer, or z/Architecture computer. See also *Virtual Machine*.

CPU. Central processing unit. The part of a computer that includes the circuits that control the interpretation and execution of instructions. Traditionally, the complete processing unit was often regarded as the CPU, whereas today the CPU is often a microchip.

CPU utilization. A measure of performance. This is a measure of how busy the CPU is at any given period of time, for example, 24 hours.

CTCA. See *channel-to-channel adapter*.

CTSS. Compatible Time Sharing System. This IBM 7094 time-sharing operating system was created at MIT Project MAC and first demonstrated in 1961. It was used as the programming and debugging tool during initial Multics programming and bring up by Project MAC, General Electric CISL, and Bell Telephone Lab personnel. In some sense the intellectual offspring of CTSS, Multics was conceived as the next step in the future of multiple-access computing.

DASD. Direct Access Storage Device. DASD is a general term for magnetic disk storage devices that has historically been used in the mainframe and minicomputer (mid-range computer) environments. The "direct access" means that all data can be accessed directly in about the same amount of time rather than having to progress sequentially through the data.

datamart. A subset of a data warehouse that contains data tailored and optimized for the specific reporting needs of a department or team. A datamart can be a subset of a warehouse for an entire organization, such as data contained in online analytical processing (OLAP) tools.

device. A mechanical, electrical, or electronic contrivance with a specific purpose. See also *DASD*.

device number. In a channel subsystem, the four hexadecimal digits that uniquely identify an I/O device.

DFSMS. Data Facility Storage Management Subsystem. An IBM feature for managing files in Shared File System (SFS) file pools, helping to move CMS minidisks between like and unlike direct access storage devices (DASD) quickly and efficiently, and providing command and Callable Services Library (CSL) interface to removable media library support.

directory. (1) In a hierarchical file system, a container for files or other directories. (2) In VM, a Control Program (CP) disk file that defines each Virtual Machine's typical configuration: the user ID, password, regular and maximum allowable virtual storage, CP command privilege class or classes allowed,

dispatching priority, logical editing symbols to be used, account number, and CP options desired.

DirMaint. Directory maintenance. A CMS application that helps manage an installation's VM directory. Directory management is simplified by the DirMaint command interface and automated facilities. DirMaint directory statement-like commands are used to initiate directory transactions. DirMaint error checking ensures that only valid changes are made to the directory, and that only authorized personnel are able to make the requested changes. Any transaction requiring the allocation or deallocation of minidisk extents can be handled automatically. All user-initiated transactions can be password-controlled and can be recorded for auditing purposes.

disaster recovery. The process used to recover from an outage in the IT environment due to the simultaneous failure of multiple key components that preclude simply restarting the failed environment. However, such a simultaneous failure is unusual. The effects can be disastrous in that the length for recovery is long and the outage impact could hurt the business. Such multiple simultaneous outages usually are related to an event that is called a "disaster," such as a fire, earthquake, or explosion.

distribution. A Linux distribution provides a collection of application, middleware, tools, kernel, device drivers, and libraries. Distributors, such as Red Hat and SuSE, ensure that key packages of a distribution are well-tested. They also provide installation and configuration capabilities as well as maintenance and support.

DMTF. Distributed Management Task Force. An alliance of computer vendors that was convened to define streamlined management of the diverse operating systems commonly found in an enterprise. For further information, see http://www.dmtf.org/

EBCDIC. Extended Binary-Coded-Decimal Interchange Code. EBCDIC is a binary code for alphabetic and numeric characters that IBM developed for its larger operating systems. It is the code for text files that is used in IBM's z/OS operating system for its zSeries servers and that corporations use for their legacy applications and databases. In an EBCDIC file, each alphabetic or numeric character is represented with an 8-bit binary number (a string of eight 0s or 1s). 256 possible characters (letters of the alphabet, numerals, and special characters) are defined.

ECC. Error correction code or error checking and correcting. ECC allows data that is being read or transmitted to be checked for errors and, when necessary, corrected on the fly. It differs from parity-checking in that errors are not only detected but are also corrected.

ESCON. Enterprise Systems Connection. A set of IBM products and services that provide a dynamically connected environment within an enterprise based upon fiber connections.

ESS. IBM TotalStorage Enterprise Storage Server. An advanced, SAN-ready disk storage system that provides high performance, scalability, and universal access across all major server platforms, and which maximizes data sharing across the enterprise.

external throughput rate (ETR). Work completed per second. For example, a Web server serving 300 pages per second can be said to have an ETR of 300 pages per second.

FCP. Fibre Channel Protocol. A standardized protocol recently implemented by IBM on its zSeries mainframe. There is a family of these protocols used for transporting SCSI over a fiber channel, instead of over copper. The zSeries FCP channel provides unique value in Linux environments. For further information on FCP, see http://www.t10.org/scsi-3.htm.

FICON. Fiber Connectivity. FICON is a high-speed input/output (I/O) interface for mainframe computer connections to storage devices. As part of IBM's zSeries server, FICON channels increase I/O capacity through the combination of a new architecture and faster physical link rates to make them up to eight times as efficient as ESCON (Enterprise System Connection), IBM's previous fiber-optic channel standard.

FORTRAN. FORTRAN (FORmula TRANslation) is a third-generation programming language that was designed for use by engineers, mathematicians, and other users and creators of scientific algorithms.

front-end. A part of an application that is the closest to the user. Typically, it contains that part of the application logic that manages the application's presentation to the user.

GDPS. Geographically Dispersed Parallel Sysplex. An IBM solution for disaster recovery and continuous availability for a zSeries multi-site enterprise. This solution mirrors critical data and efficiently balances workload between the sites. GDPS solution also uses automation and Parallel Sysplex technology to help manage multi-site databases, processors, network resources, and storage subsystem mirroring.

GPL. GNU General Public License. A software license allowing the licensed program to be passed on, on condition that the source text always remains available. Equally permissible and desirable is the fact that you can make your own improvements to the software and republish it. Linux itself is also under the GPL. For further information, see http://www.gnu.org/copyleft/gpl.html.

Guest LAN. z/VM 4.2 introduced Guest LAN support, which is implemented in the z/VM Control Program (CP). With the Guest LAN interfaces, you can define a virtual LAN. z/VM guests may communicate via TCP/IP and virtual network interfaces with other guests connected to such a virtual (Guest) LAN.

HA. High availability. Refers to a system or component that is operational for a desirably long length of time. Availability can be measured relative to "100% operational" or "never failing." A widely-held but difficult-to-achieve standard of availability for a system or product is known as "five 9s" (99.999 percent) availability.

high-availability clustering. A high-availability (HA) cluster is a group of interconnected servers, redundantly configured, that behave as an aggregate to serve a particular workload. The cluster is configured with hardware and software so that the failure of one or a few servers in the cluster does not impact the availability of the application from the users' perspective.

horizontal growth. Growing capability by adding a complete new instance of a resource. Contrasted with vertical growth, which is growing by increasing the capacity of the existing resources.

hypervisor. The licensed internal code that was developed to support the Logical Partitioning (LPAR) of an SMP system. In z/VM, it is the part of the Control Program (CP) responsible for managing the virtual environment.

IFL. Integrated Facility for Linux. An IFL is a feature of the G5, G5 and zSeries family of processors. These features are only available within a special LPAR defined to run in Linux-only mode.

internal throughput rate (ITR). A performance measurement. Units of work completed per unit of processor busy time. For example, if a Web server serves 30 pages per second and thereby shows CPU as 50% busy, then its ITR is 60 pages per second. ITR only measures the throughput from within the processor. Compare with *external throughput rate*, which measures the end users' perspective of throughput.

I/O Configuration Data Set (IOCDS). The file on the Support Element that contains an I/O and LPAR configuration definition built by the I/O configuration program (IOCP). This file is loaded at Power on Reset.

IRQ. Interrupt Request Line. An IRQ is a hardware line used in a PC by (ISA bus) devices such as keyboards, modems, sound cards, and so on, to send interrupt signals to the processor to tell it that the device is ready to send or accept data.

ISP. Internet Service Provider. An organization that provides access to the Internet for a fee.

Linux. Linux is a UNIX-like operating system that was designed to provide personal computer users with a free or very low-cost operating system comparable to traditional and usually more expensive UNIX systems. Linux's kernel (the central part of the operating system) was developed by Linus Torvalds at the University of Helsinki in Finland. To complete the operating system, Torvalds and other team members made use of system components developed by members of the Free Software Foundation for the GNU project. Linux is distributed commercially by a number of companies.

Load balancing cluster. A specific type of cluster that involves a front-end dispatcher which distributes the incoming application work to the servers within a cluster, attempting to assure that each server receives its share of the incoming work.

LPAR. Logical PARtition. LPAR is the division of a computer's processors, memory, and storage into multiple sets of resources so that each set of resources can be operated independently with its own operating system instance and applications.

MAC. Mandatory Access Control. In computer security, a means of imposing mandatory controls when restricting access to objects, based on the sensitivity, as represented by a sensitivity label, of the information contained in the objects and the formal authorization or security clearance of subjects to access information of that sensitivity, and enforced by the trusted computing base. A user only gets access to a controlled resource providing he/she passes the mandatory control test.

middle-tier. A middle-tier "lives" between the front-end (tier) and the back-end (tier). Middle-tiers usually implement the piece of the application that collects the data (input) from the end user, does some initial processing, and passes that on to the back-end (and vice versa with the results). For example, a Web server is a typical middle-tier server.

middleware. A vague term that refers to the software between an application program and the lower-level operating system functions.

minidisk. (1) A z/VM construct that is a logical subdivision (or all) of a direct access storage device that has its own virtual device number, consecutive virtual cylinders (starting with virtual cylinder 0), and a Volume Table of Contents (VTOC) or disk label identifier. (2) A virtual disk in storage.

MIPS. A measure of computer processing performance that is equal to one Million Instructions Per Second.

MTBF. Mean time between failures. For a stated period in the life of a functional unit, the mean value of the lengths of time between consecutive failures under stated conditions.

multiple preferred guests (MPF). A facility that supports up to six preferred Virtual Machines when the Processor Resource/Systems Manager (PR/SM) feature is installed in the real machine. This facility allows z/VM to provide special treatment for these guests, thus allowing nearly-native performance for those guests.

MVS. Multiple Virtual Storage. MVS was IBM's first mainframe operating system to provide separate virtual address spaces for each of its users. Over time, it was succeeded by other operating systems like OS/390 and currently z/OS.

OCO. Object code only. The format that IBM uses to ship many of its priced products. OCO refers to the fact that no source code is made available. In addition, the product license permits you to execute only the binary implementation and gives you no rights to the original product source code.

OS/MFT. Operating System/Multi-programming with a Fixed number of Tasks. OS/MFT was one of the two heavyweight real-storage operating systems on the original S/360 machines (OS/MVT was the other one).

OS/MVT. Operating System/Multi-programming with a Variable number of Tasks. OS/MVT was one of the two heavyweight real-storage operating systems on the original S/360 machines

(OS/MFT was the other one). z/OS was derived from OS/MVT.

PKI. Private Key Infrastructure. PKI is used with cryptography, and is an asymmetric key system consisting of a public key (which is sent to clients) and a private key (which stays local on the server). PKI differs from a symmetric key system in which both the client and server use the same key for encryption and decryption.

program status word (PSW). Defined by the architecture as the location containing the state indicators that reflect the execution of the current program, as well as the address of the instruction currently being executed. The PSW is implemented as a register in the hardware.

PROP. Programmable Operator. This CMS facility enables automatic filtering and routing of messages from a specified Virtual Machine's system console to another Virtual Machine. It also permits installation-defined actions to be automatically performed.

Processor Resource/Systems Manager (PR/SM) feature. Provides the logical partitioning (LPAR) capability of the real machine such that multiple system-control programs can simultaneously share the use of the processors in a single machine. It also provides support for the multiple preferred guest facility of z/VM. See also *multiple preferred guests*.

quota. The maximum amount of a resource that a resource consumer is allowed to use. Frequently this concept is used with respect to disk or file space. In UNIX and Linux systems, there is a quota command that is used to implement such a resource-capping process for file systems.

RACF. Resource Access Control Facility. An IBM licensed program that provides access control by identifying users to the system; verifying users of the system; authorizing access to protected resources; logging detected, unauthorized attempts to enter the system; and logging detected accesses to protected resources. RACF is included in OS/390 Security Server and is also available as a separate program for the z/VM environment.

RAID. Redundant Array of Independent Disks. RAID is a way of configuring redundant disks in various types of arrays so that the data can be retrieved, even if one disk in the array were to fail. There are many types of RAID configuration. The two most common configurations are: the mirroring approach of RAID1 (where each piece of data is written to two disks in the array) and the striping approach of RAID5 (where a block of data is striped across multiple disks, together with an error correction code that allows the data to be reconstructed if any disk fails). For further information, see http://www.acnc.com/04_01_00.html.

RAMAC. RAID Architecture with Multi-level Adaptive Cache. RAMAC is an older IBM disk product that attaches to the mainframe.

RAS. Reliability, availability, serviceability.

Response time. A measure of the time taken to perform a certain task, such as running a specific job. However, another understanding of "response time" is the elapsed time from the point a user hits the Send key, until the point-in-time that the first byte of data comes back. Response time is related to ETR.

REXX. Restructured Extended Executor. A general-purpose, interpretive, procedural language for end-user personal programming, designed for ease-of-use by both casual general users and computer professionals. It is also useful for application macros. REXX includes the capability of issuing commands to the underlying operating system from these macros and procedures. REXX is the automation scripting language used in z/VM.

RISC. Reduced Instruction-Set Computer. A computer that uses a small, simplified set of frequently-used instructions for rapid execution.

RSA. Rivest-Shamir-Adelman. The RSA algorithm is one of the most commonly used encryption and authentication algorithms today. The algorithm involves multiplying two large prime numbers and through additional operations deriving a set of two numbers that constitutes the *public key* and the *private key*. Both the public and private keys are needed for encryption and decryption, but only the owner of a private key ever needs to know the contents of the private key. Using the RSA system, the private key never needs to be sent across the Internet.

SAN. Storage Area Network. This concept puts sets of disk storage on an area network and allows this network of disks to be used by multiple servers. By aggregating storage, the SAN becomes a single management entity.

scalable. Pertaining to the capability of a system to adapt readily to a greater or lesser intensity of use, volume, or demand. For example, a scalable system can efficiently adapt to work with larger or smaller networks performing tasks of varying complexity. Generally, the term "scalable" is understood to mean that an entity can "grow." For example, an application can handle more users, or a mainframe can be made larger by adding more processors.

SCSI. Small Computer System Interface. The protocol that is used by most non-mainframe servers to communicate with external storage devices. There are a number of SCSI standards that can be used.

server consolidation. The process of taking a set of application serving capabilities and consolidating that into a smaller number. There are a few aspects of servers that lend themselves to consolidation. One can take a number of instances of like server function and consolidate them onto a single larger capacity server (for example, for mail or file or Web page serving), reducing the number of logical servers. Another type of server consolidation is to use a single instance of z/VM to rehost the set of servers onto one larger hardware server, that is, the zSeries processor, keeping the number of logical servers the same but reducing the number of hardware servers.

SLA. Service-level agreement. An agreement or contract between a provider of services and a customer of those services, which sets expectations for the level of service with respect to availability, performance, and other measurable objectives.

SMP. Symmetric multiprocessing. SMP is the term used to define a specific architecture for having multiple processors cooperate on a set of work. SMP means that the processors are symmetric in capabilities and share at least a common central storage.

SNMP. Simple Network Management Protocol. A standardized protocol used to manage entities on a network, everything from printers and routers to servers. SNMP is an application layer protocol. Information on devices managed is defined and stored in the application's Management Information Base (MIB).

socket. An endpoint provided by the transport service of a network for communication between processes or application programs.

SSL. Secure Sockets Layer. A security protocol that provides communication privacy. SSL enables client/server applications to communicate in a way that is designed to prevent eavesdropping, tampering, and message forgery. SSL was developed by Netscape Communications Corp. and RSA Data Security, Inc.

subchannel. (1) A division of a channel data path. (2) The channel facility required for sustaining a single I/O operation. (3) The facility that provides all of the information necessary to start, control, and complete an I/O operation.

throughput. A performance measurement. Work done per unit time.

tool. Any object or (software) becomes a "tool" when, in the perspective of its user, the object enables the task at hand to be performed more easily.

TSO. Time Sharing Option. An integrated function of the z/OS operating system that provides interactive time sharing from remote terminals.

vertical growth. Growing by increasing the capacity of a resource. Contrast this with *horizontal growth* (growing by adding yet another instance of the resource).

VIPA. Virtual IP Address. Is a feature on certain of IBM's mainframe network adapter cards. VIPA eliminates a host's dependency upon individual network adapters by virtualizing the relationship between network adapters and IP addresses. As a result, adapter failures do not affect active connections.

virtual memory. A programming concept implemented by many operating systems in which there is a virtual model of memory used by programs, which expect a particular behavior (typically, byte-of-word addressability across some range of addresses.) The under-

lying operating system provides this construct to each of the programs, while mapping each program's virtual address to some real storage address on the actual hardware.

Virtual Machine (VM). (1) A virtual data processing system that appears to be at the exclusive disposal of a particular user, but whose functions are supplied by sharing the resources of a real data processing system. (2) In z/VM, the virtual processors, virtual storage, virtual devices, and virtual channel subsystem allocated to a single user. Synonymous with virtual configuration. (3) In z/VM, the functional equivalent of a z/Architecture system. Each Virtual Machine is controlled by an operating system, such as CMS. CP controls the concurrent operation of several Virtual Machines on a processor complex.

VPN. Virtual private network. A network comprised of one or more secure IP tunnels connecting two or more networks.

VSE/ESA. Virtual Storage Extended /Enterprise Systems Architecture. The generalized term that indicates the combination of the DOS/VSE system Control Program and the VSE/Advanced Functions licensed program.

working set. The set of virtual pages a program needs to begin/resume executing, and also the set of virtual pages a program will reference during its next "time slice" on the machine. It is important that operating systems correctly restore a program's working set before dispatching the program. If not, the program will "page fault" and not use its time slice. "Thrashing" might occur if there is no way for the operating system to use the history to predict which set of pages the program will next need. In this case, the program simply continues to "page fault" and makes little progress in completing its execution.

workload consolidation. To move the functions of a given workload from many servers to fewer or even one server.

z/OS. IBM's flagship operating system for the zSeries mainframe, which was designed and developed to meet the demanding quality of service requirements for enterprise e-business.

z/VM. IBM's zSeries operating system that provides the Virtual Machine capability that allows hundreds or more guest operating systems to run on a single mainframe.

Further Reading

The available information related to Linux on the mainframe is rapidly changing and new information becomes available every day. Nevertheless, because the topic is new, we put together a selective list of what we think might be of interest to you when starting with a Linux on the mainframe project.

In contrast, the bibliography provides a more comprehensive list.

You can obtain IBM documentation through the IBM Publication Center at: http://www.elink.ibmlink.ibm.com/public/applications/publications/cgibin/pbi.cgi.

The suggested literature includes IBM Redbook publications. To obtain a list of all available Redbook publications about Linux on the mainframe, visit:

http://publib-b.boulder.ibm.com/cgi-bin/searchsite.cgi?query=linux+AND+zseries.

For a list of all IBM Redbook publications on Linux, visit:

http://publib-b.boulder.ibm.com/cgi-bin/searchsite.cgi?query=linux.

For other suggested literature, we have either provided a URL where the publication is available for download in a printable format or the ISBN to help you order it through a retailer.

Part 1, "Linux on the Mainframe – an Introduction"

Hall, Mark *Evolution of IBM's Open-Source Strategy. A Time Line of Linux and Open Source Developments.* In: Computerworld from IDG.net, October 2001. Available on Internet: http://www.computerworld.com/softwaretopics/os/linux/story/0,10801,65073,00.html.

> Provides a time line of Linux and Open Source developments through 2001 and points to other relevant articles.

Hoskins, Jim, and Bob Frank *Exploring IBM eServer zSeries and S/390 Servers: See Why IBM's Redesigned Mainframe Computer Family Has Become More Popular than Ever!* Florida: Maximum Press, 8th Edition, 2003. (ISBN: 1-855068-91-3)

> Provides a thorough look at mainframe hardware and software.

IBM *IBM eServer zSeries 900 and z/OS.* IBM Reference Guide, August 2002. (IBM Form Number: G326-3092-03)

> IBM's technical guide to the z900 machine and z/OS.

Raymond, Eric S. *The Cathedral and the Bazaar.* O'Reilly & Associates, February 2001. (ISBN: 0-596001-08-8)

> An easy-to-read book for anyone interested in learning how the Open Source community functions. The author is an early community member. From a sociologist's point of view, he explains how the "society" is formed and manages to accomplish tasks that others thought could not possibly happen.

Weiss, George *Conditions for Strategic Linux Adoption.* Gartner Research Note, May 2002. Available at the Gartner Site: http://www.gartner.com.

> Discusses Linux as a enterprise-ready operating system.

Part 3, "Is Linux on the Mainframe for Me?"

Altmark, Alan, and Cliff Laking *The Value of z/VM: Security and Integrity.* IBM Technical Paper, May 2002. (IBM Form Number: GM13-0145-00)

Provides an overview of the security and integrity characteristics of the z/VM hypervisor.

Alves, L.C, et al. *RAS Design for the IBM eServer z900.* In: IBM Journal of Research and Development, Volume 46, Numbers 4/5, Jul/Sept 2002, pp. 503–522. Available on Internet: http://www.research.ibm.com/journal/rd/464/alves.html.

Amrehn, Erich, et al. *Linux on IBM zSeries and S/390: High Availability for z/VM and Linux.* IBM Redpaper, 21 June 2002. (IBM Form Number: REDP0220)

Helps planning for and installing a high-availability solution for Linux for zSeries running under z/VM. Discusses the high-availability possibilities of a Linux for zSeries environment.

Geiselhart, Gregory, et al. *Linux on IBM zSeries and S/390: Cloning Linux Images in z/VM.* IBM Redpaper, 3 September 2002. (IBM Form Number: REDP0301)

Detailed how-to description of a cloning implementation.

Ogden, Bill, and Bill White *Getting Started with zSeries Fibre Channel Protocol.* IBM Redpaper, 13 August 2002. (IBM Form Number: REDP0205)

Helps you understand the concepts of zSeries Fibre Channel Protocol support and shows how various SCSI devices can be configured to build a zSeries FCP environment.

Schneier, Bruce *Applied Cryptography. Protocols, Algorithms and Source Code.* C. John Wiley & Sons, 2nd. Edition, 1995. (ISBN: 0-471117-09-9)

A comprehensive guide to modern day cryptography. Guides the user as well as the professional cryptographer through the algorithms, uses, and applications needed to secure data and communications.

Thomas, Stephen *SSL and TLS Essentials: Securing the Web.* John Wiley & Sons, 2000. (ISBN: 0-471383-54-6)

An introduction to Secure Socket Layer technology providing an end-to-end view of the technology behind e-commerce and the Web.

White, Bill, et al. *zSeries HiperSockets.* IBM Redbook. (IBM Form Number: SG24-6816)

This book offers a broad description of the architecture, microcode function, and operating systems support of HiperSockets. It enables you to plan and install a HiperSockets network.

Ziegler, Robert *Linux Firewalls.* New Riders Publishing, 1999. (ISBN: 0-735709-00-9)

Provides guidance for single- and multiple-system firewall solutions using Linux, along with the basics of packet filtering and the DMZ. In addition, aspects of basic system hardening, intrusion detection, and system monitoring are covered.

Zwicky, Elizabeth, Simon Cooper, and Brent Chapman *Building Internet Firewalls.* O'Reilly & Associates: 2nd Edition, June 2000. (ISBN: 1-565928-71-7)

A general guide to firewall technology. Introducing various network communications, why they need to be protected and how to build a firewall to do the job.

Part 4, "Making the Most of Linux on the Mainframe"

Compaq *Business Value Methodology in Support of Networked Storage Architectures.* Compaq White Paper. Prepared by Enterprise Storage Group Compaq Computer Corporation. February 2002. Available on Internet: ftp://ftp.compaq.com/pub/products/storageworks/whitepapers/15ZV-1201A-WWEN.pdf.

Explains the various types of network-based storage methods (for example, NAS, SAN). It is not specifically about Linux, but it lays out much of the terminology in an understandable way. It also shows how a slavish approach to TCO/ROI might lead one to wrong conclusions on the best approach to solve storage needs.

Geiselhart, Gregory, Tung-Sing Chong, and Michael Donovan *Cloning Linux Images in z/VM.* IBM Redpaper, 03 September 2002. (IBM Form Number: REDP0301)

In a LinuxWorld demonstration, IBM created thousands of Linux images averaging one new image per minute. This Redpaper gives an insight into exactly what those images could do and how the cloning process was managed.

IBM *Large Systems Performance for IBM eServer zSeries and S/390.* Available on Internet: http://www.ibm.com/servers/eserver/zseries/lspr/.

Explains the background of the Large Systems Performance Report process. Includes descriptions of the workloads as well as a recent set of measurements. The document is typically updated as new mainframe processors become available.

NTP Software *Do you need a Storage Management Policy?* NTP Software White Paper, Rev. 2.1, August 2001. Available on Internet: http://www.ntpsoftware.com/WhitePapers/docs/DoYouNeedAStoragePolicy.pdf.

This white paper argues that companies' crucial data call for explicit storage management policies to guide the organizational interaction with these data. The paper also explores how to formulate policy in a way that makes people comply with it.

Ogden, Bill, and Bill White *Getting Started with zSeries Fibre Channel Protocol.* IBM Redpaper, 13 August 2002. (IBM Form Number: REDP0205)

Gives a description on how to set up the SCSI over FCP environment for Linux on the mainframe.

Rayns, Chris, et al. *Linux on zSeries and S/390: System Management.* IBM Redbook, 04 December 2002. (IBM Form Number: SG24-6820)

Explains the "how to" aspects of Linux-on-the-mainframe systems management. Apart from a description of IBM Tivoli, this book provides descriptions of CA and BMC tools that are written by technical people from the respective companies.

Part 5, "Running Applications"

IBM   *Porting UNIX Applications to Linux. Hints and Tips.* IBM Technical Paper, January 2002. (IBM Form Number: GM13-0115)

Provides hands-on information and practical tips for those interested in the technical aspects of porting an application to Linux on the mainframe.

Wahli, Ueli, et al. *Enterprise Integration with IBM Connectors and Adapters.* IBM Redbook, 22 February 2002. (IBM Form Number: SG24-6122)

Explores how IBM connectors and adapters can be used to solve the integration problems many enterprises face when deploying e-business solutions. The book uses scenarios to show how to use a J2EE connector with an existing application and how a J2EE connector or the MQSeries Adapter Offering can be used in creating a new application.

Wakelin, Phil, et al. *Java Connectors for CICS: Featuring the J2EE Connector Architecture.* IBM Redbook, 22 March 2002. (IBM Form Number: SG24-6401)

A practical guide with technical details for integrating Java applications with CICS back-ends. The book explores several possibilities, with a focus on the J2EE Connector Architecture. It includes comprehensive code samples.

Bibliography

Books

Hoskins, Jim, and Bob Frank *Exploring IBM eServer zSeries and S/390 Servers: See Why IBM's Redesigned Mainframe Computer Family Has Become More Popular than Ever!* Florida: Maximum Press, 8th Edition, 2003. (ISBN: 1–855068–91–3)

Raymond, Eric S. *The Cathedral and the Bazaar.* O'Reilly & Associates, February 2001. (ISBN: 0–596001–08–8)

Schneier, Bruce *Applied Cryptography. Protocols, Algorithms and Source Code.* C. John Wiley & Sons, 2nd. Edition, 1995. (ISBN: 0–471117–09–9)

Ziegler, Robert *Linux Firewalls.* New Riders Publishing, 1999. (ISBN: 0–735709–00–9)

Zwicky, Elizabeth, Simon Cooper, and Brent Chapman *Building Internet Firewalls.* O'Reilly & Associates: 2nd Edition, June 2000. (ISBN: 1–565928–71–7)

IBM Redbooks

The following publications can be found on Internet: `http://www.redbooks.ibm.com` by giving the correspondant IBM Form Number in the Search Command.

Amrehn, Erich, et al. *Linux on IBM zSeries and S/390: High Availability for z/VM and Linux.* Redpaper, 21 June 2002. IBM Form Number: REDP0220.

Amrehn, Erich, et al. *Linux on IBM zSeries and S/390: Server Consolidation with Linux for zSeries.* Redpaper, 30 July 2002. IBM Form Number: REDP0222.

Amrehn, Erich, Ulrich Boche, and Manfred Gnirss *Linux on IBM zSeries and S/390: Securing Linux for zSeries with a Central z/OS (RACF) LDAP Server.* Redpaper, 21 June 2002. IBM Form Number: REDP0221.

Endrei, Mark, et al. *IBM WebSphere V4.0 Advanced Edition Handbook.* Redbook, 13 March 2002. IBM Form Number: SG24-6176.

Geiselhart, Gregory, Tung-Sing Chong, and Michael Donovan *Cloning Linux Images in z/VM.* Redpaper, 03 September 2002. IBM Form Number: REDP0301.

Geiselhart, Gregory, et al. *Linux on IBM eServer zSeries and S/390: Application Development.* Redbook, 5 August 2002. IBM Form Number: SG24-6807.

Injey, Frank *IBM eServer zSeries 900 Technical Guide.* Redbook, 06 September 2002. IBM Form Number: SG24-5975.

MacIsaac, Michael, et al. *Linux for IBM eServer zSeries and S/390: Distributions.* Redbook, 20 September 2001. IBM Form Number: SG24-6264.

MacIsaac, Michael, et al. *Linux on IBM zSeries and S/390: ISP/ASP Solutions.* Redbook, 20 December 2001. IBM Form Number: SG24-6299.

Ogden, Bill, and Bill White *Getting Started with zSeries Fibre Channel Protocol.* Redpaper, 13 August 2002. IBM Form Number: REDP0205.

Rayns, Chris, et al. *Linux on zSeries and S/390: Systems Management.* Redbook, 31 October 2002. IBM Form Number: SG24-6820.

Wahli, Ueli, et al. *Enterprise Integration with IBM Connectors and Adapters.* Redbook, 22 February 2002. IBM Form Number: SG24-6122.

Wakelin, Phil, et al. *Java Connectors for CICS: Featuring the J2EE Connector Architecture.* Redbook, 22 March 2002. IBM Form Number: SG24-6401.

IBM articles and papers

Adair, R.J., et al. *A Virtual Machine System for the 360/40.* IBM Cambridge Scientific Center Report 320-2007, Cambridge, Mass., May 1966.

Altmark, Alan, and Cliff Laking *The Value of z/VM: Security and Integrity.* IBM Technical Paper, May 2002. (IBM Form Number: GM13-0145-00). Available on Internet: http://www.ibm.com/servers/eserver/zseries/library/techpapers/.

Alves, Luiz, et al. *RAS Design for the IBM eServer z900.* In: IBM Journal of Research and Development, Vol. 46, No. 4/5, Jul/Sept 2002, pp. 503–522. Available on Internet: http://www.research.ibm.com/journal/rd/464/alves.html.

Amdahl, G.M., G.A. Blaauw, and F.P. Brooks, Jr. *Architecture of the IBM System/360.* In: IBM Journal of Research and Development, Vol. 8, No.2, 1964, pp. 87–101. (Reprinted in IBM Journal of Research and Development, Vol. 44, No.1/2, Jan/Mar 2000). Available on Internet: http://researchweb.watson.ibm.com/journal/rd/441/amdahl.pdf.

Auslander, M.A., D.C. Larkin, and A.L. Scherr *The Evolution of the MVS Operating System.* In: IBM Journal of Research and Development, Vol. 25, No. 5, Sept. 1981, pp. 471-482. Available on Internet: http://www.research.ibm.com/journal/rd/255/auslander.pdf.

Guski, Richard, et al. *Security on z/OS: Comprehensive, Current, and Flexible.* In: IBM Systems Journal, Vol. 40, No. 3, May 2001, pp. 696– 720. Available on Internet: http://www.research.ibm.com/journal/sj/403/guski.html.

Mealy, G. H., B.I. Witt, and W.A. Clark *The Functional Structure of OS/360 (Parts I, II, and III).* In: IBM Systems Journal, Vol. 5, No. 1, 1966, pp. 3-51. Available on Internet: http://www.research.ibm.com/journal/sj/.

Mueller, Michael, et al. *RAS Strategy for IBM S/390 G5 and G6.* In: IBM Journal of Research and Development, Vol. 43, No. 5/6, 1999, pp. 875–888. Available on Internet: http://www.research.ibm.com/journal/rd/435/muellaut.html.

Other IBM publications

14K Days, A History of the Poughkeepsie Laboratory. 1984.

IBM eServer zSeries Performance Reference, October 2002. Available on Internet: http://www.ibm.com/servers/de/downloads/brochures/G511_4172_06.pdf.

IBM eServer zSeries 900 and z/OS. IBM Reference Guide, August 2002. (IBM Form Number: G326-3092-03). Available on Internet: http://www.ibm.com/servers/eserver/zseries/library/refguides/pdf/g3263092.pdf.

IBM WebSphere Portal for Multiplatforms V4.1 Adds Support for Linux on zSeries. IBM Software Announcement, 24 September 2002. Available on Internet: http://www.ibm.com/software/webservers/portal/news.html.

IBM zSeries 900 and z/OS Reference Guide. 2001. (IBM Form Number: G326-3092)

Large Systems Performance for IBM eServer zSeries and S/390. IBM Technical Paper. Available on Internet: http://www.ibm.com/servers/eserver/zseries/lspr/.

Linux for S/390. Device Drivers and Installation Commands. 4th Edition, 2001. Available on Internet: http://oss.software.ibm.com/linux390/docu/l390dd03.pdf.

Porting UNIX Applications to Linux. Hints and Tips. IBM Technical Paper, January 2002. (IBM Form Number: GM13-0115). Available on Internet: http://www.ibm.com/servers/eserver/zseries/library/techpapers/gm130115.html.

Samba on Linux for zSeries. IBM Product Description, June 2001. (IBM Form Number: GM13-0088). Available on Internet: http://www.ibm.com/servers/eserver/zseries/library/specsheets/gm130088.html.

The Value of z/VM for Linux. IBM eServer zSeries Announcement, March 2002. Available on Internet: http://www.ibm.com/servers/eserver/zseries/os/linux/pdf/VM_Value_Guide.pdf.

Tivoli Storage Management Best Practices. IBM White Paper, 19 April 2001. (IBM Form Number: G325-1691)

z/Architecture Principles of Operation. December 2000. (IBM Form Number: SA22-7832). Available on Internet: http://publibfp.boulder.ibm.com/pubs/pdfs/os390/dz9zr000.pdf.

zSeries 900 System Overview. December 2000. (IBM Form Number: SA22-1027).

z/VM Performance Report. IBM VM Performance Document, 18 June 2002. Available on Internet: http://www.vm.ibm.com/perf/docs/zvmperf.html.

Other articles and papers

Aberdeen Group *CA's Unicenter TNG Framework: Entry-Level for the Industry's Best Enterprise Management Software Solution.* Announcement Profile.

Amdahl, G.M. *Validity of the single-processor approach to achieving large scale computing capabilities.* In: AFIPS Conference Proceedings, Vol. 30 (Atlantic City, N.J., Apr. 18-20). AFIPS Press, Reston, Va., 1967, pp. 483-485.

Backa, Bruce *Why have storage policies?* In: SearchStorage Tips & Newsletters, 22 January 2002. Available on Internet:
http://searchstorage.techtarget.com/tip/1,289483,sid5_gci798099,00.html

Cap Gemini Ernst&Young US LLC Angelo Salerno and Peter Kostrobala: *IBM zSeries Announcement. Changing the Cost of Ownership Paradigm for Enterprise Computing.* White Paper, October 2000. Available on Internet:
http://www.ibm.com/servers/eserver/zseries/library/whitepapers/pdf/ibm_zseries.pdf.

Claybrook, Bill *Linux is on the move - Up!* AberdeenGroup InSight, 24 July 2001. Available on Internet: http://www.ibm.com/linux/LinuxInSight.pdf

Compaq *Business Value Methodology in Support of Networked Storage Architectures.* Compaq White Paper. Prepared by Enterprise Storage Group Compaq Computer Corporation, February 2002.

Computer Associates *CA Common Services Architecture Overview.* White Paper, 24 January 2002. Available on Internet: http://www3.ca.com/Solutions/Collateral.asp?ID=1313&=2848.

da Cruz, Frank *Columbia University Computing History.* In: Academic Information Systems of the Columbia University, Feb 2001. Available on Internet:
http://www.columbia.edu/acis/history/timeline.html.

Enabling Technologies Group Fred Bothwell: *Meeting the Business Challenges of the 21st Century. Comparative Large System Capabilities and Attributes IBM eServer zSeries 900 - HP - Sun.* ETG White Paper Supplement, February 2001. Available on Internet:
http://www.etginc.com/whitepap/z900s_final2.pdf.

Gartner Kyte, A.: *24x7 Is a Management Thing.* Gartner Research Note, 17 May 2001.

Gartner Weiss, G.: *Conditions for Strategic Linux Adoption.*Gartner Research Note, May 2002.

Gribbin, Jeff *Development of 360/370 Architecture—A Plain Man's View.* Electronic Data Systems, February 1989. Available on Internet: http://pucc.princeton.edu/%7Emelinda/gribbin.pdf.

Hall, Mark *Evolution of IBM's Open-Source Strategy. A Time Line of Linux and Open Source Developments.* In: Computerworld from IDG.net, October 2001.

Hilf, Bill *Securing Linux Servers for Service Providers.* IBM Linux Technology Center, December 2001. Available on Internet:
http://oss.software.ibm.com/linux/papers/security/Securing_Linux_Servers_xSP.pdf.

Hilton, Paul *Assessing the Cost/Benefit Ratio for Storage Quotas.* In: SearchStorage Tips & Newsletters, 26 March 2002. Available on Internet:
http://searchstorage.techtarget.com/tip/0,289483,sid5_gci812453,00.html

Hurwitz Group *zSeries: Economic e-business Server.* Hurwitz Group, Inc., March 2001.

Illuminata Dianne McAdam: *Storage as Risk Management.* Illuminata Publication, 05 February 2002. Available on Internet: http://www.illuminata.com/cgi-local/pub.cgi?docid=storagerisk.

International Technology Group *Value Proposition for e-Infrastructures: Cost/Benefit Case for IBM eServer.* ITG Report, May 2002. Available on Internet: http://www.ibm.com/servers/solutions/serverconsolidation/pdf/itg.pdf.

Linuxcare *Levanta: Simplifying Server Consolidation with Linux on z/VM.* Linuxcare White Paper, 01 August 2002.

Meta Group Consulting *ERP Platform-Related Analysis Total Cost of Ownership Study. A Platform-Related Cost Analysis of ERP Applications on-Going Support Costs in the Mid-Tier.* 11 February 2000. Available on Internet: http://www.sun.com/servers/workgroup/tco/meta_study.pdf.

NTP Software *Do You Need a Storage Management Policy?* NTP Software White Paper, Rev. 2.1, August 2001. Available on Internet: http://www.ntpsoftware.com/WhitePapers/docs/DoYouNeedAStoragePolicy.pdf.

OPEN NMS *The Latest Released Version of OpenNMS is 1.0.1.*Homepage of OpenNMS. Available on Internet: http://www.opennms.org/.

Pasch, Eberhard *Optimizing with gcc on Linux for S/390.* IBM Article, Oct 2001. Available on Internet: http://www.ibm.com/servers/esdd/articles/gcc_opt/.

Van Vleck, Tom *UNIX and Multics.* 05 February 1995. Available on Internet: http://www.multicians.org/unix.html.

Varian, Melinda *VM and the VM Community: Past, Present, and Future.* SHARE 89, Sessions 9059-9061, August 1997. Available on Internet: http://pucc.princeton.edu/ melinda/25paper.pdf.

Index

Numerics

24-bit addressing 299
3-tier, hardware consolidation 273
31-bit addressing 299
3380, disk device 190
3390, disk device 190
64-bit addressing 299
9345, disk device 190
9s (levels of availability) 180

A

access control 95
   DAC 95
   for devices 194
   MAC 95
   on Linux 95
   tools 332, 333
   using z/VM (example) 195
access control list 95
   glossary definition 389
accounting 241
   tools 335, 336
ACL (access control list) 95
   glossary definition 389
acquisition, total cost of 57
adapters 285
   channel-to-channel 286
   ESCON 131, 288
   FCP 191
   FICON 131, 288
   NIC 124
   OSA-2 288
   OSA-Express 131, 286
address space 21
   access to 90
   for memory isolation 89
   glossary definition 389

address space *(continued)*
   mainframe architecture and 281
address translation, isolating images
   using 89
administration interface, z/VM 73
administration, effort for unique server
   images 115
Aduva OnStage 237
   URL 337, 362
Amanda 197
   URL 337
anti-virus 106
Apache 361
   applications in distributions 250
   availability example 184
   performance monitoring example 357
API (application programming interface)
   for framework user interfaces 168
   for incremental database backup 210
   glossary definition 389
applications 11
   adding to mainframe environment 274
   commercial 251
   examples 361
   from Linux distributions 250
   from the Internet 250
   glossary definition 389
   platforms for 361
   porting 257
   URLs 361
architecture
   definition of mainframe 16
   distinction to design 16
   Linux, independent of 32
   of CPU 17
   of memory 20
   zSeries 289

informIT

YOUR GUIDE TO IT REFERENCE

Articles

Keep your edge with thousands of free articles, in-depth features, interviews, and IT reference recommendations – all written by experts you know and trust.

Online Books

Answers in an instant from **InformIT Online Book's** 600+ fully searchable on line books. Sign up now and get your first 14 days **free**.

POWERED BY

Safari

Catalog

Review online sample chapters, author biographies and customer rankings and choose exactly the right book from a selection of over 5,000 titles.